FinTech as a Disruptive Technology for Financial Institutions

Abdul Rafay
University of Management and Technology, Pakistan

A volume in the Advances in Finance, Accounting, and Economics (AFAE) Book Series

IGI Global
DISSEMINATOR OF KNOWLEDGE

Published in the United States of America by
IGI Global
Business Science Reference (an imprint of IGI Global)
701 E. Chocolate Avenue
Hershey PA, USA 17033
Tel: 717-533-8845
Fax: 717-533-8661
E-mail: cust@igi-global.com
Web site: http://www.igi-global.com

Library of Congress Cataloging-in-Publication Data

Names: Rafay, Abdul, 1973- editor.
Title: FinTech as a disruptive technology for financial institutions / Abdul Rafay, editor.
Description: Hershey, PA : Business Science Reference, [2019]
Identifiers: LCCN 2018036430| ISBN 9781522578055 (hardcover) | ISBN 9781522578062 (ebook)
Subjects: LCSH: Finance--Technological innovations. | Financial services industry--Technological innovations. | Financial institutions--Technological innovations.
Classification: LCC HG173 .F535 2019 | DDC 332.1--dc23 LC record available at https://lccn.loc.gov/2018036430

This book is published in the IGI Global book series Advances in Finance, Accounting, and Economics (AFAE) (ISSN: 2327-5677; eISSN: 2327-5685)

British Cataloguing in Publication Data
A Cataloguing in Publication record for this book is available from the British Library.

Advances in Finance, Accounting, and Economics (AFAE) Book Series

ISSN:2327-5677
EISSN:2327-5685

Editor-in-Chief: Ahmed Driouchi, Al Akhawayn University, Morocco

MISSION

In our changing economic and business environment, it is important to consider the financial changes occurring internationally as well as within individual organizations and business environments. Understanding these changes as well as the factors that influence them is crucial in preparing for our financial future and ensuring economic sustainability and growth.

The **Advances in Finance, Accounting, and Economics (AFAE)** book series aims to publish comprehensive and informative titles in all areas of economics and economic theory, finance, and accounting to assist in advancing the available knowledge and providing for further research development in these dynamic fields.

COVERAGE

- Applied Finance
- Development Economics
- Public Finance
- Auditing
- Managerial Accounting
- Microfinance
- Behavioral Economics
- E-finance
- International Trade
- Applied economics

IGI Global is currently accepting manuscripts for publication within this series. To submit a proposal for a volume in this series, please contact our Acquisition Editors at Acquisitions@igi-global.com or visit: http://www.igi-global.com/publish/.

The Advances in Finance, Accounting, and Economics (AFAE) Book Series (ISSN 2327-5677) is published by IGI Global, 701 E. Chocolate Avenue, Hershey, PA 17033-1240, USA, www.igi-global.com. This series is composed of titles available for purchase individually; each title is edited to be contextually exclusive from any other title within the series. For pricing and ordering information please visit http://www.igi-global.com/book-series/advances-finance-accounting-economics/73685. Postmaster: Send all address changes to above address.

Titles in this Series

For a list of additional titles in this series, please visit:
https://www.igi-global.com/book-series/advances-finance-accounting-economics/73685

Maintaining Financial Stability in Times of Risk and Uncertainty
Abhishek Behl (Indian Institute of Technology Bombay, India) and Sushma Nayak (Symbiosis International University (Deemed), India)
Business Science Reference • ©2019 • 377pp • H/C (ISBN: 9781522572084) • US $265.00

Global Trends of Modernization in Budgeting and Finance
Denis Ushakov (Suan Sunandha Rajabhat University, Thailand)
Business Science Reference • ©2019 • 354pp • H/C (ISBN: 9781522577607) • US $215.00

Corporate Insolvency Law and Bankruptcy Reforms in the Global Economy
Amit Kashyap (Nirma University, India)
Business Science Reference • ©2019 • 261pp • H/C (ISBN: 9781522555414) • US $185.00

Time Bank as a Complementary Economic System Emerging Research and Opportunities
Lukas Valek (University of Hradec Kralove, Czech Republic) and Vladimir Bures (University of Hradec Kralove, Czech Republic)
Business Science Reference • ©2019 • 208pp • H/C (ISBN: 9781522569749) • US $175.00

Economic Dynamics of Global Energy Geopolitics
Ahmet Salih Ikiz (Muğla Sıtkı Koçman University, Turkey)
Engineering Science Reference • ©2019 • 305pp • H/C (ISBN: 9781522542032) • US $195.00

Co-Manufacturing and New Economic Paradigms
Giulio Focardi (Osun WES, Italy) and Lorenza Salati (Osun WES, Italy)
Business Science Reference • ©2019 • 217pp • H/C (ISBN: 9781522570899) • US $185.00

Handbook of Research on Microfinancial Impacts on Women Empowerment, Poverty, and...
Ramesh Chandra Das (Katwa College, India)
Business Science Reference • ©2019 • 452pp • H/C (ISBN: 9781522552406) • US $275.00

For an entire list of titles in this series, please visit:
https://www.igi-global.com/book-series/advances-finance-accounting-economics/73685

IGI Global
DISSEMINATOR OF KNOWLEDGE

701 East Chocolate Avenue, Hershey, PA 17033, USA
Tel: 717-533-8845 x100 • Fax: 717-533-8661
E-Mail: cust@igi-global.com • www.igi-global.com

Editorial Advisory Board

Table of Contents

Section 3
FinTech and Islamic Finance

Detailed Table of Contents

In this chapter, a study about how Italian SMEs understand and use FinTech technologies is presented. The study focuses on FinTech-aided banking services, in particular, due to the fact that these are, at present, the most widely used FinTech technologies available in Italy. The study shows how, despite FinTech entering Italy only in recently, the Italian SMEs market is very active and fruitful for digital companies. In the last years, a continuous growth of investment has seen the development of FinTech technologies in multiple areas, such as mobile networks, big data, trust management, mobile embedded systems, cloud computing, image processing, and data analytic techniques.

Technology advances at an incredible rate all around the globe. Financial technologies (FinTech) are defined as production of services that combine financial services and technology. A subdimension of FinTech, insurance technologies (InsurTech) is a system built with the purpose of creating solutions for the insurance sector using a technological approach. Making it easier for the insurance companies and the insured to manage their contracts, minimizing the risks involved, and allowing for the development of innovative technologies, InsurTech is simply the technology of insurance business. For the policy owners, these technologies bring with them the benefit of cost-effective policy solutions. This chapter focuses on the possible impact of insurance technologies on the insurance sector. Explored in this study are the estimated transformation of the insurance sector with insurance technologies and the problems likely to occur as a consequence.

The introduction of FinTech into Africa's digital financial services environment has provoked a controversy as to whether the innovative technology should be assimilated by banks and other financial service providers or not, thus creating uncertainty about the future of FinTech on the continent. This chapter, therefore, examines the issues, controversy, and problems surrounding the debut of FinTech and suggest ways to make the technology acceptable in order to harness its potentials for the overall benefit of the African society.

New empirical facts are presented to help lay the foundation for creating intraday volatility models that can overcome noise interferences in high-frequency finance data. These facts also help explain some stock market anomalies like volatility jumps and flash crashes, which favor intraday RV over the traditionally used daily RV as a reliable physical measure of market risk.

Stock markets and relevant entities generate enormous amounts of data on a daily basis and are accessible from various channels such as stock exchange, economic reviews, and employer monetary reports. In recent times, machine learning techniques have proven to be very helpful in making better trading decisions. Machine learning algorithms use complex logic to observe and learn the behavior of stocks using historical data which can be used to predict future movements of the stock. Technical indicators such as rolling mean, momentum, and exponential moving average are calculated to convert the data into meaningful information. Furthermore, this information can be used to build machine learning prediction models that learn different patterns in the data and make future predictions for accurate financial forecasting. Additional factors that are being used for stock prediction include social media influences and daily news on trading stocks. Considering these qualitative and quantitative features at the same time result in improved prediction models.

This chapter examines the effects of high-frequency trading (HFT) and algorithmic trading (AT) activities, which represent important technological developments in financial markets in the past two decades, on Borsa Istanbul in terms of volatility. To clarify stock market behaviors in terms of volatility, asymmetry, and risk return after the BISTECH transition, the GJR-GARCH-in-Mean and I-GARCH models were used. The dataset consists of the daily stock return series of the main and sub-sector indexes of Borsa Istanbul, covering the period from October 24, 2012 to June 1, 2018. Although there are mixed results for the sub-indexes, it is observed that in the post-BISTECH period, volatility increases significantly in the BIST 100 and BIST

30 indexes, where AT and HFT activities are used more frequently. In particular, the duration of volatility returns to average after shock increases about seven times for BIST 100 and about eight times for the BIST 30 in the post-BISTECH period. Overall, the results indicate that AC and HFT activities may have disruptive effects on financial markets.

Section 3
FinTech and Islamic Finance

FinTech, or financial technology, is an emerging technology in financial transaction. It is disruptive technology which is changing the banking behavior for stakeholders. The thriving emergence of FinTech not only affects the conventional finance industry but also Islamic finance industry, as Islamic finance sector is also embracing FinTech as part of financial revolution. Thus, the Islamic FinTech emerges as faith-based FinTech. This is because Islamic FinTech claimed to comply with Shariah principle in their mechanism and smart contract. There is limited discussion on smart contract and Islamic FinTech and its Shariah principles. Hence, the Shariah principle in smart contract of Islamic FinTech need to be addressed. This chapter tries to delve into the smart contract concept in Islamic FinTech and Shariah principles in the mechanism. The review found that smart contract is currently in the early stage and so is Islamic FinTech. The scholars agreed that FinTech is a Maslahah (interest) to mankind's benefit. However, the smart contract is still in discussion and review.

Blockchain and smart contracts are forming new systems to record and manage businesses with less need for intermediaries. The new systems are expected to offer high level of governance with lower cost as compared to the traditional technologies. While there is a continuous effort to apply this innovative technology in several businesses, Islamic finance in general—and Islamic social finance in particular—are facing few challenges that could be solved by such innovations. Islamic social finance

Preface

INTRODUCTION

The desire to edit a book on FinTech came out of my two decades of experience as a practitioner of finance and technology. The past decade has been an eventful one for those interested in the influence of Technology on Finance. FinTech has become a buzzword from G20 to World Economic Forum to global and national economic and tech agendas. Today FinTech is being considered as a key driver of financial growth and has enabled the birth of new industries and business models.

Financial Technology (FinTech) is defined as production of services which combine financial services and technology. In other words, computer program and any other technology which is used to provide and enable financial services is named as FinTech. During the last few years, FinTech advances at an incredible rate all around the globe. Its continuous growth has seen the development of FinTech technologies in multiple areas, such as mobile networks, big data, trust management, mobile embedded systems, cloud computing, image processing, data analytic techniques, machine learning, artificial intelligence, peer to peer lending, robotic investment advisers, blockchain technology, prophetical activity analytics, data-driven selling, crowd funding, digital currencies, ePayments. Artificial intelligence in FinTech is now playing an important role in differentiating financial services products by replacing both simple and complex human activities. As a result FinTech has dramatically changed the way of banking and financial services.

The rapid development of FinTech has also presented new challenges like digital divide, issues of privacy, security, cybercrimes, digital literacy to name a few. Disruptive innovation creates a new market and value market. It happens whenever a new technology changes the way markets operate. It is an event in the financial service which forces the financial institutes to think, when there is a technology development, about the approach used in their industry. Even the firms engaged in FinTech disrupted themselves.

WHAT THE FINTECH GURUS SAID?

Jim Marous, one of the most influential people in FinTech, has been featured on CNBC, CNN, *The Wall Street Journal, New York Times, The Financial Times, The Economist* and the *American Banker*, and has advised the White House on banking policy and spoken worldwide.

The biggest challenge for banking in this age of disruption will be to break free from the patterns and comfort level of the past and accept the realities of the new digital marketplace – it is the non-banks that are setting the expectations for the new generation of banking consumers. Financial Institutions must be able to deliver and easy to navigate, a seamless digital platform that goes beyond a miniaturized banking platform. (Marous, 2018)

Matteo Rizzi, is a partner in SBT Venture Capital, one of the first funds solely dedicated to FinTech investment. In 2008 he co-founded Innotribe, the innovation arm of SWIFT. This is where Matteo launched the Innotribe Startup Challenge, the first global challenge for FinTech entrepreneurs.

The next generation of Financial Services will be fundamentally different. Our duty is not to fight the disruption, but to embrace it. The journey to fairer, faster, ubiquitous and global access to value has just begun. (Rizzi, 2018)

Claire Cockerton is the founding director and CEO of Innovate Finance. Cockerton is also founder and chairwoman of Entiq, and set the strategy and co-led the implementation of Level39, Europe's largest technology accelerator dedicated to FinTech, retail and smart cities technologies.

We are heading towards a tipping point in finance and banking where technology will radically change every aspect of the products offered, the businesses that deliver them, and the social and economic opportunities the sector creates for society as a whole. (Cockerton, 2018)

CONTEXT AND ORGANIZATION OF THIS VOLUME

This volume is organized into three sections. Section 1 addresses the emergence and future of FinTech with a set of five chapters from disparate parts of the world, Italy, Nigeria, Pakistan and Turkey. Section 2 addresses the role of FinTech in financial markets with a set of three chapters from US, Pakistan and Turkey. Section

3 addresses the role of FinTech in Islamic Finance with a set of three chapters from Malaysia and Pakistan.

In Section 1, the first chapter, "Crypto-Currency: Future of FinTech," throws light on future of crypto-currencies. Despite substantial security risk in crypto-currency trading, it has become the most traded commodity. The second chapter, "FinTech and SMEs: The Italian Case," is about how Italian SMEs understand and use FinTech technologies. The study focuses on FinTech technologies available in Italy particularly FinTech aided banking services. The third chapter, "Emergence of Insurance Technologies (InsurTech): The Turkish Case," discusses a sub-dimension of FinTech, Insurance Technologies (InsurTech) in the context of creating solutions for the insurance sector. The study explores the possible transformation of the insurance sector with insurance technologies and the problems likely to occur as a consequence. The fourth chapter, "FinTech for Digital Financial Services: The African Case," examines the issues, controversies and problems surrounding the debut of FinTech and suggest ways to make the technology acceptable in order to harness its potentials for the overall benefit of the African society. The fifth chapter, "Security and Privacy in FinTech: A Policy Enforcement Framework," discusses several security and privacy issues being faced by FinTech stakeholders while providing financial services to the users. The main aim of this chapter is to provide a policy framework to ensure the security and privacy of users' information while using FinTech applications and services.

In Section 2, the sixth chapter, "Volatility Estimation in the Era of High-Frequency Finance," discusses the surge of high-frequency finance data that has brought disruptive revolution in modeling asset prices. The chapter reviews some general frameworks like realized volatility (RV) in estimating the latent volatility and their recent developments in the era of high-frequency finance. The seventh chapter, "Algorithmic Machine Learning for Prediction of Stock Prices," discusses Machine learning algorithms that use complex logic to observe and learn the behavior of stocks using historical data. The eight chapter, "FinTech and Stock Market Behaviors: The Case of Borsa Istanbul," examines the effects of high-frequency trading (HFT) and algorithmic trading (AT) activities in Borsa Istanbul, which represent important technological developments in the this regional capital market.

In Section 3, the ninth chapter, "FinTech and *Shariah* Principles in Smart Contracts," discusses that the thriving emergence of FinTech affects not only the conventional finance industry but also Islamic finance industry. This chapter tries to delve the concept of smart contract in Islamic FinTech. The tenth chapter, "Blockchain for Islamic Social Responsibility Institutions," explains how Blockchain and smart contract technologies can help Islamic social responsibility institutions *Waqf* for better governance, lower transaction cost, more transparency and higher trust. The eleventh chapter, "Blockchain for Islamic Financial Services Institutions:

The Case of *Sukuk* Financing," discusses how technology could be disruptive in Islamic banking and finance sector keeping *Sukuk* as a case. The authors elaborate a proposed model of blockchain that could solve the issue of traceability.

I am hopeful that this book will deepen the discourse on the role of FinTech in modern day environment. I thank the contributors and also the external reviewers who have patiently critiqued these chapters to meet the minimum acceptable standard.

Abdul Rafay
University of Management and Technology, Pakistan
Lahore, Pakistan

REFERENCES

Cockerton, C. (2018). *FinServ 25: The most influential voices in banking*. Retrieved from https://thefinancialbrand.com

Marous, J. (2018). *FinServ 25: The most influential voices in banking*. Retrieved from https://thefinancialbrand.com

Rizzi, M. (2018). *FinServ 25: The most influential voices in banking*. Retrieved from https://thefinancialbrand.com

Section 1

Emergence and Future of FinTech

Chapter 1
Crypto-Currency:
Future of FinTech

S. Iqbal
University of Management and Technology, Pakistan

Muzammil Hussain
University of Management and Technology, Pakistan

Muhammad Umar Munir
University of Management and Technology, Pakistan

Zunair Hussain
University of Management and Technology, Pakistan

Sobia Mehrban
University of Management and Technology, Pakistan

Muhammad Adeel Ashraf
University of Management and Technology, Pakistan

Salah-u-din Ayubi
University of Management and Technology, Pakistan

ABSTRACT

This chapter sheds light on the future of crypto-currencies in the world as they have become a major part of trading and are now being adopted by leading investment firms as a new way of buying and selling. Despite the substantial security risk in crypto-currency trading, it has become the most traded commodity. Many new crypto-currencies are being introduced that attract investors. Banking institutions in USA and other leading countries have started to take part in investments in crypto-currency as it has revolutionized financial technology.

DOI: 10.4018/978-1-5225-7805-5.ch001

INTRODUCTION

Ceaseless development in innovation has prompted earth shattering headways in different fields be it restorative, building, farming and so forth. As of late digital forms of money have surprised the world and have upset the region of fund and saving money. Money related innovation which is otherwise called financial technology is getting advancer step by step with new advances and thoughts. Cryptographic forms of money have turned into a piece of consistently changing budgetary innovation and have changed the entire scene of fund and managing an account. These days computerized innovation is being utilized significantly because of which real organizations and driving keeping money establishments are anxious to partake in it that is the reason digital forms of money are thought to be an extremely lucrative method of purchasing and offering.

Digital money is as yet a generally new innovation that is the reason individuals are very little mindful of it and there is a significant need of mindfulness for it. Nations, for example, Russia and China have appreciated embracing cryptographic forms of money as new method of purchasing and offering. Digital forms of money have since ruling the features with the ascent of Crypto-cash. Digital currency was fuelled by the square chain innovation which depends on Machine learning and in addition other complex advances. Square chain innovation joins very unpredictable calculations which take a shot at shared system (Velankar, Valecha & Maji, 2018).

The likelihood of cutting edge financial benchmarks has existed for a significant long time. By then, not as much as 10 years back, Crypto-cash exploded into the universe of computerized cash. By and by, Crypto-money has ended up being not only a social ponder, in any case, a political and budgetary one likewise, holding the fiscal eye of the world prisoner through its wild course. It has by and by been comprehensively discussed and used as a piece of various made countries. With the coming of IoT which is truncation of web of things numerous new digital forms of money have additionally approached in which Ethereum (Vujicic, Jagodic & S. Randic, 2018) merits specifying and specialists have hailed it as a standout amongst the most progressive cryptographic forms of money out there in the market. Budgetary innovation is quickly changing and now money related foundations are particularly keen on digital forms of money and square chain innovation as eventual fate of exchanging and speculations.

Figure 1 illustrates that in spite of the fact that Bitcoin was the primary cryptographic money which was presented and Ethereum is moderately new however has picked up significantly more consideration since it has more perplexing and more solid square chain calculations which makes it more steady and secure. That is the reason financial specialists are supporting it and specialists have thought to be

Figure 1. Comparison between bitcoin and ethereum

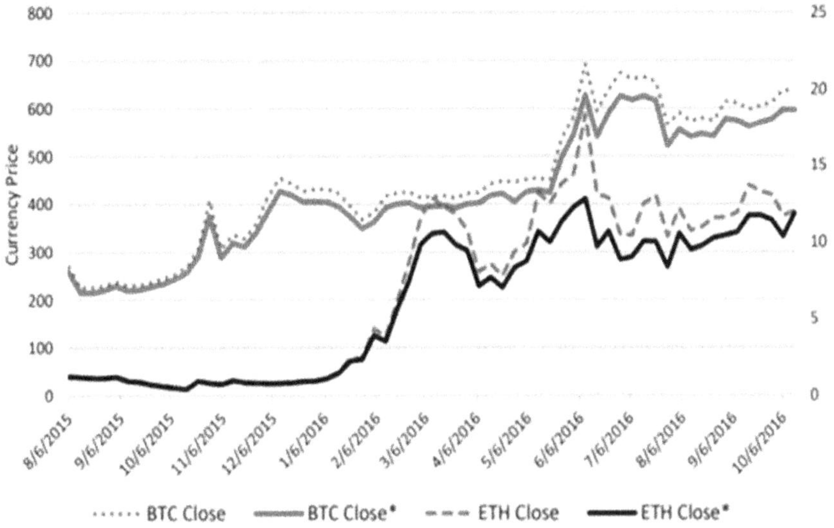

potential pioneer in digital forms of money in future (Ahram, Sargolzaei, Sargolzaei, Daniels and Amaba, 2017).

BACKGROUND

Generally, the business scene in dealing with a record has changed profoundly. After the money related emergency of 2007-2008 the monetary market authorities have braced control of the dealing with a record division, displaying new or fortifying existing standards. In addition, types of progress and change of development and monetary headways (Financial technology) have stretched out the need to search for more creative approaches moreover in sparing cash. Financial technology has changed into a fundamental piece of keeping cash. According to Accenture Report and UK Business Insider, overall financial technology wander has taken off starting late accomplishing ca. 15 billion USD in 2015 (standing out from 4.05 billion USD in 2013).

The development and joining of financial technology will reshape finance, in addition, experts starting at now call it the financial technology bother. It is strengthened by vivacious distinction in hardware (checking PDAs), programming (virtual "cloud," personalization of relationship on the web) and making centring of information progresses (ITs).

The impression of the financial technology change is to some degree conflicting. A few people from the money related associations industry see the effect in financial technology as a risk to standard dealing with a record industry. Others expect that Financial technology has changed into a test that can be changed into an open portal as it gives more essential adaptability, better an incentive in two or three zones of keeping cash business and furthermore aggregation of associations. As needs be, the progress of financial technology and its effect on the conceivable predetermination of keeping cash are unimaginably topical these days as it is illustrated in the figure 2 which explains about the global trend.

Experts in the field of finance are now looking for applying more unorthodox and unconventional solutions in the financial markets due to this crypto-currencies have become the best asset class. Although it is relatively new technology but financial experts have been very optimistic about the potential of crypto-currencies and it has been long considered to be the alternative to traditional currencies. Financial crisis of 2008, has led many leading bankers to opt for solutions that are more stable and since the crisis investors are very much more interested in crypto-currencies. With that the transactions in the crypto-currencies, as compared to traditional currencies are considered to be hundred times faster and more secure (Courtois, Emirdag and Nagy, 2017). Despite of all the advantages there are many issues revolving around the crypto-currencies as there is very little amount of regulation and it is considered to be used in illicit activities which is supposedly associated with underground deals. Along with this crypto-currencies have significant amount of risk associated with them due to massive pricing fluctuations (Lustig and Nardi, 2015).

Figure 2. Financial technology global trend

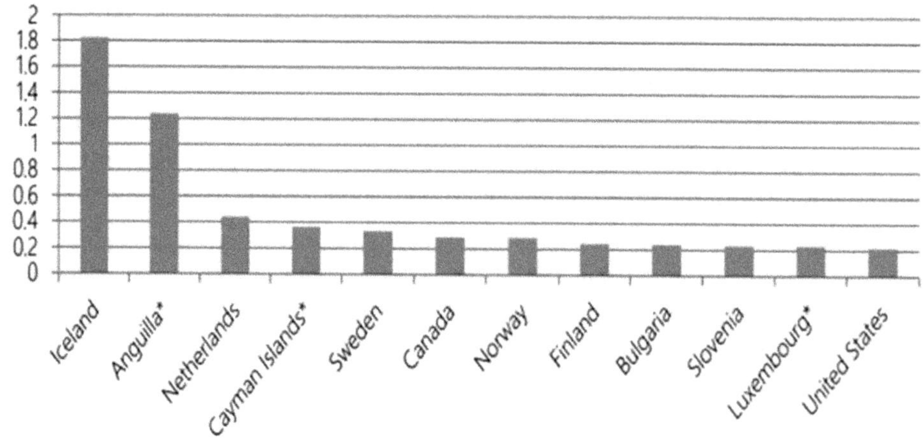

PROBLEM STATEMENT

Since the launch of crypto-currencies institutional as well as individual investors have started to trade on crypto-currencies which has led to massive speculation. Crypto-currencies are very much volatile and have significant amount of risk attached to them.

There is still no factor upon which crypto-currencies are priced due to which it makes them a highly risky investment as one can see the Figure 3 and realize about the huge fluctuations in the price of Bitcoin over the time. The prices are very much dependent on economic policies as well as geo-political climate of world. If one country bans the crypto-currencies it can cause a huge amount of depreciation in the price of crypto-currency this can lead to huge losses. People are still now much aware how the pricing is conducted due to which there is a huge possibility of loss (Fraser and Bouridane, 2017).

People with expertise are using machine learning to predict the price of crypto-currencies such as Bitcoin and Ethereum, and this is widely considered to be the best method to determine the pricing. But again, this is very technical and requires people to have a very strong knowledge of crypto-currencies and algorithms which work behind them. In addition to that there is a security concern as well because no major centralized institution insures the block chain and crypto-currencies McNally, Roche & Caton, 2018; Conti, Lal & Ruj 2018). Retail traders are also very much speculative about investing in crypto-currencies as well as the institutional traders due to significant amount of complexity involving in the crypto-currencies due to which experts need to have deep knowledge of the mathematical algorithms and functions in order to properly understand the crypto-currency.

Figure 3. Variations in the price of bitcoin over the time

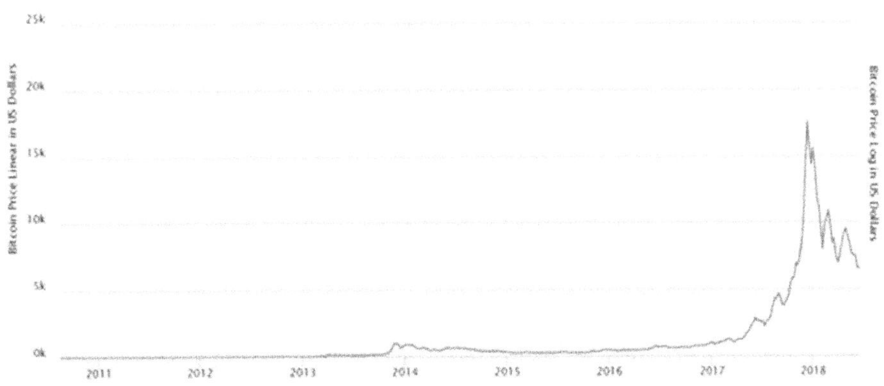

OBJECTIVE

Our genuine inspiration driving this examination is to show available development in keeping cash division that is up 'til now used as a piece of computerized types of cash. So we will probably review these open progressions and by taking a gander at these advances tell about fitting development that we used for dealing with a record division that is free from security issues and besides from trade issues. Right when piece ties at first showed up very nearly 10 years earlier as the specific spine of Bitcoin, the world's driving advanced cash, they seemed to offer the lion's share a way to deal with evacuate the budgetary operator. In any case, now the gigantic banks and other industry players are finding ways to deal with turn the new gadget additionally supporting their favorable luck. Regardless, the practicality of this technique has remained questionable a similar number of people assume that approach makers should propel opportunity and straightforwardness by drawing all in all general public to explicitly intrude and change the system for open interest. This article attempts to consolidate and separate open information with a consideration with respect to blockchain, a money related mechanical assembly that can accept a fundamental part in the supportable headway of the overall economy. The new development is depended upon to pass on immense focal points to customers, to current dealing with a record system and to the whole society when all is said in done. (Judmayer, Stifter, Krombholz, Weippl, Bertino, Sandhu, 2017)

LITERATURE REVIEW

Expert Montier (2013) says that crypto-currency price is derived from the supply and demand. In the first place, in the cash supply hypothesis, the administration prints cash and pumps it into the economy through bonds and direct spending on legislative projects. The amount hypothesis of cash expresses that MV = PY, with M being the financial supply, V being the speed of cash, P being the cost of merchandise, and Y being yield. This is the thing that market analysts call a personality, which implies that it must be valid. Since M has extended, and given a steady speed and yield, costs must ascent.

Professor John Harvey of Forbes Magazine proposes the purposeful increment in cost of a specific powerful great motivations swelling. Costs rise due to one of four variables. In the first place, showcase influencers who are safe or impervious to focused weights can raise costs. For example, the OPEC oil cartel cut the US supply of oil amid the Yom Kippur War in the 1970s, causing oil costs, as well as costs of anything that depended on oil for generation. This prompted high swelling. Second, an ascent sought after for center merchandise in respect to supply additionally climbs costs. For example, a lodging blast can lead for a request in amble, making the cost of wood increment. This expansion streams through the economy in higher costs for every related great. Third, the benefit market can add to expansion (Kaushik, Choudhary, Ektare, Thomas and Akram, 2017).

At the point when certain item prospects are exchanging at high costs, it boosts the individuals who create those products to withhold the supply with an end goal to expand the cost of those wares. At last, supply stun can cause swelling, for example, when Katrina crushed the southern US and interfered with the supply of oil. Block chain technology relies on mining heavily which needs huge amount of energy to carry on. On average a single mining setup takes a lot of energy to get created. Experts are proposing solutions to effectively mine the Bitcoins and other block chain based crypto-currencies using new methods to reduce energy consumption (Montier, 2013; Luo, Su & Huang, 2017).

METHODOLOGY

Research will be led by means of review instrument or survey. Get ready four distinctive surveys. Research papers and reports developed so far are studied to develop a comprehensive research work in order to express either the crypto-currency is the future of this global village or not?

As crypto-currency is still a nascent technology that is why there is a limited number of data and information regarding to the algorithms and designs which are used in its research.

FINDINGS

Digital currency likewise addresses the issue of trade rates. Numerous nations have precarious monetary forms. This issue is like hyperinflation, yet rather than the expansion rate going up, these monetary standards' trade rates vacillate uncontrollably. By and by, nations in war-torn regions or in turbulent areas regularly are liable to this. These monetary standards, named by financial analysts as garbage or unstable monetary forms, are set apart by fiercely fluctuating trade rates. One case of an unstable cash is Brazil's genuine. In 2012, fund serve Guido Mantega announced a cash war on the United States, planning to battle back against what he hinted were uncalled for "expansionary money related approaches" that made the genuine acknowledge. To do this, the Brazilian government broadened a six percent exchange assess on abroad advances that would develop in more than three years.

This exchange assess was intended to make the Brazilian genuine devalue, making trades less expensive and empowering the nation's economy.

The idea of Crypto-money makes it to a great extent safe to hyperinflation. To start with, it is managed by the network Crypto-money is viewed as a product cash. New "coins" can enter the trade through mining, at the end of the day there is a limited number of Crypto-currencies that can exist. This makes Crypto-money acknowledge in esteem. One diary article stated this preferred standpoint in the accompanying way: Hyperinflations have never happened when an item filled in as cash or when paper cash was convertible into a ware.

The scourge of hyperinflation has just raised its appalling head when the supply of cash had no characteristic limitations and was administered by an optional paper cash standard. Second, Crypto-cash is liable to decentralized direction, which gives it protection against supply stun and the hardships of the cash supply hypothesis. Some stress that this collapse will prompt accumulating of Crypto-cash, which would cause both instability and inaccessibility of the money.

Be that as it may, rather than having the coveted impact, the genuine conversion scale has since changed drastically. This vacillation has made three asymmetries create in the trade advertise. To start with, the mental factor of

Misfortune abhorrence becomes possibly the most important factor, which implies that amid times of either thankfulness or deterioration, the losing side feels the torment of misfortune more intensely and vocally than the less vocal winning side. This brings on additional change in financial strategy.

While Crypto-money does not offer an entire answer for this issue, it can fence against cash changes. People living in a nation such a Brazil with unusual and unstable trade rates can rather put their cash in Crypto-money. Utilizing Crypto-cash as a holding place for their cash, they at that point can either change over their Crypto-money into other, more steady monetary standards or just utilize Crypto-money as their value-based cash. Enthusiasm for Crypto-cash is as of now high in nations comfortable with this sort of instability, for example, Indonesia (Gifari, Anggorojati & Yazid, 2017).

Concept of centralization in the leading crypt-currency i.e. Bitcoin has also surfaced and will impact hugely because it can stabilize the currency as well as the whole crypto market if it is done properly.

DISCUSSION

The possibility of advanced monetary forms has existed for quite a long time. Be that as it may, in spite of some exertion with respect to software engineers, none demonstrated reasonable. At that point, not as much as 10 years prior, Bitcoin detonated into the universe of cryptographic money. Presently, Bitcoin has turned out to be a social marvel, as well as a political and financial one too, holding the monetary eye of the world hostage through its wild course. It has right now been broadly talked about and utilized as a part of numerous created nations.

Notwithstanding, proposed theory is that Bitcoin gives an unmistakable favourable position to populaces living in immature and battling economies, since it is takes care of the issues of hyperinflation, trade, duplicating, and unavailability. This paper likewise suggests that the three factors that may thwart the boundless reception of Bitcoin in these battling economies is absence of foundation, hidden issues with the Bitcoin organize itself, and dread of the obscure.

In an environment that advances exceedingly mind boggling and mysterious trades of information, the likelihood for significant system bargains (i.e. 'hacks') appears to be high. The ongoing case of the DAO assault causing 3.6 million individual units of Ether to be directed into a substitute DAO shows the likelihood and potential seriousness of such hacks. While the likelihood of a '51% assault' in which a greater part partner can essentially affect the estimation of Crypto-monetary standards, the likelihood of a noteworthy hack is improbable because of the inflexible system of Crypto-monetary standards and the relative absence of across the board utility, the main eminent special case being Crypto-monetary standards Exchange disappointments as on account of the Mt. Gox emergency. On the other hand, Ether has effectively encountered a noteworthy hack, prompting the fork amongst Ethereum and Ethereum Classic. More opportunity, more hubs, and more hazard is inborn in the Ethereum Network, and accordingly, the danger of a noteworthy hack is significantly higher. There is some danger of real hacks with respect to the different trades in which both Crypto-monetary forms and Ethereum are exchanged. These hacks while not normally characteristic of defects with the digital money's code, have verifiably appeared to affect the cost of every cash transaction.

Cryptographic forms of money have utility entirely as advanced cash as it is illustrated in below figure 4 that more and more people are trying to own crypto currencies and use them as regular means of exchange. Accordingly, Crypto-monetary forms can be relied upon to have a converse relationship to the condition of the worldwide economy. Spots ailing in monetary foundation or exceptionally swelled monetary forms will probably recognize crypto-monetary standards as an elective measure for execution. In spite of the fact that Ether ought to likewise shoulder a backwards relationship to the worldwide economy because of these same factors, the greatness of this relationship would almost certainly be reduced because of the wide cluster of employments, and the more imaginative nature of the Ethereum Network. Where Crypto-monetary forms esteems are probably going to act in an indistinguishable way from wares, Ether esteem ought to relate all the

Figure 4. Trend of using cryptocurrencies over the time

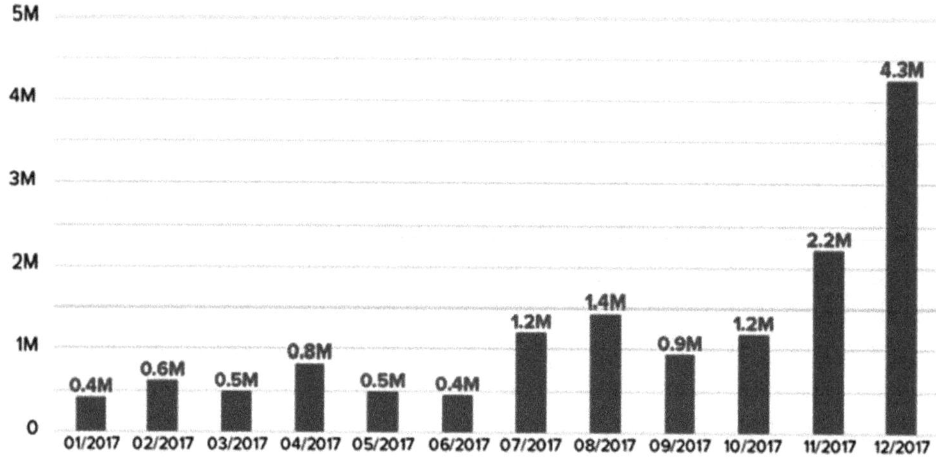

more intently to broad selection of the system and shrewd contracts (M. Saad and A. Mohaisen, 2018).

There is potential for internet business to emphatically affect the estimation of digital forms of money and in addition ether, anyway cryptographic forms of money is better situated to be utilized as a part of these exchanges. The present instalment frameworks are set up with the end goal that there are different touch directs which leads toward exorbitant exchanges (up to 10%) and long preparing circumstances. The digital forms of money dispose of the requirement for these check strategies and significantly lessen the exchange time. Cryptographic forms of money show up particularly valuable to limit these expenses and keeping in mind that the more prominent potential for hacks and security issues because of multifaceted nature for Ethereum, the probability and size of effect would be less noteworthy for Ethereum's flexible system (Beikverdi and Song 2015)

The blockchain applications for financial technology are better for the Ethereum stage as it is a more adaptable stage for these foundations to complete their activities. The advantage that is accomplished is a protected exchange and additionally a solitary record that lessens the need to accommodate over each gathering's free record (Brennan & Lunn, 2016). Where there could be benefits for the individual monetary forms is if the financial technology organizations might want to expand liquidity in low liquidity markets, anyway this is a moderately little opportunity. Because of the more extensive scope of use for the Ethereum keen contracts, we have gathered that the feasible effect of financial technology reception would be more prominent for Ethereum as they can complete applications notwithstanding utilizing the advantages of Crypto-monetary forms as a digital currency.

There have been many cases of security flaws in one of leading crypto-currencies Bitcoin as it can be manipulated with set of certain algorithms. This has resulted in value of Bitcoin significantly. Many events have taken place which have caused dramatic change in price of Bitocoin and resulted in losses of people and investors alike (Fraser & Bouridane, 2017).

PROPOSED AGREEMENT

Decentralization is the basic course of action with cutting edge money related structures innovative improvement. With the movement of IOT decentralization improvement can additionally be utilized with IOT consequently monetary headway can be given both in cell phones and in electronic building. Blockchain is seen as an open record where each online trade are recorded and everyone is allowed to relate, to send or affirm exchange2s. Toward the day's end, Blockchain is a digitized course of action of accounting records which records in unpretentious components all trades according to a logical plan of principles to prevent unlawful impedance. Research on impacts of cryptographic types of cash, decentralized record and Blockchain have shown that they are conceivably extreme gadgets to constrain costs and pass on genuine changes to the budgetary field as time goes on (V. Vallois and F. A. Guenane, 2017).

No one can undermine the brilliance of block chain technology which has brought number of innovations but the stability of crypto-currencies depends upon the reliance of more credible technology and background Internet of things is being adopted now in the world of technology due to which block chain has also amassed great innovation and new ideas (Conoscenti et. al., 2016).

REFERENCES

Ahram, T., Sargolzaei, A., Sargolzaei, S., Daniels, J., & Amaba, B. (2017). *Blockchain technology innovations. In 2017 IEEE Technology & Engineering Management Conference* (pp. 137–141). Santa Clara, CA: TEMSCON.

Beikverdi, A., & Song, J. (2015). Trend of centralization in Bitcoin's distributed network. *2015 IEEE/ACIS 16th International Conference on Software Engineering, Artificial Intelligence, Networking and Parallel/Distributed Computing (SNPD)*, 1-6. 10.1109/SNPD.2015.7176229

Conoscenti, M., Vetrò, A., & De Martin, J. C. (2016). Blockchain for the Internet of Things: A systematic literature review. *2016 IEEE/ACS 13th International Conference of Computer Systems and Applications (AICCSA)*, 1-6. 10.1109/AICCSA.2016.7945805

Conti, M., Kumar, S., Lal, C., & Ruj, S. (2018). A survey on security and privacy issues of bitcoin. IEEE Communications Surveys & Tutorials. doi:10.1109/COMST.2018.2842460

Courtois, N. T., Emirdag, P., & Nagy, D. A. (2014). Could Bitcoin transactions be 100x faster? *2014 11th International Conference on Security and Cryptography (SECRYPT)*, 1-6. 10.5220/0005102804260431

doi:10.1109/INFOTEH.2018.8345547

Fraser, J. G., & Bouridane, A. (2017). Have the security flaws surrounding BITCOIN effected the currency's value? *2017 Seventh International Conference on Emerging Security Technologies (EST)*, 50-55. 10.1109/EST.2017.8090398

Gifari, A., Anggorojati, B., & Yazid, S. (2017). On preventing bitcoin transaction from money laundering in Indonesia: Analysis and recommendation on regulations. *2017 International Workshop on Big Data and Information Security (IWBIS)*, 143-148. 10.1109/IWBIS.2017.8275116

Judmayer, A., Stifter, N., Krombholz, K., & Weippl, E. (2017). Blocks and Chains: Introduction to Bitcoin, Cryptocurrencies, and Their Consensus Mechanisms. *Synthesis Lectures on Information Security, Privacy, &. Trust*, *9*(1), 1–123.

Kaushik, A., Choudhary, A., Ektare, C., Thomas, D., & Akram, S. (2017). Blockchain — Literature survey. *2017 2nd IEEE International Conference on Recent Trends in Electronics, Information & Communication Technology (RTEICT)*, 2145-2148. 10.1109/RTEICT.2017.8256979

Luo, J., Su, W., & Huang, A. Q. (2017, July). Bit-energy: An innovative bitcoin-style distributed transactional model for a competitive electricity market. In 2017 IEEE Power & Energy Society General Meeting (pp. 1-5). IEEE. doi:10.1109/PESGM.2017.8274639

Lustig, C., & Nardi, B. (2015). Algorithmic Authority: The Case of Bitcoin. *2015 48th Hawaii International Conference on System Sciences*, 743-752. 10.1109/HICSS.2015.95

McNally, S., Roche, J., & Caton, S. (2018). Predicting the Price of Bitcoin Using Machine Learning. *2018 26th Euromicro International Conference on Parallel, Distributed and Network-based Processing (PDP)*, 339-343. 10.1109/PDP2018.2018.00060

Montier, J. (2013). *Hyperinflations, Hysteria, and False Memories*. GMO LLC.

Saad, M., & Mohaisen, A. (2018). Towards characterizing blockchain-based cryptocurrencies for highly-accurate predictions. *IEEE INFOCOM 2018 - IEEE Conference on Computer Communications Workshops (INFOCOM WKSHPS)*, 704-709. 10.1109/INFCOMW.2018.8406859

Vallois, V., & Guenane, F. A. (2017). Bitcoin transaction: From the creation to validation, a protocol overview. *2017 1st Cyber Security in Networking Conference (CSNet)*, 1-7. 10.1109/CSNET.2017.8241988

Velankar, S., Valecha, S., & Maji, S. (2018). Crypto-currency price prediction using machine learning. *2018 20th International Conference on Advanced Communication Technology (ICACT)*, 144-147.

Vujičić, D., Jagodić, D., & Ranđić, S. (2018). Blockchain technology, bitcoin, and Ethereum: A brief overview. *2018 17th International Symposium INFOTEH-JAHORINA (INFOTEH)*, 1-6. 10.1109/INFOTEH.2018.8345547

Chapter 2
FinTech and SMEs:
The Italian Case

Stefania Marrara
Consorzio per il Trasferimento Tecnologico C2T, Italy

Mirjana Pejic-Bach
https://orcid.org/0000-0003-3899-6707
University of Zagreb, Croatia

Sanja Seljan
University of Zagreb, Croatia

Amir Topalovic
Consorzio per il Trasferimento Tecnologico C2T, Italy

ABSTRACT

In this chapter, a study about how Italian SMEs understand and use FinTech technologies is presented. The study focuses on FinTech-aided banking services, in particular, due to the fact that these are, at present, the most widely used FinTech technologies available in Italy. The study shows how, despite FinTech entering Italy only in recently, the Italian SMEs market is very active and fruitful for digital companies. In the last years, a continuous growth of investment has seen the development of FinTech technologies in multiple areas, such as mobile networks, big data, trust management, mobile embedded systems, cloud computing, image processing, and data analytic techniques.

DOI: 10.4018/978-1-5225-7805-5.ch002

INTRODUCTION

In the last years, the term Financial Technology (FinTech) has been adopted in order to describe a wide range of services, aided by several financial technologies (Gabor & Brooks, 2017), for different types of organizations, which mainly address the advancement of quality of financial products and services supported by Information Technology (IT) applications. FinTech has become important due to several important factors, ranging from technical advancement, enterprises innovation, the need for reducing costs, and for improving the relationship with the customers. The high speed in which FinTech has been adopted caused a great challenge, due to the multidisciplinarity, advanced usage of integrated platforms, and increased demand for such services (Gai, Qiu, & Sun, 2018). FinTech is supported with the development of cutting-edge technologies, among which the most relevant are those that can discover hidden information from various sources and thus improve the decision-making process in SMEs, which influence security, and enable easier communication with customers.

In Italy, from the end of the first decade of 2000, almost all banks decided to follow new paths, starting a process of exploiting digital opportunities and moving clients onto more agile and less costly channels (i.e., Internet Banking and Mobile Banking) envisioning novel ways for serving clients and generating profit (Premoli, 2017).

The chapter has three goals. The first goal of the chapter is to analyze the wealth of digital possibilities, embedded as FinTech solutions and strategic partnerships, that are available for banks to improve their current portfolio of products and services. The second goal is to provide the overview of the FinTech solutions for SMEs, with the focus to Italian banks and FinTech, and to provide the overview of two main venues for increasing their competitiveness: (i) online advisory and internationalization for SMEs, and (ii) product standardization and multichannel distribution. The third goal of the paper is to analyze the main emerging and disruptive technologies in banking domain, adopted by the FinTech industry today (e.g., big data, data mining, text mining, blockchain, AI), which provide a rich source for future research directions for FinTech.

The abovementioned goals are attained by (i) conducting a comprehensive literature overview, focusing on cutting-edge research in the area of disruptive technologies (e.g., big data, data mining, natural language processing); (ii) investigating the grey-literature research in order to collect knowledge on Italian FinTech, such as case studies, white papers and industry position papers.

The chapter consists of the following parts. After the introduction, the background of the research is provided, focusing on Italian SMEs and their significance for the economy. The third chapter discusses FinTech as a new venue for advancing financial products and services, presenting the main technologies used for FinTech applications, the relationship between FinTech and innovation, and the role of FinTech as a disruptive technology in the Italian context. The fourth chapter aims at providing solutions and recommendations for FinTech and Italian SMEs, while fifth chapter provides the overview of future research directions for FinTech, such as big data, data mining, text mining, and others. Finally, a conclusion is provided.

BACKGROUND

The Relevance of SMEs in the Italian Economy

Small Medium Enterprises (SMEs) are the most widely spread companies in the European Union and are considered the true engine of economic growth. Indeed, SMEs represent 99.8% of European companies (93% are micro enterprises) in the non-financial business sector. For this reason, they also play an important role in the European labor market. Almost 90 million people were employed in SMEs in 2015 (67% of total employment), and they generated 58% of the sector's value added (Muller et al., 2015).

In Italy and Spain, in particular, the share of workers employed by small companies are equal to 79.6% and 73.1% respectively (Figure 1).

Before the financial turmoil of 2007-2008, the number of jobs in SMEs 'increased at an average annual rate of 1.9%, while the number of jobs in large enterprises increased by only 0.8%', as indicated by the report European SMEs under Pressure:

Figure 1. The share of SMEs participation in employment, and total number of firms in selected European countries
Source: Muller et al. (2015)

Annual Report on EU Small and Medium-Sized Enterprises. SME performance review (European Commission, 2010).

European Commission uses four quantitative criteria in order to define the size of the company (European Commission, 2003): '(i) the total number of employees in the enterprise; (ii) the annual volume of the turnover; (iii) and the total of the assets in the enterprise balance, and (iv) the degree of independence of the enterprise or the ownership over it'. Different values of these criteria according to four groups of enterprises according to size: micro, small, medium and large are depicted in Figure 2.

The number of employees (the 'staff headcount criterion") is the main criterion; introducing a financial and ownership 'criterion is nonetheless a necessary adjunct in order to grasp the real scale and performance of an enterprise and its position compared to its competitors' (European Commission, 2003). Therefore, to classify an enterprise, the condition a) must be present and accompanied by some employees and the size of the revenue or assets. Finally, the ultimate condition, the ownership, states that 'the participation of a big enterprise in the ownership of a small or medium enterprise should be of no more than 25% of its share capital' (European Commission, 2003, p.2). However, 'in order to encourage the creation of enterprises, equity financing of SMEs and rural and local development, enterprises can be considered autonomous despite a holding of 25% or more by certain categories of investors who have a positive role in business financing and creation' (European Commission, 2003, p.3).

Nowadays, the recovery from the financial crisis indicated the need for the economies to create employment opportunities for the citizens. Hence, given the contribution mentioned above of SMEs to employment, the growth and creation of SMEs are essential.

As shown in Figure 1, SMEs are extremely important in Italy, much more than in other European big countries, such as France and Germany. The result is expected, since many Italian SMEs, particularly in the manufacturing industry, are famous all over the world: 'made in Italy" is considered a guarantee of the high quality of the products. The downturn of 2008 has created several problems for Italian SMEs, undermining their ability to generate profit and, not less important, to generate cash.

Figure 2. Criteria for classifying companies according to size
Source: European Commission, 2010

	Employees	Revenue	Assets
Micro	< 10	< €2 million	< €2 million
Small	10-49	€2 – €10 million	€2 – €10 million
Medium	50-250	€10 - €50 million	€10 - €43 million
Large	> 250	> 50€ million	> 43€ million

From the beginning of the crisis to 2015, more than 82.000 firms have failed with the consequent loss of almost 1.000.000 employees. Many of them died not because they were not profitable anymore, but because of lack of cash. Banks were almost forced to deny credit to many small companies, more opaque and riskier than large corporates, thus deteriorating SMEs' situation.

As already said, SMEs are the basic element for the Italian economy. Hence it is fundamental to sustain them during difficult periods and help them re-finding the path of growth. This can be done both with the politic support of the government, through ad hoc fiscal policies to unburden the firms, and with the monetary support, i.e., banks that give credit to companies in order to finance their day-to-day operations and new profitable projects.

Business clients are an important market segment for the banks (Rajaobelina, Brun & Toufaily, 2013) in particular the small and medium enterprises (SMEs). First, SMEs are the vast majority of companies, both in Italy and throughout Europe. Second, even if their turnover is substantially smaller than those of large companies are, SMEs still need a variety of banking products and services in order to support their day-to-day operations (Dhliwayo & Governor, 2014). Also, SMEs are less ready, than large corporations, to move from one bank to another in order to reduce their financing costs, such as the minimum possible interest rates (Sayani, 2015). Therefore, SMEs are potentially more profitable clients for banks.

Furthermore, successful SMEs have the potential for growth, and with the right support and the right choices of financial products, they can increase their turnover, and even grow to the size of large corporations. If a bank recognizes their potential early, such fast-growing SMEs can become the most loyal clients for the bank. Above stated indicate that banks are keen to innovate the portfolio of their products and services, in order to provide an attractive offer for the SMEs, providing not only standard digital products but also pushing on value-added services, supported with digital technologies (Chen, 2016).

FinTech as a Disruptive Technology in the Italian Context

Following the 2017 report by ABI (Associazione Bancaria Italiana), innovations promoted by FinTech can not only be an opportunity to develop alternative services, but can also support the operations of banks, such as credit rating techniques (ABI (Giovanni Sabatini), 2017). Italian banks have already determined as a priority the relationship with FinTech.The present Italian scenario is made up of 136 FinTech companies that have launched 145 initiatives as shown in Figure 3.

The main Italian Groups and Banks are implementing new partnership strategies with the various FinTech start-ups through:

Figure 3. Italian FinTech initiatives
Source: Adapted from ABI (Giovanni Sabatini), 2017

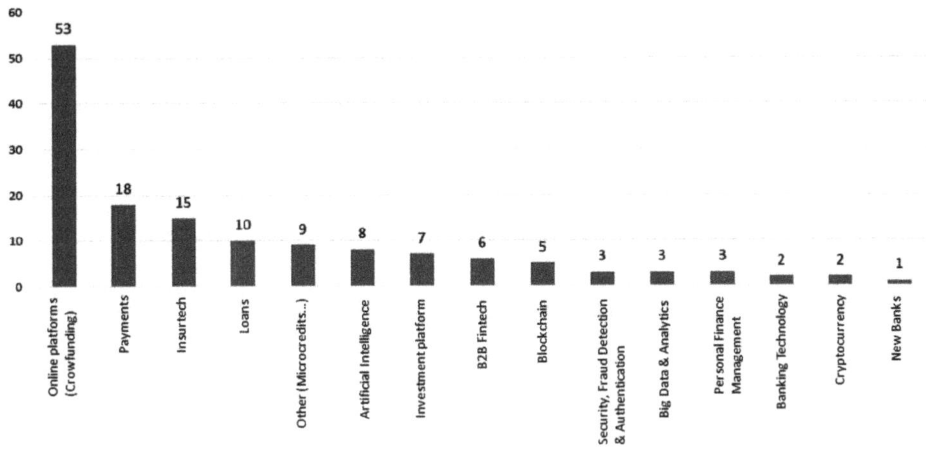

- the creation of dedicated investment funds, both Italian and international,
- commercial partnerships,
- targeted investments in the capital of certain FinTech start-ups,
- the creation of accelerators and incubators for the development of FinTech,
- international observatories for FinTech's innovation scouting activities, and
- joint research and development activities with the FinTech world.

As stated in the 2017 by the Italian FinTech Report (NetConsulting, 2017), banks and financial operators are beginning to show signs of concern about FinTech and the way it could pose a threat to traditional business, as emerges in PWC's Global FinTech Report 2017, which involved over 1,300 respondents (Financial Companies and FinTech) in 71 different countries around the world, including Italy.

The report highlights that 89% of European banks and 82% of Italian banks claim to see FinTech as a possible threat, in particular in some areas of the value- chain such as Payments, Robo-Advisoring, and Personal Financial Management. To avoid the possible threat of FinTech and turn it into an opportunity, 41% of traditional Finance operators have entered into partnerships with these start-ups, while 84% say that, in order to better face the challenges that the digital transformation requires, they intend to start cooperation programs with newly established companies in the next 3-5 years. The scenario is therefore in strong evolution, and the collaboration with FinTech represents an opportunity for banks to accelerate the process of innovation.

FINTECH AS A NEW VENUE FOR ADVANCING FINANCIAL PRODUCTS AND SERVICES

FinTech would not be possible without the advancements in the new technologies, as well as a rapid decrease in the prices of hardware and software solutions, as well as supported by numerous open-source initiatives. This, in turn, resulted in the explosion of innovations supported and developed by FinTech solutions.

The Main Technologies Used for FinTech Applications

FinTech is a term denoting financial services aided by technological innovation, which can take the form of new business models, processes or products, with a decisive effect on the financial markets, the institutions, or on the supply of services: the use of technology, therefore, constitutes a prerequisite to make financial innovation possible (Van Loo, 2018).

FinTech innovations include financial services supported with various information and communication technologies (Gomber, Kauffman, Parker & Weber, 2018). FinTech covers various services: crowd-funding, peer-to-peer lending, payment services (e.g., instant payment), virtual currencies (e.g., Bitcoin), and consulting services (e.g., roboadvisor). Also, it uses technologies for the decentralized validation of transactions (e.g., Blockchain), biometric identification (e.g., using fingerprint, retina facial recognition), and the support for the delivery of services (e.g., with the utilization of cloud computing and big data). FinTech is present in numerous banking and financial services markets. For example, it allows the entry of technological start-ups, and the giants of the information and social media technology (Google, Apple, Facebook, Amazon, Alibaba).

Morgan (2017) defines five broad technological areas currently adopted by the FinTech industry today: (i) artificial intelligence and machine learning, (ii) application technologies interfaces, (iii) Blockchain, (iv) human digital interfaces, and (v) quantum computing.

Artificial Intelligence and Machine Learning.

In recent years there have been numerous debates on the contribution that Artificial Intelligence (AI) and Machine Learning (ML) can make to the banking and financial world. In its broadest definition, AI is identified as mere cognitive computing, with the meaning that it can increase human intelligence, but not replace it. In the financial field, AI has made a fundamental contribution to the identification of innovative techniques for fraud detection. Another important area has been the definition of intelligent systems that satisfy a whole series of compliance regulations, capable of keeping companies up to date with regulations that are constantly evolving. AI-built chats are an excellent tool to help operators to handle customer requests accurately and quickly, or in some cases even to replace the human operator. In the financial sector, AI is used for simulations of financial stress situations or for building predictive models to support decision-making activities. However, its potential will be utilized to the greatest extent only if it is combined with big data, which is one of the most fruitful directions of the future research for SMEs and FinTech.

Application Technologies Interfaces (APIs)

The use of APIs has been a key element in making the landscape of new services, also in the form of mobile apps, more lively, which have made it possible to keep pace with the economic and business challenges that the financial industry has been facing for some years now. FinTech start-ups have been able to create high technological value software that has challenged, and in some cases surpassed, a consolidated but, for this reason, rigid banking sector. Banks had to incredibly increase their investments in technology both internally, improving their ability to create innovative mobile applications, and by participating in developer sandboxes through the release of APIs.

Blockchain

The blockchain is distributed architecture that make financial areas with a high risk of fraud more reliable and transparent. By establishing consortia, large financial operators are working together to create new infrastructures based on this new technology, with the aim to replace obsolete and non-integrated systems. This process is affecting both commercial financing platforms and cross-border payments. Thanks also to digital identification, Blockchain is becoming an important asset in overcoming financial mechanisms rigid due to the high rate of fraud and lack of transparency. By eliminating these rocks within business processes and by creating innovative networks, Blockchain is making the exchange of value through ecosystems effective and efficient.

Blockchain represents a type of disruptive technology having a big impact on cost-savings, labor-saving, transparency, security, and others, having significant implications in banking and finance (Cocco, Pinna & Marchesi, 2017). Guo and Liang (2016) point out issues of regulation, efficiency, and security. FinTech Network (N/A) quotes the following possible uses of blockchain: reduction of fraud, which represents one of the main challenges in the banking sector; Know Your Consumer (KYC) by including data of KYC; trading platform; new way of payments, allowing banks to operate 24h/day, and many others.

Human Digital Interfaces

Digital devices have long been part of our daily lives. Nowadays, they can accept both voice and touch screen commands. Biometric identification systems are widespread in many areas and can cover both fingerprint or face recognition and retinal scans.

Quantum Computing

A computer based on quantum computing uses qubits instead of bits, allowing it to go beyond encoding two-state information (0.1). A quantum computer can therefore greatly increase the amount of information it can store while consuming less energy. Although quantum computers cannot be expected to replace traditional computers in the foreseeable future, they are already used today to solve very complex computing problems, such as maximizing the return on investment based on a given risk profile. Through the combined use of artificial intelligence and automatic learning, they can make calculations that are extremely fast but also highly reliable. Areas such as fraud detection or money laundering are particularly promising for the use of quantum computing.

All these technologies play an important role in the Italian FinTech context as shown at the Italian FinTech Forum held in Milan on April 12th, 2018.

FinTech and Innovation

FinTech is an industry that continues to be at the forefront of innovation (Gomber et al., 2018; Leong, Tan, Xiao, Tan, & Sun, 2017). While security risks remain, the winners are consumers who see the benefit and functionality in their banking and financial experiences, thanks to these trends in FinTech technology (Lee & Shin, 2018). Therefore, the possible reasons for the success of the high number of start-ups active in FinTech and the giants of ICT, reside above all, in their inherent capacity to create technological innovation and, secondly, the speed with which these can implant the innovations achieved in old and new services, being free from pre-existing technological systems (so-called 'legacy systems'). At present, FinTech companies can offer a wide range of services of financing, payment, investment and consulting with high technological content and at competitive prices; their activity contributes to the development of non-banking sectors, closing a gap in the capital market (Gai et al., 2018).

The current and prospective demand factors are important too. The demand of financial services with a high technological content is set to increase with the growth of the share of the population familiar with digital services, in particular, young people, the so-called millennials and digital natives (Jones, Ramanau, Cross, &

Healing, 2010). However, at this moment, it is obvious that the FinTech innovations structurally simplify how customers use financial services. In that case, they will enable financial transactions to be carried out easily in each case, everywhere, and at any time, there is connectivity, using clients own mobile devices. What is even more important, even as they are primarily aimed at digital natives, FinTech also facilitates the most populous cohorts of older and less computer literate customers.

However, the future scenarios are uncertain. The first scenario is that a configuration of the financial system in which actors, currently outside the regulatory perimeter, would continue to remain outside, offering technological intermediaries and financial services preparatory to the development of new ways of intermediation (which would remain in the hands of the traditional intermediaries). The second scenario is that FinTech could mark the entry of the same computer technology giants and social media in the financial system, strongly stimulating the competitiveness of the financial system. In this case, the erosion of market shares would also occur thanks to the ability of these subjects to exploit the micro-data of their customers, profiling the characteristics of customers and offering them integrated services, including, for example, the online sale of products through payment or credit services dedicated (Aldás-Manzano, Lassala-Navarré, Ruiz-Mafé, & Sanz-Blas, 2009).

A secondary effect of the FiTtech is that the entry of new operators into the financial system already obliges intermediaries to react by investing more in technological innovation to reduce costs and to automate processes in order to re-modulate distribution channels for offering customers innovative and high-quality services. At the international level, it is estimated that the investment for the development of FinTech projects exceeded 25 billion dollars in 2016 (European Central Bank, 2016). North America is the leading region for investments (55 percent of the total), followed by Asia (34 percent) and therefore from Europe (9 percent). Investments in Italy are still limited compared to other European countries, such as the United Kingdom, Germany, France, and the Netherlands, due to a low presence of FinTech companies and a still traditional banking business model, moreover, the network of branches is not very automated and the entire system is mainly based on it.

Therefore, FinTech can be a driver for innovation in the financial industry, seeking new business models and recovering satisfactory margins of profitability. For smaller intermediaries, the probability of inaction could be even higher, due to the high investments required and the problems of coordination between a wide range of actors during the strategy definition and the implementation of platforms of services of common interest.

FinTech Solution for Italian SMEs

As claimed by the 2018 BeBeez Report on FinTech (BeBeez, 2018), the FinTech revolution began in Italy almost in silence, with the first web platforms of loans between private individuals born between 2012 and 2013. There was a jump between 2016 and 2017 in terms of new services, and now, thanks to the new European directive on payment services (Payment Services Directive 2 or PSD2), we are on the eve of another big leap, with a series of new services that individuals and businesses can use to pay, transfer money and check the status of their accounts. In this framework, all the start-ups that develop technologies to support these are then included services and thus technologies for mobile payments or services of big data analysis and structuring of Blockchain.

In the world, the FinTech sector has already attracted billions of dollars of investments by venture capital funds, but also by the private equity funds. The sector has already attracted investment of 5.42 billion euros in the retail sector. The data are from CB Insights, which specifies that this is the third value highest recorded since the beginning of 2013, after that of the third quarter 2015 at €5.5 billion and the second quarter of 2017 at €5.5 billion.

SOLUTIONS AND RECOMMENDATIONS FOR FINTECH AND ITALIAN SMES

In this chapter we focus to the main two venues for the Italian SMEs and financial institutions to utilize FinTech solutions in order to increase their competitiveness: (i) online advisory and internationalization for SMEs, and (ii) product standardization and multichannel distribution.

Online Advisory and Internationalization for SMEs

As previously stated, a great portion of NPL (i.e., the amount of non-performing loans over total loans) in banks' balance sheets derives from corporate clients, especially the smaller ones. The reason behind this evidence is straightforward: many SMEs do not have sufficient financial knowledge. This is particularly true in Italy, even if it is a general problem of SMEs from all over the world. Generally, Italian entrepreneurs have great ideas and can deliver niche products, also requested from foreign countries. Thus, the default of many SMEs is often due to a lack of financial expertise and dangerous financial choices and not because of a poor product, difficult to sell on the market. Premoli (2017) provides the recap of some of the most interesting products that came out from the analysis of the Italian bank's services. Starting from

The actual relationship between banks and firms is based on a dispute for the lowest spread on the loan or the line of credit, without reasoning on the value-added elements. Usually, what SMEs need is deep support in financial activities, such as instruments of cash flow forecasting and the right advisory on how to finance an investment or what the main movement of the markets are. Indeed, many SMEs do not have an internal solid and specialized accounting, finance, and control business unit and, consequently, do not have a Chief Financial Officer (CFO) that takes reasonable decisions with a financial viewpoint. This lack of financial knowledge often brings small firms to undertake hazardous actions that in some years lead the business to fail.

Online Advisory

In this field, the digital can have an important role. The online advisory is already a reality for the retail clients of many digital banks in Italy, such as Wediba and Fineco, and soon can affect the corporate segments. Such digital capabilities are playing a significantly greater role in the selection process of the banks. According to a research performed by The Boston Consulting Group (BCG), 'after financial stability, service excellence, and business understanding, customers rated digital capabilities the most important factor in evaluating their business-banking relationship requirements." In the same research, they highlighted the importance of human interaction that, however, must be accompanied by new digital solutions because 'banking clients expect those one-on-one relationships to be complemented with smart, tailored, digitally enabled service" (Boston Consulting Group, 2016). By now, the two leading banks in Italy, UniCredit and Intesa Sanpaolo, have developed some interesting digital tools to support their small business clients. In particular, UniCredit merchants that need a POS to run their business can activate a service that gives to business owners a set of intuitive graphs and synthetic prospects, useful to deepen their business trends and the buying habits of their customers.

Another interesting product offered by UniCredit is a tool for all the SMEs that have more than one banking account. This product offers not only an aggregated view of all the expenses and financial situation of the firm but also help it to understand what could be the most suitable financing products according to its operations and its current situation. Furthermore, it is possible to manage autonomously advanced payment of account receivables. On the other hand, Intesa Sanpaolo offers to its small business customers an online platform where they can publish request of commercial collaborations, acquisitions, sales and meet online firms also coming from foreign countries.

Internationalization

It is known that export is a fundamental component of the Italian economy and foreign countries very well appreciate Italian products. Moreover, the increasing globalization of the market is pushing several companies to find new interesting customers abroad. Sometimes this is an issue for small businesses that are used to sell their products within their border and do not have sufficient means and expertise to go out of the country. For this reason, many banks are developing online platforms, such as the Intesa mentioned above Sanpaolo, able to support SMEs in their expansion abroad.

In Italy, this kind of digital solutions is also spreading through smaller banks that want to be among the first movers of the country. A practical example is BPER, that recently launched a platform developed to increase and improve the internationalization paths of the firms, providing directly online the resources and information needed by answering four simple questions. A similar product is also offered by some European banks. An example is provided by BBVA, the second biggest bank in Spain, which offers a digital web platform that supports Spanish SMEs that would like to expand their business overseas using advisor's expert in different markets and sectors.

Nevertheless, different businesses belong to different sectors, and their related economics are different from one industry to another. For this reason, it would be better for some banks to specialize in specific industries and become a leader of that specific segment of firms. SMEs need an advisor that deeply understand the challenges of a specific market, that help them recommending where to invest and not to invest, and that can forecast possible development of the market and the connected impact on the cash flows of the firms. Logically, the choice of the target industry, such as agribusiness, energy or mechanic, will depend on the specific context of the local market, on the dimension of the industry and on the possibility to create differentiation with respect to other banks. Industry specialization would mean, for example, to create tailored products for that industry, to hire specialists coming from that industry that become valuable advisors but also useful risk managers because the economics of an agribusiness firm is radically different from the ones of an energy firm and experts would prevent to take unnecessary risks.

In Europe, Rabobank is one of the banks that provides a real application of this solution. The Dutch bank has developed, besides a generic but well-detailed platform that gives online advisory and insights of several markets, a specific platform for the agribusiness. FAR, that stands for Food & Agribusiness Research, and Advisory is a platform that provides many reports created by more than 80 food & agribusiness research analysts that collect information and spot opportunities using local knowledge and global reach.

Of course, not all the solutions described so far lead directly to an increase in the revenue of the bank. Nevertheless, they have two main effects that will be visible in the end. On one side, firms will become more autonomous and will not need to visit a branch to have financial advisory, with some clients that may ultimately opt for a digital self-service model. The digital approaches will enable the advisors to spend more one-on-one time serving as strategic advisors to high-value clients and to use digitally enabled tools and channels to streamline service and expand client reach. On the other side, banks may sustain those high-value small business clients during their growth, benefitting from the long run partnership and the different products and services that the companies may need to run their expanding business.

Product Standardization and Multichannel Distribution

Significant and unnecessary product complexity is a burden for numerous large banks (The Bain.com, 2016). This complexity brings to a wide number of superfluous costs that banks are not willing to sustain anymore. Often, each product has different risk management processes, as well as separate operations and technology. Moreover, the current banking service model is based on an undifferentiated product/service offering for each type of counterpart that carries to a strong reduction of margins, especially for small size financing.

Consequently, smaller firms have much more difficulties than larger ones in obtaining financing, avoiding them the possibility to invest and to grow. In order to manage this product complexity, some leading banks are pursuing different approaches for different segments of customers. According to Bain & Company, in general, small businesses with relatively simple needs, are interested in a modular bundle of standard products. Larger firms, instead, are more complex than SMEs and require more advanced auxiliary products and advisory solutions.

Thus, in order to make the process of funding to SMEs more efficient and to increase the satisfaction of this segment of customers, the credit offering to SMEs must be revised by the banks through new models. One possible solution is the creation of financing products easy to buy and rapid to access, similar to the ones already existing for consumer credit. Even if the rate is a fundamental component in a financing offer, it is not the only element that has to be taken into consideration by the borrower. Nowadays, banks should avoid the competition exclusively on the rate, which currently would bring just to a bloody war. Instead, the credit offering to SMEs should aim at satisfying other real needs of the firms, such as the reduction of the initial costs for the preparation of the procedure, transparency on the modality of costs calculation and reduction of both the scrutiny and issue time. Hence, among the critical success factors of SMEs financing, there are rapid credit access and a standard product offering with user-friendly interfaces and different channels. With this mind, banks should industrialize processes and build simple products regarding the offering, pricing and required guarantees with the aim of reducing the managing costs of these contracts.

One possible example of this type of product could be financing without a mortgage guarantee, with a fixed rate, sureties and definite and rapid time for the approval and the issue of credit (KPMG, 2016). This kind of product could be offered through digital channels, with the support of the digital sign, or through the net of branches, mainly to SMEs with a consolidated relationship with the bank. The simplified process is as follows: (i) SME requires small size loan, (ii) using website of the bank SME chooses the most acceptable product, (iii) SME sends the needed documentation over the web form, (iv) bank checks the eligibility of SME for financing, and (v) the amount is paid at the SME's account. The benefits stemming from this solution would be the ease of offering and issue of credit and the extension of the services offered, useful for customers' retention. Moreover, the creation of standard products would lead to a more industrialized process, with considerable benefits regarding efficiency and costs reduction. Currently, a Poland bank offers a similar product for retail customers and is aiming at doing the same also for corporates. Its process is quite simple and divided into three steps: (i) First of all the customer determine the amount and tenor of the loan, and the rata is immediately computed, (ii) Subsequently, it has to accept the terms and conditions of the loan, and (iii) at the end, the loan is available in around 30 seconds from the confirmation.

Of course, product offering must be aligned with the customers' characteristics of the specific region but is indubitable that every bank requires a digital transformation. Nowadays, many banks offer a simple internet banking platform with a limited number of actions available. Usually a firm, but the same is valid also for retail clients, can only check its balance and manage its money in a limited way, but it cannot sign up for a loan or interact directly with a representative. The future of the bank will probably lead to an integrated multichannel offering where customers can perform the same activities through each channel in the same way. Going digital does not mean giving up branches, because the physical interaction with people will remain an important component, while it means that branches have to change their functions and have to be completely integrated with the digital processes.

FUTURE RESEARCH DIRECTIONS FOR FINTECH

Big data and artificial intelligence (AI), use of machine learning (ML) together with data mining and texting or natural language processing (NLP) techniques, blockchain and new ways of human-computer interaction drive the growth of new opportunities which can influence business processes and strategies.

Analysis of researches shows the growing interest in technology innovations in the form of products which have an impact on business processes, models or strategy for the institutions. Deloitte (2018) identifies main issues critical for long-term growth: customer centricity and organizational agility, regulatory compliance aligned with business strategy, technology asset that differentiates the bank, greater protection of cyber risks, FinTech and BioTech for innovations, reinterpreting/defining new roles of the workforce with increasing automation and diversity.

Big Data

Big data is mostly analyzed through interactions among consumers, institution and technology. Big data is the key driver for successful machine learning. Banks and financial institutions use various research techniques to extract information from big data relating to structured, semi-structured or unstructured data, mostly agreeing on the following (Evry, N/A):

Big data was born out of the necessity of datasets growing so large and complex that traditional tools are no longer sufficient to process this data. By aggregating large amounts of data from many different sources makes big data very powerful for business decision-making, revealing insights and behaviors faster and better than otherwise possible with traditional BI.

Therefore, one of the most fruitful areas for the future research directions in FinTech is the *big data*, due to the fact that most of the analysis in financial sector is performed on structured data, and appearance of big data has triggered analysis from semi-structured and unstructured data, e.g. appearing in customer reviews (BaFin, 2018).

Turner, Schroeck, and Shockley (2012) indicate that big data is today business imperative for a long-standing business challenge for banking and financial sector, but still hard to find out on what financial services they are based. However, big data is useful only when the collected large databases are analyzed using data mining and text mining methods. Recently, social network analysis has also proven to be a fruitful area of big data analysis.

Financial sector and banks are among early adopters of big data technologies, showing the main trends in big data analytics of financial sector (Alexander, Das, Ives, Jagadish, & Monteleoni, 2017; Moro, Cortez, & Rita, 2015; Srivastava & Gopalkrishnan, 2015; Turner et al., 2012). Some of the possible researches include: customer analytics (such as customer understanding and activation, customer segmentation and profiling, enhancing customer engagement, retention, and loyalty; detecting customer needs, quality analytics, sentiment analysis, best offer, customer gamification, and others), development of new business models (w-banking, increase in revenue, better understanding customer needs, use of historical data for predictive models, forecasts and trading impacts with real-time view of data,, new communication channels), operational optimizations (ability to collect data, aggregation and integration of a variety of data such as reports, transactions, e-mail, logs, social media, free-form texts, external data, geo-spatial, audio, images, sensors, and others), high-capacity of warehouse, data quality management, strong analytic capabilities, risk and fraud management (risk detection, credit approval, crime management, confidential information leaking, mail spamming), and others.

Data Mining

Data mining is the process of discovering patterns in large data sets, using different methods, among which machine learning (ML) the most often used. According to Moro et al. (2015) data mining is focused to extract useful knowledge (e.g. trends, patterns) from unstructured or semi-structured file, databases, XML files in order to create data-driven models, such as classification (if output data is a categorical value) or regression model (if output data is numerical value) or clustering. Today financial institutions and banks are faced with more demanding customers who seek low-risk investments and products relevant for their needs, while financial institutions re-evaluate the market situation and customer needs, searching for hidden information in unstructured data, which can influence the decision-making process. Mak, Ho, and Ting (2011) indicate that data mining in finance domain could improve workflow and deepen understanding of investment behavior.

According to Financial Stability Board (2017), financial institutions use machine learning methods (e.g., classification, regression, clustering) to analyze data on transactions and payment history to generate credit score and speed up a decision on lending or risks. On the other side, financial institutions turn to exploit semi-structured and unstructured data to extract more subtle customer opinions (e.g. opinion on some products, willingness to pay, to raise the loan) or data from social networks, text messages or mobile phone use. According to some researches, there is an increased use of voice-to-text communication, which can generate new amounts of data, which can be then integrated with existing data. However, usage of personal data opens issues on data confidentiality, privacy, and protection.

Customer-centricity is one of the key drivers of banks' growth, as pointed out in numerous researches. Ivanauskienė, Auruškevičienė, Škudienė, and Nedzinskas (2012) analyzed factors of consumer-perceived values in the retail banking sector during the period of economic recession, conducted on customers of commercial banks in Lithuania. The study showed that in the period of economic recession in transitional economy the following factors were present: emotional/ affective factor (when contacting with bank personnel, positive atmosphere, security, trust in bank personnel, satisfaction with conducted transactions) and functional factors (quality of service, price, contact personnel competence, physical environment), but also social factor (including opinions of others, established relationship). Data mining (DM) is the method that can support banks in attaining these goals. Hassani, Huang and Silva (2018) analysed the most often used data mining implementations in banking, until 2013, indicating that data mining algorithms were exploited in the last decade mostly for improving customer satisfaction, marketing and optimization of strategic management, while recent applications target security and fraud detection, risk management and investment banking, as well as customer relationship management (CRM).

Through predictive and prescriptive analytics, banks use technology in a way to gain direct impact on business, such as possible customer churn, marketing, and sales activities, cross-selling activities, fraud detection, customer relationship management (CRM), workforce development, and others.

Asare-Frempong and Jayabalan (2017) performed an analysis of direct marketing focusing on customers who expressed likelihood by subscribing on products, offers, and other packages. They aimed to predict customer response to direct bank marketing by the classifier, i.e., neural networks, decision tree, logistic regression, and random forest, attaining the accuracy of 87%.

Sun, Morris, Xu, Zhu, and Xie (2014) presented Intelligent Customer Analytics for Recognition and Exploration (iCARE) framework to analyze banking customer behavior for retail banks from banking big data. Budale and Mane (2013) used predictive analytics in retail banking to gain insight in improving the relationship with the customer and devise mechanisms for marketing in order to prevent switching to another bank. Results were used to predict churn probability of customer, product preferences and customer lifetime value.

Somal (2017) suggested customer metrics relating to the customer itself, opinions, feelings and attitudes, customer profile and relationships, customer goals and objectives, with examples on Royal Bank of Canada, Toronto Dominian Bank, Bank of Nova Scotia, Bank of Montreal and Canadian Imperial Bank of Commerce. Levy and Hino (2016) evaluated the relationship between customers' emotional attachment towards bank service provider and card loyalty, as well as customer satisfaction.

Text Mining and Natural Language Processing

Text mining is a particular type of data mining focused on the handling of unstructured or semi-structured text documents. In the process of text mining, relevant words and relationships are extracted in order to categorize or draw conclusions. Some of possible text mining techniques include information extraction, topic detection, summarization, classification, concept linkage, information visualization, and question answering, keyword detection, named entity recognition, gender prediction, sentiment analysis, social network analysis, and others. Key-word detection aims to detect relevant keywords from any monolingual or bilingual corpus, using language-independent statistically based techniques, rule-based methods or hybrid approaches, as in Seljan et al. (2009a, 2009b, 2013, and 2017). Named Entity Recognition represents an important step in text mining (Saju and Shaja, 2017) used on large corpora, which can be used in Information Retrieval (IR), Information Extraction, further in Natural Language Processing (NLP), Machine Translation and Question-Answering System, Speech Recognition, Natural Language Generation, Chatbot conversation, Machine Learning, Image Recognition, and others. Nopp and Hanbury (2015) used sentiment analysis to detect risks in the banking system. Srivastava and Gopalkrishnan (2015) analyzed sentiments for the banking sector in order to assess the opinions on the functioning of the bank. Topic modeling or topic prediction/ extraction is based on number and distribution of terms across documents by counting the probability of belonging to a certain topic. Moro et al. (2015) performed topic detection of a large number of manuscripts using text-mining techniques when detecting terms belonging to business intelligence and banking domains.

Social network analysis (SNA) is a different type of analysis in comparison to text analysis, but it is used here to show how text analysis and its results can be integrated with this analysis. Morales et al. (2014) used SNA to estimate bank financial strength during the financial crisis.

Natural language processing (NLP) tools can help to extract and detect information relating to sentiment analysis on trust in banks, e.g. from Twitter posts or text from a newspaper article, can be used for predicting banks attitudes of clients towards the bank, and thus predict the potential business risks. Various consulting companies point out cases to acquire, develop and retain customers using sentiment analysis, in order to:

- analyze customer opinions (e.g., Barclays);
- develop 360-degree customer-view to predict future trends or ideas, as well as customer churn behavior (e.g., OCBC bank in Singapore, Bank of Austria, Tatra Bank);
- conduct customer segmentation in order to divide customers into groups that share similar characteristics (e.g., Bank of America, First Tennessee Bank);
- to improve marketing effects (e.g., by serving consumers according to lifestyle, professional life, families, and retirees, as for Singapore Citibank);

- to offer loyalty cards based on customer habits (e.g., Bank of America), as well to increase card usage (e.g.,Barclays to target students), for the next best offer to predict future purchases (e.g., Westpac bank in Australia and New Zeland);
- to choose communication channel for interaction with customers ranging from mobile apps, social networks, clickable ads, stores, TV, publication platforms, and others, in order to provide preferred content through a preferred channel or to avoid undesirable ones (e.g., HDFC bank in India, OCBC bank in Singapore);
- to personalize customer experience on the chosen channel or preferred language (e.g., Bank of China), which would support the improvement of overall marketing effectiveness (e.g., Laurentian Bank of Canada).

Human-Computer Interaction

According to Saha (2017), banks are one of the first adopters of cutting-edge technologies, including human-computer interfaces which use natural language processing and speech recognition, connected with machine learning algorithms.

Researches and implementations of chatbots in the banking sector are often used as ‘live chat”. They access data and use artificial intelligence in the background to enable conversation and offer responses to customers. There are several possible uses of chatbots: to ask specific questions to consumers and, therefore, to collect data and learn customer preferences, or when integrated with machine learning solutions, to offer personalized products and offers via preferred mobile app, or to offer right content to the customer.Okuda and Shoda (2018) presented an artificial intelligence-based chatbot service, developed by Fujitsu, which aims to support users’ needs.

Another example of human-computer interaction is voice input, for information search, online communication or integrated with other technologies. Seljan and Dunđer (2014) performed research on combined automatic speech recognition and machine translation in the domain of business correspondence. Voice-activated home banking is presented in Isobe, Morishima, Yoshitani, Koizumi, and Murakami (1996) with a success rate of 85%. Some banks use voice-recognition to check an account balance or to hear a payment-due date.

Due to security threats, banks are interested in risk prevention, where biometric technologies can apply. Banking use of selfies, fingerprints, facial recognition or voice biometrics, representing the new horizon, which enables users to enrol in banking services through smartphones or telephone banking. Piotrowska, Polasik, and Piotrowski (2017) concluded that authorization using fingerprint is secure and convenient for consumers in mobile banking.

Mobile Banking: Security and Gaming

Banks and financial institutions have to satisfy mobile banking customers with instant access, but at the same time protect customer information, transactions, banks' data from any threats in order to ensure the highest level of security. According to Vasco Data Security (2016), nearly all Android apps (95%) were hacked in 2014 and the security issue has become the main concern of financial institutions. This is of highest concern since according to Global FinTech Survey (2016), where more than 90% banks expect the raise in usage of mobile applications and 71% believe that in the next five years more than 60% of clients will use mobile applications at least once a month to use financial services. Therefore, special attention is given to the *security* aspect in mobile applications. He, Tian, Shen, and Yaohang (2015) explored blog mining as a research method to analyze blog discussion on security of mobile applications and used the current technology to simulate the scenario of emerging attacks on banking applications. They identified the main protection strategies for users and developers of mobile banking apps. Alotaibi, Furnell, and Clarke (2016) studied risks for each process from the authentication within the mobile application in order to understand various levels of risks. Hayikader, Hadi, Hanis, and Ibrahim (2016) examined issues of architecture and security issues on banking apps for everyday users.

Schaefer, Moormann, and Rosemann (2012) considered the concept of customer process to establish a customer-centric business model and presented the results of empirical research of smartphone apps for banking. The research pointed out a customer-centric approach which presented competitive advantage and important feature of the app where the customer could be present during the whole process which had a positive impact on trust, as well as value-added services. In this process, *gamification* can be used as the leverage to increase the quality of customer relationships. Torres-Toukoumidis and Marín-Mateos (2017) identified incorporation of game elements in the mobile application in the Spanish financial sector, using a sample of 38 mobile application of mobile banking, analyzing purpose, audience, technological strategy, play experience, and game mechanics. Results showed that the purpose of such applications was to enforce customer loyalty and expand influence on audience between 26-35, with technology strategy to adopt security and privacy systems and the meaning of gaming awards. Additionally, game experience was adopted in banking communication among Spanish banking entities. The research aimed to establish patterns for gamification in the banking sector, by measuring effects and effectiveness on clients and their communication.

CONCLUSION

The banking sector is strongly affected by the aforementioned disruptive technologies, challenging the traditional model, moving from purely monetary transactions to integrated financial experience which also includes technological, personal and social aspects. Use of new technologies requires specific attention given to security, privacy, data protection, and legal regulations. Banks offer new personalized approach and try to differentiate from others through customer-centric approach, effective use of technology and adapted business process. Data science combined with sophisticated analytic tools and computer power created new business opportunities.

Digital innovation is changing traditional small business banking. The continuous research of efficiency by the banks, along with the increasing demand of small business owners who are raising their expectations in their business banks, is pushing the transaction of banking institutions through digital solutions, also for small business clients. Banking is looking for ways to exploit digital innovation to support small business activities, solving their day-to-day problems and helping them to expand above their geographical border. Moreover, banks can often take advantage of the investments that have already been made in retail banking digital platform. As highlighted by Oliver Wyman in the report on European retail and SME credit, 'banks that successfully digitaze their SME offering can benefit enormously. In North America, Bank of Montreal and PNC claim significant increases in customer numbers as a result of online and mobile banking offers targeting small business owners". Nevertheless, as resulted from the analysis of the previous section, there is again room for improvement regarding a digital proposition for SMEs. For this reason, this chapter provides an outlook to the possibilities that could arise from the digitization..

The chapter focuses on FinTech aided banking services, in particular, because these are, at present, the most widely FinTech technologies available in Italy. We presented a study about how Italian SMEs understand and use FinTech technologies, indicating that despite FinTech has entered in Italy only in recent times, the Italian SMEs market is very active and fruitful for digital companies.

REFERENCES

ABI (Giovanni Sabatini). (2017). *Indagine conoscitiva sulle tematiche relative all'impatto della tecnologia finanziaria sul settore finanziario, creditizio e assicurativo* [Cognitive survey on issues related to the impact of technology]. Retrieved from https://www.abi.it/DOC_Info/Audizioni-parlamentari/Presentazione%20per%20 Audizione%20DG%20Commissione%20FInanze%20Camera%204%2012%20 2017.pdf

Aldás-Manzano, J., Lassala-Navarré, C., Ruiz-Mafé, C., & Sanz-Blas, S. (2009). The role of consumer innovativeness and perceived risk in online banking usage. *International Journal of Bank Marketing*, *27*(1), 53–75. doi:10.1108/02652320910928245

Alexander, L., Das, S. R., Ives, Z., Jagadish, H. V., & Monteleoni, C. (2017). Research Challenges in Financial Data Modeling and Analysis. *Big Data*, *5*(3), 177–188. doi:10.1089/big.2016.0074 PMID:28816500

Alotaibi, S., Furnell, S., & Clarke, N. (2016). A novel Taxonomy for mobile applications data. *International Journal of Cyber-Security and Digital Forensics*, *5*(3), 115–122. doi:10.17781/P002070

Asare-Frempong, J., & Jayabalan, M. (2017). Predicting Customer Response to Bank Direct Telemarketing Campaign. *International Conference on Engineering Technologies and Technopreneurship (ICET2T)*, 1-4. 10.1109/ICE2T.2017.8215961

BaFin. (2018). *Big data meets artificial intelligence: Challenges and implications for the supervision and regulation of financial services*. Retrieved from https://www.bafin.de/SharedDocs/Downloads/EN/dl_bdai_studie_en.pdf?__ blob=publicationFile&v=11

BeBeez. (2018). *Tutte le Fintech italiane (o fondate da italiani) finanziate da venture, angel, o altri investitori* [All the Italian Fintech (or founded by Italians) funded by venture, angel, or other investors]. Retrieved from https://bebeez.it/files/2018/06/ FintechBeBeez-giu2018.pdf

Boston Consulting Group. (2016). *Global Corporate Banking 2016: The Next-Generation Corporate Bank*. Retrieved from http://image-src.bcg.com/Images/ BCG-Global-Corporate-Banking-2016-Dec-2016_tcm80-217574_tcm9-167068.pdf

Budale, D., & Mane, D. (2013). Predictive Analytics in Retail Banking. *International Journal of Engineering and Advanced Technology*, *2*(5), 508–510.

Chen, L. (2016). From fintech to finlife: The case of fintech development in China. *China Economic Journal*, *9*(3), 225–239. doi:10.1080/17538963.2016.1215057

Cocco, L., Pinna, A., & Marchesi, M. (2017). Banking on blockchain: Costs savings thanks to the blockchain technology. *Future Internet*, *9*(3), 25. doi:10.3390/fi9030025

Deloitte. (2018). *2018: Banking Outlook: Accelerating the transformation*. Retrieved from https://www2.deloitte.com/content/dam/Deloitte/tw/Documents/financial-services/tw-2018-Banking-Outlook-English.pdf

Dhliwayo, C., & Governor, A. (2014). *Role of the banking sector in promoting growth & development of small and medium enterprises. In 2nd SME Banking* (pp. 1–17). Microfinance Summit.

European Central Bank. (2016). *Financial Stability Review*. Retrieved from https://www.ecb.europa.eu/pub/pdf/other/financialstabilityreview201611.en.pdf

European Commission. (2003). *Commission Recommendation of 6 May 2003 concerning the definition of micro, small and medium-sized enterprises*. Retrieved from https://eur-lex.europa.eu/LexUriServ/LexUriServ.do?uri=OJ:L:2003:124:0036:0041:en:PDF

European Commission. (2010). *European SMEs Under Pressure: Annual Report on EU Small and Medium-Sized Enterprises. SME performance review*. Retrieved from https://ec.europa.eu/docsroom/documents/15767/attachments/1/translations/en/renditions/native

Evry. (n.d.). *Big data in banking for marketers: How to derive value from big data*. Whitepaper. Retrieved from https://www.evry.com/globalassets/insight/bank2020/bank-2020---big-data---whitepaper.pdf

Financial Stability Board. (2017). *Artificial Intelligence and machine learning in financial service: Market developments and financial stability implications*. Retrieved from http://www.fsb.org/wp-content/uploads/P011117.pdf

FinTech Network. (n.d.). *Four Blockchain Use Cases for Banks*. Retrieved from https://blockchainapac.fintecnet.com/uploads/2/4/3/8/24384857/FinTech_blockchain_report_v3.pdf

Gabor, D., & Brooks, S. (2017). The digital revolution in financial inclusion: International development in the fintech era. *New Political Economy*, *22*(4), 423–436. doi:10.1080/13563467.2017.1259298

Gai, K., Qiu, M., & Sun, X. (2018). A survey on FinTech. *Journal of Network and Computer Applications*, *103*, 262–273. doi:10.1016/j.jnca.2017.10.011

Global FinTech Survey. (2016). *Customers in the spotlight: How FinTech is reshaping banking*. Retrieved from https://www.pwc.com/jg/en/publications/fin-tech-banking-2016.pdf

Gomber, P., Kauffman, R. J., Parker, C., & Weber, B. W. (2018). On the Fintech Revolution: Interpreting the Forces of Innovation, Disruption, and Transformation in Financial Services. *Journal of Management Information Systems*, *35*(1), 220–265. doi:10.1080/07421222.2018.1440766

Guo, Y., & Liang, C. (2016). Blockchain application and outlook in the banking industry. *Financial Innovation*, *2*(1), 24. doi:10.118640854-016-0034-9

Hassani, H., Huang, X., & Silva, E. (2018). Digitalisation and big data mining in banking. *Big Data and Cognitive Computing*, *2*(3), 18. doi:10.3390/bdcc2030018

Hayikader, S., Hadi, A., Hanis, F. N., & Ibrahim, J. (2016). Issues and security measures of mobile banking apps. *International Journal of Scientific and Research Publications*, *6*(1), 36–41.

He, W., Tian, X., Shen, J., & Yaohang, L. (2015). Understanding Mobile Banking Applications' Security risks through Blog Mining and the Workflow Technology. *36th International Conference on Information Systems*, 1-10.

Isobe, T., Morishima, M., Yoshitani, G., Koizumi, N., & Murakami, K. (1996). Voice-activated home banking system and its field trial. In *Proceedings of Fourth International Conference on Spoken Language Processing* (pp. 1688-1691). Philadelphia: IEEE. 10.1109/ICSLP.1996.607951

Ivanauskienė, N., Auruškevičienė, V., Škudienė, V., & Nedzinskas, Š. (2012). Customer perceptions of value: Case of retail banking. *Organizations and Markets in Emerging Economies*, *3*(1/5), 75–88.

Jones, C., Ramanau, R., Cross, S., & Healing, G. (2010). Net generation or Digital Natives: Is there a distinct new generation entering university? *Computers & Education*, *54*(3), 722–732. doi:10.1016/j.compedu.2009.09.022

KPMG. (2016). *Nuovi modelli distributivi nel settore bancario* [New distribution models in the banking sector]. Retrieved from https://assets.kpmg.com/content/dam/kpmg/pdf/2016/06/it-modelli-distributivi.pdf.pdf

Lee, I., & Shin, Y. J. (2018). Fintech: Ecosystem, business models, investment decisions, and challenges. *Business Horizons*, *61*(1), 35–46. doi:10.1016/j.bushor.2017.09.003

Leong, C., Tan, B., Xiao, X., Tan, F. T. C., & Sun, Y. (2017). Nurturing a FinTech ecosystem: The case of a youth microloan startup in China. *International Journal of Information Management, 37*(2), 92–97. doi:10.1016/j.ijinfomgt.2016.11.006

Levy, S., & Hino, H. (2016). Emotional brand attachment: A factor in customer-bank relationships. *International Journal of Bank Marketing, 34*(2), 136–150. doi:10.1108/IJBM-06-2015-0092

Mak, M. K. Y., Ho, G. T. S., & Ting, S. L. (2011). A financial data mining model for extracting customer behavior. *International Journal of Engineering Business Management, 3*(3), 59–72.

Morales, M., Brizan, D. G., Ghaly, H., Hauner, T., Ma, M., Reza, S., & Rosenberg, A. (2014). *Application of Social Network Analysis in the Estimation of Bank Financial Strength During the Financial Crisis.* NLP Unshared Task in PoliInformatics. Retrieved from https://www.researchgate.net/profile/Michelle_Morales4

Morgan, R. (2017). The Top Fintech Trends Driving the Next Decade. *American Bankers Association. ABA Banking Journal, 109*(5), 22.

Moro, S., Cortez, P., & Rita, P. (2015). Business intelligence in banking: A literature analysis from 2002 to 2013 using text mining and latent Dirichlet allocation. *Expert Systems with Applications, 42*(3), 1314–1324. doi:10.1016/j.eswa.2014.09.024

Muller, P., Caliandro, C., Peycheva, V., Gagliardi, D., Marzocchi, C., Ramlogan, R., & Cox, D. (2015). *Annual report on European SMEs*. Retrieved from http://ec.europa.eu/DocsRoom/documents/16341/attachments/2/translations/en/renditions/native

NetConsulting. (2017). *Le aziende del Fintech in Italia 2017*. Retrieved from https://www.pwc.com/it/it/industries/FinTech/docs/2017-FinTech-report.pdf

Nopp, C., & Hanbury, A. (2015). Detecting Risks in the Banking System by Sentiment Analysis. In *Proceedings of the 2015 Conference on Empirical Methods in Natural Language Processing* (pp. 591-600). Lisbon, Portugal: Association for Computational Linguistics. 10.18653/v1/D15-1071

Okuda, T., & Shoda, S. (2018). AI-based chatbot service for financial industry. *Fujitsu Scientific and Technical Journal, 54*(2), 4–8.

Piotrowska, A. I., Polasik, M., & Piotrowski, D. (2017). Prospects for the application of biometrics in the Polish banking sector. *Equilibrium. Quarterly Journal of Economics and Economic Policy, 12*(3), 501–518.

Premoli, F. (2017). *The impact of digital innovations on the current banks' offering towards SMEs*. Retrieved from https://www.politesi.polimi.it/handle/10589/136364

Rajaobelina, L., Brun, I., & Toufaily, É. (2013). A relational classification of online banking customers. *International Journal of Bank Marketing*, *31*(3), 187–205. doi:10.1108/02652321311315294

Saha, A. K. (2017). *Review of Design of Speech Recognition and Text Analytics based Digital Banking Customer Interface and Future Directions of Technology Adoption*. Retrieved from https://arxiv.org/ftp/arxiv/papers/1712/1712.04640.pdf

Saju, J. C., & Shaja, A. S. (2017). A Survey on Efficient Extraction of Named Entities from New Domains Using Big Data Analytics. *2nd International Conference on Recent Trends and Challenges in Computational Models (ICRTCCM)*, 170-175. 10.1109/ICRTCCM.2017.34

Sayani, H. (2015). Customer satisfaction and loyalty in the United Arab Emirates banking industry. *International Journal of Bank Marketing*, *33*(3), 351–375. doi:10.1108/IJBM-12-2013-0148

Schaefer, A., Moormann, J., & Rosemann, M. (2012). The rise of smartphone apps: Opportunities for customer-centric retail banking. *Banks and Bank Systems*, *7*(1), 73–82.

Seljan, S., Dalbelo Bašić, B., Šnajder, J., Delač, D., Šamec-Gjurin, M., & Crnec, D. (2009b). Comparative Analysis of Automatic Term and Collocation Extraction. *2nd International Conference "The future of information sciences (INFuture 2009): Digital resources and knowledge sharing"*, 219-228.

Seljan, S., & Dunđer, I. (2014). Combined Automatic Speech Recognition and Machine Translation in Business Correspondence Domain for English-Croatian. *World Academy of Science, Engineering and Technology (WASET) - International Journal of Computer, Electrical, Automation. Control and Information Engineering*, *8*(11), 1980–1986.

Seljan, S., Dunđer, I., & Gašpar, A. (2013). From digitization process to terminological digital resources. In *36th International Convention on Information & Communication Technology Electronics & Microelectronics (MIPRO)* (pp. 1053-1058). IEEE.

Seljan, S., & Gašpar, A. (2009a). First Steps in Term and Collocation Extraction from English-Croatian Corpus. *Proceedings of 8th International Conference on Terminology and Artificial Intelligence*. Retrieved from http://ceur-ws.org/Vol-578/paper21.pdf

Seljan, S., Stančić, H., & Dunđer, I. (2017). Extracting Terminology by Language Independent Methods. In L. N. Zybatow, A. Stauder, & M. Ustaszewski (Eds.), *Forum Translationswissenschaft: Translation Studies and Translation Practice* (pp. 141–147). Frankfurt am Main: Peter Lang GmbH.

Somal, H. K. (2017). Big Data & Analytics: Tackling Business Challenges in Banking Industry. *Business and Economics Journal, 8*(2).

Srivastava, U., & Gopalkrishnan, S. (2015). Impact of big data analytics on banking sector: Learning for Indian banks. *Procedia Computer Science, 50*, 643–652. doi:10.1016/j.procs.2015.04.098

Sun, N., Morris, J. G., Xu, J., Zhu, X., & Xie, M. (2014). iCARE: a framework for big data-based banking customer analytics. *IBM Journal of Research and Development, 58*(5-6), 4:1-4:9.

The Bain.com. (2016). *Divide and Conquer: A Guide to Winning SME Banking Strategies*. Retrieved from http://www.bain.com/publications/articles/divide-and-conquer-a-guide-to-winning-sme-banking-strategies.aspx

Torres-Toukoumidis, A., & Marín-Mateos, P. (2017). Gamification in mobile applications for banking services in Spain. *Revista de Ciencias de la Administración y Economía, 7*(13), 59–72.

Turner, D., Schroeck, M., & Shockley, R. (2012). *Analytics: The real-world use of big data in financial services*. Retrieved from https://www-935.ibm.com/services/multimedia/Analytics_The_real_world_use_of_big_data_in_Financial_services_Mai_2013.pdf

Van Loo, R. (2018). *Making Innovation More Competitive: The Case of Fintech. 65. UCLA Law Review. University of California, Los Angeles. School of Law, 232*. Retrieved from https://ssrn.com/abstract=2966890

Vasco Data Security. (2016). *Mobile Banking Applications: Balancing Security and Convenience*. Retrieved from https://www.vasco.com/images/Mobile-Banking-Applications-White-Paper-redux-MondayApril4_tcm42-46736.pdf

Chapter 3
Emergence of Insurance Technologies (InsurTech):
The Turkish Case

İsmail Yıldırım
Hittite University, Turkey

ABSTRACT

Technology advances at an incredible rate all around the globe. Financial technologies (FinTech) are defined as production of services that combine financial services and technology. A subdimension of FinTech, insurance technologies (InsurTech) is a system built with the purpose of creating solutions for the insurance sector using a technological approach. Making it easier for the insurance companies and the insured to manage their contracts, minimizing the risks involved, and allowing for the development of innovative technologies, InsurTech is simply the technology of insurance business. For the policy owners, these technologies bring with them the benefit of cost-effective policy solutions. This chapter focuses on the possible impact of insurance technologies on the insurance sector. Explored in this study are the estimated transformation of the insurance sector with insurance technologies and the problems likely to occur as a consequence.

DOI: 10.4018/978-1-5225-7805-5.ch003

INTRODUCTION

The common practice in an insurance company used to quote for a casco policy is to base their calculation on the age of the vehicle in question, the information of the insured, no-claim status, etc. which play a role in the price of an insurance policy (Cappiello, 2018). InsurTech analyzes the vehicle and the behavior/driving habits of the insured and offers the right insurance policy accordingly. Minimizing the risks, it contributes to the development of the insurance sector. The purpose of insurance, on the other hand, is to offer complete insurance services to the clients in order to meet their needs and to reduce the risks involved in their operations. Insurance companies need to offer innovative and impeccable services if the sector is to grow and develop. Any innovative entrepreneur who places importance on their business and who knows how to offer the best services to their clients may benefit from the development of the insurance sector and may secure millions or even billions of dollars of growth for their business if they develop a business model based on the InsurTech.

Among the nations with the greatest advancements made in InsurTech are the USA, the UK, Germany, and the Netherlands. Receiving state incentives backed by leading insurance companies, these startups take on very large tasks. Even the reassurance companies are now investing in InsurTech. For example, Trov, an Axa-backed InsurTech company based in the UK, offers insurance policies for personal belongings such as cameras, PCs or mobile phones. “We track the risks in real-time,” said Scott Walchek, CEO of Trov, a company focusing on smartphone insurance. “As soon as you turn on a device, your insurance is enabled and it is disabled as soon as you turn it off. Then, the time elapsed is calculated for billing purposes,” he added (Machler, 2016).

Another example is Lemonade; the company receives unprecedented financial support from US-based investment companies. Able to obtain your quote in an average of 30 seconds, this system guarantees the payment of compensation for damages within 3 minutes. Lemonade builds on AI and digital technologies. Offering its services using a chatbot, Lemonade’s customers just need to text this chatbot to receive the best insurance solution for themselves (Carney, 2017). Chatbots, then, present the customer with insurance options customized based on the information given. After deciding the best option designed for themselves, the clients can sign up to the system using their credit card and mobile signature, and purchase the insurance policy (Schanz, 2015). Another example is Bought by Many, the company aims to operate in a segment none of the insurance companies dare to invest, such as the travel insurance for recovering cancer patients.

InsurTech startups not only adopt a user-friendly approach but also build a close relationship with the insurance customers and offer a service where the client is protected at all ends while preventing damages to the insurance company with risk prevention efforts, warning, and guidance services. Startups aim to define any possible risk using smart devices in segments such as Accident, Health or Hazard Insurance and to minimize or even eliminate those risks.

A Blockchain is a concept with possible ties to InsurTech and it is a topic drawing recent interest in Turkey. Developed with the purpose of bringing the customers and the intermediary together, Blockchain is a database where any transaction is controlled by the users without the need for a corporation to offer security over the transactions, thanks to the Blockchain ledger. This system offers a secure and transparent method for transactions which ensures the efficiency and productivity of all (Shelkovnikov, 2016). Minimizing printed material costs and transaction costs between companies, it also allows for rapid processing. The requests received are filtered by the Blockchain software automatically allowing for the drafting of smart contracts. A promising new technology for fields such as supply chain, product lifecycle, secure data collection, transparent data sharing, the Blockchain technology has drawn the attention of tech companies, entrepreneurs and the governments all around the world.

Blockchain technology gains more recognition in FinTech every day and it is expected to prevent any fraud or scam in this filed with even increased impact on both FinTech and InsurTech initiatives. Expected to grow even more valuable for several sectors, the blockchain system is believed to help several products and services to be kick-started over time. In Turkey, InsurTech is currently overshadowed by FinTech. Established with the aim to bring the financial technology ecosystem under the same umbrella, the "FinTech Istanbul" Platform can be a good example for the future of InsurTech. It is highly possible that the InsurTech investments in Turkey will grow in the near future (Acer, 2017).

In this chapter, the development of the insurance technology market has been discussed in Turkey. Technological innovations in the insurance sector are mentioned. Possible problems that may arise during the technological development stage are mentioned. The possible effects of insurance technologies on insurance companies, insurers, claims payments, insurance premiums have been discussed.

DEVELOPMENT OF INSURTECH

The number of financial technology initiatives which build on the advancing technology in order to ensure customer satisfaction and a service-oriented approach (FinTech) grows every day (Berger, 2017). A closer look into FinTech companies at a global scale shows that they have received an approximate amount of $35 bil. in capital investment in 2018 and that there are around 4,500 startups operating in this segment. It is expected that the total investment will add up to $40 bil. by the end of 2018 with the addition of new startups (KPMG, 2017).

On the other hand, InsurTech companies focusing on insurance services and solutions as part of this ecosystem received an approx $5 bil. investment in 2018 and there are almost 400 startups operating in this segment now. It would be fair to say that the insurance sector is the third largest after the banking and telecommunication sectors and that it has a great potential for development. The current situation allows the so-called InsurTech companies to grow and the people prefer these services at an increasing rate (Larimer, 2016).

So, what is the purpose of InsurTech companies? What are the elements of insurance they are here to change and maybe even demolish? What kind of values do they offer their clients and what are the elements of technology they use? In order to be able to answer these questions, we need to be talking about the advancing technology (Cappiello, 2018). There are a number of new concepts we are all familiar with and they are here to stay with the facts of our times. Taking a closer look at the advancements of today, technologies like the Internet wearables, the blockchain, mobile devices, robots, robotic advisors/chatbots, telematics, cybersecurity solutions, and AI have a disruptive effect on traditional business processes, perceived services and insurance products. The technological developments, on the other hand, bring about new ways of doing things and new job descriptions; among these are sharing economy, P2P, and usage-based billing. InsurTech firms lead the insurance world with brand new solutions for any relevant field (Yalçın, 2018).

Among these are, as follows:

- **Product Design:** Among the new products offered to the individual insurance products segment are mile-based auto insurance (traffic + casco), home insurance, life insurance, drone insurance, and auto, yacht, housing, and private jet insurance as part of sharing economy. For the corporate, products such as cybersecurity, sensor-based home, office, and logistics vehicle insurance, new solutions for IT companies, drone insurance, etc. are being developed.
- **Marketing and Channels/Distribution:** With the advanced technology, we now have more channels and points of contact to reach out to the consumer. For example, it is now possible to offer our services to our clients using robots on a social network and to satisfy their insurance needs right away and also the related marketing activities. Very soon we will see scenarios where a vehicle equipped with a telematics device will send an automated warning to the insured when they travel outside of the insurance coverage zone which leads to the purchase of additional products (McKinsey, 2017).

- **Technical Assessment:** Using their analytical skills to the fullest, these corporations are able to offer innovations and competitive solutions for their technical assessment and pricing processes. Among these solutions are discount home/office insurance for those who use sensor-based tracking for their vehicles, or discount and usage-based billing and technical assessment for those with fleets equipped with telematics.
- **Policy Management:** With the advancing technology, policy creation/ management and services are now easy and rapid. The best example of this is the possibility offered to clients to create their own policies with the conditions they need to use online and mobile channels without the need for an agency or an intermediary. For the insurance companies, this is similar to self-service and it allows for substantial cost reduction (Larimer, 2016).
- **Damage Management & Support:** Damage management stands out as the most customer-oriented field in the value chain. With tools like analytics, big data and telematics, the developments in this field are quite impressive. And examples of the uses of these tools are the collection of data such as the severity of an accident and the damage caused by the accident starting from the moment of a traffic accident. A similar procedure is the sensor-backed homes and offices. The whole process can be taken onto mobile channels in order to offer the insured a transparent, rapid and informative damage claims processing. With this, the insured are informed of each step of the process at all times as part of the reflection of self-service concept in this system.

The advantage brought in by InsurTech makes insurance companies much more accessible for the consumer and reduces the intermediary costs in doing so. The recent development and modification of damage and risk models allowed the tech companies to introduce their new software.

The following is a breakdown of the innovations made very recently in the InsurTech market (Carney 2017), (Machler, 2016), (Yalçın, 2018);

1. Telematics
2. User-based/User-centered Technologies
3. Big Data
4. Self-driving Car Technologies & Smart Homes
5. Cyber Insurance
6. Aviation & Drones

- **Telematics:** Think about Fitbit and similar wearable technology products. As these products collect information such as the steps you have taken or the calories you have burned, they are actually creating a data warehouse for you. The creation of custom solutions for consumers or new products based on this vast collection of information, on the other hand, is rather easy (Cappiello, 2018). Telematics solutions are no different from smart wristbands. Digitalizing a huge amount of data about vehicles and therefore their drivers, this technology allows for a comparison between a good driver and a bad one which helps with the insurance policy quoting.

Today, we even have access to apps and software which calculate your chances of getting involved in a traffic accident. Not to mention those apps and features which inform the authorities in case of an accident.

- **User-based / User-centered Technologies:** The Do-it-yourself generation. A consumer type which would like to take care of their own business, they consider online banking as a part of their lives. Once required us to physically go to a bank branch and place the request to a teller, now we can just click our way into any banking transaction (Cappiello, 2018). It is Financial Technologies a.k.a. FinTech which have brought in the biggest advancements in terms of user-based and user-centered technologies in the world. And the flagship is the banking and insurance practices. With the developing mobile technology, now it is possible for the users to log in to banking and insurance services using their smartphones.

Thus, it is not only allowing the users to manage their purchase or contracts but also collects data about the consumer's behavior. As it is the case in mobile banking apps, mobile insurance apps make it possible for the users to purchase any type of insurance using their smartphones. Availability of mobile apps focusing on basic insurance offerings is no longer an added value, but a necessity for insurance companies.

- **Big Data:** As the insurance sector is built on the ability to foresee the possible future outcomes and to measure the risk/value involved, datasets offering the volume, velocity, veracity, and variety needed have become indispensable for insurers. Thanks to data sources such as telematics, sensors, state-owned data, customer interactions, and social media, the possibility to utilize big data in the insurance sector has never been this attractive. Today, big data technologies are being used in the insurance sector to define the risks involved, to cater to consumer needs, and to improve customer experience. This, on the other hand, leads to a higher predictive accuracy in the measurements of the insurance companies (Bakshi, 2012) (Elgendy, 2013).

- **Autonomous Car Technologies & Smart Homes:** Google, Tesla, and many other tech giants invest billions of dollars into autonomous or self-driving car technologies and insurance may be the sector which will experience the most significant consequences. Google is designing not only self-driving cars but also cars integrated with the rest of the city. They are working towards a technology which knows the color of the traffic lights one mile ahead and adjusts the vehicle speed accordingly. Maybe the time when insurance is no longer relevant with self-driving cars is not that far away. And we can find the examples of this scenario in modern collective housing projects, security systems, air conditioning units which can be operated remotely, surveillance systems which send notifications if something out of ordinary happens at home, etc.
- **Cyber Insurance:** Having drawn the attention of the public recently, cybersecurity insurance will also be one of the trending topics in 2018. As the available insurance products are expensive and not able to meet the real needs of the businesses, the InsurTech market is presented with a great opportunity for development in this segment (Yeşilyurt, 2015).
- **Aviation & Drones:** Although considered a niche market, this field is believed to grow at an unprecedented rate in the near future. Among the examples of the possible use of drones and UAVs in the insurance sector is the remote investigation of an area affected by a natural disaster or the investigation of hard-to-reach accident locales (Yalçın, 2018).

In Turkey, the current battle between the insurance sector and technology is fought by the intermediaries. The local sector is indifferent to the technological developments, dedicating their time mostly on issues such as who issued the policy or who provided the services. Similar issues were dealt with by the banking sector in the past. Insurance sector will very soon need to leave these issues behind and focus on technological developments for the future. Insurance companies which are ready for the technology will benefit in the future.

BLOCKCHAIN TECHNOLOGY IN INSURTECH

The term ‘blockchain’ was first implied in an article titled ‘Bitcoin’ written by Satoshi Nakamoto and published in 2008. Although this article did not use the exact term, the technological component behind cryptocurrency was defined as a number of data blocks chained to each other cryptographically. Bitcoin was the first take on the blockchain technology (Iansiti and Lakhani, 2008). And it was a great step towards the widespread use of this technology. The reaction of juridical science and lawmakers to the widespread adoption of this technology was about how to regulate Bitcoin (Shcherbak, 2014), (Tu and Meredith, 2015).

Among the major reasons behind these developments and fundamental changes is the Blockchain technology which finds its way into our lives every day. It seems like blockchain will come in handy to prevent fraudulent actions which may prevail as the innovations in InsurTech are introduced (Schanz, 2015). Nevertheless, among the most important developments expected from the blockchain are privacy and reputation of the user. For example, a project named "social credit score" was introduced very recently in China and it is closely connected with this subject. It is expected that such projects will pave the way for InsurTech firms to develop new solutions such as "ensuring reputation."

Today, we transfer data using a large number of media (multimedia, communication, web interface, etc.) on the internet. Blockchain technology, on the other hand, is a decentralized database which allows us to transfer value-attached assets along with these data. Suggested by Satoshi Nakamoto (a pseudonym) in 2008, the Bitcoin cryptocurrency introduced a new international currency to the world. Once just considered as a currency, Bitcoin was very soon explored for the blockchain technology it was built on with for other possible areas of use. Briefly defined, a blockchain eliminates the need for providers or a trustable authority and distributes the centralized trust on the Internet. Blockchain technology is commonly associated with digital currencies such as Bitcoin and Ethereum. However, this technology actually has a lot more to offer (http://blokzincir.bilgem.tubitak.gov.tr/blok-zincir.html).

Among the most common areas of use of blockchain are, as follows: (Usta and Doğantekin, 2017).

1. Banking
2. FinTech
3. Money Transfer
4. Creation and Storage of Important Documents
5. e-Commerce and Payments
6. Stocks & Stock Markets
7. e-Notary Services
8. P2P Lending & Distributed Crediting Systems
9. Crowdfunding Systems & Micro-Payments
10. Cloud Computing & Secure Cloud Storage

Although it is still in development, this technology is explored by many firms and even governments for its potential uses.

"Trust" is the critical aspect of transaction ledgering and blockchain technology offering a trustless system which offers the ultimate transparency. It may seem contradictory to use blockchain in a field like insurance which is directly based on trust, however, major players of the insurance sector such as Axa, Generali, and Allianz are already investing in blockchain technology.

Here are some of the possible areas of use for blockchain in insurance (Çipil, 2016):

1. It may be used for its decentralized and trustless transaction structure, for the purpose of improving fraud detection and data management, and to offer cost advantages.
2. It may offer a reliable and cheaper method for sensitive personal information sharing, including medical history.
3. It may offer the basis for P2P insurance products with its reliable and transparent transaction infrastructure.
4. It may ensure the widespread use of micro-insurance practices through this P2P structure.
5. Damage management and payment processes may be accelerated and the operational costs involved may be reduced.

Even though we are just at the beginning of this process, it is obvious that the blockchain technology will create a great commercial and economic value for the sector. Among the possible benefits of blockchain for insurers are, as follows:

1. Better efficiency,
2. Advanced pricing and risk management,
3. Improved reliability with a better compensation experience,
4. Ability to offer services to an increased number of clients,
5. Demand for new insurance products and services,
6. New 'smart' contract models (KPMG, 2017)

Improvement of the results obtained from blockchain depends heavily on the networking effect; in other words, the effect will be increased as the number of systems available and users of such blockchain-based applications increase.

INSURTECH ECONOMY IN TURKEY

It is a fact that the InsurTech initiatives will change the dynamics of the Turkish insurance sector and the companies which act fast will be one step ahead of their competition (Yıldız, 2017). The reasoning behind this statement can be explained, as follows:

The insurance sector puts a lot of effort into conforming regulations. Developments in non-life insurance, casco, and private pension schemes have required the insurance sector to invest in conforming the laws for the past 2 years. They have allocated their IT and R&D resources to this aspect (Eroğlu, 2018). On the other hand, some companies have commissioned internal innovation programs in order to be able to catch up with the developments in the mobile and digital world. However, it takes some time for these internal efforts to be translated into products and services. In a time like this, it would be the smart move to collaborate with startups and to integrate the products and services of these startups into their own products and channels to offer new products.

Consumer expectations are high for private insurance products. The insured are now able to visit insurance company websites and to place queries through call-centers and agencies. However, the consumers are already familiar with performing many of their transactions online and they would like to access insurance services through mobile channels. Calling a taxi using a mobile phone, sending/receiving wire transfers, ordering a meal, purchasing a flight ticket, renting an apartment, etc. are just some of the examples of what we use our mobile devices these days. Being able to view private pension funds available, to buy/sell funds, to view health limitations, to confirm the provision of services after a doctor's visit... These and many others could be services which bring convenience to the insured. In fact, making such applications available will become a necessity with the very first changes to be made in traffic insurance (Eroğlu, 2018). With the advancements in smart and self-driving cars, concepts such as driver, accident, responsibility, and insurance are being reshaped. Involved in a traffic accident, two smart vehicles communicate the data they collected at the moment of an accident to the insurance center for the calculation of liability in the accident.

Who are the actual customers of insurance companies? Reaching out to the insured through agencies and banking corporations, insurance companies feel the need for direct contact with their customers in order to be able to make customized offers. They are aiming not only for the ability to contact the customer at the moment of a claim but also for the ability to contact them before such a claim is requested and being a part of their lives. The firms which find the right solution for reaching out to their customers via mobile channels without disturbing the available agency relationships which they had invested dearly will be steps ahead of their competition.

The term, "the World is Flat," applies to insurance as it is the case for all of the other sectors. Especially increasing in number in the Internet and mobile field, unicorn companies are gaining traction. First started in California in 2010, Uber is now available in 81 countries and 563 cities. The success stories are everywhere with examples such as Netflix, Spotify, ebay, and many others. After being born in some distant part of the world, any disruptive insurance venture will penetrate the Turkish market in a short time (Acer, 2017).

These trends make it clear that insurance companies should act fast to partner with InsurTech startups to offer new products. An important aspect of this shift will be updating the regulations based on the provision of digital insurance products in order for the insurance companies to catch up with the changes in the world. The Insurance Information and Monitoring Centre (SBM) invests, on behalf of the sector, in both intercorporate processes and the digitalization of the services offered to the insured. Considering that we now have a practical application named 'Mobile Accident Report,' there is sufficient reason to believe that the necessary changes can be rapidly made to the regulations if the common good is proven.

It is believed that many of the insurance giants will leave aside the traditional methods and turn into rapidly growing InsurTech firms. We anticipate that Turkish insurance companies will invest heavily in InsurTech firms building partnerships. Among the segments where the InsurTech investments are expected to grow in the Turkish insurance sector are, as follows:

1. Commercial fields and reassurance,
2. Correspondence bot's firms use before the claims resolution, decision support systems, and the use of artificial intelligence for virtual assistance,
3. Internet of Insurance with the world becoming more interconnected every day,
4. Technology supported cyber insurance solutions and services,

It is expected that this transformation will have an effect on many fields and that not only firms but also technological manpower will turn their attention towards the traditional insurance sector (Eroğlu, 2018). Today, insurance companies are led by financial, insurance, risk and actuary specialists, while tech specialists assume lower positions. In 2016, new IT-based positions were created in order to change this situation and talents from other sectors were recruited by insurance companies, and this trend is expected to continue (KPMG, 2017).

In Turkey, InsurTech ecosystem is used most commonly to prevent insurance frauds. With the use of SAS (Fraud Framework for Insurance) technology, insurance frauds are reduced in number in Turkey.

The vision of Insurance Information and Monitoring Center (SBM) is to ensure the growth of the sector and to produce solutions to increase the profitability of the Turkish insurance sector. Thus, one of the main strategies of this center is to battle with the problem of insurance misconduct which has a significant and negative impact on the profitability of the sector. Building on this vision, Insurance Information and Monitoring Center has been looking for technological solutions to achieve the best results in this respect. The number of claims filed in Turkey adds up to 2.5 million annually (Acer, 2017) (Yıldız, 2017). A total number of 16 million traffic insurance and 5 million casco policies are issued every year. An advanced analytical solution was needed in order to uncover the fraud networks, having processed all these data. Turkish Insurance Information and Monitoring Center built a system based on Fraud Framework for Insurance software in order to fight fraud (Güzey, 2018). This system interprets all the data made available by insurance companies using the embedded analytical models and populates a risk score for the insured based on the relationships between the stakeholders. Introduced as a social network analysis, this network allows the Insurance Information and Monitoring Center (SBM) to view the relationships between all stakeholders. The system also searches for files similar to those previously defined as fraudulent. Then, SBM shares the risk scores it has produced with the insurance companies. Nevertheless, any organized crimes are investigated by the Fraud Prevention Office operating under the Insurance Association of Turkey and necessary actions are taken to charge these organizations.

Turkey is very promising in terms of InsurTech. And the reason behind this is the social structure, i.e. the young population. Therefore, there will always be investors if there are startups which can read the current situation. The important thing here is for the investors to know the logic behind insurance. Insurance companies may build mechanisms which will attract good startups. Banks once had taken such an approach and we will see the same happening for the insurance sector. We also need to work on the widespread recognition of InsurTech. The finance sector is now becoming familiar with the meaning of FinTech. The next thing to think about is how to actualize the financial solutions in the insurance sector and we need to read the international examples very carefully. This task is not only the responsibility of insurance companies but also regulatory bodies and associations such as Insurance Association of Turkey (https://fintechistanbul.org/category/insurtech/).

The most important step to be taken for the development of fuse technology in Turkey is the protection of personal data. Protection of personal data is also one of the most controversial issues of insurance. For some insurance branches, full compliance with the rules related to the sharing of personal data, which is vital, can hurt the business of insurance companies (Ünan, 2018). In Turkey on April 7, 2018 the Date of Protection of Personal Data Act entered into force. According to the law, personal data cannot be transmitted without the clear consent of the person concerned. It cannot be transferred abroad without the person's open recourse. Insurance companies must pass their business processes in a timely manner in accordance with the new regulations.

POSSIBLE ISSUES OF INSURANCE TECHNOLOGIES

The importance of the concept of InsurTech increases for the insurance companies which try to get their services and processes up-to-date with the technological advancements. What kind of changes InsurTech is bound to bring to the insurance sector? (Eroğlu, 2018). Creating new opportunities on one side, will it threaten the existence of others? Here are the possible issues which may be caused by the insurgence of InsurTech in Turkey and the global insurance market:

1. Inability to create customer-oriented solutions,
2. Possible issues in insurance distribution channels,
3. Possible issues in insurance companies,
4. The possibility of failure of digital projects.

- **Inability to Create Customer-Oriented Solutions:** Insurance companies operating in Turkey may invest in a failing project if they cannot embed InsurTech in every aspect of their operation from the production, to sales, from claims management to customer satisfaction. InsurTech organization matters, however, the companies will need to alter their ways of contacting the client and also their service quality (Güzey, 2018).

If it is unable to use the service quality and claims management in the most efficient way possible, and if it is unable to sort out the process as soon as possible, then the insurance system will be negatively affected. It could be said that the insurance sector should not only focus on price competition in a time where speed and service quality matter, and should focus on creating awareness with damage management and should be able to contact the client in any stage between policy sales to damage claim. Here, InsurTech emerges as an important parameter in this process.

- **Possible Issues in Insurance Distribution Channels:** There are three points of sales in the insurance sector: agency, bank, and broker. And the digitalization must be designed with these points of sales. Turkish insurance companies possess a number of structural faults. Turkish insurance companies depend heavily on agencies among other sales channels. Sixty percent of the insurance policies are processed by the agencies. Therefore, it is necessary to support the insurance agencies (https://fintechistanbul.org/category/insurtech/).

Turkish insurance agencies consider digitalization as their new competition. It is necessary to prove them wrong and to solve this issue. They must be informed that this is an opportunity for them and that those who do not take this opportunity are bound to lose out. Using a holistic approach, the agencies must be included in the InsurTech system (Çavuşoğlu, 2018).

- **Possible Issues in Insurance Companies:** InsurTech companies are divided into two, namely, 1st generation and 2nd generation InsurTech companies. The 1st generation consists of entrepreneurs who believe that they can "take a piece of the pie with online policy sales". They plan to offer services to make a profit with competitive prices. In such a competitive environment, no business may prevail if they cannot produce value. Insurance is not only about selling products, services or consultancy service (Çavuşoğlu, 2018). Entrepreneurs commonly believe the following is a fact: If the production processes are online, then the winner of the game is Google. Your chances of successfully competing with such giants are very thin. Innovation and entrepreneurship are being redefined all around the world, which brings us to the concept of the 2nd generation of InsurTech. Startups are everywhere. These entrepreneurs realize that agencies are not the enemy, that agencies can make the process easier for them, that the market will grow if they can develop solutions to add value to people's lives, and in doing so, they will also prevail. Entrepreneurs remodeling their business plans with this approach in mind and they are able to offer new solutions.

Some just bring convenience to the daily operations of the agencies and others develop products to eliminate their digital handicaps. Startups recognize that agencies are indispensable in the insurance sector and that they offer valuable input in terms of consultancy services and they are building on these strengths in creating solutions (Abacı, 2018). Insurance companies have set their course as the 1st generation of InsurTech firms at the beginning. However, it is necessary for them to reconsider this approach. It would be beneficial for all if they act fast to complete their transition to the 2nd generation of InsurTech firms. The advantages of such a transition will very soon be enjoyed by both InsurTech firms and the intermediaries.

The possibility of failure of digital projects. The transition can be a painstaking process for insurance companies. Looking at the global examples of such transitions, we can see that more than 80% of the digital projects are failed (Abacı, 2018). Large companies make substantial investments, however, most of the time they cannot have a return on investments. The reason behind this is that such projects are not embraced by the employees of the company. Another reason is that these companies are clueless about what exactly to focus on. It is very common that they invest their time and resources in the wrong project.

It is commonly underlined that the reason behind the slow development of InsurTech in Turkey, when compared to the EU, is the regulations in effect. Regulations are welcomed in the insurance sector, however, it is at least necessary to have such regulations updated as the sector develops. This is also the case in the banking system. We can see that certain structures in Europe have their regulators engaged in the process with a hands-on approach. They work in the ecosystem and not outside of it. And this approach makes it possible for us to see what the regulators are capable of. In countries such as the UK where InsurTech and FinTech are highly advanced, there are testing media for regulations called "sandbox." Thus, the companies are not restrained by the regulations once they are established and received their license (https://fintechistanbul.org/category/insurtech/).

CONCLUSION

The purposes of InsurTech can be summarized as the creation of new platforms for technical, claims and distribution channels, improvement of the customer experience, and accelerating the insurance processes using new software. Looking back at the reason behind this change in the insurance sector, we can observe the need for attracting more and more investors to the sector. Having considered insurance as a complicated and inefficient business process, investors had stood clear of the insurance sector which resulted in the lack of resources necessary for the development of the sector. With the idea that there are a lot of aspects of the sector which needs to be altered, startups started to promote their innovative solutions to insurance companies presenting them with the opportunity to team up for the tech revolution they need to go through in order to meet the changing customer demands.

There is a great resemblance between the insurance system in Babylon and the InsurTech startups of today. You build your own pool and the claims are paid from this pool when the damage occurs. This system was not built in one day. It is a result of the widespread digitalization in the world. Insurance sector offers a lot of opportunities. Among these opportunities is IoT (Internet of Things). It draws attention as it can be used with wearables. The smartwatch you wear can now collect any data about you such as the steps you have taken or your heart rate and many others. Insurance companies are now using the data they collect from these products and they offer insurance policies customized for you based on this information.

Telematics is another element of the equation. As part of telematics systems, a device is connected to the vehicle to collect data. Such devices collect all the driving data. Another system to be used in damage assessment and expert opinion is the use of drones. Drones are especially handy when damage assessment and expert opinion is needed for a hard-to-reach or risky area. Another common practice is the use of surveillance cameras. Today, the sales representatives are catering to their customers using tablets provided by their employer. Using the cameras on these devices, it is possible to obtain expert opinion right away.

Another medium is the payment systems... It can be said that Turkish citizens are very familiar with debit/credit card payments. And also there are many examples of digital wallet use. BKM Express is just one of these apps. This system allows for instant payments. Such digital integrations allow the insurance companies to collect payment of a policy while setting reminders and automatic payment options.

Telematics is also used in agriculture. They come in handy to reduce the irrigation costs of the farmer while protecting the crops. Although these technologies may seem user-oriented, they also reduce the claims paid by the insurance company. On a macro scale, they reduce the burden of reassurance. And this translates into contribution not only to the local economy but also to the global one.

How will the widespread use of these technologies affect agencies? The insurance sector has always been a growing one thanks to the intermediaries, which may justify the opposition in the face of these developments. There are also a number of applications for agencies. It is possible for the agencies to act as information and consultation providers and not as fund collection centers. These are not unprofitable fields. Here, the specialty of the agency matters and the agency is paid for their specialized services. In order to be able to do this, an agency must have a professional level of know-how.

In terms of offering innovative and creative solutions based on customer problems and needs, InsurTech startups are waiting for the insurance companies to optimize their advantages. In this respect, the Turkish insurance sector and the international insurance sector must place importance on the following aspects.

All the rings of the insurance value chain are being digitalized. InsurTech startups offer opportunities for all the rings of the insurance value chain, and not those motivated only by the sales, offering optimal solutions.

It is not a viable approach for a company if it attempts to offer the perfect solution for all the rings of the value chain. On the contrary, the companies which create the shared platform necessary for the collaboration with specialized InsurTech startups which produce the perfect solutions will prevail.

InsurTech startups commonly focus on B2B and B2B2C models, and solutions to add value to the corporations and the consumer via these corporations, instead of pursuing schemes which are disruptive to the current actors and the available system.

It is clearly a need to focus on human behavior and customer needs without being sidetracked by a sole focus on technology.

As insurance products are integrated to many aspects of the lives of individual and corporate clients, insurance companies and startups need to see beyond the insurance and keep an open mind about being a part of a wider ecosystem and platform. Section title should be "Conclusion," not "Conclusions." Provide discussion of the overall coverage of the chapter and concluding remarks.

REFERENCES

Abacı, M. (2018). *IT Yatırımlarımızın Yüzde 41'i Dijitalleşmeye Gidiyor*. Retrieved from http://m.sigortagundem.com/uploads/documents/akilliyasamdergisi-ocak2018-qnWW.pdf

Acer, F. (2017). *Insurance Sector to Develop with InsurTech*. Retrieved from https://www.bankasurans.com.tr/sigorta-sektoru-insurtech-ile-gelisecek/

Bakshi, K. (2012). Considerations for Big Data: Architecture and Approaches. *Proceedings of the IEEE Aerospace Conference*. 10.1109/AERO.2012.6187357

Berger, R. (2017). *Copy Them? Work with Them? or Buy Them?* InsurTechs and the Digitalization of Insurance.

Cappiello, A. (2018). Digital Disruption and InsurTech Start-ups: Risks and Challenges. In *Technology and the Insurance Industry*. Springer.

Carney, M. (2017). *The Promise of FinTech—Something New Under the Sun?* Retrieved from www.bankofengland.co.uk/publications/Documents/speeches/2017/speech956.pdf

Çavuşoğlu, R. (2018). *İkinci Nesil Insurtech Şirketine Dönüşmek İçin Çalışıyoruz*. Retrieved from http://m.sigortagundem.com/uploads/documents/akilliyasamdergisi-ocak2018-qnWW.pdf

ÇipilM. (2016). Retrieved from https://tr.linkedin.com/pulse/blockchain-sigortac%C4%B1l%C4%B1%C4%9F%C4%B1-nas%C4%B1l-etkileyecek-mahir-%C3%A7ipil

Elgendy, N. (2013). *Big Data Analytics in Support of the Decision Making Process* (MSc Thesis). German University in Cairo.

Eroğlu, M. A. (2018). *Her Aşamada Müşteriye Dokunmalıyız*. Retrieved from http://m.sigortagundem.com/uploads/documents/akilliyasamdergisi-ocak2018-qnWW.pdf

Güzey, P. (2018). *Dijital projelerin yüzde 80'inden fazlası başarısızlıkla sonuçlanıyor*. Retrieved from http://m.sigortagundem.com/uploads/documents/akilliyasamdergisi-ocak2018-qnWW.pdf http://blokzincir.bilgem.tubitak.gov.tr/blok-zincir.html https://fintechistanbul.org/category/insurtech/

Iansiti, M., & Lakhani, K. (2017). The Truth About Blockchain. *Harvard Business Review, 95*(1), 118–127.

KPMG. (2017). *Sigortacılık, Teknolojiyle Yeniden Doğdu* [Rebirth of insurance business with technology]. Retrieved from https://home.kpmg.com/tr/tr/home/media/press-releases/2017/07/sigortacilik-teknolojiyle-yeniden-dogdu.html

Larimer, D. (2016). *Blok Zinciri Ve Sigorta*. Retrieved from https://www.blokzinciri.org/yazi/blok-zinciri-ve-sigorta/

Machler, M. (2016). *InsurTech Paving the Way to Change the Insurance Regulatory Landscape?* Retrieved from http://www.icir.de/fileadmin/Documents/Policy_Platform/180426_ICIR_JB_PP_InsurTech.pdf

McKinsey. (2017). Blockchain Technology in the Insurance Sector. In *Proceedings of the Quarterly Meeting of the Federal Advisory Committee on Insurance (FACI)*. McKinsey & Company.

Schanz, K. U. (2015). *The Technology and Data Revolution in Insurance: A Brave New World?* Middle East Insurance Review.

Shcherbak, S. (2014). How should Bitcoin be regulated? *Eur. J. Legal Stud.*, *7*, 41.

Shelkovnikov, A. (2016). *Blockchain Applications in Insurance; Deloitte Report*. London, UK: Deloitte LLP.

Tu, K. V., & Meredith, M. W. (2015). Rethinking virtual currency regulation in the Bitcoin age. *Washington Law Review (Seattle, Wash.)*, *90*, 271.

Ünan, S. (2018). *Sigortacılığın Kişisel Veri İmtihanı*. Retrieved from http://www.sigortacigazetesi.com.tr/sigortaciligin-kisisel-veri-imtihani/

Usta, A., & Doğantekin, S. (2017). *Blockchain 101*. İstanbul: Kapital Medya Hizmetleri A.Ş.

Yalçın, G. F. (2018). *Sigorta Teknolojileri İçin Üretim Zamanı* [Time to Produce Insurance Technologies]. Retrieved from http://fintechtime.com/tr/2018/02/sigorta-teknolojileri-icin-uretim-zamani/

Yeşilyurt, H. (2015). Cyber Security Risks And Solutions in The Financial Services Sector: Payment Systems And Supply Chain Integrity. *CBÜ Sosyal Bilimler Dergisi, 13*(2).

Yıldız, Y. (2017). *Turkey's digital insurance innovation*. Retrieved from https://www.worldfinance.com/markets/turkeys-digital-insurance-innovation

KEY TERMS AND DEFINITIONS

Autonomous Car: Also known as self-driving cars, these cars use a number of sensors to identify its surroundings and they are able to move autonomously without the need for human interference.

Blockchain: It is a recording system made up of blocks which are connected using cryptography, making the system a lot more secure.

Broker: Private and independent professional insurance intermediary who acts as the consultant and/or representative of the person who purchases an insurance policy.

FinTech: This is a technological development which aims to compete with traditional finance methods. It represents the technology allowing for mobile banking and the use of mobile devices for investment and making financial services readily available for the users.

Insurance: A risk transfer system where a certain amount of money is paid by individuals exposed to the same type of risk and their damages are compensated only when such risk is actualized using the money collected in the pool.

Insurance Policy: The written and legal proof of the contract signed between the insurer and the insured. An insurance policy consists of information about the insurer and the insured, definitions of the type and coverage of the insurance, the cost of insurance, the duration of a contract, premium payment information, issue date, and liabilities and responsibilities of the parties.

Insurer: The insurance company which contracts an engagement with the insured undertaking all the responsibilities of the insured with regards to the insurance type.

Premium: The payment made by the insured on a regular basis in exchange for the assurance provided by the insurer in the face of the risks available.

Reassurance: The partial or full transfer of the liabilities of one insurer to another insurer.

Smart Home: Building technologies are the reflection of common industrial control systems into our daily life; home automation can be defined as the use of this technology customized according to personal preferences and needs. Smart homes allow the user to remotely control any functions and systems embedded in a home.

Chapter 4
FinTech for Digital Financial Services:
The African Case

Benjamin Enahoro Assay
Delta State Polytechnic Ogwashi-Uku, Nigeria

ABSTRACT

The introduction of FinTech into Africa's digital financial services environment has provoked a controversy as to whether the innovative technology should be assimilated by banks and other financial service providers or not, thus creating uncertainty about the future of FinTech on the continent. This chapter, therefore, examines the issues, controversy, and problems surrounding the debut of FinTech and suggest ways to make the technology acceptable in order to harness its potentials for the overall benefit of the African society.

INTRODUCTION

In a competitive environment dominated by technology, the growth of modern business is closely linked with technological innovations. Betz (1998 p.23) described technological innovation as the invention of new technology and the development and introduction of the technology into the market place. Technological innovations comprised modified products and processes that improve on performance characteristics (OECD, 2002).

DOI: 10.4018/978-1-5225-7805-5.ch004

For businesses to thrive in this digital era there is need for such business entities to continue to innovate in order to deliver quality products and services to consumers as well as compete effectively in the industry. According to the Oslo manual, an innovation is defined as the implementation of a new or significantly improved product (good or service), or process, a new marketing method, or a new organizational method in business practices, workplace organization or external relations (Eurostat and OECD, 2005). The Oslo manual further stated that the minimum requirement for an innovation is that the product, process, marketing method or organizational method must be new (or significantly improved) to the firm. Innovations activities are all scientific, technological, organizational, financial and commercial steps which actually, or are intended to lead to the implementation of innovations. Innovations activities also include Research and Development that is not directly related to the development of a specific innovation.

Shukla (2017), while defining innovation as exploiting new ideas leading to the creation of a new product, process or service said it is not just the invention of a new idea that is important, but it is actually, 'bringing it to market', putting into practice and exploiting it in a manner that leads to new products, services or system that add value or improve quality. According to him, innovation also means exploiting new technology and employing out-of-the-box thinking to generate new value and to bring about significant changes in society. Berry and Taggart (1994 p. 341) viewed innovation as the total process from the inception of an idea through to the manufacture of a product and finally, to its ultimate sale. They further added that innovation includes invention as the many stages of implementation such as research development, production and marketing.

It is obvious from the foregoing that innovation may have slightly different meanings depending on the industry but its core is universal. Jacob Beckley in an article he wrote for Business NewsDaily said innovation embodies the improvement of something that has come before and it is the evolution of convenience, efficiency and effectiveness. As the Fusion 92 vice president put it, the companies that do their best are the ones that will ultimately have sustained success:

In the vast sea of innovation, companies that take the largest risk, close the biggest gaps and identify the newest opportunities are rewarded with the title of true innovators and leaders by their consumers and peers. These true innovators are setting themselves apart from any and all competition (Business NewsDaily 2013, September 23).

Innovation helps businesses to stay ahead of the competition as the market and trend continue to shift. ImagineNation (2018) asserted that innovation enables businesses to achieve a range of key business outcomes including: (1) engaging and aspiring people to tap into the power of the internal crowd, and empower people to create, invent and innovate new products, processes and services; (2) increasing their return on investment (ROI) to shareholders; (3) achieving business growth goals and improving bottom line results; (4) increasing business value making the business attractive to shareholders, mergers and acquisitions; (5) making productivity and efficiency gains to increase profitability; (6) competing successfully to respond to industry disrupters, increase market share and extend product lifecycles; and (7) responding quickly by developing the internal capability in both human and technology resources to change direction and do things differently.

Businesses that are unable to innovate by recognizing their current resources, opportunities for development, response to customer or organizational needs and anticipation of future trends, run the risk of operating inefficiently (Innovation Xchange, 2018) as well as face decline and extinction. Technological innovations are therefore key enablers of businesses growth and development (Moore 2017; George, McGahan & Prabhu 2012).

One key innovative technology that is poised to revolutionize the financial services sector in Africa is Fintech. Simply put, Fintech is the application of innovative technology to financial services and dates back to the invention of double entry bookkeeping. However, since the turn of the century, the term has expanded and now presents a very valid challenge to traditional banking as an increasing number of startups are providing services more efficiently and less expensively. Amid all the hype, Fintech is greatly reducing the cost of transferring money and giving hundreds of millions of people access to financial services for the very first time in the African continent.

The financial services sector consists of diverse group of companies that goes beyond banks and credit unions. Companies in the financial services industry are in the business of managing money. Globally, the financial services industry leads the world in terms of earnings and equity market capitalization. Large conglomerates dominate this sector, but it also includes a diverse range of smaller companies. Commercial banking services are the foundation of the financial services group (Investopedia, 2018a).

The digitalization of financial services is contributing to an expansion in offerings. For the past decade the financial services sector in sub-Saharan Africa, as with many other less developed markets has leveraged digital technology to help underserved clients interface with financial products and services from which they were previously excluded. For several years, there had been little product diversification beyond digital payments and transfers. Lately, however, the broader shift to digital is leading to more modes of engagement, tools and offerings and ultimately contributing to an expansion in the pool of use of cases.

Users are now able to interact with financial services via various digital channels of engagement. Modes of engagement range from the original USSD mobile money services, accessed through feature phones, to services accessible through smart phones applications and social messaging platforms. With 55% of sub-Sahara Africa's network connections predicted to come through smart phones by 2020 (MobileWorldLive, 2017) there is no doubt that the face of digital finance is changing. Increased smart phones adoption has led many local Fintechs (such as Branch, Tala) as well as banks and mobile network operators (such as Eazzy Bank, Tigo Pesa) to offer their services through applications either in conjunction with or as a substitute for a USSD service.

Undoubtedly, Fintech is the new buzzword sweeping across Africa. As with many new phrases that land on the shores of the African continent, there is enthusiasm to embrace it, partly in order to avoid being seen as behind the times. Yet, clearly, there is still considerable confusion about exactly what it is and where and for what purpose it can be applied. This chapter thus examines the future of Fintech in Africa's digital financial services environment. The objectives of the chapter are:

1. To find out the areas where Fintech can be applied effectively
2. To highlight the benefits and challenges of the new innovative technology
3. To ascertain why its acceptance is still shrouded in controversy
4. To come out with recommendations that would help to overcome the challenges and make Fintech acceptable in the African continent.

The next discussion will feature the following sections: background, main focus of the chapter (issues, controversies, and problems), solutions, recommendations, and conclusion.

BACKGROUND

Concept of Fintech

Fintech is a combination of the words "financial" and "technology". It is a broad category that refers to the innovative use of technology in the design and delivery of financial services and products. The application of Fintech cuts across multiple business segments, including banking, insurance, investment management and payments, lending, advice and other areas related to finance. Many Fintech companies harness mobile technologies, big data and superior analytics to tailor products for various customer segments. Fintech is fast changing the way in which companies interact with their customers in today's digital world. The proliferation of Fintech has had a number of positive impacts for society, including increased competition, a reduction in prices paid by customers and wider access to financial services among the traditionally underserved.

Fintech is defined differently in the literature. Researchers such as Sweeny (2015) cited in Ryu (2018 p.3864) and Kuo Chuen and Teo (2015) defined Fintech as products or services in financial service companies that were created on highly innovative and disruptive service technologies. Ernest and Young (2015) cited in Ryu (2018 p 3864) defined Fintech as an innovation in financial services where technology is the key enabler. Lee (2015) referred to Fintech as a type of business using hardware and software technologies to provide financial services. Amer, Barberis & Buckley (2015) also referred to Fintech as technology enabled financial solutions.

According to Kawai (2016 p.1) Fintech denotes companies or representatives of companies that combine financial services with modern, innovative technologies. Schueffel (2017 p.32) defined it as a new financial industry that applies technology to improve financial activities, while Sanicola (2017) described Fintech as the new applications, processes, products, or business models in the financial service industry, composed of one or more complementary services and provided as an end-to-end process via the internet. Accenture (2018a) averred that Fintech is all about applying evolving technological advances to improve financial services – either reinventing or simplifying a process, increasing its functionality and making it more engaging for user. The 'tech' in Fintech, as Accenture puts it, is the emergence of brand new technologies such as AI (Artificial Intelligence), blockchain, analytics and big data.

Blockchain represents the new economic revolution of the twenty first century with a vast possibility of its application in several areas of the economy such as finance, medicine, agriculture, insurance, voting system etc. (Okonji, 2018 p. 30). For African governments and businesses struggling under the weight of outdated administration techniques, overbearing bureaucracies, and competing asset ownership claims, the attractions of blockchain are obvious (African Business, 2018 February p. 14). Defined by Iansiti and Lakhani (2017) as "an open, distributed ledger that can record transactions between two parties efficiently and in verifiable and permanent way", blockchain allows contracts to be embedded in code and "stored in transparent, shared data bases, where they are protected from deletion, tampering, and revision".

Although Fintech is generally seen as an economic industry composed of companies that use technology to make financial services more efficient, it encompasses companies that simply provide the technology (such as software solutions) to financial service providers (Dorfleitner, Weber, Schmitt & Hormuf, 2017 p.5).

Contrary to popular belief, Fintech is not new. It has been around in one form or another virtually as long as the financial services industry itself. After the global financial crisis of 2008, however, Fintech has evolved to disrupt and reshape commerce, payments, investment, asset management, insurance, clearance and settlement of securities and even money itself with cryptocurrencies such as Bitcoin. In the last few years, Fintech companies have defined the direction, shape, and pace of change across almost every financial services subsector. Customers now expect seamless digital onboarding, rapid loan approvals, and free person-to-person payments – all innovations that Fintech made popular. And while they may not dominate the industry today, Fintechs have succeeded as both stand alone businesses and vital links in the financial services value chain (World Economic Forum, 2017).

According to World Economic Forum (2017), disruptive forces that have reshaped the Fintech industry include, but are certainly not limited to:

1. The growth of online shopping, which is expanding quickly at the expense of in-person shopping, leading to the dominance of online, cashless solutions for transactions.
2. A shifting balance of power that swings from banks and other financial services to those who own the customer experience. Banks are eliminating in-person services and looking to Fintech and large technology companies for other ways to engage customers.
3. New trading platforms that are collecting data to create an aggregated market view and using analytics to uncover trends.
4. Insurance products, which are becoming more tailored to customers who, in turn, are demanding coverage for specific locations, uses and timeframes. That is driving insurers to collect and analyze additional data about their clients.
5. Artificial intelligence, which now plays a role in differentiating financial services products as it replaces complex human activities.
6. Transaction process improvement and middle ware, both of which remain expensive. This is pushing traditional financial services firms to consider partnership with market place lenders for Fintech solutions that do not require a full infrastructure overhaul.

The rise of Fintech has changed the world's business landscape. Fintech companies are now directly competing with banks in most areas of the financial sector to sell financial services and solutions to customers (Chima, 2017 p. 27). Mostly due to regulatory reasons and their internal structures, banks still struggle to keep up with Fintech startups in terms of innovation speed. Fintechs have realized that financial services of all kinds - including money transfer, lending, investing, payments etc - need to seamlessly integrate in the lives of the tech-savvy and sophisticated customers of today to stay relevant in a world where business and private life have become increasingly digitalized.

Fintech and the Business World

Once thought to be unfailingly secure due to their size, scope, influence and the high barriers to market entry, banks, insurance companies and investment houses have come under assault from a new technological wave that threatens their status quo, if not their existence. Fintech is said to be moving at such a rapid pace that, by 2020 as much as 25% of the financial industry's revenue will be at risk. According to a PriceWaterHouseCoopers' (PWC) report titled: "Financial Services Technology 2020 and Beyond", the convergence of financial services and technology, which has come to be known as Fintech, has become such a disruptive force in such a short time period that established financial institutions must quickly reconsider their business models or risk obsolescence in significant parts of the financial services value chain (Investopedia, 2018b).

There is no doubt that Fintech has changed the world of finance for customers in a myriad of ways. Customers can now open a bank account over the internet without physically visiting the bank. They can link the account to their smartphone and use it to monitor their transactions. They can as well turn the smartphone into a 'digital wallet' and use it to pay for things using money in the account. Fintech is also rapidly changing the insurance and investment industries, car insurance providers now sell 'telematics-based' insurance where driving is monitored using data collected via a smart phone or a 'black box' fitted in one's car. This data can then be used to determine how much is paid for an insurance policy. In the future, it may be possible to buy insurance on a short-term or 'pay as you go' basis.

As an innovative and emerging field, Fintech has attracted public attention and growing investment (Ryu, 2018 p. 3864). According to an Accenture report titled "The Future of Fintech and Banking Digitally Disrupted or Reimagined?" global investment into Fintech companies and startups have risen dramatically from $930m in 2008 to over $12billion by the beginning of 2015. Europe experienced the highest growth rate, with an increase of 215% to $1.48billion in 2014 (Accenture 2018b). This figure is likely to increase tremendously in the years ahead.

Fintech and Africa's Emerging Market

Africa is a vast continent with diverse economies and a total population growth of 1.2 billion people living in 54 independent countries spread over 30 million square kilometers. As a market, the continent has all the prerequisites to serve as a firm foundation for growth and development. Among the key data points characterizing Africa's state of financial system, the SWIFT Institute (2017) has outlined the following:

1. In 47 out of the 89 markets where mobile money is available, both banks and nonbanks are allowed to provide mobile money service.
2. Half of almost 300 million registered mobile money accounts globally are located in sub-Saharan Africa.
3. In addition, there are 226 million mobile money agents in developing countries around the world, many more than the number of alternative financial access points comprising ATMs (1.38 million), commercial bank branches (524,000), post offices (501,00) and Western Union locations (500,000).

As at the end of 2017, there were more than 300 Fintech African startups across the continent. Disrupt Africa's innovating for Africa: Exploring the Fintech startup Ecosystem Report 2017 concludes that African startups' growth since 2015 has been nothing short of tremendous. Mulligan (2017) notes:

With so many of Africa's citizens still without access to basic financial services the work being done by the continent's Fintech innovations is of crucial importance and impact. We are glad to report such thriving activity among Africa's Fintech community, and believe these local entrepreneurs are creating a new model for financial services – and financial inclusion – in Africa.

The record shows over US $100 million in Fintech funding has been secured across the continent over the last two years, with South Africa, receiving 34.2 percent of the total and Nigeria following closely with 34 percent. South Africa has the most Fintech Startups with 94, followed by Nigeria with 74 and Kenya 56. Oladeji (2018) identify the following as the factors and drivers behind the growth of Fintech in Africa's emerging market.

Payment Made Easy

Fintech has made payments and remittances more convenient across the continent. Most traditional banks are located in cities and commercial areas, making them difficult to access from remote areas. Tanzania, for example, has about 50 million people sparsely distributed across an area nearly four times the size of the United Kingdom. In Nigeria, banks used to be packed with customers queuing to pay their utility and Cable TV bills, school fees and so on. It could take hours to make a simple transaction.

In 2012, a cashless policy was introduced by the Central Bank of Nigeria to curb excess handling of cash and reduce the volume of money in circulation. The policy has facilitated many Nigerian Fintech startups' market penetration and expansion. Customer transportation costs, waiting times and the loss risks attached to cash have been eliminated by the smartphone- based Fintech services provided by these startups. About 100 of Africa's Fintech startups are focused on streamlining money transfers. According to Tayo Oviosu, founder and CEO of Nigerian mobile payment platform Paga, "Nigerian banks have traditionally focused on retail. Paga has built the single largest network of financial access points in Nigeria. We are going to leverage that to deliver financial services to the mass market".

Market Confidence

One of the significant drivers of African Fintech startups is high confidence in the market. Early Fintech startups demonstrated that the market is strong, and the growth trend has continued, attracting Silicon Valley-based accelerators. Fintech startup funding is presently one of the most attractive investments on the continent. In 2017, over 30% of the US $195 million in VC funding raised by Africa startups went to the Fintech sector. Safaricom's M-Pesa mobile money service has had a great impact in Kenya, and Nigeria's Paga, South Africa's Zoona, Kenya's BitPesa and others across the continent are garnering increased funding as investors become more confident.

Influencing the Traditional Banking System

Since the inception of Fintech, there have been dramatic changes in the continent's traditional banking system. Banks and financial institutions are under pressure to match the innovative solutions and services being offered by Fintech startups which have reached millions of people who have mobile phones but not bank accounts. Now, banks and financial institutions are introducing a variety of strategies and tactics to invest in, acquire or collaborate with Fintech startups. This is a trend that is expected to continue.

More Africans Connected to the Internet

Nigeria, South Africa, Egypt, Ethiopia and Kenya are among the most significant mobile markets in Africa. Although 80 million Nigerians – 47 percent of the population do not have bank account, 142 million Nigerians have mobile network access and 103 million are internet users, according to the regulator of the telecommunications industry, Nigerian Communication Commission (NCC).

The penetration of mobile phones and the internet has enabled Fintech to influence how financial services and products are developed and delivered, as more Africans plug into digital financial services across the continent. Kenya's M-Pesa is being used by more than half of the country's adult population, and has recorded transactions worth more than half the country's GDP since its debut. Similar success stories have been told by the likes of South African startup Zoona, Nigeria's Paga and others.

Filling the Vacuum

A World Bank report notes that Nigeria, like many countries in sub-Sahara Africa, has a growing population that lacks easy access to traditional financial services and Fintech innovators are filling the vacuum by connecting these people. This differs from the situation in advanced economies with strong financial institutions, where Fintech startups are cast instead as disrupting the traditional banking industry. For example, China's Wechat is a popular messaging app with a wallet feature that enables users to send and receive money, make payments and so on from within the Wechat app, without connecting to a bank account for many transactions.

Competition and Regulations

Among the factors responsible for African Fintech growth are strong competition and loose regulations. Presently across the continent, there are few or no strict regulations compared to advanced economies. Startups can operate relatively tax-free and with less government interference, leaving them to chart their courses and develop their products with little regulatory interference.

There is also increasing integration from service providers, many of which are partnering with Fintech startups to make transactions more convenient for customers. For example, Cable TV companies such as DSTV, HiTV, and TSTV have introduced Fintech alternatives to their traditional bank payment models. As more banks and financial institutions acquire or partner with Fintech startups, the trend is being seen not so much as financial industry competition but as industry reinvention that has improved financial service companies' profiles, reach and products and services; and is beneficial to banks, startups and customers alike. Fintech has thus become one of the most vibrant investment options in the African tech space.

Going Forward

In recent years, African Fintech Start-ups have been outperforming banks in delivering digital financial services. Iyin Aboyeji, Chief Executive of digital payment technology startup flutterwave, describes Fintech as a financial element that will drive the digital economy in Africa over the coming years. Investors and companies are expected to get even more involved in African Fintech market because the opportunities are tremendous.

Fintech Ecosystem in Africa

Since the Fintech startup boom began in earnest in 2015, the Disrupt Africa's Finnovating for Africa research found that the continent's Fintech startups have secured millions of dollars in investment. While the payments and remittances, and lending and financing subsectors saw the highest values of investment secured, a novel trend uncovered by the data is that blockchain startups have proven the most likely group of startups to raise external funding – with 38.9 percent of Africa's blockchain startups securing funding since the beginning of 2015. This point to the fact that investors are drawn both to startups busy addressing the lack of basic financial services on a local level, as well as those innovating around globally relevant cutting-edge technologies.

Reflecting on the vibrancy of Fintech in Africa's ecosystem, Tom Jackson, co-founder of Disrupt Africa enthused:

Fintech is clearly a vibrant space with the African tech scene, perhaps the most vibrant of all. Increasingly, investors are seeking the huge potential the space has to offer. We hope this report will provide valuable insights and leads to both, startups and funders in space, and contribute to the evolution of the sector for the benefits of all.

MAIN FOCUS OF THE CHAPTER

Issues, Controversies, and Problems

Issues

The debut of Fintech in the financial services sector in Africa has led to the introduction of startups and innovative solutions by Fintech companies. These startups and solutions deployed by the Fintech companies are disrupting existing financial services as well as creating opportunities for many who were hitherto not served by the banks and other financial institutions. As a result, the Fintech companies are considered a threat to the existence of most banks. The threat, identified as real has continued to engender fear amongst stakeholders (policy makers, professionals, and employees) in the financial industry.

Echoes of the fear resounded recently in Lagos, Nigeria when the Central Bank Governor, Mr. Godwin Emefiele admitted that Fintech companies pose a big threat to the banking industry. Emefiele raised the alarm at the investiture of Mr. Uche Messiah Olowu as the 20th President and Chairman of Council of the Chartered Institute of Bankers of Nigeria. While calling on bankers to urgently address the threats posed by Fintech companies, he urged the CIBN to embark on advocacy campaign to avoid crisis in the financial sector. Immediate past president of CIBN, Mr. Segun Ajibola also admitted that banks face huge threats from Fintech companies (Asu, 2018).

The fears and worry over the negative impact of Fintech on the financial services sector show how disturbing the situation could be in all the countries where the innovative technology has made remarkable progress in driving the exponential growth in digital payment. Threatened by disruption from Fintech companies, and the fear of being obsolete in the years ahead, African banks have been on the forefront of collaboration between startups and corporates.

Controversies

Since the emergence of Fintech in Africa's digital financial space, established players (banks and other financial companies) are in a quandary as to whether to compete by adopting the new technology or stick to what they know best. While some are urging them to assimilate Fintech and deploy it appropriately for the benefit of society, others want the banks and other companies to either fight or tread softly.

Reflecting on the dilemma faced by the established players in the financial services sector, the Bank of England's Governor, Mark Carney warned that competition offered by Fintech could reduce the stability of funding of incumbent banks. He added that the challenge for policy makers is to ensure that Fintech develops in a way that maximizes the opportunities and minimizes the risks for society. Ford (2017 p.20) noted that while it can be difficult for mainstream banks to replicate the services offered by Fintech operators at similarly low cost, mobile money firms can usually provide alternative versions of the products offered by traditional banks. For example, M-Pesa now allows customers to save for a specific purpose via its M-Shwari service, replicating similar savings accounts offered by high street banks that enable customers to buy a car, pay school fees or meet other specific outlays.

Global consultancy Accenture calculates that Fintech threatens more than a third of traditional bank's revenue due to the march of technological innovation and the emergence of more attractive investment regimes, the challenge posed by Fintech is only likely to grow. The Chief Executive Officer of cloud banking services Mambu, Eugene Danilkis, commented that: "Africa is in the early but rapid phases of Fintech development. Having started off on the payments side, it will move quickly and leapfrog to more complex financial service as smart phones penetration deepens. There is a big opportunity for extensive growth with a population of 1.2bn, which will double over the next 30 years" (Ford, 2017 p.20).

However, Dave Van Niekerk, the CEO of MyBucks, said it is hard for traditional banks to change traditional operations because it is not viable for them to offer accounts with very small balances to millions of people. He added that in the very near future, the poorest of the poor will use technology to educate themselves and access financial products and services, anywhere and at any time. In view of the many challenges posed by Fintech to the financial services sector in Africa, the banks and financial companies must therefore decide whether to defend its position or evolve in line with market trends.

Problems

The financial service sector in Africa has grown to be one of the most popular for technology innovations. Today, all eyes are now fixed on the sector globally, and the changes that are set to occur in the nearest future. Across Africa, more and more Fintech companies are innovating, putting the continent on the global landscape. These companies leverage technology to provide innovative financial service, including payment, lending, savings, financial advice and financial infrastructure, resulting in greater efficiency, better service and lower costs (CPAFRICA, 2018).

In the words of Phillippe Gelis, CEO of Kantox, "Fintech is changing the finance sector just like the internet changed the written press and the music industries". The words of Gelis aptly describe the rate at which Fintech has grown in the last few years, changing the traditional financial service sector we used to know, and impacting how increasing numbers of individuals and businesses alike conduct their financial transactions (CPAFRICA, 2018).

One of the biggest problems of the innovative technology (Fintech) is the lack of interoperability between the various services and mobile operators in different countries. Until recently, while Kenyans living abroad were able to transfer money to family and friends at home via M-Pesa, it was more difficult for Kenyans to send money to people living in other African countries.

However, cooperation and interoperability agreements are being concluded between different mobile and platform operators, Vodafone, which partly owns M-Pesa, and MTN group signed a deal in early 2015 that allowed their customers to transfer money between the two networks. Some weeks later, the British company concluded another agreement that allowed M-Pesa to transfer to seven African countries via Vodafone's network. Other mobile operators were forced to follow Vodafone's lead. East Africa has been at the forefront of this trend as Central banks and telecoms regulators in the region have required operators to allow transfer between platforms (Nelson, 2017 p.25).

Solutions

In spite of the threat it poses to banks and financial service providers, it is instructive to note that Fintech has become the next big thing in Africa. In the next few years, going by the way it is disrupting traditional processes, it would take over the financial service sector in the continent. In view of the prospect Fintech holds for Africa's financial industry, the following solutions are hereby proposed to address the issues raised in this work.

1. In order to harness the benefits of Fintech for the growth and development of the financial service sector in Africa, established banks should assimilate the innovative technology rather than fight it.
2. For the financial sector to achieve maximum growth in this digital age, banks and other financial service providers should collaborate with Fintech companies and take advantage of the numerous opportunities it presents to improve their traditional offerings.
3. Companies in the financial service sector and outside hoping to flourish should also leverage the potential of Fintech by having a top-down approach, embracing new technologies in every aspect of their businesses, shifting their thinking to better meet customer needs, constantly tracking technological developments and integrating digitalization into their activities.

Recommendations

Based on the issues, controversies and problems presented in this chapter, the following recommendations are made.

1. There is no doubt that the emergence of Fintech companies pose serious challenges to banks and the traditional payment methods. In view of this, banks are therefore, encouraged to become equally innovative to compete effectively with the new entrants.
2. Established banks and other financial institutions should position themselves to take advantage of the tide of financial technological innovations in Africa.
3. E-payment providers who are worried by the emergence of disruptive technologies like Fintech should rather focus on how to use them to add value to their services and the financial ecosystem.
4. Established banks should seek to compete with Fintech companies by becoming incubators for the innovative technology. Banks like Standard Bank and Barclays have both launched startup support program with the most successful companies taken under their wings at the end of the periods of supports.

5. Established banks should seek out Fintech startups that fit into their existing corporate, technological and business systems rather than opting for those that are truly disruptive in nature.
6. Established banks and mobile network operators in Africa should work together to promote interoperability to ease the transfer of money within the continent, as well as between platforms.
7. Fintech companies should reach out to low income earners and people in the rural areas in order to boost economic growth and increase the Gross Domestic Products (GDP) of African countries.
8. The Fintech companies should also play important role in the development of the economy and the promotion of financial inclusion in Africa.
9. Lastly, there is a need for constant dialogue between all stakeholders in the financial service sector so that the current obstacles to the adoption and use of Fintech could be removed.

FUTURE RESEARCH DIRECTIONS

Technology has no doubt changed the way the world works and communicates. In this digital age where almost everything is leveraged by technology, more and more disruptive technologies are being introduced into various world ecosystems to ease the conduct of business, reach more people and provide them with exciting opportunities to enhance their wellbeing. Fintech is one of such technologies that is constantly disrupting the way things are being done in the financial service sector in Africa.

This chapter discusses the future of Fintech in Africa's digital financial services environment. It aligns with the title of the book which has to do with Fintech as a disruptive technology for financial institutions. The model which captures the essence of this work is the technological innovation model. Pratali (2003) averred that the application of technological innovation to processes or products yields a strategic weight that enables decision makers to evaluate the increase in business value.

Pratali's technological innovation model is composed of four sub-models: the first is an analysis of process/ product competitiveness aimed at identifying competitive priorities and therefore appropriate technologies; the second sub-model identifies the priorities of technological intervention from amongst the competitive technologies selected; the third sub-model correlates the two previous models and thereby expresses "strategic weight" of the technological projects with respect to the competitive priorities of the processes or products; the fourth and the last sub-model applies scenario simulation and sustainable growth verification to estimate the impact of strategic project innovation in terms of increased business value.

As the technology spreads one would expect the key players in the financial service sector to embrace and utilize the various genuine Fintech startups and solutions for the overall benefit of the African society. Banks and other financial service providers' readiness to assimilate the innovative technology will help promote financial inclusion and ultimately determine the future of Fintech in the continent. The level of compliance in the adoption and use of Fintech in individual countries and how businesses benefit from it will likely form the nucleus of future research in this domain.

CONCLUSION

Despite the fears expressed by key players about the negative impact of Fintech on the financial service sector of the African economy, the innovative technology offers several advantages that far surpass the challenges it pose to banks and other financial institutions. It is glad to note that it can be cheaper to operate and more efficient in terms of manpower, money and data, and it can more easily reach those currently without access to financial services. Fintech is also credited with cutting remittance costs to a fraction.

Consultants Mckinsey has revealed that about 2,455m people around the world – or 53% of the global adult population – do not use any financial institution. An incredible 78% of all adult Africans lack access to bank services. Yet at the same time, there are 220m registered mobile money accounts on the continent, more than in the rest of the world put together.

M-Pesa and similar services allow users to send and receive money from anywhere with a mobile signal via a mobile handset and at far lower cost than by traditional banks and money transfer services. Most customers want just four services: banking, borrowing, money transfer and insurance, so platforms can be fairly simple, relying on access to mobile phones. The proportion of adults with mobile phones is roughly the same in Nigeria and the US, although smart phone penetration is more advanced in the latter.

However, Fintech developer MyBucks gets around even the lack of mobile technology by offering customers a basic mobile handset as part of its package.

Fintechs, as the Director Non Traditional channels West Africa, Mastercard, Uwa Uzebu noted are one of the forces driving digital payment. Digital payments in 2015 alone accounted for eight percent of total global retail payment of $16 trillion and it is projected to grow to 24 percent in 2020 when global retail payments would have increased to $21 trillion. The number of Fintech startups has tripled and funding has grown seven times over the last decade.

The payment industry has recently witnessed the entry of diverse non bank digital players – both technology giants and startups who are presenting increased competition for banks. While these categories of entrants have generally not been major threats to the banking and payments industry in the past, the aggressive nature of the digital players, the prominence of smart phones as a channel and rapidly evolving customer expectations have all made a difference in recent past. To maintain customer relationships and stay relevant, there is need for all stakeholders to respond to these changes with new strategies, capabilities and operating models.

REFERENCES

Accenture. (2018a). *What is Fintech and where is it headed?* Retrieved from https://www.accenture.com/ng-en/insight-fintech-did-someone-cancel-revolution/

Accenture. (2018b). *The future of Fintech and banking: Digitally disrupted or reimagined?* Retrieved from https://www.accenture.com/us-en/insight-future-fintech-banking/Accessed/28/5/2018

African Business. (2018, February). *Beyond the hype: what block chain could mean for Africa*. Author.

Amer, D. W., Barberis, J. N., & Buckley, R. P. (2015). The evolution of Fintech: A new-crisis paradigm? University of Hong Kong.

Asu, F. M. (2018). Fintech, threat to banking industry- CBN. *CIBN*. Retrieved from https://punch.ng.com/fintech-threat-to- banking-industry-cbn-cibn/Accessed 28/5/2018

Beckley, J. (2013). Innovation: Key to successful business. *BusinessNewsDaily*. Retrieved from https://www.businessnewsdaily.com/5167-innovation.html

Berry, M. M. J., & Taggart, J. H. (1994). Managing technology and Innovation: A review. Research & Development Management, 24(4).

Betz, F. C. (1998). *Managing technological innovations: Competitive advantage from change*. New York: Wiley.

Chima, O. (2017, February 1). Expanding financial services through digital payments. *ThisDay*.

CPAFRICA. (2018). *The rise and rise of Fintech in Africa*. Retrieved from https://www.cp-africa.com/2018/51/30/rise-rise-fintech-africa/

Dorfleitner, G. H., Weber, M., Schmitt, M., & Hormuf, L. (2017). *Fintech in Germany*. New York: Springer International Publishing, AG. doi:10.1007/978-3-319-54666-7

Eurostat & OECD. (2005). *Guidelines for collecting and interpreting innovation data-the Oslo manual* (3rd ed.). Paris: Author.

Ford, N. (2017). Should established banks fight or assimilate Fintech? *African Banker, 41*.

Geroge, G., McGalan, A. M., & Prabhu, J. (2012). Innovation for inclusive growth: Towards a theoretical framework and a research agenda. *Journal of Management Studies*, *49*(4).

Iansiti, M., & Lakhani, K. R. (2017). The truth about blockchain. *Harvard Business Review*. Retrieved from https://hbr.org/products/the-truth-about-blockchain/R1701J-PDF-ENG

ImagineNation. (2018). *8 reasons why innovation is important to businesses today*. Retrieved from https://www.imaginenationa.com.au/innovation-blog/8reasons-innovation-important-business-today/Accessed 28/5/2018

Innovationxchange. (2018). *Importance of innovation in business*. Retrieved from https://www.ixc-uk.com/importance_of_innovation_in_Business.html/Accessed 28/5/2018

Investopedia. (2018a). *What is the financial services sector?* Retrieved from https://www.investopedia.com/ask/answers/030315/what-is-the-financial-services-sector.asp/Accessed 28/5/2018

Investopedia. (2018b). *Why fintech will drive business models of the future?* Retrieved from https://www.investopedis.com/articles/markets/080716/why-fintech-will-drive-business-models-future.asp/Accessed 28/5/2018

Kawai, Y. (2016). Fintech and the IAIS. *IAIS Newsletter, 52*. Retrieved from https://www.iaisweb.org/file/61139/iais-newsletter-june-2016-final

Kuo Chuen, D.L.., & Teo, E.G. (2015). Emergence of fintech and the LASIC Principles. *Journal of Financial Perspectives, 3*(3).

Lee, M. C. (2015). Factors influencing the adoption of internet: An integration of TAM and TPB with perceived risk and perceived benefit. *Electronic Commerce Research and Applications*, *8*(3), 130–141. doi:10.1016/j.elerap.2008.11.006

MobileworldwideLive. (2017). *Bharti Airtel identifies African consolidation markets*. Retrieved from https://www.mobileworldwide.com/featured-content/top-three/bharti-airtel-identifies-african-consolidation-markets

Moore, R. (2017). *Technology is an enabler of business growth*. Retrieved from https://m.fin24.com/Tech/opinion/technology-is-an-enabler-of-business-growth-20170612

Mulligan, G. (2017). *Over 300 fintech start-ups active in Africa*. Retrieved from https://www.disrupt-africa.com/2017/06/0ver-300-fintech-startups-active-in-africa/

Nelson, C. (2017) Fintech marches on. *African Banker, 41*.

Okonji, E. (2018, July 9). FG urged to adopt blockchain technology to boost FDI. *Thisday*.

Oladeji, A. (2018). *African Fintech startups are revolutionizing banking*. Retrieved from https://syncedreview.com/2018/03/17/african-fintech-startups-are-revolutionizing-banking/

Organization for Economic Cooperation and Development. (2002). *Frascati Manual*. Retrieved from https://stats.oecd.org/glossary/detail.asp?ID=2688

Pratali, P. (2003). Strategic management of technological innovations in the small to medium enterprise. *European Journal of Innovation Management*, *6*(1), 18–31. doi:10.1108/14601060310456300

Ryu, H. S. (2018). Understanding benefit and risk framework of fintech adoption: Comparison of early adopters and late adopters. *Proceedings of the 51st Hawai International conference on system sciences*. Retrieved from https://hdl.handle.net/10125/50374

Sanicola, L. (2017, February 13). What is fintech? *Huffington Post*.

Schueffel, P. (2017). Taming the beast. A scientific definition of Fintech. *Journal of Innovation Management, 4*(4).

Shukla, A. (2017). *What is innovation? Why innovation is important?* Retrieved from https://www.paggu.com/getting-into-roots/what-is-innovation-why-innovation-is-important

Society for Worldwide Interbank Financial Telecommunication. (2017). *63 companies shaping Africa's fintech ecosystem*. Retrieved from https://medium.com/@gomedici/63.companies-shaping-africas-fintech-ecosystem-352720312629

World Economic Forum. (2017). *Beyond fintech: A pragmatic assessment of disruptive potential in financial services.* Retrieved from https://www.weforum.org/reports/beyond-fintech-a-pragmatic-assessment-disruptive-potential-financial-serrvice

KEY TERMS AND DEFINITIONS

Business Ecosystem: Is a network of interlink companies such as suppliers and distributors, who interact with each other, primarily complementing or supplying key components of the value propositions with their products or services.

Digital Payment: Is a way of paying for services or goods via an electronic medium without the use of cash or check. It is also known as electronic payment system or e-payment.

Disruptive Technology: This refers to any enhanced or completely new technology that replaces and disrupts an existing technology, rendering it obsolete.

Financial Service Providers: They are financial institutions that provide services to consumers. The most typical of the service providers are banks, payment providers, insurers, receivables managers, intermediaries, funds and investment fund.

Fintech Companies: They consist of both startups and established financial technology companies trying to replace or enhance the usage of financial services provided by existing financial companies.

Innovative Technology: Is a technology that is newly invented or is being utilized in new ways.

Mobile Network Operator: Is a telecoms entity that provides services for mobile phone subscribers.

Remittance: Is the funds a foreign worker sends to his or her country of origin via wire, mail or online transfer.

Chapter 5
Security and Privacy in FinTech:
A Policy Enforcement Framework

Muzammil Hussain
University of Management and Technology, Pakistan

Sobia Mehrban
University of Management and Technology, Pakistan

Muhammad Waqas Nadeem
University of Management and Technology, Pakistan

Syeda Nisar Fatima
University of Management and Technology, Pakistan

S. Iqbal
University of Management and Technology, Pakistan

Owais Hakeem
University of Management and Technology, Pakistan

Ghulam Mustafa
University of Management and Technology, Pakistan

ABSTRACT

Financial technology (FinTech) has dramatically changed the way of banking and financial services. Computer programs and other technology which used to provide and enable financial services is named as FinTech. However, these services face several security and privacy issues while providing financial services to the users. These services and applications must be secured to enhance the acceptance and usability of these services among the users. The main aim of this research is to provide a policy framework to ensure the security and privacy of user information in financial technology, since FinTech applications and services carry quite sensitive data of its users. This policy framework provides a comprehensive set of policies to secure FinTech services. These policies must be implemented in each organization providing FinTech services.

DOI: 10.4018/978-1-5225-7805-5.ch005

INTRODUCTION

In past decade, Financial Technology (FinTech) is rapidly proliferating technology, and FinTech is emerged as new technical term that mainly describes the financial technology sectors for various operations relating to enterprises or organization, which mainly provides with the service quality using Information Technology (IT) applications. Usage of multiple technologies in FinTech such as mobile embedded systems, mobile networks, big data, data analytic techniques, cloud computing and mobile cloud computing, have been played a vital role in the development of FinTech, as discussed in (Li, Dai, Ming, & Qiu, 2016).

In financial industry threats are major issues. Financial Service Institutes (FSIs) face threats imposed by daily innovations in information systems. Some of the risks within an anticipated scope are data abuse, malware attacks and networking errors (Morgan, 2015). In cloud computing masked operations enhances the probability of information breaches and the provided security gadgets cannot effectively cope with threats (Traynor, Butler, Bowers, & Reaves, 2017). The threats manners often raise as financial crisis, disorientation, and execution hindrance (Gai, Qiu, Sun, & Zhao, 2016).

By giving flexible service deployment, the cyber risk management have been powered by implementation of cloud computing. For example, many researches (Gai, Qiu, & Elnagdy, 2016; Gai, Qiu, & Sun, 2017) have proved the efficacy of cloud-based cyber risk management system in the financial industry. This approach classifies information releases that can cause potential privacy breach using organized learning methods.

In modern world, cyber security serves financial industry and is important to reduce security risks (Gai, Qiu, & Elnagdy, 2016). Cyber security is a need of modern days for Financial Service Institutes (FSIs) to reduce the risks of cyber-attacks. Financial industry has a critical concern when higher level security of information is needed and Financial Service Institutes (FSIs) is giving network based remedy (Gai, Qiu, & Elnagdy, 2016; Sharma & Panigrahi, 2013).

A number of solutions are required to avoid cyber-attacks. There should be awareness against cyber in general public and to deal with a cyber-risk is a challenging task due to nature of its diversity, cyber risks are divided into three layers tactical, strategical, and operational layers. The protection of information is based on three principals, availability, integrity and confidentiality (Elnagdy, Qiu, & Gai, 2016; Gai, Qiu, & Elnagdy, 2016). This study provides a policy model to mitigate the aforementioned privacy and security issues.

This study provides a brief background on privacy and security issues in FinTech, such as threats, attacks, adversaries, and malicious behaviors. The main of objective of this study is to propose a policy enforcement framework to ensure the security and privacy of applications used in FinTech. In addition, the objective of this study is to make policies to ensure security and privacy of services and applications used in financial service institutes. The proposed framework ought to address the security and privacy issue mainly faced by FinTech applications that includes lack of reliable authentication and access control systems, threats due to the usage of cloud computing in FinTech, users of FinTech are susceptible to privacy threats, information leakage in the usage of FinTech applications, risks involve in FinTech applications and usage of FinTech mobile applications and services, and cyber concerns involve in the usage of FinTech.

BACKGROUND

There are many researches who has given their data on the efficacy of preventing specific information from a cyber-risk. Gartner's research (Morgan, 2015) shows the importance of security in financial institutes. Moreover, in another survey by silicon bank only 35% of companies are confident of their information security ("SVB: Cybersecurity report 2015," 2015). There should be awareness regarding security breach of information system by different malwares and anticipated cyber risks (Gai, Qiu, Sun, et al., 2016).

Financial service institutes are frustrated by financial frauds. Glancy et al. (Glancy & Yadav, 2011) developed a model for detecting financial frauds. Many models are made to detect frauds but these models could not ensure maximum detection security because they use quantitative approach. Researchers (Kou, Peng, & Wang, 2014) are working to use clustering algorithms for financial risk analysis. Since there were some serious financial accounting frauds were reported in well reputed organizations such as Enron, Lucent, WorldCom and Satyam, in the course of the most recent decade, the need of detecting, defining and reporting financial frauds is rapidly increasing (Ryu, 2018; Yue, Wu, Wang, Li, & Chu, 2007).

Economically and financially, financial accounting fraud is turning into an undeniably major issue and effectively identifying fraud has constantly been an essential assignment for accounting experts (Ngai, Hu, Wong, Chen, & Sun, 2011; Stewart & Jürjens, 2018). If the internally available auditing system of an organization fails to detect account then the organization has to use other professional procedures and processes to identify financial accounting fraud those procedures together named as forensic accounting. Forensic accounting is the main source to detect those financial frauds which are nearly impossible to detect through internal auditing by applying auditing, accounting and investigative skills (Lim, Kim, Hur, & Park, 2018; Romānova, Grima, Spiteri, & Kudinska, 2018; Singleton & Singleton, 2010; Wells, 2007). A review of data mining-based financial fraud and attacks detection research is presented in (Phua, Lee, Smith, & Gayler, 2010), including credit exchange misstate, telecoms membership fraud, automobile insurance fraud, militant detection, financial crime detection, interruption and spam identification. Others scientist have surveyed on frauds relating to insurance (Derrig, 2002) and financial account fraud (Macedo, 2018; Shadrin & Leonov, 2018; Yue et al., 2007).

The security threats to the financial industry have rapidly increased since the introduction of electronic-based financial applications and services in financial industry. Past researches have mostly resolved the conventional security and privacy attacks, for example, malware attacks, network worms, and information abuse (Hu et al., 2011; Qiu et al., 2013). Contemporary financial institutions are racing towards utilizing maximum web-related technologies to provide modern services, better quality services and to facilitate their user with new and digital services. This improvement has been amazingly affecting on the modern development in financial industry and new technologies' utilization [1]-[4] (Gai, Qiu, Jayaraman, & Tao, 2015; Gai, Qiu, Tao, & Zhu, 2016; Qiu, Ming, Wang, Yang, & Xiang, 2014). As an evolving marketing paradigm, data sharing has turned into nan essential approach for finance related firms to strengthen their perspectives. Cloud computing is another most attractive stage for financial industry to communicate, share and exchange their information [5]-[12] (Gai, 2014; Gai & Li, 2012; Gai, Qiu, Zhao, Tao, & Zong, 2016; J. Li et al., 2012; Y. Li, Dai, Ming, & Qiu, 2016; Qiu, Chen, & Liu, 2014; Qiu, Ming, Li, Gai, & Zong, 2015; Qiu et al., 2008).

Similar to other new technologies, IT applications relating to FinTech have to face certain challenges despite their exciting benefits. Services and applications related to FinTech are facing the usual Privacy and security issues, such as enforcing

Figure 1. Taxonomy of FinTech trends

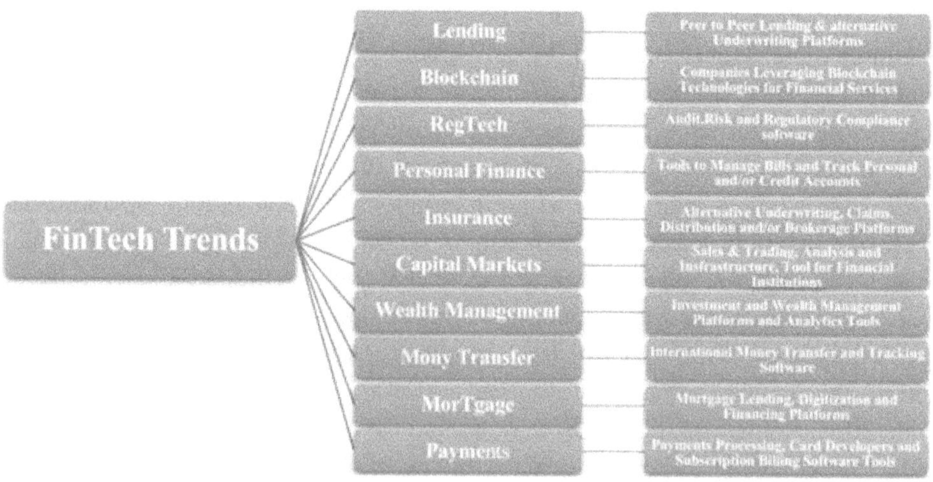

confidentiality, integrity, and availability through authentication, access control and authorization. It is quite important to highlight privacy and security issues to improve the adoption of information technology application and services in FinTech (Gai, Qiu, Sun, et al., 2016; Traynor et al., 2017).

A number of financial technology trends exits in finance market, and these FinTech trends provides a number of useful facilities to the users so they can manage their money and business efficiently. FinTech provides different types of services and applications, such as FinTech finance services are provided on demand which is much embraced idea for customers by using mobile and cloud computing. Figure 1 presenting taxonomy on the trends of FinTech which is based on the report presented in (Cb Insights, 2018), this taxonomy is demonstrating the motivation of this research and highlighting the importance of Financial Technology in the modern financial market.

POLICY FRAMEWORK

This policy framework is based on multiple modules that include policies that must be ensured by any organization using FinTech applications or providing FinTech services. A brief description of the modules is as follows; a security module is proposed which is based on a context-aware access control system that access control system deals with the access control in FinTech on the basis of location and time, second module deals with the fraud involved in the usage of financial technology, third module defines policies and protection mechanism related to secure mobile base applications for different threats, and proposes a strong authentication mechanism deals with risks involved in the distribute applications usage in financial technology. The proposed policy framework is shown in Figure 2.

The details of these security modules are in the following sub-sections.

Policies to Detect Fraud in FinTech

This section proposes a conceptual framework from the available literature which is based on the usage of data mining methods and applications to detect financial accounting fraud (Ahmed, 2004; Mitra, Pal, & Mitra, 2002; Sharma & Panigrahi, 2013). The conceptual framework is rely on literature-based knowledge on data mining research (Ahmed, 2004; Mitra et al., 2002; Sharma & Panigrahi, 2013), fraud detection research (Bolton & Hand, 2002; Derrig, 2002; Phua, Lee, Smith, & Gayler, 2010; Sharma & Panigrahi, 2013; Yue, Wu, Wang, Li, & Chu, 2007; Zhang & Zhou, 2004), this framework is shown in phase-I of Figure 2.

A financial fraud framework is proposed in (Ngai, Hu, Wong, Chen, & Sun, 2011) which is based on a framework of financial crime of the United States Federal Bureau of Investigation, and it is one of the reputable frameworks or schema to detect financial fraud. Phase I of the Figure 2 contains two layers, the first layer consist of four different data mining applications classes of classification, prediction, clustering and visualization (Bolton & Hand, 2002; Derrig, 2002; Fawcett & Provost, 1997; Phua et al., 2010; Sánchez, Vila, Cerda, & Serrano, 2009), a set of algorithmic approaches support these data mining application classes to obtain the related relationships in the data (Turban, Sharda, & Delen, 2010). The policy framework for services and applications of FinTech is shown in Figure 2.

1. **Data Mining Techniques toward FinTech Fraud Detection:** A brief description of the policy framework relating to fraud detection, the four application classes of data mining (i.e., classification, prediction, clustering and visualization), and each component of this framework is elaborated in further detail in the subsequent sections
    a. **Classification:** FinTech services or applications are secured through classification in which training a data set model and target set are used to predict categorical labels of unknown objects and the categorical labels are predefined and discrete. Some important techniques which are used for classification includes Neural Network, Naive Bayes and Support Vector Machines (Zhang & Zhou, 2004). Different FinTech services are secured by classifications which are credit card fraud, corporate fraud and other types of fraud. Classification is more powerful technique which is proposed to secure FinTech services and application in case of fraud detection.
    b. Clustering: Clustering protects the security of FinTech services and applications by partition of object in to similar and dissimilar groups and clustering also known as data segmentation. The data point of a cluster is similar and should be dissimilar from other cluster. K-nearest neighbour and Naive Bayes are important techniques of clustering. Fraud detection in FinTech must be protected through clustering. Clustering appears to be a far better solution to secure FinTech services and applications against emerging threats of financial technology sector.
    c. **Prediction:** The FinTech applications have several security threats which are harmful for FinTech services and these attacks are based on some factors prediction estimates numeric and ordered value on the basis of patterns of data set which assure the threats for Financial Technology. The prediction techniques can be used to secure the FinTech service and

Figure 2. Policy framework to ensure the security and privacy in FinTech

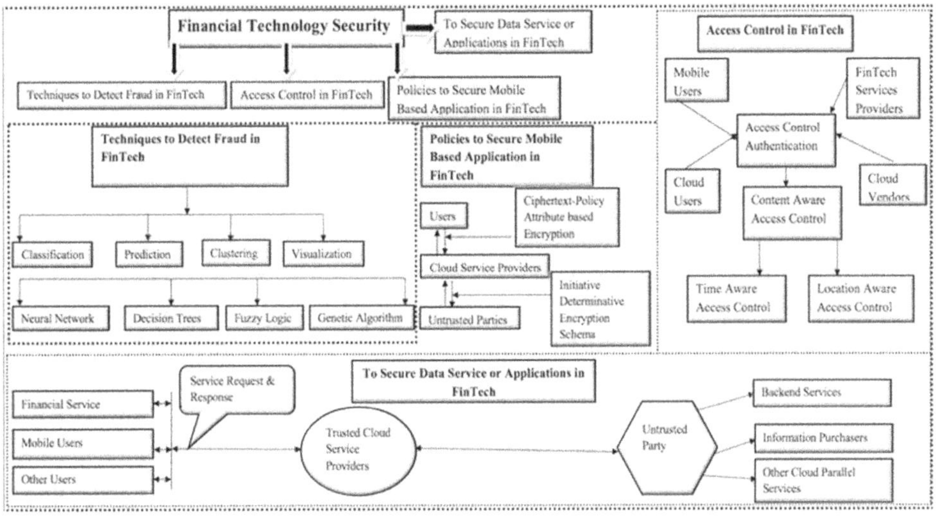

applications are Neural Networks and Logistic model. These techniques must be used by financial services provider to secure sensitive information of the users.

d. **Visualization:** In FinTech services the visualization provides the presentation of data which are more complicated and not understandable in simpler form and facilitates users to view quite complex patterns in data mining process. The data which are related to FinTech security sometime it is rather complex, in that case, visualization is suitable way to deliver complex data and patterns into clear presentation of functions or data, so user and services providers can easily understand and can protect their data from adversaries.

e. **Neural Networks:** The FinTech services and applications must use the Neural Networks base model to ensure the security of applications and services provided by Financial institute of services because neural networks are non-linear statistical data models work like a human brain. Neural Network is mostly applied in classification and clustering due to its adaptive and robust models. In FinTech services, Neural Network can be applied for credit card and corporate fraud detection. Financial institute of services can use neural network as a financial fraud detection tool and can be applied on financial data. To predict event of corporate fraud neural network plays an important role. Fraud is a significant issue in FinTech services which can be secured through neural network.

f. **Decision Trees**: Another tool that can be used to secure FinTech services and applications is Decision tree. Decision trees are applicable to ensure the security threats in FinTech applications and services and this is a decision support tool where node represent test attribute and branch represent its possible consequences. ID3, CART and C4.5 algorithms can be used for planting decision trees. In this policy framework, FinTech decision tree proposed for credit card and corporate fraud detection. CART algorithm identifies and predicts financial statements related fraudulent in Fin Tech.

g. **Genetic Algorithm:** The security of FinTech services and application is most important phenomenon, and Genetic algorithm is quite substantial technique which must be utilized to ensure the security of services of FinTech. Genetic algorithm is a classifier which auditor decision in a fraud. FinTech services face many security problems among of these credit cards related fraud is being solved by genetic algorithm along with support vector machines (SVM) (Welch, Reeves, & Welch, 1998). Genetic algorithm is best technique to protect the FinTech services and applications against various security threats.

h. **Fuzzy Logic:** The services and applications providing by Financial Institute of Services is vital and changes the way of working of financial institutions. Fuzzy logic is a best technique to ensure the security and privacy of FinTech services because it is a mathematical technique that classifies and assigns data to a group or cluster on the base of degree of possibility. Fuzzy logic increases the performance of data due to its numerical representation and enhances the range of operations on data. In FinTech a fuzzy logic model proposed in (Lenard & Alam, 2004) can be applied to detect fraud in an Excel spreadsheets. Fuzzy logic detects fraud in non-financial and financial data. Fuzzy logic expert system is designed to identify the elements which are involved in fraud and FinTech security. Fraud in FinTech services can also be detected though fuzzy logic system discussed in (Deshmukh, Romine, & Siegel, 1997; Pathak, Vidyarthi, & Summers, 2005). The expert fuzzy systems play an important role to detect the privacy and security threats in FinTech services and Applications.

2. **Fine-Grained Context-Aware Access Control Model in FinTech:** This section presents the fine-grained context-aware access control policies of this framework. According to (Conti, Nguyen, & Crispo, 2011; Hussain, Al-Haiqi, et al., 2018; Hussain, Zaidan, et al., 2018), the following aspects can be considered as context: status or condition of few variables (i.e., physical location, temperature, time, light, noise), or an existence of other devices and sensors. In this policies model, security and privacy rules depend on the context

(i.e., location and time), and the idea is based on context-aware access control systems (Conti et al., 2011; Hussain, Al-Haiqi, et al., 2018; Hussain, Zaidan, et al., 2018). This research considers only geographical location and time for context-aware access control in FinTech applications and services.

The context-based access control model illustrated in Figure 2 is exclusively responsible to detect, report and thenceforth updating the context condition of the user's device and its related applications in financial technology. Mainly, these types of policies are entirely relied on the theory of context-based (aware) access control system. The context-based policy system acquires the geographical location parameters (Cell ID, Wi-Fi, GPS parameters) via different sensors, devices and forward collected parameters to the central context-aware system upon request. This type of context checks allows the framework to enable the user of enforcing run-time constraints and restrictions on the use of sensitive services and applications in Fintech based on multiple contexts such as time and location. The users have the facility to define constraints and restrictions on the basis of their requirements. The policies and rules relating to context-based access control system are described in following sub sections.

3. **Policy Conditions for Context-Aware Access Control in FinTech:** Access control context-aware policies are imposed on the following basis, different contexts, context conditions and policies; these are elaborated in the subsequent sections.
    a. **Context Conditions:** In this policy framework, geographical location of the user and the time period are considered as context, in other words these are the factors being used to secure Fintech applications and services on basis of time and location. The user device physical location data is collected via GPS and user can allocate names of the location where the user device is placed. A policy time period presented in policy framework is a particular time interval within which a policy must be imposed. The following format is used to represent the date and time for context policies;
    $DD - MM - YYYY - hh : mm : ss$
    Additionally, this framework considered to use the R flag to specify periodic or repeated events. The value of flag R is taken out of the Set $\left[OO, ED, WK, MT, AN\right]$
    This is specifying the frequency of an event:
    $OO \rightarrow$ Only $Once$, $ED \rightarrow$ every Day, $WK \rightarrow Weekly$,
    $MT \rightarrow Monthly$, and $AN \rightarrow Annualy$

Time and date both describe the policy time period and on basis of the value of R an event is recurred (i.e., the frequency is defined by the value of R with which that specific policy context-condition must be verified). For instance, to set a particular event which occurs every Monday from 9:30 AM to 5:30 PM for eight months R would be set to W and the time period would be set as an event of date-time, for example, beginning at $15-02-2018-09:30:00$ and finishing on $15-10-2016-17:30:00$.

b. **Definition 1 - Context-Aware Condition:** The geographical location and time are considered as context in this policy framework, and the c is the notation to represent context. A policy-context is a check or condition to impose associated restrictions. A context-aware policy can be defined as the combination of context-condition and restrictions associated to this context. A single particular context could be linked with only a policy restriction and only single policy restriction could be linked with only a context (i.e., one-to-one relation).

   Suppose L represents the name of a location and demonstrating the specific location and suppose $\left[f,\ S,E\right]$ respectively are the frequency, start time, and end time, which specify once a particular context-policy would be imposed. So, the conditions for the context-policies are specified as a tuple of $\left[L,\left(f,S,E\right)\right]$.

c. **Definition 2 – Active Context Condition (Active Policy) for FinTech Services:** A particular context condition c is named as active context condition at a specified time $\boldsymbol{t}$, if all the compulsory restrictions which a context describes are confirmed. An active policy $\boldsymbol{P}$ which is linked to the active context condition $\boldsymbol{C}$ is named as the active policy. There is the possibility that multiple contexts can be active at the same time.

4. **Policies to Secure Distributed and Mobile Based Applications/Services in FinTech:** Figure 2 shows the procedure of suggested conceptual framework in operating a mobile transaction and other services which is based on (Gai, Qiu, Thuraisingham, & Tao, 2015), and it defines the procedure of transaction using P2DS (Architecture of Proactive Dynamic Secure Data Schema), and the details of P2DS model can be found in (Gai et al., 2015). To control their financial operations the anonymous and distrustful services providers also required a particular level of authorization and authentication. Thus, merely blocking the distrustful parties is not an adequate effort. The aim or objective of the suggested scheme it assists multiple service supporters without disclosing or revealing the sensitive data or information.

The suggested framework encrypts and secures the part of the clients' information, and it provides the information to the unknown parties only in case it is highly essential to deliver or provide the particular information or services. The information will be forbidden to and kept hidden from all other services, parties and usages which do not have one-to-one or direct relationship with transaction services. The key elements of the services or applications relating to the user's privacy data such as their real name, address or phone number, would be encrypted and converted by this framework in non-human understandable formats.

Figure 2 also shows the policy model required for financial service institutes and their clients. There is always risk of breach in sensitive information, the procedure or framework is made in such a way that even involvement of third party to ensure delivery services cannot keep financial organizations unaware of all issues. The P2DS model proposed in (Gai et al., 2015) ensures that only authorized people should have access to data. It uses three algorithms, first the Static Decryption Attribute Algorithm (SDAA) is designed to assign authority and to scrutinize the status of trusted party. Next one Corresponded Decryption Attribute Algorithm (CDAA) is to assign decryption attributes with decryption authorizations and in last Proactive Determinative Encryption Algorithm (PDEA) is proposed to determine whether the attributes need to be encrypted.

By applying this model and it policies, the following two security goals can be achieved; first, which protects users' related information while using cloud computing and other distributed services. Second, this model concentrates on the privacy and security requirements of the FinTech industry which can protect sensitive information from different security risks.

This section provided a mechanism that can be used to secure sensitive information of financial clients who perform online transactions using mobile applications running on mobile devices, for example, tablets or smart phones. The motivation of using our proposed model is to secure the implemented services accessing by multiple organizations.

FUTURE RESEARCH DIRECTIONS

The implementation of the proposed policies of FinTech is a future objective of this research; there are four different phases of this policy framework. In future, time-aware and location-aware security framework will be implementing, and further it is planned to explore further policies that might help to ensure security and privacy of FinTech applications and services users. Furthermore, it would be a big challenge to consider other factors in fine-grained context-aware access control environment such as, the existence of other devices and sensors, and make policies to protect the FinTech services related to it.

CONCLUSION

This research proposed a policy framework that provides various policies for different security issues of FinTech; this framework covers three different aspects of FinTech services and provides security policies to secure FinTech services. A proper guidelines and policies are proposed in this framework to detect fraud in FinTech. A fine-grained context-aware access control model has also been proposed in this research which controls the access according to the contexts. A solution to protect mobile and distributed applications and services is also provided in this study. This framework will increase the acceptance of technology in financial sectors and will remove the barriers between the financial service providers and information technology. Furthermore, this framework will develop the trust of the users of FinTech on financial services so users can reliably use the services and facilities of FinTech.

REFERENCES

Ahmed, S. R. (2004). *Applications of data mining in retail business.* Paper presented at the Information Technology: Coding and Computing, 2004. 10.1109/ITCC.2004.1286695

Bolton, R. J., & Hand, D. J. (2002). Statistical fraud detection: A review. *Statistical Science*, 235–249.

Cb Insights, R. R. (2018). *Fintech Trends to Watch in 2018. A look back at fintech trends in 2017 and exploring what's ahead in 2018.* Retrieved from https://www.cbinsights.com/research/report/fintech-trends-2018/

Conti, M., Nguyen, V. T. N., & Crispo, B. (2011). CRePE: Context-related policy enforcement for Android. In *Information Security* (pp. 331–345). Springer. doi:10.1007/978-3-642-18178-8_29

Derrig, R. A. (2002). Insurance fraud. *The Journal of Risk and Insurance*, *69*(3), 271–287. doi:10.1111/1539-6975.00026

Derrig, R. A. (2002). Insurance fraud. *The Journal of Risk and Insurance*, *69*(3), 271–287. doi:10.1111/1539-6975.00026

Deshmukh, A., Romine, J., & Siegel, P. H. (1997). Measurement and combination of red flags to assess the risk of management fraud: A fuzzy set approach. *Managerial Finance, 23*(6), 35–48. doi:10.1108/eb018629

Elnagdy, S. A., Qiu, M., & Gai, K. (2016). *Understanding taxonomy of cyber risks for cybersecurity insurance of financial industry in cloud computing.* Paper presented at the Cyber Security and Cloud Computing (CSCloud), 2016 IEEE 3rd International Conference on. 10.1109/CSCloud.2016.46

Fawcett, T., & Provost, F. (1997). Adaptive fraud detection. *Data Mining and Knowledge Discovery, 1*(3), 291–316. doi:10.1023/A:1009700419189

Gai, K. (2014). A review of leveraging private cloud computing in financial service institutions: Value propositions and current performances. *International Journal of Computers and Applications, 95*(3), 40–44. doi:10.5120/16578-6268

Gai, K., & Li, S. (2012). Towards cloud computing: a literature review on cloud computing and its development trends. Paper presented at the Multimedia Information Networking and Security (MINES), 2012 Fourth International Conference on. 10.1109/MINES.2012.240

Gai, K., Qiu, M., & Elnagdy, S. A. (2016). *Security-aware information classifications using supervised learning for cloud-based cyber risk management in financial big data.* Paper presented at the Big Data Security on Cloud (BigDataSecurity), IEEE International Conference on High Performance and Smart Computing (HPSC), and IEEE International Conference on Intelligent Data and Security (IDS), 2016 IEEE 2nd International Conference on. 10.1109/BigDataSecurity-HPSC-IDS.2016.66

Gai, K., Qiu, M., Jayaraman, S., & Tao, L. (2015). Ontology-Based Knowledge Representation for Secure Self-Diagnosis in Patient-Centered Teleheath with Cloud Systems. Paper presented at the Cyber Security and Cloud Computing (CSCloud), 2015 IEEE 2nd International Conference on. 10.1109/CSCloud.2015.72

Gai, K., Qiu, M., & Sun, X. (2017). A survey on FinTech. *Journal of Network and Computer Applications.*

Gai, K., Qiu, M., Sun, X., & Zhao, H. (2016). *Security and privacy issues: A survey on FinTech.* Paper presented at the International Conference on Smart Computing and Communication.

Gai, K., Qiu, M., Tao, L., & Zhu, Y. (2016). Intrusion detection techniques for mobile cloud computing in heterogeneous 5G. *Security and Communication Networks, 9*(16), 3049–3058. doi:10.1002ec.1224

Gai, K., Qiu, M., Thuraisingham, B., & Tao, L. (2015). *Proactive attribute-based secure data schema for mobile cloud in financial industry.* Paper presented at the High Performance Computing and Communications (HPCC), 2015 IEEE 7th International Symposium on Cyberspace Safety and Security (CSS), 2015 IEEE 12th International Conferen on Embedded Software and Systems (ICESS), 2015 IEEE 17th International Conference on. 10.1109/HPCC-CSS-ICESS.2015.250

Gai, K., Qiu, M., Zhao, H., Tao, L., & Zong, Z. (2016). Dynamic energy-aware cloudlet-based mobile cloud computing model for green computing. *Journal of Network and Computer Applications*, *59*, 46–54. doi:10.1016/j.jnca.2015.05.016

Glancy, F. H., & Yadav, S. B. (2011). A computational model for financial reporting fraud detection. *Decision Support Systems*, *50*(3), 595–601. doi:10.1016/j.dss.2010.08.010

Hu, F., Qiu, M., Li, J., Grant, T., Taylor, D., McCaleb, S., ... Hamner, R. (2011). A review on cloud computing: Design challenges in architecture and security. *CIT. Journal of Computing and Information Technology*, *19*(1), 25–55. doi:10.2498/cit.1001864

Hussain, M., Al-Haiqi, A., Zaidan, A., Zaidan, B., Kiah, M., Iqbal, S., ... Abdulnabi, M. (2018). A security framework for mHealth apps on android platform. *Computers & Security*, *75*, 191–217. doi:10.1016/j.cose.2018.02.003

Hussain, M., Zaidan, A., Zidan, B., Iqbal, S., Ahmed, M., Albahri, O., & Albahri, A. (2018). Conceptual framework for the security of mobile health applications on Android platform. *Telematics and Informatics*, *35*(5), 1335–1354. doi:10.1016/j.tele.2018.03.005

Kou, G., Peng, Y., & Wang, G. (2014). Evaluation of clustering algorithms for financial risk analysis using MCDM methods. *Information Sciences*, *275*, 1–12. doi:10.1016/j.ins.2014.02.137

Lenard, M. J., & Alam, P. (2004). The use of fuzzy logic and expert reasoning for knowledge management and discovery of financial reporting fraud. *Organizational data mining: Leveraging enterprise data resources for optimal performance*, 230-262.

Li, J., Qiu, M., Ming, Z., Quan, G., Qin, X., & Gu, Z. (2012). Online optimization for scheduling preemptable tasks on IaaS cloud systems. *Journal of Parallel and Distributed Computing*, *72*(5), 666–677. doi:10.1016/j.jpdc.2012.02.002

Li, Y., Dai, W., Ming, Z., & Qiu, M. (2016). Privacy protection for preventing data over-collection in smart city. *IEEE Transactions on Computers*, *65*(5), 1339–1350. doi:10.1109/TC.2015.2470247

Li, Y., Dai, W., Ming, Z., & Qiu, M. (2016). Privacy protection for preventing data over-collection in smart city. *IEEE Transactions on Computers*, *65*(5), 1339–1350. doi:10.1109/TC.2015.2470247

Lim, S. H., Kim, D. J., Hur, Y., & Park, K. (2018). An Empirical Study of the Impacts of Perceived Security and Knowledge on Continuous Intention to Use Mobile Fintech Payment Services. *International Journal of Human-Computer Interaction*, 1–13. doi:10.1080/10447318.2018.1507132

Macedo, B. E. (2018). Security in the Future of WealthTech. *The WealthTech Book: The FinTech Handbook for Investors, Entrepreneurs and Finance Visionaries*, 279-281.

Mitra, S., Pal, S. K., & Mitra, P. (2002). Data mining in soft computing framework: A survey. *IEEE Transactions on Neural Networks*, *13*(1), 3–14. doi:10.1109/72.977258 PMID:18244404

Ngai, E., Hu, Y., Wong, Y., Chen, Y., & Sun, X. (2011). The application of data mining techniques in financial fraud detection: A classification framework and an academic review of literature. *Decision Support Systems*, *50*(3), 559–569. doi:10.1016/j.dss.2010.08.006

Ngai, E., Hu, Y., Wong, Y., Chen, Y., & Sun, X. (2011). The application of data mining techniques in financial fraud detection: A classification framework and an academic review of literature. *Decision Support Systems*, *50*(3), 559–569. doi:10.1016/j.dss.2010.08.006

Pathak, J., Vidyarthi, N., & Summers, S. L. (2005). A fuzzy-based algorithm for auditors to detect elements of fraud in settled insurance claims. *Managerial Auditing Journal*, *20*(6), 632–644. doi:10.1108/02686900510606119

Phua, C., Lee, V., Smith, K., & Gayler, R. (2010). *A comprehensive survey of data mining-based fraud detection research.* arXiv preprint arXiv:1009.6119

Phua, C., Lee, V., Smith, K., & Gayler, R. (2010). *A comprehensive survey of data mining-based fraud detection research.* arXiv preprint arXiv:1009.6119

Qiu, M., Chen, Z., & Liu, M. (2014). Low-power low-latency data allocation for hybrid scratch-pad memory. *IEEE Embedded Systems Letters*, *6*(4), 69–72. doi:10.1109/LES.2014.2344913

Qiu, M., Ming, Z., Li, J., Gai, K., & Zong, Z. (2015). Phase-change memory optimization for green cloud with genetic algorithm. *IEEE Transactions on Computers*, *64*(12), 3528–3540. doi:10.1109/TC.2015.2409857

Qiu, M., Ming, Z., Wang, J., Yang, L. T., & Xiang, Y. (2014). Enabling cloud computing in emergency management systems. *IEEE Cloud Computing*, *1*(4), 60–67. doi:10.1109/MCC.2014.71

Qiu, M., Sha, E. H.-M., Liu, M., Lin, M., Hua, S., & Yang, L. T. (2008). Energy minimization with loop fusion and multi-functional-unit scheduling for multidimensional DSP. *Journal of Parallel and Distributed Computing*, *68*(4), 443–455. doi:10.1016/j.jpdc.2007.06.014

Qiu, M., Zhang, L., Ming, Z., Chen, Z., Qin, X., & Yang, L. T. (2013). Security-aware optimization for ubiquitous computing systems with SEAT graph approach. *Journal of Computer and System Sciences*, *79*(5), 518–529. doi:10.1016/j.jcss.2012.11.002

Romānova, I., Grima, S., Spiteri, J., & Kudinska, M. (2018). The Payment Services Directive 2 and Competitiveness: The Perspective of European Fintech Companies. *European Research Studies Journal*, *21*(2), 5–24.

Ryu, H.-S. (2018). Understanding Benefit and Risk Framework of Fintech Adoption: Comparison of Early Adopters and Late Adopters. *Proceedings of the 51st Hawaii International Conference on System Sciences*. 10.24251/HICSS.2018.486

Sánchez, D., Vila, M., Cerda, L., & Serrano, J.-M. (2009). Association rules applied to credit card fraud detection. *Expert Systems with Applications*, *36*(2), 3630–3640. doi:10.1016/j.eswa.2008.02.001

Shadrin, A., & Leonov, P. (2018). Risks Evaluation of Financial-Economic Activity and Their Management in the System of Economic Security of the Organization. *KnE Social Sciences*, *3*(2), 427–435. doi:10.18502/kss.v3i2.1573

Sharma, A., & Panigrahi, P. K. (2013). *A review of financial accounting fraud detection based on data mining techniques*. arXiv preprint arXiv:1309.3944

Singleton, T. W., & Singleton, A. J. (2010). *Fraud auditing and forensic accounting* (Vol. 11). John Wiley & Sons. doi:10.1002/9781118269183

Stewart, H., & Jürjens, J. (2018). Data security and consumer trust in FinTech innovation in Germany. *Information & Computer Security*, *26*(1), 109–128. doi:10.1108/ICS-06-2017-0039

SVB. (2015). *Cybersecurity report 2015*. Retrieved from https://www.svb.com/uploadedFile/Content/TrendsandInsights/Reports/CybersecurityReport/cybersecurity-report-2015.pdf

Traynor, P., Butler, K., Bowers, J., & Reaves, B. (2017). FinTechSec: Addressing the Security Challenges of Digital Financial Services. *IEEE Security and Privacy*, *15*(5), 85–89. doi:10.1109/MSP.2017.3681060

Turban, E., Sharda, R., & Delen, D. (2010). *Decision Support and Business Intelligence Systems (required)*. Prentice Hall Learning Outcomes.

Welch, O. J., Reeves, T. E., & Welch, S. T. (1998). Using a genetic algorithm-based classifier system for modeling auditor decision behavior in a fraud setting. *International Journal of Intelligent Systems in Accounting Finance & Management*, *7*(3), 173–186. doi:10.1002/(SICI)1099-1174(199809)7:3<173::AID-ISAF147>3.0.CO;2-5

Wells, J. T. (2007). Forensic Accounting and Fraud Investigation for Non-Experts. *The CPA Journal*, *77*(2), 14.

Yue, D., Wu, X., Wang, Y., Li, Y., & Chu, C.-H. (2007). *A review of data mining-based financial fraud detection research*. Paper presented at the Wireless Communications, Networking and Mobile Computing, 2007. WiCom 2007. International Conference on. 10.1109/WICOM.2007.1352

Yue, D., Wu, X., Wang, Y., Li, Y., & Chu, C.-H. (2007). *A review of data mining-based financial fraud detection research*. Paper presented at the Wireless Communications, Networking and Mobile Computing, 2007. WiCom 2007. International Conference on. 10.1109/WICOM.2007.1352

Zhang, D., & Zhou, L. (2004). Discovering golden nuggets: Data mining in financial application. *IEEE Transactions on Systems, Man and Cybernetics. Part C, Applications and Reviews*, *34*(4), 513–522. doi:10.1109/TSMCC.2004.829279

Section 2

FinTech in Financial Markets

Chapter 6
Volatility Estimation in the Era of High-Frequency Finance

Sibo Yan
KPMG LLP, USA

Da Yan
The University of Alabama at Birmingham, USA

ABSTRACT

Over the last two decades, ultra-high frequency (or tick-by-tick) transaction data has become increasingly available. This surge of high-frequency finance data has brought disruptive revolution that makes modeling asset prices as continuous-time processes more possible than ever before. This is because we can now witness market microstructures and stock market volatility over tiny time intervals. This chapter reviews some general frameworks like realized volatility (RV) in estimating the latent volatility and their recent developments in the era of high-frequency finance. New empirical facts are presented to help lay the foundation for creating intraday volatility models that can overcome noise interferences in high-frequency finance data. These facts also help explain some stock market anomalies like volatility jumps and flash crashes, which favor intraday RV over the traditionally used daily RV as a reliable physical measure of market risk.

DOI: 10.4018/978-1-5225-7805-5.ch006

1. INTRODUCTION

Investors have long dreamed of knowing how stock prices fluctuate. This desire dates back to the time when option contracts were invented in the late 17th century. At that time, Japanese samurai were paid in rice instead of Japanese Yen for their bodyguard services. Because it is hard to control the price of rice, they created a "Rice Exchange" where people can trade rice with a lock-in price before the delivery to avoid a price increase. Since then, many financial instruments have been created all over the world to hedge the risk of various businesses and volatility, and the primary measure of risk starts to frequently come out from the mouths of wealth managers in Wall Street.

While in economic literature, volatility is not that popular until the 20th century. In March 1900, the founding father of mathematical finance, Louis Bachelier, published the thesis entitled "The Theory of Speculation", which later becomes the beacon to modern finance research. In that book, he showed that stock prices can be approximated by a motion process where volatility is the only predefined parameter. He also named volatility as the "coefficient of instability" which amplifies the uncertainty of future prices.

1.1. Volatility in Finance

Following Louis Bachelier, many researchers continued to explore broader uses of volatility in various fields:

- *In portfolio allocation,* volatility helps determine how portfolio investments are to be rewarded given the risk they bear (Markowitz, 1952). In finance, this is called the risk-return tradeoff. For example, index funds average about 12% return per year in the long run but U.S. government bonds commonly reach a maximum annual return of only 6%; however, there is still a large group of investors choosing government bonds because index funds could double the loss than the bonds when bad time hits. In fact, Sharpe (1964) and Lintner (1965) prove that if two stocks have the same correlation with the market index, stocks with more volatility tend to have higher positive returns in good times and higher negative returns in bad times. In the hedge fund industry, this risk-return tradeoff is often used to evaluate fund performance (Carhart, 1997; Fama & French, 2010).
- *In financial engineering,* volatility is the only unobserved parameter of the most recognized stock option pricing model, the Black-Scholes-Merton model (BSM model) (Black & Scholes, 1973; Merton, 1976). The BSM model provides a unique solution to option pricing regardless of the return

distribution of the underlying asset. Because of this feature, this model is widely used by investment managers in Wall Street to price options under various market conditions which leads to the prosperity of the finance industry before the Great Financial Crisis in 2008 (Hull, 2012).

- *In corporate finance,* volatility is broadly used to help companies make appropriate financial and investment decisions (Shiller, 1981; Schwert, 1989). For example, after Tesla, Inc. bought SolarCity to expand its exposure to the energy industry, its stock price nearly doubled in the next two months. However, the long-term value of Tesla increased slower than its stock price after acquiring SolarCity stocks with a much higher volatility. The increase in stock volatility makes the Tesla business riskier. Increase in the riskiness of the business reduces people's expectation of future revenue brought by the business, and could finally discount the overall value of Tesla, Inc.
- *In market timing research,* volatility is closely related to the right time in buying/selling stocks in the market. Persistent high levels of market volatility usually signal a bad time to buy-in as stock prices are not stable and may be incorrectly valued. Moreover, unexpected market crashes often come after a long period of frequent market fluctuations (Ross, 1989; Fleming, Kirby, & Ostdiek, 2003; Banerjee, Doran, & Peterson, 2007).

1.2. Volatility Estimation at Low Frequency and Its Limitations

Since volatility plays an important role in nearly every aspect of finance, numerous efforts have been spent on modeling and measuring asset price volatility. Since volatility is not directly observable, it can either be implied from 1) historical volatility, 2) the market price of financial derivatives or 3) time series models (Britten-Jones & Neuberger, 2000; Bollerslev, Gibson, & Zhou, 2011; Canina & Figlewski, 1993), which we describe as follows:

1. **Historical volatility:** It is usually calculated by standard deviations of stock prices over a fixed time period. This trivial method has two problems. First, historical fluctuations may not necessarily imply movements in future prices, as some of the volatility may be transient. (Anderson & Bollerslev, 1998b). This is especially true in recent years where large swings in price movements become more apparent which is regarded as a sign for structural changes in volatility data (Brailsford & Faff, 1996). Second, volatility pattern changes with sampling frequency. The common paradigm for mathematical finance is constrained by the "no-arbitrage" principle, which says that stock prices should follow a continuous process and that no one could profit from trading the stock without taking any risks (Merton, 1980). Under this principle, prices should be

sampled with infinitely high frequency so as to see the actual price volatility. In fact, volatility often cannot be inferred from the low frequency finance data because data look quite different under different sampling frequencies as Figure 1 illustrates.

Specifically, the figure exhibits stock price volatility over 100-second time intervals for SPDR S&P 500 ETF Trust (SPY), an exchange traded fund that tracks the S&P 500 index. Volatility exhibited in both Figures 1(a) and 1(b) are calculated by the so-called Realized Volatility (RV) which will be introduced in detail in Section 2.2 as an important measure of actual volatility. RV accumulates the price changes from the

Figure 1a. Volatility described by low frequency and high frequency data

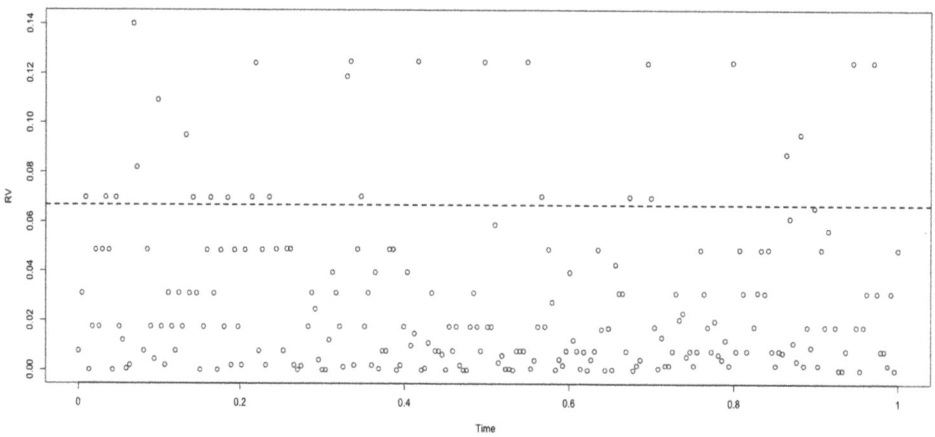

Figure 1b. Volatility described by low frequency and high frequency data

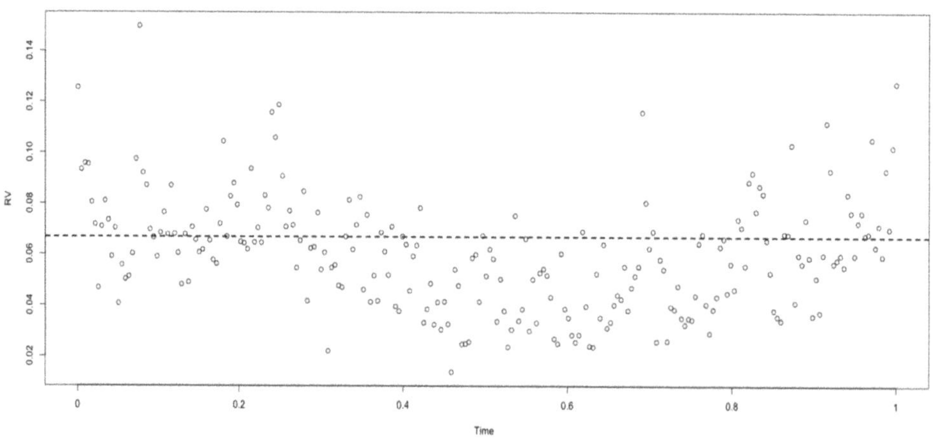

start of a trading day. In the two subfigures, RVs are computed from prices sampled at every 100 seconds and at every second correspondingly. The dashed line in the middle of each subfigure indicates the daily volatility average. Volatility movements are different in the two subfigures due to different price sampling frequency. In Figure 1(a), some large volatilities are at the top of the figure but most of the others stay at the bottom; volatilities are not clustered but rather separated. In contrast, in Figure 1(b), except for large volatilities at the beginning and the end of the day, volatilities are clustered and oscillate together around the average.

2. **Implication from financial derivatives:** Asset volatility can be implied from financial derivatives because the intrinsic value of a derivative depends on the volatility of the underlying asset. For example, consider the value of a European call option that gives investor the right to buy a stock at a fixed price. The option value is $\max(0, S-K)$ as an investor could choose to exercise the option or not where K is the fixed buying price and S is the current market price of the stock. In the formula, the option value increases with S. A larger volatility of the underlying stock means a better chance for S to be much higher than K and hence higher expected profit from the option. Thus, large market price of the option usually implies a large volatility in the underlying stock as well. Option pricing models like BSM provides a deterministic function to calculate the implied stock volatility from the option price (Hull, 2016). However, this also indicates that different formulas may lead us to different results of implied volatility.

Apart from the above model-dependence issue, the estimation is usually not unbiased because of *volatility risk premium*. This premium refers to the gap between stock option-implied volatility and the actual volatility, which is consistently negative in the historical data (Dai, 2015; Anderson & Benzoni, 2009). This gap exists because option pricing models are constructed under the so-called risk neutral statistical measure different from the measure of real world data (Shreve, 2004). This risk neutral measure ensures option price equals to the present value of expected future payoff of the option so as to conform with the "no-arbitrage" principle.

3. **Time series models:** Since the direct use of historical volatility to estimate future volatility have biases, researchers come up with some time series models to describe the volatility process with the entire history of stock prices. Typical examples include *Autoregressive moving average* (ARMA) and *Autoregressive conditional heteroskedastic* (ARCH) models (to be introduced in detail in Section 2) (Anderson & Bollerslev, 1998b). These models assign weights to historical volatility of different periods and aggregate them for

the current volatility. The prediction would therefore rely less on the recent volatility changes. Some randomness is also allowed in the model to explain the gap between model predictions and volatilities calculated from the price (Bollerslev, 1986; Engle, 1982). However, volatility process in these models has to be stationary and decays slowly in time. Such a model would also fail if there are some breaks or abrupt changes in the data. Besides, these models usually have many parameters so estimation of the model is usually nontrivial. (Anderson & Benzoni, 2009).

1.3. High-Frequency Volatility Estimation

High-frequency data was expected to significantly improve volatility estimation when it first emerged in the late 1990s because such data enable us to witness the tiny fluctuations of asset prices. In fact, technology is so advanced these days that we can not only see nearly-continuous changes of asset prices but also the number of orders submitted within each second (Johnson, 2010; Jacob, 2015). The micro-changes of stock prices may reflect some market activities that would not have been noticed with low-frequency data. (Aït-Sahalia & Jacod, 2014; Engle, 2000).

Figure 2 plots the price of SPY at every second on the "Flash Crash" day (Kirilenko, Kyle, Samadi, & Tuzun, 2017), an example where high-frequency data provides an advantage of detecting severe changes in price: around 2:40PM on the 6th of May 2010, the S&P 500 index suddenly plunged about 9% within 20 minutes but returned to the level before the crash right after. Since SPY moves closely to the S&P 500 index, we are able to see a clear path of price movements during the

Figure 2. Stock market at the "Flash Crash"

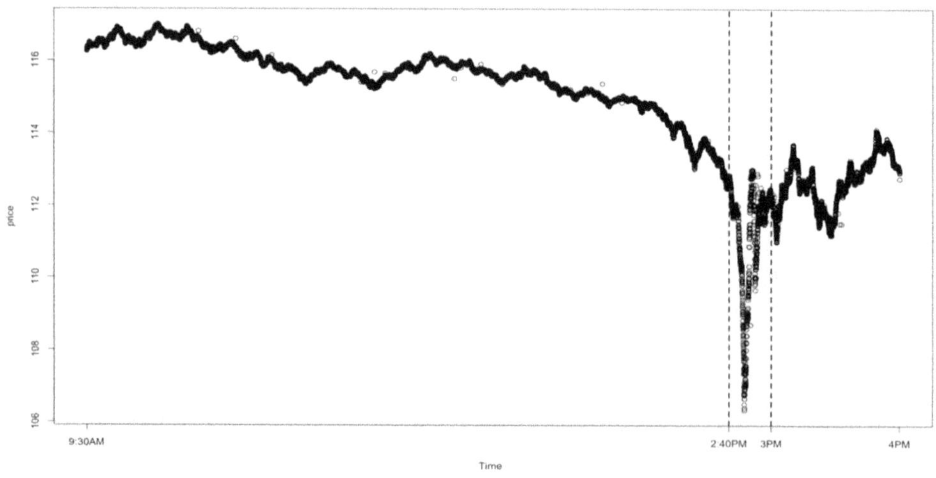

"Flash Crash" and the increase in price volatility after the event. The low-frequency data may not deliver such an ability to trace the movements with so many details.

Another advantage of high-frequency data is that it allows researchers to abandon strong econometric assumptions and rely on model-free definitions of volatility to measure the latent volatility. As have been mentioned in Section 1.2, volatility patterns change with different sampling frequencies. Nonparametric approaches hence were not very useful in approaching the continuous volatility in the low-frequency finance era but are popular with ultra-high frequent sampling of prices.

However, high-frequency data have not been used much in empirical finance research over the past two decades mainly because of two reasons. First of all, the data is assumed to have "noises" between the observed prices and the model-predicted prices (Aït-Sahalia & Jacod, 2014). They cannot be handled by data cleansing techniques that makes high-frequency volatility measures unstable (Aït-Sahalia, Mykland, & Zhang, 2005; Anderson, Bollerslev, Diebold, & Labys, 2003). There are many reasons that generate the noise including rounding errors, discretization of prices, and asymmetric information that will be explained in detail in Section 3. High-frequency trading activities is also believed to be a reason: to discover profit opportunities, frequent trades incur huge transaction costs and are believed to add extra volatility in the market prices (Zhang (2010)). To reduce the impact of microstructure noises, some econometricians argued for a maximum sampling frequency and a minimum time scale for volatility measurement (Aït-Sahalia et al., 2005; Hansen & Lunde, 2005; Bandi & Russell, 2008).

This infrequent sampling approach wastes a lot of high-frequency data. To reconcile this issue, econometricians search for other ways to handle noises and produce stable estimates. Some of them try to calibrate the noise distribution with high-frequency price data and control their behavior in volatility estimates over time (Hansen & Lunde, 2005; Bandi & Russell, 2005; Jacod, Li, & Zheng, 2017). Others treat noises as stochastic components in volatility measures and rely on statistical convergences to estimate volatility processes (Ellickson, Sun, Whang, & Yan, 2018). Also, some recent evidences show that high-frequency behavior may help to reduce uncertainties in the market and restore prices to an efficient level. (Brogaard & Hendershott, 2014; Budish, Carmton, & Shim, 2015; Smith, 2010).

How to model jumps is the second difficulty in studying high-frequency finance data. Structural breaks and jumps are very common in high-frequency price and volatility processes. This makes it hard to model price as a continuous-time process as required by the usual mathematical finance paradigms. At this stage, we still know little about jumps as their arrivals are random and sizes are unpredictable. A lot of efforts have been spent on discovering jump properties and some recent progress shows that jumps are at least not explosive and usually clustered (Aït-Sahalia & Jacod, 2014; Todorov, 2009; Mykland & Zhang, 2005). Some people explore strange behaviors of high-frequency volatility before the arrival of jumps and try to construct alarm time windows for investors to adjust their stock inventory before market crashes (Kirilenko et al., 2017; Yan, 2018). These researches pave the way for the future development of better estimation approaches for high-frequency volatility.

1.4. Chapter Organization

The rest of this chapter is organized as follows. Section 2 presents some famous parametric time series models like ARCH/GARCH and stochastic volatility. We discuss their success in predicting low-frequency volatility as well as their limitations at high frequency. We also introduce a nonparametric volatility measure called Realized Volatility (RV) that is frequently used in high-frequency finance. Section 3 describes some popular causes of microstructure noises and their impact on volatility estimation at high frequency. We then move to intraday volatility modeling with the help of RV in Section 4, which aims to overcome the weaknesses of low-frequency approaches that use daily volatility. Section 5 introduces the concept of "jumps" in intraday volatility, their empirical properties, and the potential of modeling jumps to improve intraday RV modeling. Section 6 reviews other related works and Section 7 concludes this chapter.

2. VOLATILITY MODELS FOR LOW-FREQUENCY DATA

This section introduces some recognized models of volatility measurement in the low frequency era. During the last 3 decades, researchers find more and more statistical properties in price data as the sampling frequency increases. These properties demonstrate the existence of violent fluctuations in prices, which deviates from the traditional assumption that stock prices follow a normal distribution (Manderlbrot, 1963; Fama, 1965). Here are some of the stylized facts about financial data discovered so far (Jacob, 2015).

- **Irrelevance:** Returns of asset prices at different time have very little correlation
- **Heavy-Tail/Excess Kurtosis:** Empirical return distributions have thicker tails and more peaked centers than the standard normal distribution;
- **Asymmetry/Skewness:** Observable returns are mostly asymmetric in favor of large deviations from the mean;
- **Volatility Clustering:** Large price fluctuations in one period tend to be followed by equally large price fluctuations in the next period;

- **Jumps:** Large and sudden moves of prices are evidence that empirical observations cannot be implied by diffusion-type continuous process alone but rather with jumps incorporated.

While many parametric volatility models are inspired by some of the above facts in the 1990s, ARCH-type models outshine other low-frequency volatility measures because they are both intuitive and accurate in predicting volatility changes. The following subsections introduce these models in detail.

2.1. ARCH Models

A fundamental question in volatility modeling is how to use data to forecast mean and variance[1] of asset return conditioned on past observations. While many specifications have considered using mean return to forecast volatility in future returns, the ARCH model introduced by Engle (1982) proves that direct specifications on conditional volatility would work as well. In this model, returns on an asset over time, $X(t)$, are defined as follows:

$$X(t) = \mu(t) + \varepsilon(t) \tag{1}$$

$$\varepsilon(t) = \sqrt{h(t)}\eta(t),\ \eta(t) \sim N(0,1) \tag{2}$$

$$h(t) = a(0) + \sum_{i=1}^{q} a(i)\varepsilon(t-i)^2, \tag{3}$$

where $\mu(t)$ is the historical average of $X(t)$ up to time t and $\varepsilon(t)$ is the error term of using $\mu(t)$ to predict the current return, $X(t)$. The error term $\varepsilon(t)$ is $\sqrt{h(t)}$ scaled by $\eta(t)$, where $h(t)$ is volatility of the error term and hence the conditional volatility of the return, which is computed by the weighted moving average of the past $\varepsilon(t)$ terms, and $\eta(t)$ is an independent, standard normal variable. The weights $a(i)$ must be estimated from historical data. The idea behind this model is simple: volatility clustering could be explained by volatility moving slowly over time; in other words, current volatility could be modeled as a function of all the error terms in the return series from a rolling time window of length q. To ensure the price process is stationary[2] so the mean and variance are non-explosive, the long-term average of the ARCH volatility is assumed to be constant and $\sum_{i=1}^{q} a(i) < 1$. Bollerslev (1986) generalizes the model to add historical $h(t)$ directly into predicting the current volatility $h(t)$ (aka GARCH model). Mathematically, a GARCH (p, q) model redefines Equation (3) above as

$$h(t) = a(0) + \sum_{i=1}^{q} a(i)\varepsilon(t-i)^2 + \sum_{i=1}^{p} \beta(i)h(t-i).$$

The most popular GARCH model assumes $p = q = 1$. In this version of GARCH, the variance in the next period is a weighted average of the long-run average variance $a(0)$, the variance predicted for previous period $h(t-1)$ and new information brought by the error term in prices $\varepsilon(t-1)$.

Although ARCH/GARCH models make economic sense in addressing volatility clustering in daily price data, the model limitations are also apparent. First of all, the difficulty of parametric estimation increases linearly with the number parameters $a(i)$. Moreover, in ARCH/GARCH model, mean and variance are independently forecasted; however, in real finance data we observe the so-called "leverage effect" where asset returns are generally negatively correlated with changes of volatility (Christie, 1982; Schwert, 1989; Bekaert & Wu, 2000). Also, $\eta(t)$ is the only source of randomness in this model but randomness in prices may not fully explain the randomness in volatility. For example, changes in the base interest rate by the federal government may increase market uncertainty and hence the volatility, but it may not have a noticeable impact on the asset returns. In this case, volatility should have its own source of randomness. This leads to another famous category of volatility models, stochastic volatility (SV) that are described next.

2.2. Stochastic Volatility Models

Stochastic volatility (SV) models refer to any models in which not only the asset return process is stochastic but the variance of a return process is randomly distributed as well. One of the most typical SV models is the Heston (1993) model defined as follows.

Assume return on the asset $X(t)$ follows a stochastic differential equation given by

$$dX(t) = b(t)dt + \sigma(t)dW(t), t \geq 0, \tag{4}$$

where $W(t)$ is a Brownian motion (aka random walk)[3], $b(t)$ is the moving average of the return and $\sigma(t)$ is mean-reverting conditional volatility of asset returns over time (volatility tend to move to its average over time). Processes b and σ can be any stochastic non-anticipating process, meaning that they cannot see into the future . Let $c(t) = \sigma^2(t)$ to simply the notations, then

$$dc(t) = \kappa(\overline{c} - c(t))dt + \gamma c(t)dB(t)(t \in [0,1]), \tag{5}$$

where $B(t)$, $t \geq 0$ is another random walk process, possibly correlated with W in the price process. There are three parameters in this volatility process.

- The parameter $\overline{c}$ is the asymptotic mean of the volatility process. It is also regarded as the long-term equilibrium of volatility, which could be daily or monthly average volatility depends on what time scale the volatility is measured on.
- The parameters κ is the rate of reversion to the asymptotic mean. Volatility has the tendency to move towards the long-term equilibrium and κ measures the time it takes for an off-equilibrium volatility to converge to the equilibrium.
- The parameter γ is the variance of volatility. Because the volatility process now has its own source of randomness, γ is the coefficient of the random walk process $B(t)$.

All the three parameters are assumed to be strictly positive and to obey the Feller condition $2\kappa\overline{c} > \gamma^2$ (Heston, 1993) ensures that $c(t)$ remains strictly positive with probability one (Shreve, 2004). Heston model is popular at pricing financial derivatives because it helps to explain the "volatility smile" phenomenon where implied volatility plotted against the strike price is a U-shape (Hull, 2012). In later sections, we will see how the mean-reversion structure and extra stochasticity introduced in volatility would help to explain the features of high-frequency volatility.

The common challenge for an econometric volatility model is whether it would maintain the same form when used at different time scales. We have seen in Section 1.2 that patterns found at high-frequency data disappear at a low frequency. Thus, successful low-frequency volatility models like ARCH/GARCH may not work at a high frequency (Drost & Nijman, 1993; Christoffersen, Diebold, & Shuermann, 1998). Drost and Nijman (1993) even provide a formula to aggregate volatility processes over time and find that fluctuations of volatility tend to disappear when time interval gets large. Therefore, a non-parametric approach that is invariant with respect to different time scales is in demand to exploit the high-frequency data to estimate volatility. Under this circumstance, the realized volatility measure was brought upfront in the finance research which will be introduced in the next subsection.

2.3 Realized Volatility Measure

Unlike ARCH/GARCH models that rely on parameters to describe the latent volatility process, the realized volatility measure is model-free. Conceptually, it is calculated by the cumulative variations in returns over a given time horizon. Realized volatility is also invariant for any type of data generating process, which makes it ideal for high-frequency volatility estimation.

This subsection defines realized volatility and explains how it helps to estimate the latent volatility regardless of sampling frequency. Suppose prices are sampled at evenly spaced discrete points over a given time interval $\left[t,t+h\right]$, and the sampling grids of the interval are $t=t+\frac{h}{n},\ldots,t+\left(n-1\right)\frac{h}{n},t+h$, where n is a positive integer representing the sampling frequency. Let $t_i=t+\frac{i}{n}$, where $i=1,\ldots,nh$. the return of asset price over a period $\left[t_i,t_j\right]$ is denoted as $X\left(t_i,j-i\right)=S\left(t+\frac{j}{n}\right)-S\left(t+\frac{i}{n}\right)$ where $S\left(s\right)$ is the logarithmic asset price at time s. The realized volatility over $\left[t,t+h\right]$ is then defined as (Anderson & Bollerslev, 1998a)

$$RV\left(t,h,n\right)=\frac{1}{h}\sum_{i=1}^{nh}X^2\left(t+\frac{i}{n},\frac{1}{n}\right) \tag{6}$$

This formula will also work even when the subintervals $\left[t_i,t_j\right]$ are not evenly spaced in $\left[t,t+h\right]$.

To give an example how realized volatility would look like, let's assume the return process $X(s)$ is generated by: $dX(s) = b ds + \sigma dW(s),\ t \leq s \leq t + h$. The process is the same as in the Heston model for asset returns (c.f. Equation (4)) except that now the theoretic average return b and conditional volatility σ are constant. Merton (1980) proves the following results by Taylor series expansion

$$\mathbb{E}\left[RV(t,h,n)\right] = \frac{b^2}{n} + \sigma^2 \tag{7}$$

and

$$Var\left[RV(t,h,n)\right] = 4\frac{b^2\sigma^2}{n^2} + 2\frac{\sigma^4}{n} \tag{8}$$

When $n \to \infty$, $RV(t,h,n)$ converges to σ^2 and the variance of $RV(t,h,n)$ vanishes (Merton, 1980). In other words, the realized volatility will be close enough to the actual unobserved volatility when the sampling frequency is large enough. This result is derived under the condition that the market data is frictionless, meaning that no noises or jumps are in the price process within a fixed time interval $\left[t, t+h\right]$.

2.4 Realized Volatility in a General Framework

We have seen why realized volatility would work in high-frequency finance data when asset returns are sampled from a Brownian motion. This subsection shows how realized volatility works in a more general framework like in Equation (4) where return average and volatility themselves are both stochastic processes (Anderson & Bollerslev, 1997; Anderson et al., 2003). Recall that

$$dX(t) = b(t)dt + \sigma(t)dW(t), t \geq 0, \tag{9}$$

where process *b*(*t*) has finite variation and $\sigma(t)$ is strictly positive and square integrable, i.e., $E\left[\int_0^t \sigma^2(s)ds\right] < \infty$. As $\sigma(t)$ is random and time-varying, finance researchers use the integrated variance (IV) over a certain time period as the underlying variance of asset returns. Specifically, IV is defined as

$$IV(t,h) = \frac{1}{h}\int_{t}^{t+h}\sigma^2(s)\,ds \tag{10}$$

In other words, IV (aka quadratic variation) is the instantaneous volatility. The definition of IV implies that the volatility process of asset returns is not impacted by the return average $b(t)$. The property holds even if we accumulate returns over a very short time interval *h*.

Meanwhile, the realized volatility of this process still follows the same definition by Equation (6). Recall from the previous subsection that realized volatility is biased but approaches the actual volatility when sampling frequency goes to infinity. The same result holds when the return process follows a much general form here: realized volatility is a consistent estimator of the underlying actual volatility (Anderson et al., 2003). Mathematically,

$$RV(t,h;n) \to IV(t,h)\, as\ n \to \infty \tag{11}$$

This finding supports realized volatility as the direct measure for the underlying volatility process in a general stochastic volatility setting. However, some special features in the high-frequency data has tripped the use of realized volatility in the last decade, which will be introduced in the next section.

3. INTERFERENCES OVER HIGH-FREQUENCY FINANCE DATA

While the advent of ultra-high frequency finance data brings the hope of applying the concept of realized volatility to the maximum extent, some microstructure noises create difficulties for volatility modeling. These noises which can be largely categorized into two groups: price discreteness, and errors by market activities.

1. **Price discreteness:** Refers to the inherent gap between observed price and the latent continuous price decided by the "no-arbitrage" principle, as even for the most liquid asset, high-frequency data cannot be entirely treated as continuous. Table 1 displays the distribution of trades for SPY, one of most active exchange-traded funds. The first row "# of trades per second" of the table shows the average number of trades per second and the second row "% inactive" shows the average number of seconds with no trade. Those seconds are called inactive seconds. There are on average 12 to 15 trades in one second but still

18% to 30% percent of the seconds are inactive. In other words, transactions are jammed in disconnected time intervals.

Not only there are substantial gaps between clustered trades, the trade arrival rates seem to differ from the traditional assumptions as well. Poisson distribution is usually the primary choice to model trade arrivals and jumps in mathematic finance because it is "memoryless" (Merton, 1980; Shreve, 2004; Bauwens & Hautsch, 2009). In other words, the number of trades arrive in two non-overlapping time intervals are independent and the arrival time of the trade is uncorrelated with the time waited. These properties are consistent with real stock market intuitions. However, if we assume that trade arrival follows a Poisson distribution, then an arrival rate of 12 trades per second would indicate the probability of no trade in a given second to be 6.1×10^{-6}, a very small number[4] comparing to around 20 percent chance in reality. In fact, the high-frequency trade process may not follow any of the existing stochastic processes according to the recent findings. (Guilbaud & Pham, 2013; Kent, 2015; Yan, 2017).

2. **Errors by market activities:** Except from price discretization, other sources of measurement error are usually caused by market issues like manual faults of price recording, dealer stock inventory control, bid-ask bounce backs, etc., that are introduced as follows:
   a. **Recording error:** Factual errors that may be attributed to the manual recording process. They are random noises uncorrelated with the price processes and stay around zero most of the time. These errors could be eliminated by "cleaning" the data at the expense of a few missing observations.
   b. **Rounding error:** Factual errors that occur in every measurement of any kind. The rounding error may be small compared with the order of magnitude in biological or physical science but it cannot be ignored in the case of finance. In fact, the magnitude of log returns between two

Table 1. Trades per second and inactive time stamps for SPY

Year	**2007**	**2008**	**2009**	**2010**	**2011**	**2012**	**2013**	**2014**
# of trades per second	13.4	12.1	14.1	12.9	13.4	13.5	13.5	**15.0**
% inactive	**34.4**	**17.0**	**18.1**	**20.2**	**17.6**	**25.1**	**26.7**	**22.6**

consecutive seconds is very small, usually at the magnitude of 10^{-6}, which may not be of a larger magnitude than the rounding error.

c. **Bid-ask bounce backs:** Stock transaction happens in a clearing process when the market maker assigns a buy order to a sell order, under the condition that bid price is higher than the ask price. The difference between the bid and ask price is called the "bid-ask spread". The observed price *bounces* between bid and ask prices before the market clearing, depending on which side submits the order first. These "bounce-backs" usually happen in a tiny price range and should not be regarded as volatility in transaction prices. Although bid-ask bounce-backs occur all the time, they may be eliminated by a manual process. The eliminated prices are usually replaced by the average price of the remaining shares traded.

d. **Small variations in prices due to a block trade:** Block trade is a privately negotiated transaction that could cause a market turbulence if submitted publicly. In United States, trades exceed 10,000 shares would usually be suggested exercising through block trade. Since block trades happen after negotiation between the buy and sell side, they close very quickly with an agreed price that might be different from the current market price. These transactions happen so fast that they may not be noticed by a third party, but the stock price is disturbed on a short time interval.

e. **Price spread due to dealer inventory control:** This is the system level of price adjustment due to the diverge of actual and desired inventory positions.

Earlier finance literature justify that microstructure noises emerge when sampling frequency increases (Anderson et al., 2003; Aït-Sahalia & Jacod, 2014). They argued that the optimal sampling frequency may not be the highest available, but rather some intermediate frequency. This frequency should be ideally high enough to produce a volatility estimate with negligible sampling variation, yet low enough to avoid microstructure bias (Anderson et al., 2003; Mykland & Zhang, 2005). To find this optimal sampling frequency, Anderson et al. (2003) even introduce a tool called "volatility signature plot" which plots the average of daily realized volatility against the frequency of sampling stock prices. On that graph, the daily realized volatility spikes at high sampling frequency and decays when sampling frequency decreases. Although the graph does not indicate which sampling frequency is optimal, Aït-Sahalia et al. (2005) conjecture that the average daily RV stabilizes at sampling frequency equal to every 5 minutes or lower. They claim that RV should be measured over longer time span, for example daily, to mitigate the impact of sampling variability because of microstructure noises[5].

4. VOLATILITY ESTIMATION WITH HIGH-FREQUENCY DATA

Recall from Section 2.4 that realized volatility (RV) is the direct measure of the underlying volatility process when noise-free price data are sampled at a high-frequency. However, Section 3 indicates that microstructure noises exist in high-frequency data, which trip the use of realized volatility in the last 2 decades. In this section, we introduce how this issue has been dealt with in recent research of volatility estimation, which demonstrates that RV could still be used to approach the actual volatility in the short run.

4.1. Daily Volatility Models

As mentioned in Section 3, an effective approach to avoid noise interferences in high-frequency data is to sample prices at a frequency of every 5 minutes or lower and measure volatility on a daily basis (Anderson et al., 2003; Aït-Sahalia et al., 2005; Bandi & Russell, 2008). This suggestion leads to a large stream of daily volatility models.

Early daily volatility models aggregate realized volatility over the entire trading day into a constant called daily realized volatility (abbr. daily RV) and examine this daily RV over many days or weeks. They use models with long-term memory like ARCH/GARCH as the basis to explain the clustering of daily volatilities. They also add additional components in ARCH/GARCH models to account for the impact of market news or activities on intraday prices. (Andersen & Bollerslev, 1997, 1998; Bandi & Russell, 2008; Bollerslev & Zhou, 2002; Giot, 2005[6]). We remark that most of these studies use data from currency exchange rate or S&P 500 index futures rather than the actual stock prices to estimate model parameters.

However, researchers soon find out that these models cannot well forecast intraday prices at 5-minute time intervals if the only features considered are those of daily volatilities. Therefore, some researchers start to incorporate simple features related to intraday volatility into the daily volatility models. Boudt, Croux and Laurent (2011) and Engle and Sokalska (2012) try to introduce a concept of *periodicity of intraday volatility* while looking at prices sampled at 10 minutes interval for many days. This periodicity is induced by the so called "U-shape" diurnal effect which refers to an empirical observation that volatility of stock returns tends to be large at beginning and end of the day but to stay low around lunch time. To accommodate with this periodicity, Engle and Sokalska (2012) define assume stock returns in the ARCH model as $X(i,t) = \mu(i,t) + \sqrt{s(i)h(t)}\eta(i,t)$. Similar to Equation (1) in Section 2.1, $\mu(i,t)$ is the moving average of stock return, where t is the date and i indexes the 10-minute time intervals of a day; $\eta(i,t)$ is an independent and random error term. The difference from the standard ARCH model of Equation (1) is that volatility here is decomposed into two parts where $h(t)$ is the daily volatility that is constant for the day t and scales $h(t)$ for each time interval i in the day $s(i)$.

4.2. From Daily Volatility to Intraday: An Overview

As mentioned in Section 4.1, forecasting prices at a high frequency leads to a low accuracy if only coarse-grained daily RV is considered. In Section 4.3, we will see more empirical patterns in intraday volatility which hints that daily volatility models are not enough to capture intraday volatility dynamics. A better way to handle microstructure noises and model intraday volatility using high-frequency data is essential, and we shall discuss some of these efforts in Sections 4.4 and 4.5. Finally, Section 4.6 compares intraday RV with the market volatility index (VIX) to show the significance of using intraday RV to capture market risks.

We summarize the following reasons to switch volatility modeling from daily to intraday:

1. Sampling at a frequency of every 5 minutes or lower is a huge waste of high-frequency data. If prices at every second are collected, we can get up to 234,000[7] prices in a single day. Sampling the prices at a frequency of every 5-minutes will lose more than 99% of the data. The waste is actually more severe as current stock transactions happen in the speed of every millisecond (Whang, 2012).
2. Treating volatility as a constant during a day annihilates the dynamics of intraday volatility in asset returns. In fact, intraday volatility impacts not only return fluctuations within a day but across several days as well (Anderson, Thyrsgaard, & Todorov, 2018; Ellickson et al., 2018).
3. Compared with the daily volatility process, intraday volatility of stock prices is more likely to be a continuous process. This is because there are 17.5 hours of overnight time gap between two trading days but there is no trading gap within the day, and hence, daily volatilities should be independent of each other (Engle & Sokalska, 2012).
4. Intraday volatility performs better than what the previous literature suggests (Anderson et al., 2018; Hecq, Laurent, & Palm, 2012; Ellickson et al., 2018). We will see in the next subsection that many features of intraday volatility are observable even with microstructure noises present, which cannot be fully explained by the simple diurnal "U-shape" effect (Anderson et al., 2018; Christensen, Hounyo, & Podolski, 2017; Rossi & Fantazzini, 2015).

5. In Section 2.2, we already mentioned that parametric models like ARCH/ GARCH do not generate consistent parameter estimators with different data sampling frequencies. Thus, successful settings of daily volatility models may work differently when data is stretched to intraday level.

4.3. Empirical Patterns of Intraday Volatility

We now show some empirical properties of intraday volatility observed with the help of high-frequency price data. These properties inspire the intraday volatility models to be discussed in the next subsection. In this section, we analyze intraday RV as a direct measure of the unobserved latent volatility.

Figure 3 shows a typical trading day for SPY using prices sampled at every second on February 7th, 2007. Figures 3(a) and 3(b) show the intra-second prices and logarithmic prices. Figure 3(c) plots cumulative RV over 100-second time interval and Figure 3(d) plots the sequence of 100-second RV[8]. Since the magnitude of change is very small, we factor the log returns by 10^2 and realized volatilities by 10^4.

Two important features can be observed in these figures: 1) Prices follow a non-random walk process and volatility is not a constant. Specifically, if prices follow a Brownian motion, the cumulative RV in Figure 3(c) should be a straight line as RV is constant under random walk (Merton, 1980; Anderson et al., 2003). 2) Intraday volatility in Figure 3(d) is generally of a "U-shape" but that does not fully explain volatility dynamics: there are volatility clusters and jumps in Figure 3(d) which cannot be observed from the price process.

Although intraday volatility looks noisy, the impact of the microstructure noises may be less severe than expected. Figure 4 plots the daily volatility calculated with

Figure 3a. A typical trading day, SPY

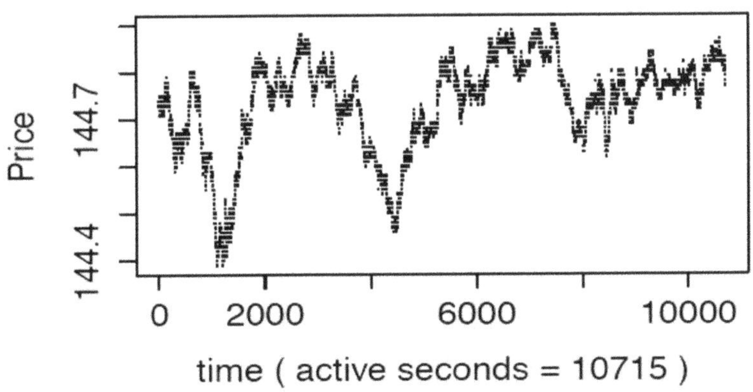

Figure 3b. A typical trading day, SPY

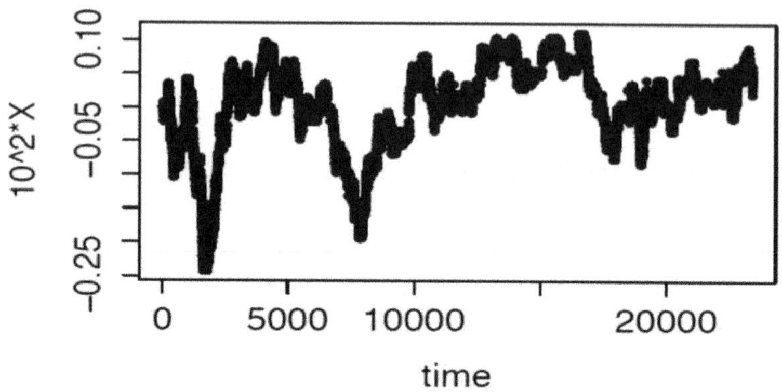

Figure 3c. A typical trading day, SPY

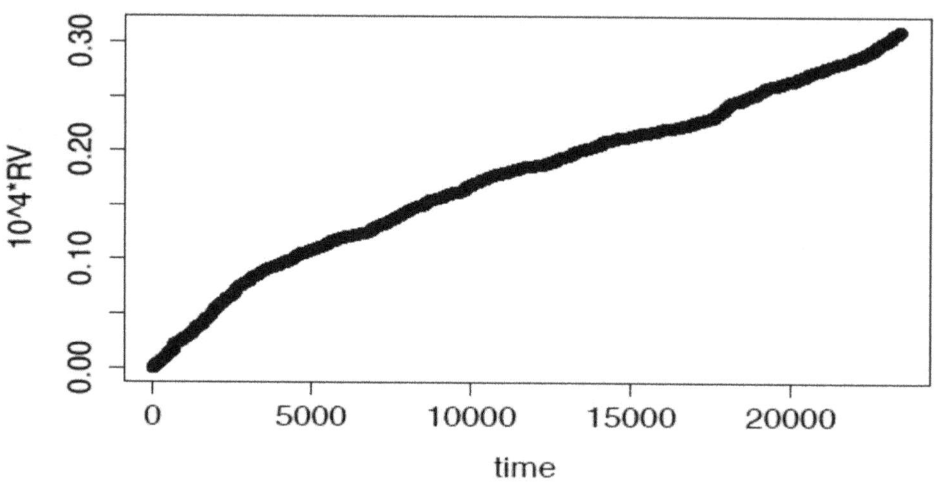

prices of SPY sampled at 5-minute frequency on the horizontal axis and the daily average of 100-second RV calculated with prices sampled every second on the vertical axis from Year 2007 to 2014. The average 100-second RV is noisy but still lie reasonably close to the daily RV except for a few outliers.

Figure 4 essentially indicates that the mean of observed intraday volatility is generally stable. Now we further consider the variances and autocovariances of intraday volatility, which have never been studied in low-frequency finance. Recent studies on high-frequency finance find that microstructure noises tend to increase the variance but not necessarily the autocovariance of intraday volatility (Ellickson et al., 2018; Sun, 2016; Yan, 2017), as Figure 5 below empirically shows.

Figure 3d. A typical trading day, SPY

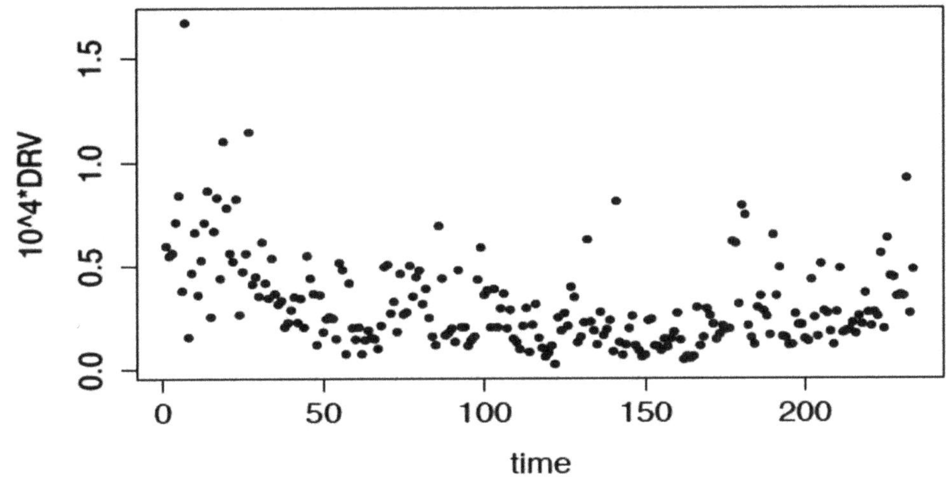

Figure 4. Daily RV vs. the average of intraday RV

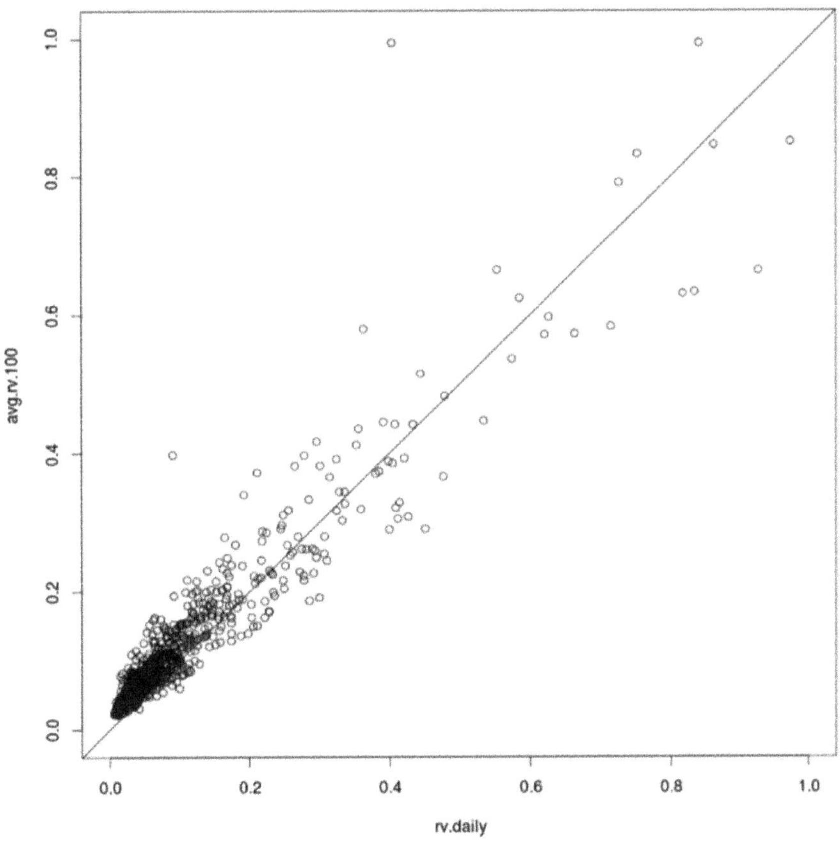

Figure 5 shows the box plots[9] of autocorrelations and their ratios for 100-second RV of SPY over Years 2004-2014[10]. Autocorrelation $R_j = V_j / V_0$, where V_j are the asymptotic autocovariances[11] for lag $j \geq 0$ and V_0 is the variance for the intraday RV. The predicted R_1 in stochastic volatility models are usually above 0.90, way above the median of R_1 shown in the graph (0.57). While the median of R_2 / R_1 and R_3 / R_1 are 0.87 and 0.8, respectively, close to what the literature suggests (0.9 and 0.81). This occurs when variance term V_0 is in the denominator of R_1 but is canceled out in R_2 / R_1 and R_3 / R_1. (Christensen, Oomen, & Podolski, 2014; Ellickson et al., 2018; Garcia, Lewis, Pastorello, & Renault, 2011).

4.4. Modeling the Intraday Volatility Process

From the observations presented in the previous subsection, we summarize the following empirical properties of observed intraday volatility for high-frequency data:

- **Mean-reverting:** Intraday volatility usually starts way above its long-term average but quickly settles to a dynamic balance between the inflow of additional market volatility and the reduction of uncertainty by market activities.
- **Stochastic:** Intraday volatility is not only time variant but also nondeterministic. It should be studied separately from the price process.

Figure 5. Box plot of autocorrelations for intraday volatility

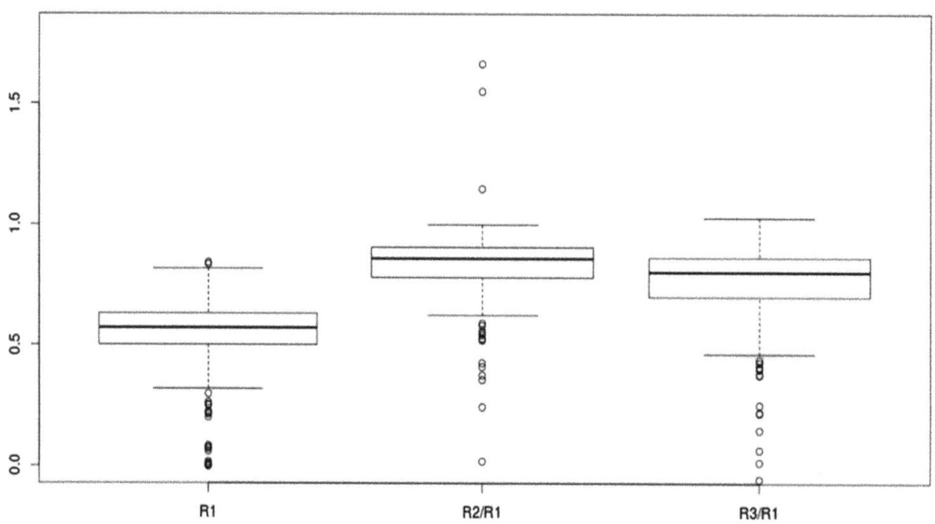

- **Stable mean and autocovariance:** The mean and autocovariances of intraday volatility behave better than expected even with the microstructure noises present.

Because of these properties, it is natural to think of using a mean-reverting stochastic volatility model to describe the dynamics of intraday volatility. It turns out that the Heston model introduced in Section 2.2 is one of the best candidates. (Anderson et al., 2018; Christensen et al., 2017; Ellickson et al., 2018).

Recall from Section 2.2 that there are three fundamental parameters in the Heston model: 1) the long-term average $\overline{c}$ which is roughly the daily average of intraday volatility; 2) the speed of mean reversion β which measures the time for an off-equilibrium volatility to go back to the long-term average; 3) variance of the volatility γ^2. The Heston model assumes that intraday volatility itself is random but with a constant variance.

The Heston model has played an important role in estimating daily volatility using high-frequency price data. Bollerslev and Zhou (2002) used the Heston model to characterize the motion of the continuous-time volatility process of the 5-minute "Deutsche Mark – Dollar" exchange rate return. They used Equation (5) to derive moment conditions of the three Heston model parameters[12] for the sequence of daily RVs. These moment conditions make it possible to estimate Heston model parameters using the generalized method of moments (GMM)[13]. The econometric technique in Bollerslev and Zhou (2002) paves the way to estimate a stochastic volatility model. Some researchers soon apply it to model the daily volatility of intraday stock prices (Corradi & Distaso, 2006; Garcia et al., 2011; Bergantini, 2013).

However, none of these researches model the intraday volatility until Ellickson et al. (2018). This paper finds that the Heston model is not only useful in describing daily volatility but also the intraday volatility process. They construct similar moment conditions as in Bollerslev and Zhou (2002) and estimate the model using 100-second RVs with microstructure noises. Except from the pioneering approach of constructing RV over a time interval less than one day as a proxy of the latent volatility, Ellickson et al. (2018) also incorporate the microstructure noises to the volatility process directly as measurement errors. As a result, they are able to provide stable and unique estimates for parameters of the Heston model with any price forms, as long as volatility follows the rule of mean-reversion as specified in Equation (5). However, microstructure noises do inflate the parameters as $\sqrt{\overline{c}}$ is estimated to be 29% in Ellickson et al. (2018) while the annual standard deviation of post-war U.S. stock return was 16% (Cochrane, 2005). Despite the slight inflation, their estimates for $\overline{c}$ still lie fairly close to the daily average of intraday RV, with 79% of the estimates lie in the 99% confidence interval of the daily average for 100-second RVs. Similar results are also derived between the autocovariance of model-implied volatility and that of intraday RV. Furthermore, Ellickson et al. (2018) attribute statistically insignificant estimates to volatility jumps (c.f. Section 5).

4.5. Other Volatility Estimation Models for High-Frequency Data

Except for the Heston model based approach, some researchers try to modify the GARCH model so that it may explain some features of intraday volatility. For example, the *fractionally integrated periodic GARCH* (aka FI-PEGARCH) (Rossi & Fantazzini, 2015) and *multiplicative component GARCH* (aka McsGARCH) (Diao & Tong, 2015) models build on intraday volatility over many days. They improve the GARCH model by allowing current volatility to depend on a random fraction of volatility memories (i.e., historical volatilities within a time window). It also treats the "U-shape" effect as a seasonal component in intraday volatility and use an operator to handle this seasonality. Anderson et al. (2018) propose a regime-switching[14] approach to explain why volatility tends to stay low at lunch time but to surge at market close. They empirically show that intraday volatility may not be reduced by market activities during the day but rather accumulate till market close.

On the other hand, some efforts have also been spent on mitigating the impact of microstructure noise in high-frequency prices so as to allow RV to approach the latent volatility directly (Hansen & Lunde, 2005; Zhang, 2006; Barndorff-Nielson, Hansen, Lunde, & Shepard, 2008; Jacod et al., 2017). These researchers found that noises are time-dependent and are correlated with the latent "arbitrage-free"[15] price. Some of them reduce the impact of microstructure noise using a "kernel estimation" technique that smooths the intraday RV process by replacing the current RV with a weighted average of the lagged RVs (Barndorff-Nielson et al., 2008; Jacod et al., 2017). Others show that the difference of RV at different time scales could be noise-free. They thus find by trial-and-error the right time scale to produce a stable RV estimate with certain statistical assumptions on the noises[16] (Zhang, 2006).

Some recent innovations on volatility forecasting involve machine learning algorithms. For example, Lahmiri and Boukadoum (2015) build an ensemble learning[17] system to hybridize the traditional GARCH model and artificial neural networks to forecast volatility under separate assumptions on mean, variance and skewness of the intraday RV distribution. Their model provides a higher accuracy in volatility forecasting than individual GARCH models.

4.6. Measuring Market Risk: Intraday RV vs. VIX

Intraday RV provides another channel to measure the market risk. Currently, the CBOE (Chicago Board Options Exchange) Volatility Index (aka VIX) is probably the most popular measure for the overall risk of the stock market. One unit of VIX represents 100 basis points of change in the expected annualized volatility of the market index, which are implied from the S&P 500 index option price. The difference between VIX and any physical volatility measure represents how much the investors are willing to pay as a premium to hedge volatility risk (aka the volatility risk premium, or VRP).

Figure 6 plots the estimated $\overline{c}$ (dotted line) of the Heston model for intraday volatility of SPY in Ellickson et al. (2018) and the daily VIX (solid line) for Years 2007-2014. We can see that VIX usually lies above $\overline{c}$ but they are fairly close. In other words, VRP is negative if $\overline{c}$ is taken as a physical measure of volatility which agrees with the literature (Bakshi & Kapadia, 2003; Dai, 2014). Figure 6 also shows three spikes of $\overline{c}$ in periods when the actual market risk is also large: 1) the Great Financial Crisis at the end of 2008, 2) the Sovereign Debt Crisis in the middle of 2010 and 3) the downgrading of U.S. Government Debt in the third quarter of 2011.

5. JUMPS IN HIGH-FREQUENCY FINANCE DATA

The volatility models introduced in the previous section are mostly continuous in order to conform to the "no-arbitrage" principle commonly assumed in mathematical finance paradigms. However, such a setting is restrictive as asset prices often exhibit sudden discrete movements when unexpected news hit the market. An attractive extension to volatility models is hence to allow for jumps.

Figure 6. Intraday RV vs. VIX

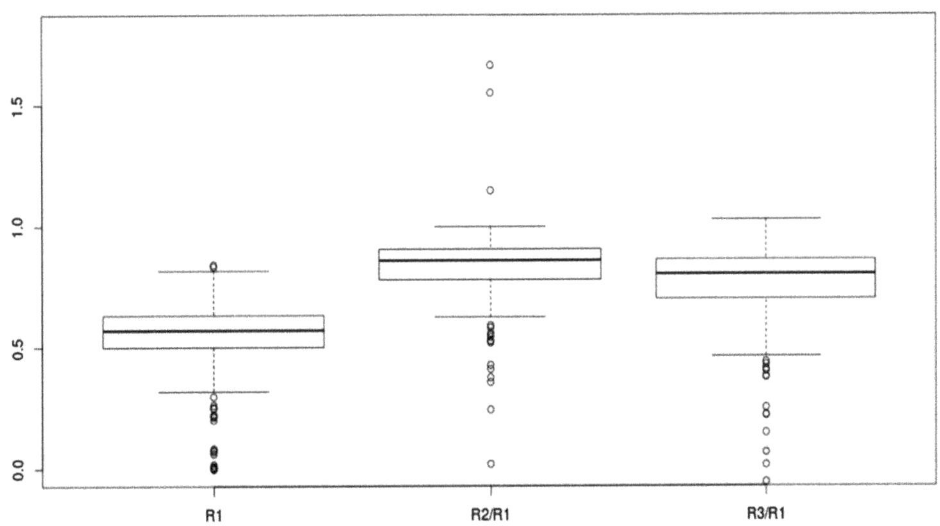

However, forecasting jumps is a non-trivial task as jump arrivals are random and jump sizes are unpredictable. We have demonstrated in Section 3 that the arrival of prices is not Poisson and may be memoryless. In this section, we continue to present more empirical findings about jumps in historical high-frequency data, which shed light on future studies on jump modeling.

5.1. Empirical Features of Volatility Jumps

In this subsection, we show some empirical features of volatility jumps occurred when the market is shocked by an event. Figure 7 plots the sequence of 100-second RVs over the week from 6/17/2013 to 6/21/2013 impacted by a Federal Open Market Committee (FOMC) announcement, which is about a rise of the federal funds rate (i.e., base interest rate). The RVs are constructed by prices of SPY sampled at every second. The announcement happened at 2pm on 6/19/2013, which is indicated on the graph by a vertical dashed line.

Several distinctive data features of volatility jumps can be observed in Figure 7, which are common in a time series of intraday volatility (Christensen et al., 2014; Yan, 2017):

1. **Mean Reversion:** Volatility rocketed 20 times over its original level after the announcement, revealing an abrupt increase of market uncertainty. However, this impact does not violate the mean-reversion rule, as volatility still settled to a balance around the new long-term volatility average in the next day.

Figure 7. FOMC announcement impact on volatility

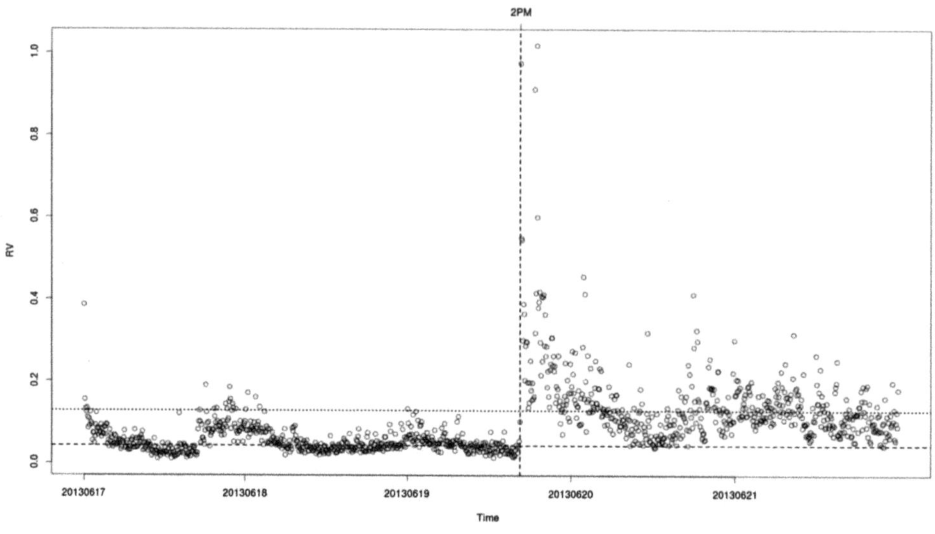

2. **Regime Switch:** Volatility jump elevates not only intraday volatility, but long-term average as well. In Figure 7, the two horizontal dashed lines refer to the estimated $\overline{c}$ using the Heston model specified in Ellickson et al. (2018) before and after the announcement, respectively. We can see a clear elevation of the long-term risk level, and that the intraday volatility also becomes a lot noisier for next couple of days.
3. **Cascades:** A large volatility jump tends to be followed by a series of small volatility jumps. This is clear in Figure 7, where volatilities within 2 hours after the big jump are clearly off-equilibrium. This feature is a side-effect of mean-reversion as the market takes time to digest a shock.
4. **"Sanity":** This feature refers to the property that extremely large jumps are rare (c.f. Section 5.2) and that the size of jumps is not "crazy". Taking Figure 7 as an example, most of the large RVs are still within 10 times of its long-term average. The market might be shocked by the announcement at the beginning but volatility immediately settled to a reasonable range.

These features demonstrate that jumps (signaled by large RVs) may be better-behaved than we expected. The next subsection further explores the magnitude distribution of intraday RVs. Empirical facts listed in these two subsections can help detect jump behaviors, which we shall briefly touch upon in Section 5.3.

5.2. Magnitude Distribution of Intraday RV

Large RVs are often caused by jumps, rather than microstructure noises which usually have a limited impact on the change of RV magnitudes; this is especially the case when continuous-time models of intraday RV fail to capture a surge in RV magnitude (Barndorff-Nielsen & Shephard, 2007; Christensen et al., 2014, 2017; Ellickson et al., 2018; Yan, 2017).

Since large RV magnitude deviation (from the average) may signal jumps, it is interesting to empirically examine the distribution of intraday RV magnitude over a reasonably long period of time (to be statistically meaningful) to find RV outliers with "exceptionally large" values, which could be jumps.

To account for the difference in the average levels of intraday RVs over different years, Yan (2017) constructs a measure called *Relative Realized Volatility* (RRV) which divides each intraday RV of a time block i by the average RV of the week containing block i. This measure endeavors to capture large deviations from the average RV level that are not explained by mean reversion or stochastic volatility, and hence likely to be jumps.

Table 2. Distribution of relative RV for SPY: 2007-2014

Magnitude	Good Week	Bad Week	Total
[10, ∞)	365 (0.11%)	582 (0.43%)	947 (0.20%)
[5, 10)	1,291 (0.39%)	659 (0.48%)	1,950 (0.41%)
[2.5, 5)	13,875 (4.15%)	5,649 (4.13%)	19,524 (4.14%)
[0, 2.5)	319,089 (95.36%)	129,766 (94.36%)	448,855 (95.22%)
[0, ∞)	334,620 (100.00%)	136,656 (100.00%)	471,276 (100.00%)

Table 2 shows the distribution of RRV over all 100-second time blocks from Year 2007 to Year 2014 for SPY. We divide the value range $[0,\infty)$ of RRVs into four intervals, namely $[0, 2.5),[2.5,5),[5,10)$, and $[10, \infty)$. Table 2 shows the number of blocks falling into each interval. The second column shows the distribution of blocks falling into the "good" weeks, and the third column shows the distribution into the "bad" weeks. A "good" week refers to the case when the Heston model is statistically significant[18] while a "bad" week refers to when the model is not statistically significant. The percentages of blocks falling into "good" (and "bad") weeks are shown in the parenthesis (e.g., 365/334,620 = 0.11%). The add-up of all the numbers in this table is the total number of 100-second blocks for the entire 8 years. Some key takeaways from the RRV distribution are listed as follows:

1. **Continuous time models fail to capture jumps:** Bad weeks differ only slightly from good weeks on the percentage of RRVs in $[0,2.5),[2.5,5)$ or $[5,10)$, but the percentage of large RRVs in $[10,\infty)$ for bad weeks is 3 times more than that of good weeks. This serves as an empirical evidence that a jump component is necessary when modeling intraday volatility. Models with only a continuous component often perform poorly in handling the outliers as observed in (Aït-Sahalia & Jacod, 2014; Ellickson et al., 2018).
2. **Large jumps are rare:** The finance literature typically categorize jump activities into large jumps and small jumps and assume the number of large jumps are finite and the number of small jumps are infinite (Anderson & Benzoni, 2009; Barndorff-Nielsen & Shephard, 2007). Table 2 demonstrates that extremely large RVs only account for less than 1% of the 8-year data sample but a large number of small RVs are less than 2.5 times their long-term mean. This finding coincides with a recent study by Aït-Sahalia and Jacod (2014) where they use the so-called Blumenthal-Getoor index[19] to show that jumps are mainly composed of infinite number of small jumps. Small jump activities are likely to be signs of microstructure noise which may not impact the estimation of

continuous time model if properly handled (Christensen et al., 2014; Ellickson et al., 2018; Jacod et al., 2017).

3. **U-shape:** We find that over 80% of the small RRV jumps within $\left[2.5,5\right)$ actually occurred within 30 minutes after the market opening and 30 minutes before the market close (Yan, 2017). This matches with the "U-shape" phenomenon discussed in Section 4.1. In fact, volatility usually starts above its long-term average when market opens. Market may need the entire day to resolve uncertainty so that volatility could go back to its long-term average.

5.3. Modeling Jump Activities

Although the theoretical development of jump detection is still at its infancy because of the difficulty in forecasting the jump arrival time and jump sizes, the empirical findings presented in the previous two subsections provide some clues to model jumps in volatility and prices.

One of the most recognized approaches is the *bi-power* and *multi-power variations* developed by Barndorff-Nielsen and Shephard (2004). Their model assumes that asset returns are governed by

$$dX\left(t\right)=\mu\left(t\right)dt+\sigma\left(t\right)dW\left(t\right)+\xi\left(t\right)dq\left(t\right), \tag{12}$$

where the occurrence of jumps is "added" to the return process with the new term $J(t) = \xi(t)dq(t)$. Here, $dq(t)$ is number of jump arrivals at time t and $q(t)$ counts the total number of jump occurrences up to time t; $\xi(t)$ is a scaling factor denoting the magnitude of a jump that occurs at time t. The finite activity counting process q is uncorrelated with W. Under this new setting, Equation (10) in Section 2.4 no longer holds and should be modified as

$$IV\left(t,h\right)=\frac{1}{h}\int_{t}^{t+h}\sigma\left(s\right)ds+\sum_{t\leq s\leq t+h}J^{2}\left(s\right) \tag{13}$$

where $\sum_{t\leq s\leq t+h}J^{2}\left(s\right)$ is the cumulated squared jumps in $\left[t,t+h\right]$. If we denote the return of asset price over a period $\left[t,t+h\right]$ as $X\left(t,h\right)=S\left(t+h\right)-S\left(t\right)$ where $S\left(t\right)$ is the logarithmic asset price at time t similar to Section 2.3. The multi-power variation (MPV) for $X\left(t\right)$ would be

$$MPV\left(t,h,n\right)=\frac{\pi}{2}\sum_{i=k+1}^{nh}\left\{\left|X\left(t+\frac{ih}{n},\frac{1}{n}\right)\right|\bullet\left|X\left(t+\frac{\left(i-k\right)h}{n},\frac{1}{n}\right)\right|\right\}^{k} \tag{14}$$

Setting $k=1$ in the above equation yields the bi-power variation (BPV) $BV\left(t,h,n\right)$. Unlike RV which aggregates squared return, BPV aggregates product of returns separated by a time interval of length h to avoid aggregating large changes in consecutive returns that may contain jumps. Barndorff-Nielsen and Shephard (2004) prove that Equation (11) can be modified as

$$\lim_{n\to\infty} RV\left(t,h,n\right)-BV\left(t,h,n\right)=\sum_{t\le s\le t+h} J^{2}\left(s\right).$$

In other words, the difference between realized volatility and bi-power variation approaches the cumulative squared jump component when sampling is infinitely frequent.

One defect of this approach is that the number of jumps is assumed to be finite, and therefore, the approach is not robust when there are infinite number of jump activities. Later on, Aït-Sahalia and Jacod (2005) use maximum likelihood estimation to disentangle the continuous component ($\mu\left(t\right)dt+\sigma\left(t\right)dW\left(t\right)$) from Equation (12) so that the last discontinuous term $\xi(t)dq(t)$ stand out, which is related to possibly infinite number of jumps. bi-power variation is also found to be less effective than multi-power variation with $k\ge 3$ when prices are contaminated by the microstructure noises20.

Truncation is another approach often used to get rid of the jump component (Mancini, 2003, 2004). This method assumes that the truncated RV follows:

$$TRV\left(t,h,n\right)=\frac{1}{h}\sum_{i=1}^{nh}X^{2}\left(t+\frac{i}{n},\frac{1}{n}\right)\bullet I[X\left(t+\frac{i}{n},\frac{1}{n}\right)<r].$$

In other words, only if the return between two consecutive time intervals is less than a predetermined threshold will it be included in the calculation of the realized volatility. This method gets rid of abrupt surges of stock prices (and hence large jump activities) but it heavily relies on the appropriate choice of threshold value r. Aït-Sahalia and Jacod (2014) improve upon this method by using a two-step learning procedure that automatically chooses the threshold for truncation. However, their analysis is still theoretical and not straightforward to implement for analyzing real data. We are still in need of a better approach in the detection of jumps for general price settings.

5.4. Jumps in the Flash Crash

We would like to conclude this section by a case study on the infamous 2010 Flash Crash event. In particular, we would like to examine the time series of intraday volatility around the incident and how intraday RV may help us avoid such a market crash. We have seen the price changes on the Flash Crash day in Figures 2 of Section 1.3. Figure 8 plots 5 days of 100-second RRVs with the price of SPY sampled at every second. The second day (5/6/2010) is the Flash Crash day, and the vertical dashed line marked with "2:20PM" on top indicates the time when the crash happened. The graph is truncated on top at RRV = 10 so that we may see details of the majority of volatilities.

Figure 8 provides the stunning details of volatility during the Crash, which shows that intraday RV follows largely the same 4 features identified in Section 5.1 even under extreme market conditions:

- Because of the Flash Crash, intraday RV jumps up to 1500 times the pre-crash average (cannot be seen in Figure 8), but soon returns back to below 10 times of the pre-crash average. This feature restates that large RVs are rare and jumps are dominated by infinite number of small jump activities.

Figure 8. RRV of SPY at the flash crash (truncated)

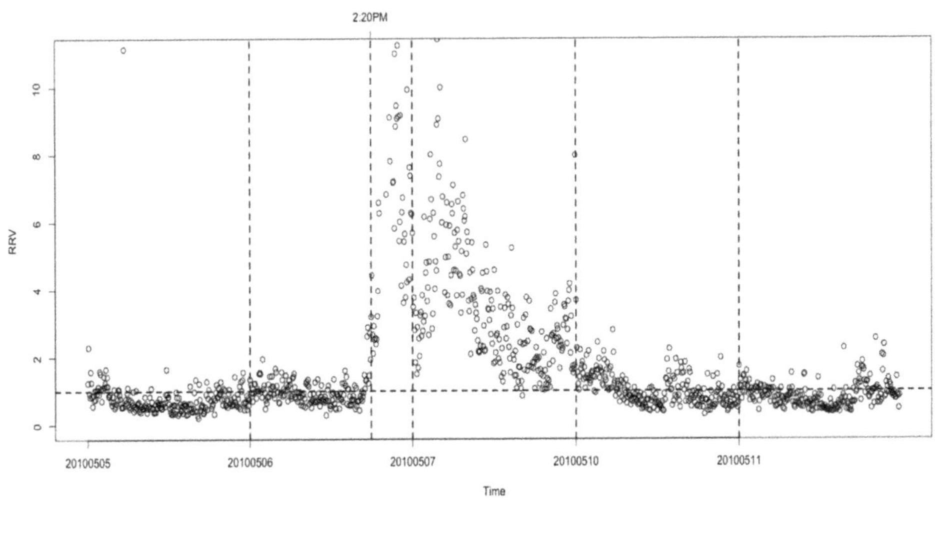

- Although the market does not cool down until the end of the next day, we could still observe the efforts by intraday RVs to revert back to the long-term mean. In fact, Yan (2017) provides a counter-factual analysis by removing RVs during the crash and re-estimating the Heston model. He finds that the long-term average barely changes before and after the crash. However, the market impact is so large that the speed of recovery (mean-reversion) is much lower than usual.
- Figure 8 also shows that the incident has asymmetric impact on price and volatility. As mentioned in Figure 2, market price plunged 9% but reverted back to its original within 20 minutes. However, volatility stayed high not only on the Flash Crash day but the next day as well.

Moreover, intraday RV could even provide signals on the time to sell (or not buy) stocks to avoid financial losses at the occurrence of the market crash. Taking Figure 8 as an example, intraday RV did not jump instantly to a high level but instead climbed up before the incident (which is not near market close). Yan (2017) looks over 8 years of high-frequency prices for 80 stocks and finds that over 80% of the volatility jumps have the "climb-up" phenomenon. Therefore, it may be a bad signal to buy in (or hold) if we see a series of intraday RVs climbing. In the cool-down period, we may further use the Heston model to calculate the reversion time by treating the largest RV as the starting point of mean reversion. Yan (2017) shows that this time is around 55 minutes for the Flash Crash.

6. OTHER RELATED WORK

Instead of modeling the volatility of a single stock, some researchers try to characterize the *realized covariation* (RC) of volatility processes for multiple stocks using high-frequency data. The realized covariance is calculated as the sum of multiplications of two asset returns. Similar to realized volatility, Barndorff-Nielsen and Shephard (2004) show that realized covariance of two assets converges to their unobserved instantaneous covariance when the sampling frequency goes to infinity. Bandi and Russell (2005) show, on the other hand, that this convergence does not hold with microstructure noise, so they propose a method for selecting a lower sampling frequency to trade-off unbiasedness for estimation efficiency (i.e., the need for fewer samples). Bandi and Russell (2005) and Andersen et al. (2003) also discover the *Epps effect*[21] which introduces additional microstructure effect as a downward bias in the realized covariance estimates. They cope with this issue by incorporating leads and lags in the RC calculation. Recent study by Hayashi and Yoshida (2006) considers an alternative estimator based on overlapping tick-by-tick stock returns instead of calendar time returns so that return values of any pair of stocks are available at any time and thus the covariance estimator would not be biased. Among the other works, Zhang (2011) shows that the RV and RC of less liquid assets are more likely to be bothered by the Epps effect and noises; Li et al. (2017) use a linear model to fit the relationship between jumps of two different realized volatility process and use that model to estimate risks of market jumps. While assessing the applicability of the Heston model on different assets, Yan (2017) also discovers strong empirical evidence that there is a common latent process behind intraday RV of different assets.

7. CONCLUSION

This chapter provided an overview of the major research status of volatility estimation so far in the era of high-frequency finance. Since volatility is such an important topic in modern finance, many efforts have been spent on modeling and forecasting the unobserved volatility with observed asset prices. Models like ARCH/GARCH successfully explained features like volatility clustering but failed to provide consistent parameter estimates when data is stretched from daily to intraday. This limitation gives rise to nonparametric measures like *Realized Volatility*.

Bothered by microstructure noises in high-frequency finance data, researchers start to model daily volatility with prices sampled at every 5 minutes or an even lower frequency. This leads to a huge waste of data and annihilates intraday volatility dynamics. To overcome these problems, recent researches endeavor to build intraday volatility models by extending the daily models and/or mitigating the impact of noises.

Continuous-time models sometimes fail when jumps present, and large RVs are usually assumed to contain jumps. Although we are still at an early stage in modeling jump activities, studying the plots and magnitude distribution of intraday RV is found to be helpful in detecting large volatility jumps and market crash.

Undoubtedly, volatility will continue to play a crucial role in financial areas like portfolio risk management, pricing derivative securities, and corporate valuation. In the foreseeable future, rapid developments of FinTech (or, financial technology) and artificial intelligence will increase the trading speed remarkably. We will be able to sample prices even more frequently and view market microstructure more clearly. This may help us resolve many remaining problems in volatility estimation like modeling jumps and noise distributions in realized volatility. How to disentangle noises from jumps is also a non-trivial question to be answered by future volatility research.

Meanwhile, volatility estimation is expected to be used more frequently in the design of new financial products. For example, variance swap is a recent financial derivative designed based on short-term realized volatility. This security helps to hedge volatility risk of the underlying asset and pays the difference between realized volatility and a fixed amount when exercised[22].

Modeling short-term volatilities with high-frequency price data will also benefit investment management. Previous literature suggests that stocks with low volatility historically tend to outperform stocks with high volatility (Blitz & van Vliet, 2007; Baker, Bradley, & Wurgler, 2011). This finding has been used to construct stock portfolios with weights rebalanced each week/month based on their historical volatility. These portfolios seem to outperform the market index consistently (Frazzini & Pederson, 2014; Moreira & Muir, 2017). We may further replace their historical volatility with intraday RV and manage the portfolio at much higher frequency to avoid risk.

Multi-factor asset pricing model has prevailed the asset management literature where excess returns in individual stocks are explained by risk factor premiums (Fama & French, 1993, 2006; Carhart, 1997). High-frequency volatility estimation could help to discover more empirical features of these risk premiums in the short run.

High-frequency finance data can also help us understand the linkage between financial markets and the general economy. Macroeconomic indicators like GDP, inflation and unemployment rate constantly impact stock market performance. Risk level in financial markets could imply investors' view towards these indicators. Engle, Ghysels and Sohn (2008) is one of the earlier studies linking macroeconomic variables to long-run volatility movements, but it is yet to be discovered if the same findings hold for intraday volatility as well.

DISCLAIMER

The views and opinions expressed herein are those of the authors and do not necessarily represent the views and opinions of KPMG LLP.

REFERENCES

Aït-Sahalia, Y., & Jacod, J. (2014). *High-frequency financial econometrics*. Princeton, NJ: Princeton Press.

Aït-Sahalia, Y., Mykland, P., & Zhang, L. (2005). How often to sample a continuous-time process in the presence of market microstructure noise. *Review of Financial Studies, 18*(2), 351–416. doi:10.1093/rfs/hhi016

Andersen, T. G., & Bollerslev, T. (1997). Intraday periodicity and volatility persistence in financial markets. *Journal of Empirical Finance, 4*(2), 115–158. doi:10.1016/S0927-5398(97)00004-2

Andersen, T. G., & Bollerslev, T. (1998a). Deutsche Mark-Dollar volatility: Intraday activity patterns, macroeconomic announcements, and longer run dependencies. *The Journal of Finance, 53*(1), 219–265. doi:10.1111/0022-1082.85732

Anderson, T. G., & Benzoni, L. (2009). *Realized volatility. In Handbook of Financial Time series, Part III.* Springer Science & Business Media.

Anderson, T. G., & Bollerslev, T. (1998b). Answering the skeptics: Yes, standard volatility models do provide accurate forecasts. *International Economic Review, 39*(4), 885–905. doi:10.2307/2527343

Anderson, T. G., Bollerslev, T., Diebold, F., & Labys, P. (2003). Modeling and forecasting realized volatility. *Econometrica, 71*(2), 579–625. doi:10.1111/1468-0262.00418

Anderson, T. G., Thyrsgaard, M., & Todorov, V. (2018). Time-varying periodicity in intraday volatility. *CREATES Research Paper.*

Baker, M., Bradley, B., & Wurgler, J. (2011). Benchmarks as limits to arbitrage: Understanding the low-volatility anomaly. *Financial Analysts Journal, 67*(1), 40–54. doi:10.2469/faj.v67.n1.4

Bakshi, G., & Kapadia, N. (2003). Volatility risk premiums embedded in individual equity options: Some new insights. *Journal of Derivatives, 11*(1), 45–54. doi:10.3905/jod.2003.319210

Bandi, F., & Russell, J. (2005). *Realized covariation, realized beta and microstructure noise* (Unpublished paper). Graduate School of Business, University of Chicago.

Bandi, F., & Russell, J. (2008). Microstructure noise, realized variance and optimal sampling. *The Review of Economic Studies, 75*(2), 339–369. doi:10.1111/j.1467-937X.2008.00474.x

Banerjee, P., Doran, J., & Peterson, D. R. (2007). Implied volatility and future portfolio returns. *Journal of Banking & Finance, 31*(10), 3183–3199. doi:10.1016/j.jbankfin.2006.12.007

Barndorff-Nielsen, O., Hansen, P., Lunde, A., & Shephard, N. (2008). Designing realized kernels to measure the ex-post variation of equity prices in the presence of noise. *Econometrica*, *76*(6), 1481–1536. doi:10.3982/ECTA6495

Barndorff-Nielsen, O., & Shephard, N. (2004). Power and bipower variation with stochastic volatility and jumps. *Journal of Financial Econometrics*, *2*(1), 1–37. doi:10.1093/jjfinec/nbh001

Barndorff-Nielsen, O., & Shephard, N. (2007). Variation, jumps and high frequency data in financial econometrics. *Advances in Economics and Econometrics. Theory and Applications, Ninth World Congress, CUP*, 328-372.

Bauwens, L., & Hautsch, N. (2009). *Modelling financial high frequency data using point processes. In Handbook of financial time series* (pp. 953–979). Berlin: Springer.

Bekaert, G., & Wu, G. (2000). Asymmetric volatility and risk in equity markets. *Review of Financial Studies*, *13*(1), 1–42. doi:10.1093/rfs/13.1.1

Bergantini, D. (2013). Moment-based estimation of stochastic volatility. *Journal of Banking & Finance*, *37*(12), 4755–4764. doi:10.1016/j.jbankfin.2013.08.008

Black, F., & Scholes, M. (1973). The pricing of options and corporate liabilities. *Journal of Political Economy*, *81*(3), 637–654. doi:10.1086/260062

Blitz, D., & van Vliet, P. (2007). The volatility effect: Lower risk without lower return. *Journal of Portfolio Management*, *34*(1), 102–113. doi:10.3905/jpm.2007.698039

Bollerslev, T. (1986). Generalized autoregressive conditional heteroskedasticity. *Journal of Econometrics*, *31*(3), 307–327. doi:10.1016/0304-4076(86)90063-1

Bollerslev, T., Gibson, M., & Zhou, H. (2011). Dynamic estimation of volatility risk premia and investor risk aversion from option-implied and realized volatilities. *Journal of Econometrics*, *160*(1), 235–245. doi:10.1016/j.jeconom.2010.03.033

Bollerslev, T., & Zhou, H. (2002). Estimating stochastic volatility diffusion using conditional moments of integrated volatility. *Journal of Econometrics*, *109*(1), 33–65. doi:10.1016/S0304-4076(01)00141-5

Boudt, K., Croux, C., & Laurent, S. (2011). Robust estimation of intraweek periodicity in volatility and jump detection. *Journal of Empirical Finance*, *18*(2), 353–367. doi:10.1016/j.jempfin.2010.11.005

Britten-Jones, M., & Neuberger, A. (2000). Option prices, implied price processes, and stochastic volatility. *The Journal of Finance*, *55*(2), 839–866. doi:10.1111/0022-1082.00228

Brogaard, J., Hendershott, T., & Riordan, R. (2014). High-frequency trading and price discovery. *Review of Financial Studies, 27*(8), 2267–2306. doi:10.1093/rfs/hhu032

Budish, E., Carmton, P., & Shim, J. (2015). The high-frequency trading arms race: Frequent batch auctions as a market design response. *The Quarterly Journal of Economics, 130*(4), 1547–1621. doi:10.1093/qje/qjv027

Canina, L., & Figlewski, S. (1993). The informational content of implied volatility. *Review of Financial Studies, 6*(3), 659–681. doi:10.1093/rfs/5.3.659

Carhart, M. M. (1997). On persistence in mutual fund performance. *The Journal of Finance, 52*(1), 57–82. doi:10.1111/j.1540-6261.1997.tb03808.x

Christensen, K., Hounyo, U., & Podolskij, M. (2017) Is the diurnal pattern sufficient to explain the intraday variation in volatility? a nonparametric assessment. *CREATES Research working paper.*

Christensen, K., Oomen, R. C., & Podolskij, M. (2014). Fact or friction: Jumps at ultra-high frequency. *Journal of Financial Economics, 114*(3), 576–599. doi:10.1016/j.jfineco.2014.07.007

Christie, A. A. (1982). The stochastic behavior of common stock variances: Value, leverage and interest rate effects. *Journal of Financial Economics, 10*(4), 407–432. doi:10.1016/0304-405X(82)90018-6

Christoffersen, P., Diebold, F. X., & Shuermann, T. (1998), Horizontal Problems and Extreme Events in Financial Risk Management. The Handbook of Risk, 234, 155.

Cochrane, J. (2005). *Asset Pricing* (Revised Edition). Princeton, NJ: Princeton University Press.

Corradi, V., & Distaso, W. (2006). Semi-parametric comparison of stochastic volatlity models using realized measures. *The Review of Economic Studies, 73*(3), 635–667. doi:10.1111/j.1467-937X.2006.00390.x

Dai, W. (2014). *Statistical methods in finance* (Unpublished doctoral dissertation). Princeton University, Princeton, NJ.

Diao, X., & Tong, B. (2015). Forecasting intraday volatility and VaR using multiplicative component GARCH model. *Applied Economics Letters, 22*(18), 1457–1464. doi:10.1080/13504851.2015.1039696

Drost, C. D., & Nijman, T. (1993). Temporal aggregation of GARCH processes. *Econometrica, 61*(3), 909–927. doi:10.2307/2951767

Egloff, D., Leippold, M., & Wu, L. (2010). The term structure of variance swap rates and optimal variance swap investments. *Journal of Financial and Quantitative Analysis, 45*(5), 1279–1310. doi:10.1017/S0022109010000463

Ellickson, B., Sun, M., Whang, D., & Yan, S. (2018). *Estimating a local Heston model.* SSRN Archive. doi:10.2139srn.3108822

Engle, R. (1982). Autoregressive conditional heteroscedasticity with estimates of the variance of United Kingdom inflation. *Econometrica, 68*(1), 1–22. doi:10.1111/1468-0262.00091

Engle, R. (2000). The econometrics of ultra-high-frequency data. *Econometrica, 68*(1), 1–22. doi:10.1111/1468-0262.00091

Engle, R., Ghysels, E., & Sohn, B. (2008). *On the economic sources of stock market volatility.* SSRN Electronic Journal. doi:10.2139srn.971310

Engle, R., & Sokalska, M. (2012). Forecasting intraday volatility in the US equity market. multiplicative component GARCH. *Journal of Financial Econometrics, 10*(1), 54–83. doi:10.1093/jjfinec/nbr005

Fama, E. F., & French, K. R. (1993). Common risk factors in the returns on stocks and bonds. *Journal of Financial Economics, 33*(1), 3–56. doi:10.1016/0304-405X(93)90023-5

Fama, E. F., & French, K. R. (2006). Profitability, investment and average returns. *Journal of Financial Economics, 82*(3), 491–518. doi:10.1016/j.jfineco.2005.09.009

Fleming, J., Kirby, C., & Ostdiek, B. (2003). The economic value of volatility timing using "realized" volatility. *Journal of Financial Economics, 67*(3), 473–509. doi:10.1016/S0304-405X(02)00259-3

Frazzini, A., & Pederson, L. H. (2009). Betting against beta. *Journal of Financial Economics, 111*(1), 1–25. doi:10.1016/j.jfineco.2013.10.005

Garcia, R., Lewis, M., Pastorello, S., & Renault, E. (2011). Estimation of objective and risk-neutral distributions based on moments of integrated volatility. *Journal of Econometrics, 160*(1), 22–32. doi:10.1016/j.jeconom.2010.03.011

Giot, P. (2005). Market risk models for intraday data. *European Journal of Finance, 11*(4), 309–324. doi:10.1080/1351847032000143396

Guilbaud, F., & Pham, H. (2013). Optimal high-frequency trading with limit and market orders. *Quantitative Finance, 13*(1), 79–94. doi:10.1080/14697688.2012.708779

Hansen, P. R., & Lunde, A. (2005). Realized variance and market microstructure noise. *Journal of Business & Economic Statistics*, *24*(2), 127–161. doi:10.1198/073500106000000071

Hayashi, T., & Yoshida, N. (2006). *Estimating correlations with nonsynchronous observations in continuous diffusion models* (Unpublished Working Paper). Columbia University, New York, NY.

Hecq, A., Laurent, S., & Palm, F. (2012). Common intraday periodicity. *Journal of Financial Econometrics*, *10*(2), 325–353. doi:10.1093/jjfinec/nbr012

Heston, S. (1993). A closed-form solution for options with stochastic volatility with applications to bonds and currency options. *Review of Financial Studies*, *6*(2), 327–343. doi:10.1093/rfs/6.2.327

Hull, J., & Basu, S. (2016). *Options, futures and other derivatives*. Pearson Education India.

Jacob, F. (2015). *Risk estimation on high-frequency financial data*. Wiesbaden, Germany: Springer. doi:10.1007/978-3-658-09389-1

Jacod, J., Li, Y., & Zheng, X. (2017). Statistical properties of microstructure noise. *Econometrica*, *85*(4), 1133–1174. doi:10.3982/ECTA13085

Johnson, B. (2010). *Algorithmic Trading & DMA: An introduction to direct access trading strategies* (Vol. 200). London: 4Myeloma Press.

Kenny, R., Hope, B., DeBold, T., & Yang, S. (2015). *'Flash Crash' a perfect storm for markets*. Retrieved from http://graphics.wsj.com/flash-crash-timeline/

Kent, A. (2015). *High Frequency Decomposition and Trade Arrivals* (Unpublished Working Paper). University of Colorado, Boulder, CO.

Kirilenko, A., Kyle, A. S., Samadi, M., & Tuzun, T. (2017). The Flash Crash: High-frequency trading in an electronic market. *The Journal of Finance*, *72*(3), 967–998. doi:10.1111/jofi.12498

Lahmiri, S., & Boukadoum, M. (2015). An ensemble system based on hybrid EGARCH-ANN with different distributional assumptions to predict S&P 500 intraday volatility. *Fluctuation and Noise Letters*, *14*(1), 1550001. doi:10.1142/S0219477515500017

Li, J., Todorov, V., & Tauchen, G. (2017). Jump regressions. *Econometrica*, *85*(1), 173–195. doi:10.3982/ECTA12962

Mancini, C. (2003). *Statistics of a Poisson-Gaussian process* (Unpublished Working Paper). Dipartimento di matematica per le Decisioni, Universita di Firenze, Florence, Italy.

Mancini, C. (2004). Estimaton of the characteristics of jump of a general Poisson-diffusion process. *Scandinavian Actuarial Journal*, *1*(1), 42–52. doi:10.1080/034612303100170091

Markowitz, H. (1952). Portfolio selection. *The Journal of Finance*, *7*(1), 77–91.

Merton, R. C. (1976). Option pricing when underlying stock returns are discontinuous. *Journal of Financial Economics*, *3*(1-2), 125–144. doi:10.1016/0304-405X(76)90022-2

Merton, R. C. (1980). On estimating the expected return on the market: An exploratory investigation. *Journal of Financial Economics*, *8*(4), 323–361. doi:10.1016/0304-405X(80)90007-0

Moreira, A., & Muir, T. (2017). Volatility-Managed Portfolios. *The Journal of Finance*, *72*(4), 1611–1644. doi:10.1111/jofi.12513

Mykland, P. A., & Zhang, L. (2005). A tale of two time scales: Determining integrated volatility with noisy high-frequency data. *Journal of the American Statistical Association*, *100*(472), 1394–1411. doi:10.1198/016214505000000169

Ross, S. A. (1989). Information and volatility: The no-arbitrage martingale approach to timing and resolution irrelevancy. *The Journal of Finance*, *44*(1), 1–17. doi:10.1111/j.1540-6261.1989.tb02401.x

Rossi, E., & Fantazzini, D. (2015). Long memory and periodicity in intraday volatility. *Journal of Financial Econometrics*, *13*(4), 922–961. doi:10.1093/jjfinec/nbu006

Schwert, G. W. (1989). Why does stock market volatility change over time? *The Journal of Finance*, *44*(5), 1115–1153. doi:10.1111/j.1540-6261.1989.tb02647.x

Sharpe, W. (1964). Capital asset prices: A theory of market equilibrium under conditions of risk. *The Journal of Finance*, *19*(3), 425–442.

Shiller, R. (1981). Do stock prices move too much to be justified by subsequent changes in dividends. *The American Economic Review*, *75*, 421–436.

Shreve, S. E. (2004). *Stochastic calculus for finance II: continuous-time models*. Springer Science & Business Media. doi:10.1007/978-1-4757-4296-1

Sun, M. (2016). *Modeling volatility using high-frequency data* (Unpublished doctoral dissertation). UCLA, Los Angeles, CA.

Todorov, T. (2009). Estimation of continuous-time stochastic volatility models with jumps using high-frequency data. *Journal of Econometrics*, *148*(2), 131–148. doi:10.1016/j.jeconom.2008.10.005

Whang, D. (2012). *Volatility at High Frequency* (Unpublished doctoral dissertation). UCLA, Los Angeles, CA.

Yan, S. (2017). *Estimating stochastic volatility within a trading day* (Unpublished doctoral dissertation). UCLA, Los Angeles, CA.

Zhang, F. (2010). The effect of high-frequency trading on stock volatility and price discovery. *SSRN eLibrary*.

Zhang, L. (2006). Efficient estimation of stochastic volatility using noisy observations: A multi-scale approach. *Bernoulli*, *12*(6), 1019–1043. doi:10.3150/bj/1165269149

Zhang, L. (2011). Estimating covariation: Epps effect, microstructure noise. *Journal of Econometrics*, *160*(1), 33–47. doi:10.1016/j.jeconom.2010.03.012

ENDNOTES

1 In this chapter, volatility and variance will be used interchangeably.

2 In statistics, weak stationarity means the mean and auto-covariance of the process do not vary with respect to time.

3 A Brownian motion W has the following properties (Shreve, 2004): 1) $W(0) = 0$ 2) With probability 1, the function $t \rightarrow W(t)$ is continuous in t 3) $W(t)$ has stationary, independent increments 4) The increment $W(t + s) - W(t)$ follows a Normal distribution with mean 0 and variance s.

4 In a Poisson process, the probability of a random variable $N(t)$ being equal to n is given by $P\{N(t) = n\} = \frac{(\lambda t)^n}{n!} e^{-\lambda t}$. In the calculation, $n = 0$, $\lambda = 12$, and $t = 1$

5 More discussion can be found in Chapter 7 of Aït-Sahalia and Jacod (2014) and Part II of Anderson and Benzoni (2009).

6 Even more research papers on daily volatility estimation can be found at the Oxford-Man Institute of Quantitative Finance Realized library: https://realized.oxford-man.ox.ac.uk/research/literature

7 The stock market opens at 9:30AM and closes at 4PM, so in total we have 6.5 hours (or 23,400 seconds equivalently) open for trade.

8 In Figure 3(a), 3(b) and 3(c), a trading day is divided into 23,400 seconds and "time" indicates which second in the day since the market opens. In Figure 3(d), since RV is measured at every 100 seconds, "time" indicates which 100-second in the day since the market opens.

9 For a box plot, the horizontal line within the box refers to the median. The upper and lower sides of the box indicate the upper and lower quantiles of the distribution. The isolated points above the "whiskers" indicate the outliers.

10 Source from Ellickson et al. (2018).

11 Here the asymptotic variance/covariance means variance/covariance at infinite sampling frequency.

12 A moment condition is an equation between theoretic moments and data implied moments which is usually a deterministic function of model parameters. Moment is the general term for statistical measures of the data shape. For example, the first moment is the mean and second moment of a distribution is the variance.

13 Method of Moments refers to the parameter estimation procedure by solving the moment conditions. Method of moments usually uses linear moment conditions. GMM deals with nonlinear moment conditions as well. For more knowledge on GMM, please see Hayashi (2000).

14 The idea behind regime-switching model is that volatility is usually fairly consistent (mild), and occasionally very high (i.e., at market crash). At different regimes, not only does the volatility differ in magnitude, but the behavior of volatility is different as well.

15 Refers to prices follow the "no-arbitrage" principle.

16 These assumptions include noises are autocorrelated or stationary with zero means and constant variance

17 Ensemble learning is a machine learning paradigm where multiple learners are trained to solve the same problem. Ordinary machine learning approaches try to learn only one hypothesis from the training data at a time.

18 Instead of estimating the Heston model daily, this exercise pools intraday day data to a 5-day week and estimates the Heston model. A Heston model is significant when all of its parameters are statistically significant and model specification test is passed with significance.

19 Please see Blumenthal and Getoor (1961) for more details. The index equals 0 if jump activity is finite; otherwise, jump activity is infinite.

20 More discussions on jump detection with noises present can be found in Chapter 7 of Aït-Sahalia and Jacod (2014).

21 In econometrics and time series analysis, the Epps effect, named after T. W. Epps, is the phenomenon that the empirical correlation between the returns of two different stocks decreases with the length of the interval for which the price changes are measured. The phenomenon is caused by non-synchronous/ asynchronous trading.

22 More discussions about the term structure of variance swaps and their use for investments can be found in Egloff, Leippold and Wu (2010).

Chapter 7
Algorithmic Machine Learning for Prediction of Stock Prices

Mirza O. Beg
National University of Computer and Emerging Sciences, Pakistan

Mubashar Nazar Awan
National University of Computer and Emerging Sciences, Pakistan

Syed Shahzaib Ali
National University of Computer and Emerging Sciences, Pakistan

ABSTRACT

Stock markets and relevant entities generate enormous amounts of data on a daily basis and are accessible from various channels such as stock exchange, economic reviews, and employer monetary reports. In recent times, machine learning techniques have proven to be very helpful in making better trading decisions. Machine learning algorithms use complex logic to observe and learn the behavior of stocks using historical data which can be used to predict future movements of the stock. Technical indicators such as rolling mean, momentum, and exponential moving average are calculated to convert the data into meaningful information. Furthermore, this information can be used to build machine learning prediction models that learn different patterns in the data and make future predictions for accurate financial forecasting. Additional factors that are being used for stock prediction include social media influences and daily news on trading stocks. Considering these qualitative and quantitative features at the same time result in improved prediction models.

DOI: 10.4018/978-1-5225-7805-5.ch007

INTRODUCTION

Machine Learning refers to a concept in which a machine has been programmed to learn specific patterns from historical data using powerful algorithms and make predictions in future based on the patterns it learnt. Machine learning is a branch of Artificial Intelligence (AI), the term proposed in 1959 by Arthur Samuel who defined it as the ability of computers or machines to learn new rules and concepts from data without being explicitly programmed.

This idea has stretched out its effect to the financial markets because of the rapid and revolutionary advancements in Artificial Intelligence (AI) and Machine Learning (ML). Since last two decades, markets have turned out to be more inclined towards high frequency trading as compared to traditional trading schemes. Stock markets generates huge amount of information on daily basis which can be accessible from various channels such as stock exchange, economic reviews, employer monetary reports etc. Therefore, it is helpful to analyze market data and get useful insights about securities to make better trading decisions. In the past, several studies have been done to predict stock prices. Different natural inspired algorithms have been proposed for stock prediction. Genetic algorithms have been studied with neural networks (Fang et. al, 2014). Different hybrid evolutionary algorithms have been proposed (Bisoi and Dash, 2014). Five algorithms Flower Pollination Algorithm (FPA), Bat algorithm (BA), Modified Cuckoo Search (MCS), Artificial Bee Colony(ABC), and Particle Swarm Optimization (PSO) were proposed. These algorithms selected the best parameters to train and optimize Least Square- Support Vector Machine (LS-SVM). The problem with those algorithms was that they couldn't overcome the overfitting and were falling in local minima (Hegazy, Soliman, and Salam, 2015). Not only the statistical data of stocks but also the textual information can make huge effects on stocks. News articles have been used with the stock prices for prediction (Li, Xiaodong et. al, 2014). Twitter sentiment analysis has been done on stocks (Ranco et. al, 2015). By incorporating the textual information with the financial information also gives better results than models which uses financial information only (Lee, Surdeanu, MacCartney, and Jurafsky, 2014). Topic modeling has been studied where topic based sentiment analysis was done by using LDA tool (Nguyen and Shirai, 2015). The events occuring in the real world can make significant effects on stock markets. Event driven stock price prediction has been studied in detail where the information about the events was extracted from the web-scale data (Ding, Zhang, Liu, and Duan, 2014). Deep learning models have proposed by using news text (Ding, Zhang, Liu, and Duan, 2015). Following the events, the news on media and public sentiments can also change the behaviour of investors and can have great influence over stock market (Li, Qing et. al, 2014). Multiple classifiers have been trained for short term and long term stock price prediction by using the historical data stocks (open, high, low & close prices) ((Patel, Shah, Thakkar, and Kotecha, 2015) Ballings, Van den Poel, Hespeels, and Gryp, 2015).

Hedge fund traders are now more biased towards the programs that will take over their daily trading business in order to maximize returns. Quantitative hedge funds have been developing and creating different machine learning based algorithms to make trading decisions. AI based programs make statistical analysis for a security, become aware of buying and selling correlations, examine market developments, and make trading decisions based on the overall findings. As the quantity of data increases, these prediction models can enhance their overall performance through the years. That is what makes them a smart bet for stock marketplace traders seeking to take emotion out of the equation. Over the time, approaches have been enhanced, which uses sophisticated and efficient algorithms to parse the content of news feed and calculating their impact on particular company's stock price. As for a long term trading decision, news about the particular security can significantly impact its price over the time. Machine learning algorithms can be used to analyze sentiments from that information and calculate its impact on a security.

It has likewise been persuasive in instructing personal computers to drive autosand in addition, interpreting languages, and now, investors are depending on this technology to make better trading decisions. Certainly that Artificial Intelligence based trading system are making significant advances towards accomplishing the objectives and this has truly changed how we see the stock trading system.

As described earlier, there are several algorithms which has been used in the area of stock prediction, it includes Naive Bayes', Linear Regression, K-Nearest Neighbors (KNN), Neural Network, Linear Discriminant Analysis (LDA), Support Vector Machine (SVM), and Random Forest. The US stocks data has been used for the training and testing purposes. Random forest was simply the best classifier in all the previous works.

In this chapter, there is a technical analysis for prediction and trading for a shorter period (i.e. 3,4, or 5 days) instead of long term predictions. Different technical indicators has been explained for short term predictions and machine learning algorithms have been trained to predict the 5th day closing price of stocks.

DATA EXPLOITATION

Data Collection

There are plenty of sources available on the internet which provides historical data of stocks like Google finance, Yahoo finance or Quandl. They provide very easy way to pull out cleaned and formatted data either manually or by API calls through code. Data contains following attributes or columns (in days interval):

- **Date:** The date on which the information is recorded.
- **Open:** The starting price (in US Dollars) at which the trading open.
- **High:** The highest price at which the stock traded in a day.
- **Low:** The lowest price at which the stock traded in a day.
- **Volume:** Total amount of stocks traded in a day.
- **Close:** The last price at which the stock traded.
- **Adjusted Close:** Little bit different from closing price, price adjusted after stock splits or dividend payments.

Data Sources

Google Finance

Google Finance can be used to get the free historical data for most of the stocks in several frequencies in which one minute being the lowest time frame. Source [1] can be used to get the data from google finance.

- PERIOD indicate the frequency or interval (in seconds). For example, for 5 minute interval, its value should be 300 (i.e. 5 * 60)
- DAYS refers to the total number of past p days for which the data is needed.
- TICKER is the symbol of the stock (i.e. for Apple stock it should be 'AAPL')

Yahoo Finance

Yahoo Finance is another very useful resource to get historical data for several stocks in different intervals, one minute being the lowest. Source [2] can be used to download data from yahoo finance.

Finam

Finam is a website which provides useful historical data for limited but popular set of stocks. Several months of data can be downloaded even for the lowest interval or time frame (i.e. one-minute). Source [3]can be used to download the historical data from finam.

Data Preprocessing

As the matter of fact that financial data is really effective for financial analysis and research. It is considered to be perfectly recorded and formatted data as stored by computers. It's an assumption that the data is accurately and consistently recorded minute by minute without having missing data points. Actually, the stock price is not the same on all the exchanges, for a particular stock, it may be traded at NYSE (New York Stock Exchange), NASDAQ, and BATS at the same time with different prices. The actual data is made up from the combination of all different data sources and providers. The other thing is not every stock trade all the time, sometime they quit existing or trading and there is no data available for that time period. So, it should be kept in mind that data can be faulty or inconsistent containing missing or null values. Therefore, after collecting or gathering data from any reliable source, it must be checked and corrected for these errors otherwise noisy or inconsistent data would lead to a bad prediction model because the model highly depends on the quality of the data it has been trained on.

Dealing With Missing Values

As explained above, data may contain missing or null values. As this is a purely time series based challenge, it is important to deal with the missing values. Below figure shows some missing values of a stock price (i.e. no trading occurred) for some intervals.

Figure 1. Stock data with missing values

Now the challenge is to fill these values in such a way that should not negatively affect the prediction model.

Intuitively, one can think of interpolating the missing values, the fact is there is no trading done and price available for that range. Therefore, it is unwise to interpolate any random value to fill null values because doing so will have a huge negative impact on the calculation of technical indicators (Rolling mean, Daily returns, Bollinger bands etc.) which can directly affect the prediction model as it would be based on self-made data points.

The best and safe way to fill these values are to use last known values as it reflects what was going on with the data.

There are two steps involved known as forward fill and backward fill. As shown in the above figure, red line represents forward fill approach. All the missing prices are filled with the last known price for that stock. Similarly, green line at the start indicates backward fill operation, which eventually uses the actual starting known price to fill unknown backward values. These should be applied in a sequence such that forward fill has to done before backward fill.

Feature Engineering

One of the most important step for any good prediction model is to generate artificial features from existing features or data. Adding relevant information to the model decreases the chance of predicting incorrect prediction. A number of statistical measures can be computed using historical data which are called technical indicators.

Figure 2. Forward/backward approach to fill missing values

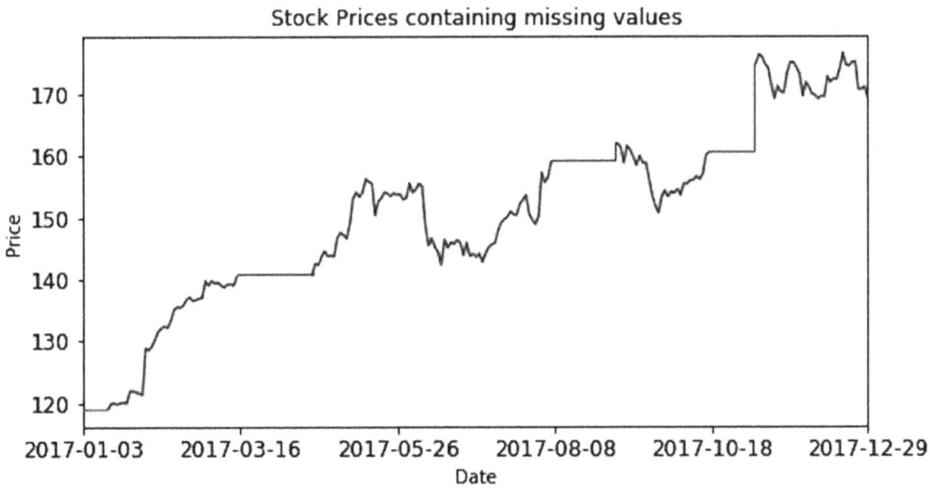

These indicators are heuristics and provides hint to buy or sell a particular stock. Use of multiple indicators at the same time is more effective than using a single indicator at a time. Also, use of technical analysis for prediction and trading for a shorter period (i.e. 3, 4, or 5 days) of time is more reliable than predicting for longer term (e.g. 5, 7, or 12 months). As over long term prediction of a stock price movement is more dependent on stock's fundamental analysis like company worth, market value, global events etc. Hence, long term analysis depends on a lot of factors which also changes over time and involves some complex decisions which should be taken by humans. On the other hand, short term prediction and high frequency trading can be done by computers by using machine learning techniques. Some useful technical indicators for short term prediction are explained as follows:

Daily Returns

It is considered to be the most effective and important statistical indicator used in financial analysis. It is simply the measurement which indicates the change in the price of the stock on t-th day compared to (t-1)-th day. It is calculated as follows:

$$\textit{Daily Return}\left(t\right) = \frac{\left(price\_at\_t\right) - \left(price\_at\left(t-1\right)\right)}{price\_at\left(t-1\right)} \tag{1}$$

Price at day t represents the t-th day adjusted closing price of the stock whereas price at day (t-1) indicates the last or previous day adjusted closing price of the stock. For example, if the current price of the stock is $110 and the last day closing price was $100, by putting the values in the above equation, it results in 0.1 which is equal to 10% percent. According to this, there is a +10% change (rise) in the stock price relative to previous day.

Above figure shows daily rate of change for the Apple's stock over the year of 2017.

Some other statistical measures like mean, standard deviation (how far individual measurements deviate from mean) and kurtosis (curved arching) of daily returns can also be useful for analysis. The figure below shows that how many values of daily return falls in a particular range. The mean, standard deviation and kurtosis values are 0.15, 1.12 and 5.29 respectively. In simple words, for the year 2017 average daily return of apple's stock is approximately 0.15%.

Kurtosis comes from a geek word that means curved or arching. It is the measure of extreme values on the tail of the distribution in which small or large excursions along the tail is indicated by negative (skinny tails) and positive (fat tails) kurtosis

Figure 3. Daily change in APPL's stock of year 2017

Figure 4. Distribution of daily return

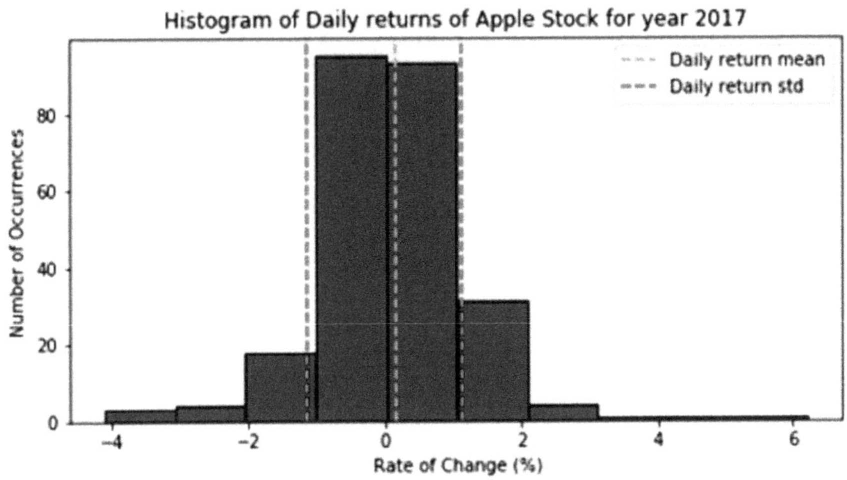

respectively. It is considered to be fat tails (positive kurtosis) when there are frequently more occurrences on the tails as compared if that was a Gaussian or normal distribution. Similarly, skinny tails (negative kurtosis) when there are less occurrences on tails. In the above figure, as the kurtosis has a positive value of 5.29. So, it is defined as fat tails or positive kurtosis.

Momentum

It is the measure of the stock's price strength or weakness over some time interval. Momentum is similar to the daily return except the one day interval is replaced with the n-th day's interval. Such that, the price change (return) is calculated as the percentage difference between the price at (t-th) day and the price at (t-n)-Th day.

$$\boldsymbol{Momentum}\left(\boldsymbol{t}\right) = \frac{\left(\boldsymbol{priceatt}\right) - \left(\boldsymbol{priceat}\left(\boldsymbol{t} - \boldsymbol{n}\right)\right)}{\boldsymbol{priceat}\left(\boldsymbol{t} - 1\right)} \tag{2}$$

Rolling Mean (Simple Moving Average (SMA)

It is the average adjusted closing price of the stock over some time frame. E.g. n day's simple moving average (SMA) is the mean value of last n day's closing price with respect to t-th day. Intuitive decisions can be made by looking into the pattern of rolling mean that is how much the actual price deviates from the moving average at particular instance creating an opportunity to buy or sell.

$$\boldsymbol{RollingMean}\left(\boldsymbol{t}\right) = \frac{\left(\boldsymbol{priceatt} - 1\right) + \left(\boldsymbol{priceatt} - 2\right) \ldots + \left(\boldsymbol{priceatt} - \boldsymbol{n}\right)}{\boldsymbol{n}} \tag{3}$$

The below figure shows the rolling mean or simple moving average for the 20 days (n=20) of window. Unlike the spikes shown for the price value of AAPL, the movement of the stock price can be easily perceived in rolling mean due to its smoothness.

Weighted Moving Average (WMA)

It is similar to the simple moving average (rolling mean) except the price values are given some weights on the basis of their importance that is why it is called weighted moving average. It is a weighted average or mean taken for last n prices. Usually, most recent prices are given more weight since they are significantly more important. It can be calculated as follows:

Figure 5. Rolling mean / simple moving average (SMA)

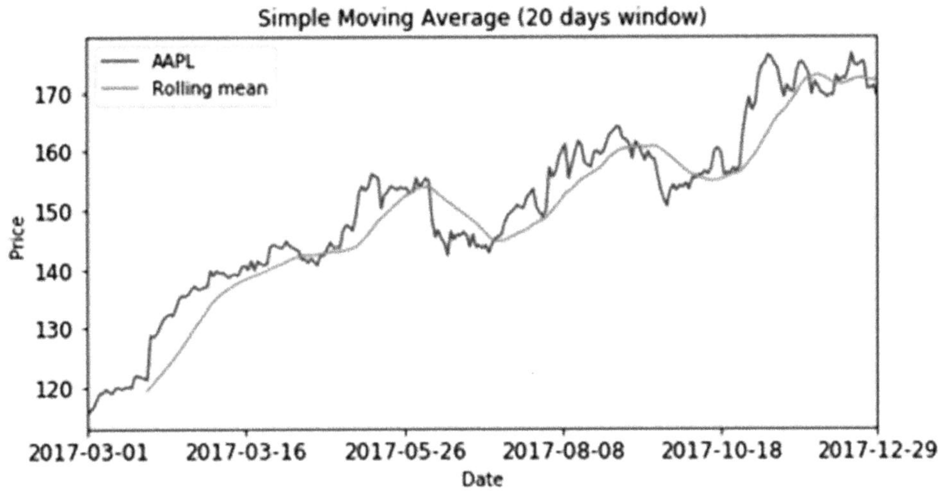

$$WMA(t) = \frac{(W*(priceatt-1)) + ((W-1)*(priceatt-2))\ldots n}{n} \tag{4}$$

In the above equation, W indicates the weight assigned to each value of the price. It must be noted that there is a difference of 1.0 between two consecutive weights which means the rate of decrease is consistent.

Exponential Moving Average (EMA)

Unlike the weighted moving average where the decreasing rate of weights are consistent, in exponential moving average (EMA) rate of decrease in weights are exponential between two consecutive prices. This technique shows quicker behavior than simple moving average because more weight is assigned to recent prices and less to past prices. Exponential weighted values for prices can be calculated as follows:

$$EMA(t) = ((closingprice) - EMA(t-1)) * \left(\frac{2}{n+1}\right) + EMA(t-1) \tag{5}$$

In the above equation, n represents the time frame window for which the average is be calculated and EMA (t-1) is the exponential moving average of previous day or record.

Figure 6. Exponential moving average (EMA)

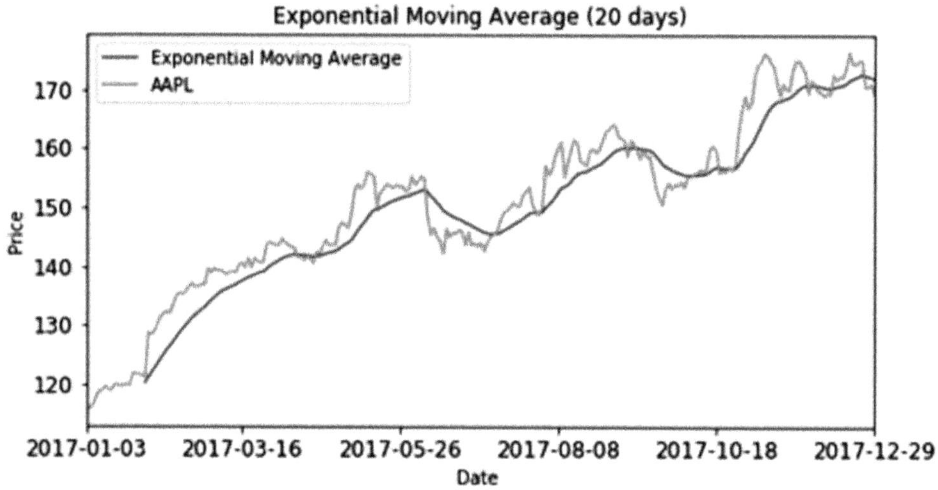

Return Moving Average

It is the measure of average return value (price change) over some interval which means n days return moving average is the mean value of last 'n days return' with respect to t-th day.

$$\textit{ReturnMovingAverage}(t) = \frac{\textit{Return}(t-1) + \textit{Return}(t-2)\ldots + \textit{Return}(t-n)}{n} \tag{6}$$

Bollinger Bands®

How much deviation from the rolling mean indicates buy/sell signal. To measure that, John Bollinger proposed a technical indicator called Bollinger bands® in 1980s which consists of two standard deviations above and below the simple moving average. For N-window moving average, an upper band should be calculated as K times N-window standard deviation added to the N-window moving average (MA + Kσ).Similarly, the lower band is defined as K times N-window standard deviation subtracted to the N-window moving average (MA - Kσ). The default value of K is 2 and N is 20, but can be changed according to the requirement and behavior of the pattern.

Figure 7. Bollinger (upper and lower) bands of Apple's stock for year 2017

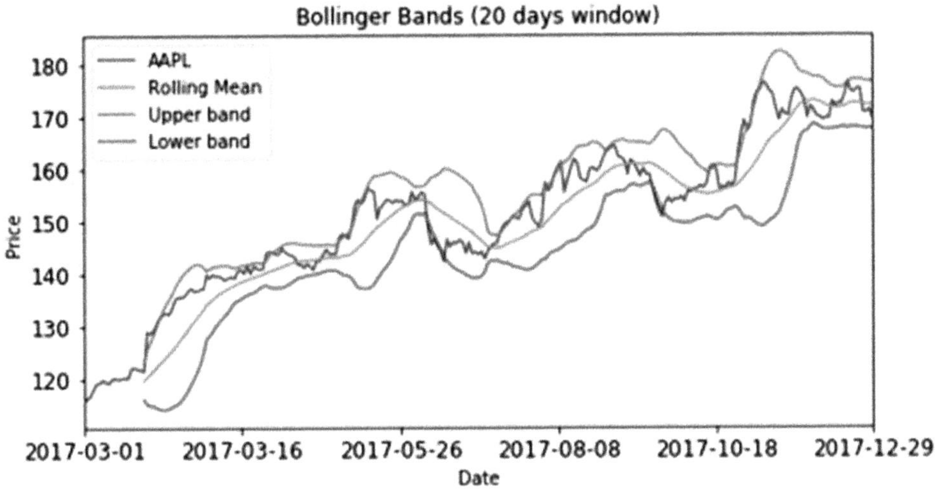

The above figure shows the visual representation of the Bollinger bands. Changing the window size and the value of K will also change the behavior of the upper and lower bands. It may be notice that some starting data points of rolling mean, lower and upper bands are not visualized, it is because of the window size which is 20. When calculating these indicators, there must be an equal number of preceding data points as the window size. People use these indicators to buy or sell stocks, the intuition is when the stock price hits or overlaps the lower band value, it is potentially considered to be the buying time as it might rise up again. Similarly, selling time is when the stock price value approaches to upper band value. But, one should not rely only on this and start trading, as there are some other factors involved which should not be over looked (e.g. sharp ratio).

Relative Strength Index (RSI)

It is one of the most popular momentum based oscillator developed by J. Welles Wilder which measures the magnitude and velocity of recent price movements. Its value oscillates between 0 and 100 which shows the trading trend for a particular security. Usually, the security/stock is considered overbought when its RSI value surpasses above 70 and oversold when the value is below 30. It is calculated as follows:

$$RSI\left(t\right) = 100 - \left(100 \; / \left(1 + \frac{Ndaysaverageupwardreturn}{Ndaysaveragedownwardreturn}\right)\right) \tag{7}$$

Where N is the total number of days or the time frame for which the value of RSI is to be calculated.

Stochastic Oscillator (%K)

It is another momentum based oscillator developed by George C in late 1950's which measures the closing trend with respect to the range of previous high and low prices over a specific period of time. In general theory, when the market trend is upward, the closing price are often near high price whereas when the market trend is downward, closing prices are near low. The formula for Stochastic Oscillator is as follows:

$$\%K(t) = 100 * \frac{(ClosingPrice(t-1) - L(N))}{(H(N) - L(N))} \tag{8}$$

In the above equation, L (N) and H(N) represents the lowest and highest price recorded for previous N days respectively.

Figure 8. Relative strength index (RSI) of Apple's stock for the year 2017

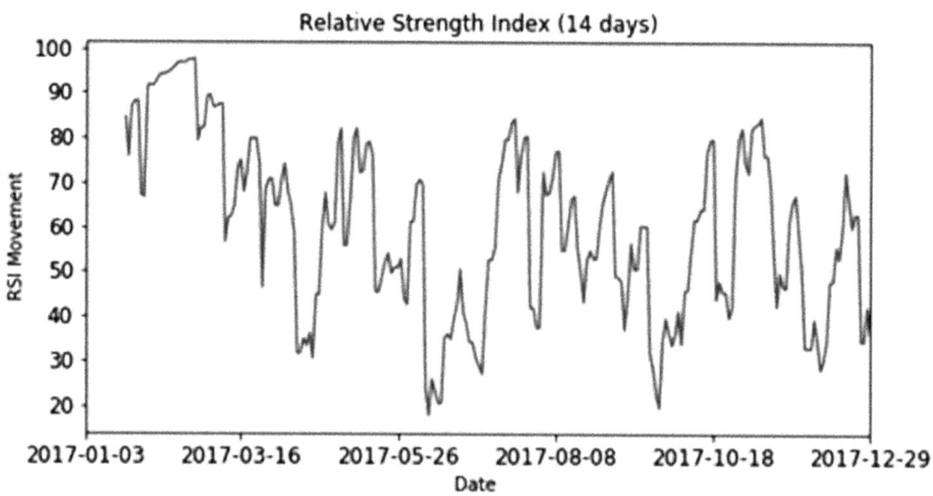

Figure 9. Stochastic oscillator %K of Apple's stock for the year 2017

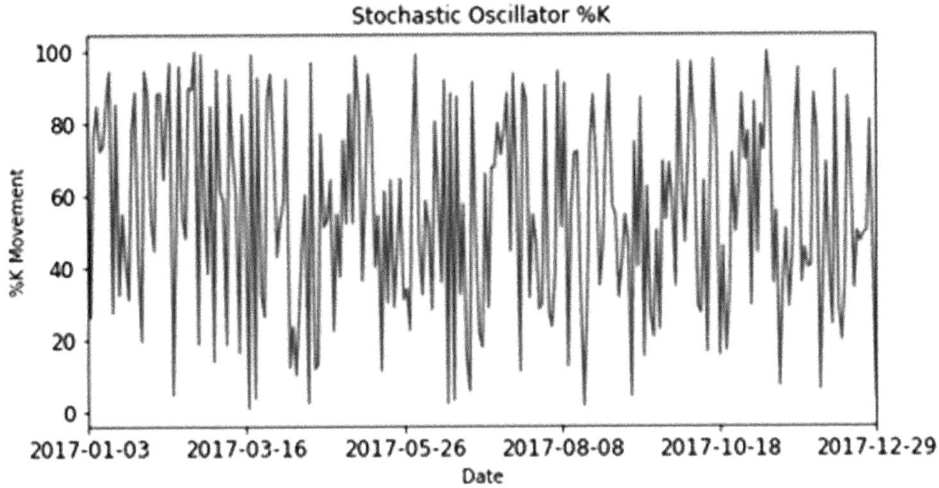

Stochastic Oscillator (%D)

It is simply the moving average (i.e. simple, weighted or exponential) of %k for D-period (time range). Usually, the three period (D=3) moving average is used to observe the market trend for buy/sell signal.

$$\%\boldsymbol{D}\left(\boldsymbol{t}\right)=\frac{\%\boldsymbol{k}\left(\boldsymbol{t}-1\right)+\%\boldsymbol{k}\left(\boldsymbol{t}-2\right)\ldots+\%\boldsymbol{K}\left(\boldsymbol{t}-\boldsymbol{D}\right)}{\boldsymbol{D}} \tag{9}$$

Moving Average Convergence Divergence (MACD)

Another momentum oscillator developed by Gerald Appel, is calculated by subtracting the longer exponential moving average (i.e. 26 days) from shorter exponential moving average (i.e. 12 days). This way, it combines the following trend of both long and short term momentum. As the name implies, it identities the convergence and divergence of two moving averages, it converges when these two move towards each other and diverges when they move away from each other. MACD oscillates above and below the 0 for which the value of MACD is positive when the shorter EMA value is greater than the longer EMA. Positive MACD indicates that the momentum is upward. On the other hand, negative MACD indicates the downward momentum such that the value of shorter EMA diverges below the longer EMA.

$$MACD(t) = EMA(t-12) - EMA(t-26) \tag{10}$$

Number of days for shorter and longer moving averages can be varied according to the trading goals.

Accumulation/Distribution (A/D) Oscillator

An Oscillator developed by Marc Chaikin to identity the pattern of the money flow in a security. It uses stock price and its volume to analyze the supply and demand behavior of investors for a particular stock. It identifies the buying (accumulation) or selling (distribution) trend of investors by calculating the close location value and then multiplying it with corresponding volume for a given range. It is formulated as follows:

$$A/D(t) = \frac{\left(\left(ClosePrice - L(N)\right) - \left(H(N) - ClosePrice\right)\right)}{\left(H(N) - L(N)\right)} * Vol(N) \tag{11}$$

In above equation, L (N) and H (N) represents the lowest and highest price of last N prices. Similarly, Vol (N) indicates the total volume for a given range. The direction of A/D line indicates the buying or selling pressure for that security in a market. If the direction is upward, the chances of buying pressure prevails whereas a selling pressure for the downward movement.

Commodity Channel Index (CCI)

A technical indicator developed by Donald Lambert which indicates about the ending of existing trend or a start of a new trend. It measures the current price levels relative to the moving average over the given period of time. CCI value is high when the prices are much higher as compared to their average price and its value is relatively low when prices are low with respect to their averages. It can also be used to identify the overbought and oversold behavior of the stock in a market. The value of CCI can be calculates as follows:

$$TypicalPrice(t) = \frac{High(t) + Low(t) + Close(t)}{3} \tag{12}$$

$$CCI(t) = \frac{TypicalPrice(t) - NPeriodSMAofTypicalPrice}{NPeriodStandarddeviationofTypicalPrice} \tag{13}$$

For a given range (i.e. days, weeks, months), Commodity Channel Index can be calculated using above equation in which N represents the time period (range). High reading values of CCI (e.g. above +100) indicates the start of an upward movement whereas low readings (e.g. below -100) indicates the start of downward trend of a stock.

BUILDING ALGORITHMIC MODELS

Data Sampling for Algorithm

Before applying any algorithms on data it is very important to split the data into at least two samples called training and testing/validation. Training set is used to train the model which learns the patterns from data whereas validation set is used evaluate the performance of the model for unseen examples. If the algorithm is tested over the same data it was trained on, it would not be properly evaluated, as it already goes through all the exact training samples. The algorithm should be tested on the data which it has not seen yet. The process of evaluating model for test set is called out of sample testing.

Creating a Training Set

Independent Variables (X)

These are the input parameters like rolling mean, momentum, exponential moving average etc. computed using historical data. These are eventually the basis for prediction model, algorithm tries to learn the behavior of depended variable (i.e. rise/fall price signal) with respect to different independent variables.

Dependent Variable (Y)

The output parameter is called the dependent or predictor variable. In case of stock movement or price prediction, the dependent variable is either the rise/fall signal or the stock price of the future.

Creating a training set purely depends on the requirement of the prediction problem. To create a model which predicts the next day price movement of a stock, the training data for the machine learning algorithm should be structured in a way that the input parameters (i.e. daily returns, simple moving averages, momentum etc.) of current day should be aligned against the dependent variable Y (i.e. daily return (rise/fall signal)) of next day.

Example

Consider the following sample for training data.

In order to create a training set and dependent variable for the prediction of stock movement for next day. The daily return column values has to be shifted one place above.

Creating a Validation Set

Test set does not contain dependent variable Y, in fact this set is used to predict its value. Therefore, there is no preprocessing like training set is required on the test set other than calculating the predictor variables (e.g. Bollinger bands, daily return, simple moving average etc.)

Table 1.

Date	Close (X1)	Rolling Mean (X2)	Momentum (X3)	Daily Return (X4)
June, 4 2018	46.52	48.03	-5.03	-0.41 - Fall
June, 5 2018	45.37	47.44	-5.91	-2.49 - Fall
June, 6 2018	46.96	46.96	-4.81	+3.50 - Rise
June, 7 2018	46.91	46.38	-5.81	-0.10 - Fall

Table 2.

Date	Close (X1)	Rolling Mean (X2)	Momentum (X3)	Daily Return (X4)	Next Day Change (Y)
June, 4 2018	46.52	48.03	-5.03	-0.41 - Fall	Fall
June, 5 2018	45.37	47.44	-5.91	-2.49 - Fall	Rise
June, 6 2018	46.96	46.96	-4.81	+3.50 - Rise	Fall

Machine Learning Algorithms

This is the core step for which all the above processing have been done such that data collection, preprocessing, feature generation, and data sampling. There are several machine learning algorithms developed for different type of problems which is whether the problem is supervised or unsupervised learning. Supervised learning is the approach of creating a model using an algorithm in which it learns to map an input (X) to an output (Y) using historical data. On the other hand, unsupervised learning models are the one which create groups or clusters for similar set of items. The majority of machine learning problems are based on supervised learning.

Machine Learning model refers to a model artifact which is created in the process of learning algorithm using historical or training data. Regression and classification models are based on supervised machine learning. In regression, model predicts the future numerical (e.g. stock price) value (Y) given a set of parameters (X). On the other hand, classification model predicts the categorical value (e.g. stock movement rise/fall) based on the input data. A number of different models can be created using different machine learning algorithms.

Linear Regressions

An algorithm which finds the best value of parameters for an equation to fit the training data. For the simple linear approach, the equation is as follows:

$$y = mx + c \tag{14}$$

As it can be noted that it is the equation of line in which m and c are the parameters for which the algorithm finds the best value considering the input x (i.e. features). Whereas, y is the output/depended variable (e.g. next day stock price). It is also known as parametric modeling. For a parametric approach, there is no need for a trained model to use the historical data while prediction, as it has already learnt the best parameters for an equation to predict a value. But, the model should be retrain and update its parameter values when the new or additional training data is gathered or added.

Pros:

- Easy to understand and implement.
- Useful to find the relationship between variables.

Cons:

- Sensitive to the anomalies or noise in a data set (i.e. outliers).
- Under perform for the non-linear data set (i.e. relationship between dependent and independent variables are not linear).

K Nearest Neighbor (KNN)

It is one of the most popular machine learning technique which has an instance based and data centric approach. The algorithm predicts the Y value by taking a vote of its 'K' nearest neighbors. For example if the value of k is 3, for any new test example b, it computes the distance of b from all the training samples (by using x values) and select Y values of 3 nearest samples. Further, the maximum occurring Y value out of those 3 is selected for example b. Unlike, linear regression where the data is not being used after the parameter finding. KNN uses or consult the historical data for every prediction it makes. This approach is hard to apply when there are large number of data points as each data point needs to be considered while prediction. But, there is no need to train a model again since it does not require any parameters (i.e. m and c) like regression based model.

Pros:

- Implementation of Algorithm is not complex.
- Easy to add new features
- Can also handle Multi-class problems

Cons:

- High computation cost for large set of data.
- As it is a distance based learning, which type of distance function should be used can be a problem to consider.
- Need to ascertain the value of K.

Decision Tree

As the name suggests, the model is based on a structure like a tree. A prediction is made by traversing the nodes of the tree one by one. On every node, there is a calculation involve on the input values (x) which eventually approaches to an outcome. A model is formed by the training algorithm in such a way that the features or input parameters which are highly correlated with an output are placed on the upper node of the tree.

Pros:

- Easily consider discrete and categorical features at the same time.
- Handle both regression and classification problems.
- Visualization and interpretation is easy.

Cons:

- Likely to over-fit as the depth of tree increases.
- Under perform for diagonal decision boundaries.

Random Forest Classifier

It is one of the most powerful algorithm which works just like the decision tree but instead of one tree, it is composed of several decision trees (weak learners) which are trained or created on random chunk of data from training set. The predictions of several models are combined to give a final result or output. It is called random because for every model a chunk of data is randomly selected from training set, further it also randomly select the limited set of features or nodes (i.e. $n = \sqrt{Total\ number\ of\ features}$) to create a decision tree for that model.

The algorithm uses a concept called bagging which is defined as creating several models from same algorithm (e.g. Support Vector Machine, K- Nearest Neighbour, Neural Net etc.) trained on a subset of randomly selected training data (known as bags of data). For a test sample prediction, all the individual predictions from models are averaged together to get the final prediction. It also helps to reduce high variance (over-fitting) while keeping the possession of bias (under-fitting).

Pros:

- Easily consider discrete and categorical features at the same time.
- Handle both regression and classification problems.
- Smartly handle multiple correlated features.
- Reduce variance and over fitting due to decorrelation between trees.

Cons:

- Likely to over-fit when the number of trees increases in case of boosted trees.
- Visualization and interpretation is not easy.

AdaBoost Classifier

AdaBoost which is a short form for adaptive boosting. Unlike the bagging approach used by random forest algorithm, it uses an adaptive boosting concept which is defined as a set of several subsequent weak learners (models) of same algorithm. Each weak learner model tries to correct the misclassifications of previous model. Thus, creating a strong learning model from several weak learners.

Ensemble Models

Combination of several algorithms for the purpose to predict something is called ensembles. It is not an algorithm but a collection of different weak learner models (i.e. KNN, Linear Regression, Random Forest etc.) combined together to build a single model. The final prediction value is calculated by using the output value of all the models. For a regression problem, the prediction value is calculated by taking the average value of the prediction of all models. Similarly, voting based approach is used for a classification problem. Use of ensemble learners often reduces the chance of over-fitting as the output is not biased on a single model or algorithm. It also minimizes the overall absolute error and improve accuracy. It should be noted that Random Forest and AdaBoost are also ensembles because instead of using several algorithms for different models, they uses the same algorithm with random data for different models.

Model Evaluation Metrics

Models are evaluated for their correctness of predictions. It is one of the major step to check how accurate the model is for future predictions of a problem. There are many evaluation metrics available for different nature of problems. Accuracy measure and Root mean square error (RMSE) are the most popular metrics for classification and regression problems respectively. In case of over-fitting, in sample (training set) error decreases and out of sample (test set) error increases.

Accuracy

In case of classification models, accuracy measure is used to evaluate model's perfection for predictions. It is the percentage of the number of correct predictions made by the model. For example, if a model correctly predicts 80 samples out of 100 then the accuracy of the model is 80%.

$$Accuracy = \frac{NumberofCorrectPredictions}{NumberofTotalPredictions} \times 100 \tag{15}$$

Root Mean Square Error (RMSE)

For a regression model which predicts a numeric value, RMSE can be used to evaluate a model. As the prediction value is numerical, accuracy metric would not be a good choice for a regression model because it gives an approximate prediction value for numerical inputs. Root mean square error is basically an average error of the overall predictions made by the model. It is calculate as follows:

$$RMSE = \sqrt{\frac{\sum\left(ActualValue\left(Y\right) - PredictedValue\left(Ytest\right)\right)^2}{TotalNumberofPredictions\left(N\right)}} \tag{16}$$

The equation above simply takes a squared difference of the actual and predicted value for all the predictions. Further, it computes square root of their mean. The square of a difference is taken to avoid negative values, as the error cannot be negative.

Bias and Variance in Models

When the model is trained, it is very important to analyze it for bias (over-fitting) and variance (under-fitting). Higher bias indicates that the model is performing too well for the training data but not on test data whereas high variance indicates that the model is not working well on training data as well as on test data. In other words, a highly over-fitted model tightly learns the training examples and fails for the testing sample. Whereas, an under-fitted model does not even understand the training examples properly. Therefore, an ideal model should have low bias and low variance.

It can be noticed in the above figure that when the number of parameters increases from 5, the difference between train and test error increases which indicates over-fitting of the model. On the other hand, when the number of parameters are set to 1 or 2, it is considered an under-fitted model.

Figure 10. Train/test performance sample

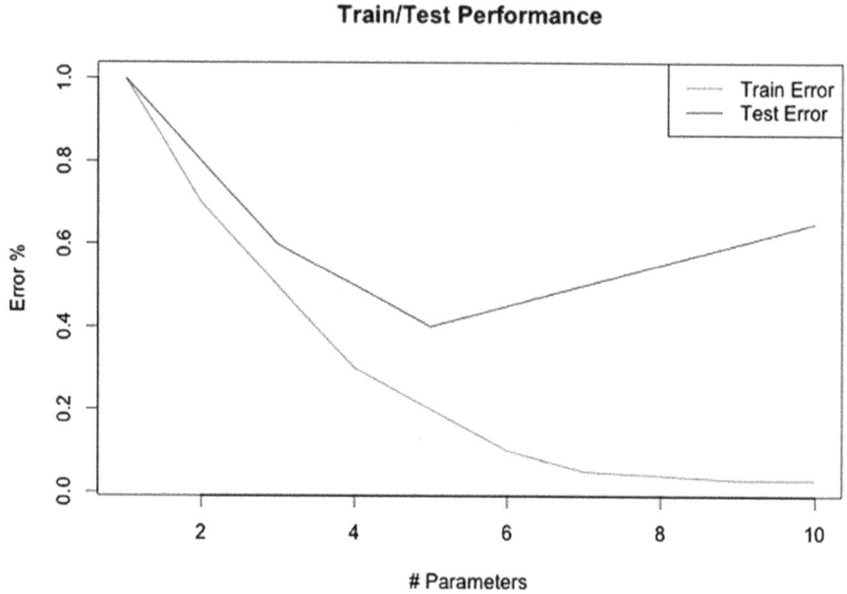

SAMPLE USE CASE

There are two different scopes in the prediction of stocks which are to predict the actual value of the stock price for the future or to predict the stock price movement (i.e. rise or fall in price) for the future. For this particular example, the goal is to predict the 5th day closing price movement of apple's stock which is a supervised learning and classification problem.

Four years (2013-2017) of apple's daily historical data was collected from yahoo finance and preprocessed before feature generation. The following additional features (technical indicators) were generated out of data to train a learning model.

The performance of some machine learning algorithms on this data are as follows:

Performance on K-Nearest Neighbors (KNN)

The algorithm is tested for its performance for different values of K and the highest accuracy (i.e. ~60%) is achieved on the test data when the value of k is set to 3. The performance of the algorithm also depends on the number of features generated and considered. It can be noted that for the training set, the accuracy of the model is 100% when the k is set to 1 that is because the testing is performed on the same data.

Table 3.

Technical Indicators
1. Rolling Mean (Simple Moving Average of 10 days)
2. Weighted Moving Average (10 days)
3. Relative Strength Index (RSI) of 10 days
4. Momentum (10 days)
5. Moving Average Convergence Divergence (MACD)
6. Stochastic K%
7. Stochastic D% (10 days)
8. Accumulation/Distribution (A/D) Oscillator (10 days)
9. Commodity Channel Index (CCI) of 10 days

Figure 11. K-nearest neighbor performance on test/train data

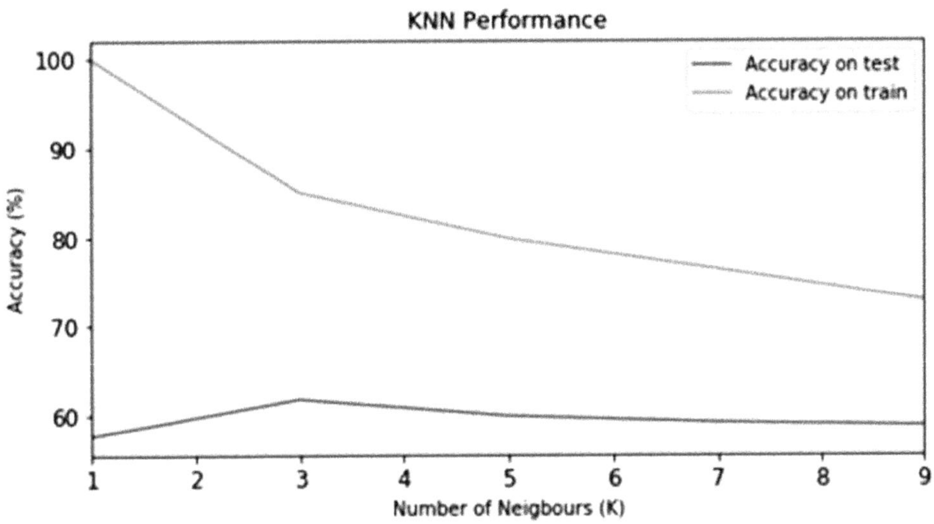

Performance on Random Forest Classifier

As compared to KNN, random forest performs slightly better when it was tested on the validation set. The performance of the model was tested on different number of trees in which the highest accuracy (i.e. ~62%) is achieved when the number of random trees were set to 160. Number of trees is a hyper parameter which vary according to the nature of the data and should be tuned with respect to training and testing data performance (i.e. low variance and bias).

Figure 12. Random forest performance on test/train data

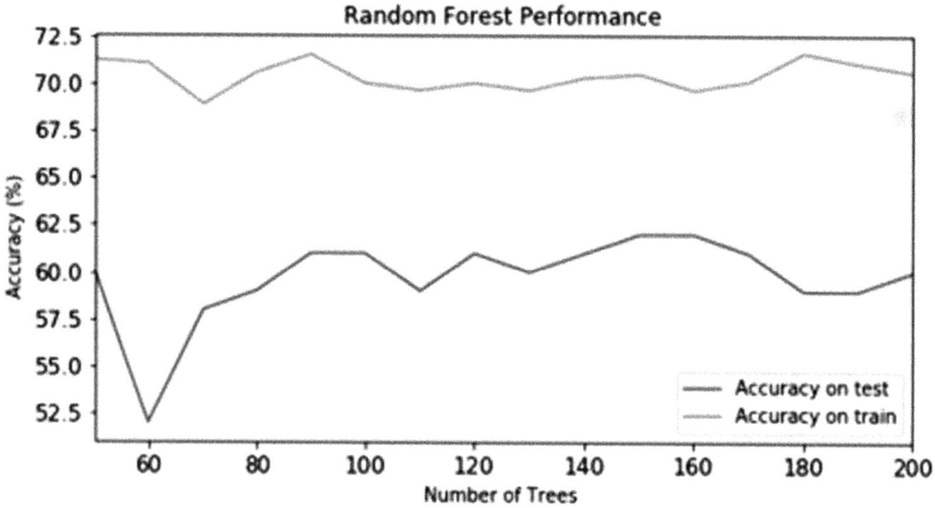

Performance on AdaBoost Classifier

The performance of AdaBoost algorithm was also tested on different number of trees and the best result (i.e. approx. 60%) on test set was achieved when the number of trees were set above 120. The algorithm does not perform better than KNN or Random Forest. This judgement is purely based on the quality of data and features generated out of historical data.

It can be noted that increasing the number of trees improve the accuracy of training set. But on the other hand, when the number of trees are increased above120. The accuracy on test set does not show much improvement which means the modelis over-fitting the training data. This behavior can be observed in AdaBoost algorithm because of its subsequent weak learner approach. Increasing the number of trees tightly learns the training set as each model (tree) tries to correct the misclassification of previous model.

FUTURE WORK

So far there has been many advancements in the field of machine learning and artificial intelligence which support and handle complex behaviors of daily stock markets. In this chapter, only technical analysis of stock market is being considered for the sake of prediction. But, there are other factors which might useful in the improvement of long term predictions. This includes the influence of social media

Figure 13. AdaBoostPerformance on test/train data

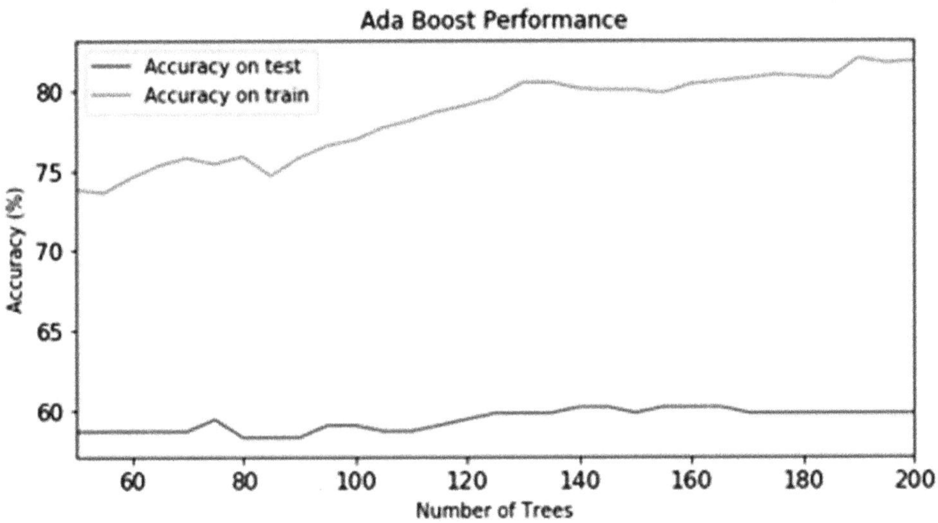

and daily news on particular security and stock market. Recently, there has been much improvement in the area of Natural Language Processing (NLP) and Deep Learning techniques. These advancements can be really helpful in calculating and interpreting the impact of daily news on particular stock. Many implementations are there on the sentiment analysis of text. But, there is a plenty of room for its improvement in the field of financial market such that calculating the exact impact of a news on a stock. Similarly, fundamental analysis is yet another technique which evaluate the intrinsic value of a stock. Considering these qualitative and quantitative features at the same time would result in the improved prediction models.

CONCLUSION

The above use case illustrate that how artificial intelligence and machine learning techniques can play significant role in stock trading. Incorporating machine learning in trading strategies can help investors and traders to capture more alpha. Over the past some years, there have been several advancements occurred in field of machine learning according to the rate of improvement in computer performance. When dealing with the complex, non-linear and dynamic behavior of financial markets the use of more sophisticated trading algorithms is necessary. In search for methods to address these weaknesses and thanks to the advances in computing and technology, research focuses on the various tools of computational intelligence. The most popular algorithms reported in literature are Logistic Regression, K-Nearest Neighbors, Neural Networks, and Support Vector Machine. Furthermore, results of predictions can be improved by analyzing the strength and weakness of the security and taking the sentiment of its information into account.

REFERENCES

Ballings, M., Van den Poel, D., Hespeels, N., & Gryp, R. (2015). Evaluating multiple classifiers for stock price direction prediction. *Expert Systems with Applications*, *42*(20), 7046–7056. doi:10.1016/j.eswa.2015.05.013

Bisoi, R., & Dash, P. K. (2014). A hybrid evolutionary dynamic neural network for stock market trend analysis and prediction using unscented Kalman filter. *Applied Soft Computing*, *19*, 41–56. doi:10.1016/j.asoc.2014.01.039

Ding, X., Zhang, Y., & Liu, T., & Duan. (2015). Deep learning for event-driven stock prediction. *IJCAI (United States)*, 2327–2333.

Ding, X., Zhang, Y., Liu, T., & Duan, J. (2014). Using structured events to predict stock price movement: An empirical investigation. *Proceedings of the 2014 Conference on Empirical Methods in Natural Language Processing (EMNLP)*, 1415-1425.

Fang, Y., Fataliyev, K., Wang, L., Fu, X., & Wang, Y. (2014). Improving the genetic-algorithm-optimized wavelet neural network for stock market prediction. *International Joint Conference on Neural Networks (IJCNN)*, 3038-3042. 10.1109/IJCNN.2014.6889969

Hegazy, O., Soliman, O. S., & Salam, M. A. (2015). Comparative study between FPA, BA, MCS, ABC, and PSO algorithms in training and optimizing of LS-SVM for stock market prediction. *IJACR, 35*.

Lee, H., Surdeanu, M., MacCartney, B., & Jurafsky, D. (2014). On the Importance of Text Analysis for Stock Price Prediction. *LREC*, 1170-1175.

Li, Q., Wang, T. J., Li, P., Liu, L., Gong, Q., & Chen, Y. (2014). The effect of news and public mood on stock movements. *Information Sciences*, *278*, 826–840. doi:10.1016/j.ins.2014.03.096

Li, X., Xie, H., Chen, L., Wang, J., & Deng, X. (2014). News impact on stock price return via sentiment analysis. *Knowledge-Based Systems*, *69*, 14–23. doi:10.1016/j.knosys.2014.04.022

Nguyen, T., & Shirai, K. (2015). *Topic modeling based sentiment analysis on social media for stock market prediction*. Association for Computational Linguistics.

Patel, J., Shah, S., Thakkar, P., & Kotecha, K. (2015). Predicting stock and stock price index movement using trend deterministic data preparation and machine learning techniques. *Expert Systems with Applications*, *42*(1), 259–268. doi:10.1016/j.eswa.2014.07.040

Ranco, G., Aleksovski, D., Caldarelli, G., Grcar, M., & Mozetic, I. (2015). The effects of Twitter sentiment on stock price returns. *PLoS One*, *10*(9), e0138441. doi:10.1371/journal.pone.0138441 PMID:26390434

ENDNOTES

1 https://www.google.com/finance/getprices?i=[PERIOD]&p=[DAYS]d&q=[TICKER]

2 https://finance.yahoo.com/quote/[TICKER]

3 https://www.finam.ru/analysis/profile041CA00007/default.asp

Chapter 8
FinTech and Stock Market Behaviors:
The Case of Borsa Istanbul

Taner Sekmen
Eskisehir Osmangazi University, Turkey

Mercan Hatipoglu
Cankırı Karatekin University, Turkey

ABSTRACT

This chapter examines the effects of high-frequency trading (HFT) and algorithmic trading (AT) activities, which represent important technological developments in financial markets in the past two decades, on Borsa Istanbul in terms of volatility. To clarify stock market behaviors in terms of volatility, asymmetry, and risk return after the BISTECH transition, the GJR-GARCH-in-Mean and I-GARCH models were used. The dataset consists of the daily stock return series of the main and sub-sector indexes of Borsa Istanbul, covering the period from October 24, 2012 to June 1, 2018. Although there are mixed results for the sub-indexes, it is observed that in the post-BISTECH period, volatility increases significantly in the BIST 100 and BIST 30 indexes, where AT and HFT activities are used more frequently. In particular, the duration of volatility returns to average after shock increases about seven times for BIST 100 and about eight times for the BIST 30 in the post-BISTECH period. Overall, the results indicate that AC and HFT activities may have disruptive effects on financial markets.

DOI: 10.4018/978-1-5225-7805-5.ch008

INTRODUCTION

In recent years, there has been a significant increase in both high-frequency trading (HFT) and algorithmic trading (AT) activity in financial markets. Most of the transaction volume in developed markets is created by HFT. Despite this rapid increase in AT and HFT activities, our knowledge about their effects on financial markets is limited. Some researchers say that these developments have benefits like price discovery efficiency, while others note that they may lead to an increase in volatility and adverse selection problems. Although these debates continue, this technological transformation, which began in the U.S. in the 1990s, has spread rapidly to developing countries in recent years. In parallel with these developments, Borsa Istanbul and NASDAQ signed a strategic cooperation agreement in 2014. The first stage of the "Technology Transformation Program" is called BISTECH, a stock market transaction system that was put into operation in 2015, along with Genium INET software and other technological components. The first stage of BISTECH, which consists of many large-scale and years-long programs, was put into practice on November 30, 2015. Borsa Istanbul and NASDAQ announced that Borsa Istanbul has started to use nine leading technologies, including transaction systems, data distribution, index calculation, market surveillance, reporting, and pre- and post-transaction risk management. With the BISTECH Project, Borsa Istanbul has increased the number of orders processed from 4,000 messages to 100,000 messages per second, and the transmission speed of orders has decreased from 1 millisecond to 100 microseconds with the FIX standard protocol. The second phase of the program, the Futures and Options Market (VIOP), began operating on the BISTECH system on March 6, 2017. According to policymakers, these transformations are expected to lead to a reliable, high-performance, fast and multi-instrumental structure in the VIOP. The VIOP, which complies with international standards in terms of technical features, is becoming an international market where investors can use the existing technological systems of foreign institutional investors, which operate by using a similar technological infrastructure.

Although these technological innovations can provide advantages such as increased liquidity, reduced transaction costs and increased competition, high-frequency trading and algorithmic trading may have some negative effects on other market participants. These effects could include the adverse selection problem, increased trading volume and market volatility. Since the introduction of AT strategies, the limit order submissions and cancellations as well as intraday price volatility have increased in some markets (Hagströmer and Norden, 2013). AT might also increase volatility because many algorithms are similar, and therefore their trades are highly correlated, as suggested by Chaboud et al. (2014) and Kalejian and Mukerji (2016). Another concern about HFT activities is that they may increase price movements in a stock market and thus disrupt stability in financial markets. Consequently, understanding the effects of HFT on stock volatility can provide information on controlling the activities of these traders.

According to Martinez and Rosu (2013), an increase in trading volume and market volatility is desirable as long as HFT boosts the efficiency of market pricing by using available information immediately. Brogaard et al. (2014) stress that the main concern about HFT is the possibility of creating market instability, but there is no evidence in their work regarding that point. In Brogaard's 2010 and 2012 studies, no evidence is obtained that HFT increases market volatility. Jones (2013), who reviews the theoretical and empirical literature, classifies the positive effects generated by HFT, while also emphasizing that the negative effects of HFT could not be determined in most of the prior studies. The author also adds that stock price instability may negatively occur during periods of unexpected volatility. However, Zhang (2010) finds some evidence that the stocks with higher HFT ratios increase volatility. Biais and Woolley (2011) list the potential negative effects of HFT as follows: (i) it may lead to manipulation in various forms; (ii) adverse selection can arise because non-HFT traders are slower and less informed than HFT traders; (iii) there can be imperfect competition resulting from the high fixed costs of the infrastructure of the HFT; (iv) there could be an increase in systemic risk resulting from HFT activities having similar strategies. Although there is more evidence in the literature supporting the positive effects of HTF, the concerns mentioned above have not yet been fully addressed.

Furthermore, almost all the studies discussed in the literature analyze developed markets. HFT and AC activities are a relatively new phenomenon for emerging markets. The relevant literature does not say anything about the effects of HFT and AC in those countries that have different economic and market foundations. Despite the fact that the studies on developed markets are generally presented as evidence of the advantages of HFT and AC, the impact of these activities on emerging markets may be quite different. Therefore, more evidence is needed on developing countries in order to understand the effects of HFT and AT activities more clearly. According to our observations on Turkey, which is an emerging market, stock market volatility has increased in the BIST 30 (the 30 largest companies listed on Borsa Istanbul) and BIST 100 indexes (the 100 largest companies listed on Borsa Istanbul), as well as some specific stocks after the transition to the BISTECH system. Abnormal movements, especially in the stock prices of companies in the BIST 30, which have had relatively low volatility levels for years, were observed during this period. Most traders and analysts say that these movements are largely caused by the newly introduced algorithms. All these observations make us skeptical concerning some findings in the literature. For this reason, this study is based on the idea that the technological developments that occurred in Borsa Istanbul may also have had some disruptive effects. In this sense, the study analyzes how stock market behaviors were affected by the introduction of HFT and AT transactions in Borsa Istanbul. More specifically, it focuses on comparing volatility, risk, return and asymmetry behaviors before and after the implementation of BISTECH. Unlike in other studies, a long-term and macro perspective is preferred. The risk, return and asymmetry issues have not been examined before by taking into account HFT in Borsa Istanbul. Therefore, this study allows for a deeper understanding of the effects of HFT on the stock market of a developing country, and a comparison of the results obtained from this developing country with developed countries.

In order to reveal how stock market behaviors changed in the post-BISTECH period, we use daily price data for the main and 15 sub-sector indexes in Borsa Istanbul. The dataset covers the period from October 24, 2012 to June 1, 2018. The study uses the GJR-GARCH-in-Mean approach to model further empirical investigation of volatility. GJR-GARCH-in-Mean makes it possible to simultaneously capture both the risk premium and asymmetry. In addition, we check the GJR-GARCH-in-Mean model's findings on volatility using the I-GARCH method.

Our results suggest that the impact of volatility of the previous period on current volatility increases for most of the indexes in the post-BISTECH period. The I-GARCH model does not reveal that the effects of shocks on volatility have changed significantly, but the GJR-GARCH-in-Mean model shows that there are significant changes in the impact of sudden shocks on volatility for sub-indexes in the post-BISTECH period. Also, the existence of asymmetries for most indexes is determined in both periods. We observe that the risk return relationship has changed for most indexes in the post-BISTECH. The findings on BIST 100 and BIST 30 show us that volatility increases significantly in these indexes for the post-BISTECH period. In particular, the duration of volatility returns to average after shock increases about 7 times for BIST 100 and about 8 times for BIST 30 after the BISTECH transition.

Although the findings from the GJR-GARCH-in-Mean model do not allow for a definite judgment, the volatility of the BIST 30 and BIST Banks indexes, which are considered to be more intensive in HFT and AT activities, seems to increase. However, the results are not very generalizable and need to be supported by further research. This study is designed as follows: Section II reviews the literature on HFT and AT activities in stock markets. Section III identifies the model and data. Section IV deals with the model estimates and the last section is the conclusion.

BACKGROUND ON HIGH-FREQUENCY TRADING AND ALGORITHMIC TRADING

Empirical studies on AT and HFT discuss their effects on different dimensions such as price discovery, adverse selection, price spreads, market quality, liquidity and the volatility of asset prices. In addition, most of these studies focus on the short-term consequences of AT and HFT, and the two concepts are often used interchangeably. However, HFT and AT are different concepts. AT is defined as "the use of computer algorithms to automatically make trading decisions, submit orders, and manage those orders after submission" (Hendershott and Riordan, 2009). Both HFT and AT use automatic decision mechanisms generated by computers, but these two concepts are different from one another in terms of the duration of the positions. Positions are preserved for a very short time in HFT and are usually closed at the end of the day. There is no such a restriction for AT, and so HFT is actually a type of AT (Brogaard, 2010). For this reason, the studies examining the effects of AT and HFT in the literature are categorized separately. In the last part of this section, the findings on studies that analyze the effects of AT and HFT on stock market and price volatility are evaluated.

Hendershott et al. (2011) assess the impact of algorithmic trading on market quality and especially on liquidity for NYSE stocks, using IV regressions and data from February 2001 to December 2005. They find that algorithmic trading improves liquidity for large-cap stocks. Statistically significant results cannot be obtained for small-cap stocks. Furthermore, AT narrows spreads, while also reducing price discovery and adverse selection. Hendershott and Riordan (2013) focus on the role of algorithmic traders on the liquidity supply and demand by using data from a total of 13 days, between January 1 and January 18, 2008, for 30 Deutscher Aktien Index stocks. Their findings are based on probit regression estimations. They conclude that algorithmic traders are likely to reduce liquidity volatility, as they provide liquidity when it is expensive, and algorithmic traders consume liquidity when it is cheap. Chaboud et al. (2014) examine the impact of algorithmic trading on price discovery for three currency pairs: euro-dollar, dollar-yen and euro-yen in the global foreign exchange market by using a structural VAR model and Granger causality tests. Using the three major currencies, and HFT data from 2003–2007, the authors find that AT reduces arbitrage opportunities and high-frequency excess volatility, thus improving price efficiency. However, high correlations between different traders' AT strategies lead to excess volatility. Frino et al. (2017a) investigate the effect of earnings announcements on trading activities. Their dataset is obtained from the Australian Securities Exchange (ASX) for the period October 27, 2008 to October 23, 2009. The authors calculate cumulative average returns and cumulative adjusted average returns to study asymmetries. They also use the (vector autoregressive model) VAR model to examine the relationship between AT and non-AT volume balances and returns. Analyses were conducted for both algorithmic and non-algorithmic trades in the periods immediately before and after corporate earnings announcements. As a result, they state that the algorithms react more quickly and accurately than non-algorithmic traders and thus increase market efficiency. Frino et al. (2017b) examine the effect of algorithmic trading on market liquidity during the high information asymmetry periods for Borsa Italiana. Their dataset covers the period from August 2, 2009 to November 20, 2012 for 35 FTSE MIB stocks. They first calculate different proxies for AT, then provide summary statistics and use the regression method. The authors highlight that market depth decreases and bid-ask spreads widen in the pre-AT period, while bid-ask spreads do not change and market depth does not decrease in the post-AT period. As a result, it is noted that AT increases market liquidity during periods of high information asymmetry.

Brogaard et al. (2014) focus on the impact of HFT trading, as well as price discovery and price efficiency during days of high permananent volatility. The authors analyze 120 randomly selected stocks for 2008 and 2009 listed on NASDAQ and the NYSE. Their estimations are based on correlation analysis and the state space model. The findings of the study indicate that HTFs generally reduce temporary pricing errors while facilitating price efficiency. Despite the debate on whether HFTs may lead to market instability, there is no direct evidence in the study that HFTs contribute to market instability. In another study investigating the effects of high-frequency trading on the foreign exchange market, Manahov et al. (2014) analyze the effects of HTF in terms of technical analysis and market efficiency. They perform AR-GARCH model and K nearest neighbor model based on Strongly Typed Genetic Programming (STGP), using data from August 27, 2012 at 10 pm (GMT) to February 12, 2013 at 10:59 am (GMT). The authors, working with the currency pairs EUR/USD, USD/JPY, GBP/USD, AUD/USD, USD/CHF and USD/CAD, conclude that HFT improves market efficiency, and it is important in the price discovery process in terms of increasing information and reducing pricing errors. Aitken et al. (2015) examine the relationship between HFT and end-of-day price dislocation in 22 stock markets, including in Australia, Canada, China (Shanghai and Shenzhen), Germany, Hong Kong, India (Bombay and the National Stock Exchange of India), Japan, Korea (KOSDAQ and Korea Stock Exchange), Malaysia, New Zealand, Norway, Singapore, South Korea, Sweden, Switzerland, Taiwan, the U.K. and the U.S. (NASDAQ and NYSE) for the January 2003–June 2011 period. According to their panel data estimations, they suggest that the presence of HFT reduces the frequency and severity of end-of-day price dislocation. Conrad et al. (2015) investigate the relationship between high-frequency quotation and the behavior of stock prices for the 2009–2011 period in the U.S., and for the 300 largest stocks on the Tokyo Stock Exchange. They design unconditional tests to provide cross-sectional evidence and use a reduced VAR model for different market types. They emphasize that the presence of high-frequency quotes reduces trading costs while improving liquidity and price efficiency. Jain et al. (2016) examine whether high-frequency quoting and trading (HFQ) increases systemic risks for 150 stocks on the Tokyo Stock Exchange. The Arrowhead high-speed trading platform was introduced in Tokyo on January 2010. The sample is divided into two sub-samples, covering the pre- and post-Arrowhead periods. The authors test the impact of the Arrowhead platform by using multiple regression models after they calculate systemic risk through the value at risk (VaR) and ΔCoVaR methods. It is observed that liquidity improves after the introduction of the Arrowhead high-speed trading platform. However, this platform increases shock propagation risk and quote-stuffing risk. The Arrowhead platform leads to systemic risk based on two different measures in study. Baron et al. (2017), meanwhile, use data on the 25 largest Swedish stocks from January 4, 2010 to December 30, 2014, focusing on the role of competition among high-frequency traders. They estimate regression models using ordinary least squares (OLS) and probit regressions. The study shows that faster HFT firms earn more trading revenues than others. Moreover, the faster HFTs capture more trading opportunities and obtain more risk-adjusted revenues.

When we look at the effects of AC and HFT on volatility, mixed and contradictory results are observed in the literature. Gsell (2008), one of the earliest studies investigating the effects of algorithmic trading on markets, focuses on price formation and price volatility through the simulation approach. The study implies that low latency leads to lower market volatility, and large volumes to execute by the algorithmic trader negatively affect market prices. Zhang (2010), examining the effects of high-frequency trading on stock price volatility and price discovery in the U.S. capital market, generally provides evidence on the potentially harmful effects of HFT. He estimates a fixed-effect model by using quarterly data containing 391,013 firm-quarter observations from 1985Q1 to 2009Q2. He finds a positive correlation between HFT and stock price volatility. This positive correlation is larger for stocks with high institutional holdings and for those among the top 3,000 stocks in market capitalization. When HFT volume is high, stock prices overreact to news about firm fundamentals. Therefore, it is suggested that HFT is weak when it comes to transferring information about firm fundamentals to asset prices. Brogaard (2010) analyzes the impact of high-frequency traders on the U.S. equity market. The dataset covers 2008 and 2009 years, as well as the period from February 22, 2010 to February 26, 2010 for 120 stocks. The findings, which come from OLS regressions and ordered logit regressions, point to HFTs contributing to the price discovery process and providing the best bid and offer quotes. In the study, it is also stated that HFTs do not increase volatility but in fact can reduce it. On days when volatility is high, HFT trading levels show little change. Kirilenko et al. (2011), examining the effects of HTFs in the Flash Crash event in E-mini S&P 500 stock index futures on May 6, 2010, emphasize that HFTs accelerated downward price movements during the Flash Crash. The regression estimates are based on data from May 3, 2010 through May 6, 2010. The authors also state that HFTs did not trigger the Flash Crash but increased market volatility. In another study analyzing whether algorithmic trading activities increase volatility, Groth (2011) presents evidence that algorithmic traders do not increase volatility more than normal traders in the stock market. The high-frequency dataset, which covers October 8, 2007 to October 12, 2007, used in study is obtained from the German Frankfurt Stock Exchange. The evidence is based on OLS regression and Two-Stage Least-Squares Regression (2SLS). In addition, it is argued that algorithmic trading participation does not increase volatility, and that algorithmic traders do not lead to a decrease in liquidity during periods of high volatility. Liu (2012) uses the difference-in-difference-in-differences (DDD) approach and data from 2006 and 2008 to investigate the impact of high-frequency trading on stock volatility in the Swedish stock market. According to the findings of the study, HFT reduces intraday volatility in the normal market environment. The removal of HFT activity leads to increased stock volatility for liquid stocks. Hagströmer and Norden (2013) use data on 30 Swedish large-cap stocks traded on the NASDAQ-OMX Stockholm and analyze only two months of data, from August 2011 and February 2012. The authors use the event study, as well as some descriptive statistics. They conclude that market-making HFTs take 63–72% of trading volume and 81–86% of limit order traffic. Moreover, market-making HFTs have lower latency and reduce intraday price volatility. Scholtus et al. (2014) assess the importance of speed for HTF strategies in responding to macroeconomic news. Their regression is based on data from the highly liquid S&P 500 ETF traded on NASDAQ from January 6, 2009 to December 12, 2011. The authors conclude that a delay of 300 milliseconds reduces the returns of trading strategies based on macroeconomic news. Moreover, this effect is greater on days with high volatility. The study also suggests that in the minute after the arrival of macroeconomic news, the best quota trading volume and depth increase, but algorithmic trading activities increase the volatility and reduce overall depth. Boehmer et al. (2015) analyze data from 42 stock markets for the 2001–2011 period to examine the effects of algorithmic trading on liquidity, short-term volatility and information efficiency. They use panel regressions and the instrumental variable (IV) approach. The findings show that AT improves liquidity and information efficiency, while also increasing volatility. The authors note, however, that this increase in volatility is not due to the faster price discovery or increased AT activity during periods of high volatility, as is often emphasized in previous studies. In addition, AT systematically affects the liquidity and volatility of small and low-priced stocks. Kalejian and Mukerji (2016) focus on the effects of high-frequency algorithmic trading on long-term volatility and non-AT investors. Their data includes 200 of the most frequently traded companies in the S&P 500 during the period from May 1, 1985 to May 31, 2012. Their estimations are based on a general spatial two-stage least squares model. The authors emphasize that HFT increases the volatility resulting from news, as well as volatility spillovers between industries. Since the introduction of AT, the variance and covariance of return volatility has increased in most industries. Hasbrouck (2018) focuses on the impact of high-frequency quoting on short-term volatility in bids and offers in U.S. equity market. The study uses a linear fixed effects panel regression model and U.S. equity data for April 2011. It indicates that bids and offers are more volatile than implied in the long term.

MAIN FOCUS OF THE CHAPTER

Econometric Models

The Gjr-Garch model developed by Glosten et al. (1993) captures volatility asymmetry with an additional leverage parameter. The model, which only considers negative shocks, can be seen in Equation (1):

$$\sigma_t^2 = \omega + \alpha\varepsilon_{t-1}^2 + \lambda 1_{\{\varepsilon_{t-1}<0\}}\varepsilon_{t-1}^2 + \beta\sigma_{t-1}^2 \quad (1)$$

In this equation, if $\varepsilon_t < 0$, the indicator function $\lambda 1_{\{\varepsilon_{t<0}\}} = 1$; otherwise, it is 0. The effect of negative shocks or positive shocks is therefore determined.

In the literature on volatility, the expected return of stocks depends on their volatility. A riskier investor, therefore, will endure higher risk for higher returns. Engle et al. (1987) developed the GARCH-in-Mean model to test this phenomenon.

The model can be explained with the help of the following Equations (2) and (3):

$$r_t = u + \delta\sigma_t^2 + a_t, \qquad a_t = \sigma_t \in_t \quad (2)$$

$$\sigma_t^2 = \omega + \theta a_{t-1}^2 + \beta\sigma_{t-1}^2 \quad (3)$$

In Equation (2), the parameters u and δ are constant, and the parameter δ is called the risk premium. The positive parameter δ indicates a linear relationship between expected return and risk. Furthermore, the significance of the δ coefficient is also considered to be the reason for the autocorrelation observed among past observations of the return series. The reason for the negative relationship between risk and return is that investors see the future as riskier than the present (Alexander, 2001).

This study uses the GJR-GARCH-in-Mean approach to model a further empirical investigation of volatility. In order to capture both the risk premium and asymmetry simultaneously, we combine the two models by integrating the risk premium parameter in the mean equation. The GJR-GARCH-in-Mean (p,q) model can be represented by the following equation as presented by Hamzaoui and Regaieg (2016):

$$r_t = u + \delta\sigma_t^2 + a_t \tag{4}$$

$$\sigma_t^2 = \omega + \alpha\varepsilon_{t-1}^2 + \lambda 1_{\{\varepsilon_{t-1<0}\}}\varepsilon_{t-1}^2 + \beta\sigma_{t-1}^2 \tag{5}$$

In addition, we can calculate the half-life of volatility, which measures the persistence of volatility in the GJR-GARCH-in-Mean model. It can be calculated in the model with the following equation (Alexander, 2008):

$$\sigma^2 = \frac{\omega}{1-\left(\alpha+\beta+\frac{1}{2}\lambda\right)} \tag{6}$$

When analyzing the financial time series with ARCH models, the sum of the coefficients α and β, depending on the number of observations, does not provide the stability condition of these models. For such cases, Engle and Bollerslev (1986) developed the Integrated GARCH model to provide the stability of the process. The following model was developed to get rid of the effect caused by permanent autocorrelation in the absolute value of the yield series (Rachev, 2007, p. 302):

$$\sigma^2 = \omega + \alpha\varepsilon_{t-1}^2 + \left(1-\alpha\right)\sigma_{t-1}^2 \tag{7}$$

In this model, parameters α and β satisfy the condition that $\alpha + \beta = 1$, and the process is stable.

Data Description

The daily stock return series are used to analyze the effects of AT and HFT activities on stock market volatility. The data covers the period from October 24, 2012 to June 1, 2018 and includes 15 sub-sector indexes, as well as the BIST 100 and BIST 30 indexes. These sub-sectors are BIST Bank; BIST Basic Materials; BIST Chem., Petrol, Plastic; BIST Corporate Governance; BIST Electricity; BIST Food, Beverage; BIST Hold. and Investment; BIST Technology; BIST Insurance; BIST Leasing, Factoring; BIST Metal Products, Mach.; BIST Real Estate; BIST Sports; BIST W. and Retail Trade and BIST Wood, Paper, Printing. All data was obtained from Datastream. The analyses are carried out by dividing the period into two sub-periods, before and after the BISTECH transition.

The stock return series are calculated as follows:

$$R_t = lnP_t - lnP_{t-1} \tag{8}$$

where R_t represents the stock return at time t, and ln indicates the natural logarithm. P_t is the stock market index at time t, and P_{t-1} is the stock market index at time $t-1$. According to this formula for computing the returns, the prices of the stocks and indexes are adjusted by the stock exchange for corporate events such as dividends and share capital increases.

SOLUTIONS AND RECOMMENDATIONS

In this section, we present the estimates for the GJR-GARCH-in-Mean model and I-GARCH model with the Gauss distribution, the Student's t-distribution and the Generalized Error Distribution (GED). The estimates of the GJR-GARCH-in-Mean model and I-GARCH model of Borsa Istanbul's main and sub-indexes are given in Table 1 through Table 17. The tables show estimates for the periods before and after the BISTECH transition. The ARCH-LM statistics in the tables help us to determine whether the returns series contain the ARCH effect. The values in the tables show the ARCH-LM statistic and probability values. The probability values for the ARCH-LM statistics indicate that there are no ARCH effects in most of the estimated models before and after BISTECH transition. Thus, the variance equations are correctly specified in most of our models. We also investigated the autocorrelation in our models. Lag(5) values in the tables represent weighted Ljung-Box test statistics on standardized residuals until the 5th lag. Insignificant Ljung-Box statistics show that there is no autocorrelation of the standardized residuals. The model comparison is done by evaluating the Akaike (AIC), Bayesian (BIC) and Hannan-Quinn (HQ) information criteria. The lowest values for the AIC, BIC and HQ statistics represent the best model. As a result, when the information criteria and residuals tests are examined, there are at least one appropriate estimated model for each sub-sector.

According to the AIC, BIC and HQ criteria, the normal distribution is the most appropriate distribution for all estimated models regardless of model type and period. Therefore, the findings of the normal distribution are used when interpreting the results. However, in the models where the diagnostic tests for the normal distribution estimates are not consistent, the second-best model is preferred according to the information criteria. In addition, the I-GARCH model is better than the GJR-GARCH-in-Mean model for modeling volatility in the pre-BISTECH period; however, the I-GARCH model for the BIST Basic Materials and BIST Real Estate indexes has autocorrelation and an ARCH effect. The results of the GJR-GARCH-in-Mean model are interpreted for these indexes. In the post-BISTECH period, the GJR-GARCH-in-Mean model is the best fit model for the BIST 100; BIST 30; BIST Bank; BIST Chem., Petrol, Plastic; BIST Corporate Governance; BIST Hold. and Investment; BIST Metal Products, Mach.; BIST Sports; BIST W. and Retail Trade; BIST Technology and BIST Insurance indexes.

The α parameter shows the effect of unexpected shocks to the return series on volatility. This parameter appears to be insignificant for the BIST 100 and BIST 30 in the GJR-GARCH-in-Mean model pre- and post-BISTECH. Thus, it is not possible to argue for the impact of sudden shocks on the volatility of the main indexes. When the other sub-sectors are examined, unexpected shocks have a significant impact on the volatility of BIST Chem., Petrol, Plastic; BIST Electricity; BIST Food, Beverage; BIST Leasing, Factoring; BIST Metal Products, Mach.; BIST Real Estate and BIST W. and Retail Trade indexes for post-BISTECH period, while they are insignificant in the pre-BISTECH period. On the other hand, the BIST Technology; and BIST Wood, Paper, Printing indexes are insignificant in the post-BISTECH period. The sudden shocks have a significant impact for BIST Insurance and BIST Sports in both periods.

We check the robustness of the GJR-GARCH-in-Mean model estimates by running the I-GARCH model. The results of the two models are substantially different from each other, especially for the pre-BISTECH period. The I-GARCH model predicts that the α parameter is statistically significant in all models in the pre- and post-BISTECH period except for the BIST Hold. and Investment and BIST Insurance indexes. The impact of unexpected shocks on volatility for these indexes is statistically significant just for the post-BISTECH period. The I-GARCH model does not reveal that the effects of shocks on volatility have changed significantly. However, the results of both models are evaluated together; our findings for the alpha parameter based on the estimates of the GJR-GARCH-in-Mean model and I-GARCH model provide

Table 1. BIST 100

	Model	Dist.	Parameters						In-Sample Criteria			Residuals Tests		
			c	ω	α	β	δ	λ	AIC	BIC	HQ	Lag(5)	ARCH-LM(5)	Half-Life
Pre-BISTECH Period	**GJR-GARCH-in-Mean (1,1)**	**Gauss**	0.003** (0.001)	0.000*** (0.000)	0.000 (0.012)	0.850*** (0.016)	-0.214* (0.113)	0.168*** (0.033)	5.670	5.635	5.657	3.309 (0.35)	0.950 (0.74)	10.31
		Student	0.002** (0.001)	0.000*** (0.000)	0.000 (0.012)	0.879*** (0.016)	-0.148 (0.017)	0.127*** (0.035)	5.755	5.714	5.739	3.685 (0.29)	1.32 (0.63)	11.97
		GED	0.002 (0.001)	0.000*** (0.000)	0.000 (0.006)	0.865*** (0.017)	-0.123 (0.122)	0.141*** (0.036)	5.750	5.710	5.735	3.76 (0.28)	1.16 (0.68)	10.53
	I-GARCH (1,1)	**Gauss**	0.000* (0.000)	0.000** (0.000)	0.111*** (0.025)	0.888			5.620	5.602	5.613	3.788 (0.28)	1.315 (0.64)	
		Student	0.000** (0.000)	0.000 (0.000)	0.061*** (0.017)	0.938			5.736	5.713	5.727	4.382 (0.20)	3.128 (0.27)	
		GED	0.000** (0.000)	0.000 (0.000)	0.084* (0.050)	0.915			5.728	5.705	5.719	4.104 (0.24)	1.801 (0.51)	
Post-BISTECH Period	**GJR-GARCH-in-Mean (1,1)**	**Gauss**	0.003* (0.001)	0.000 (0.000)	0.004 (0.010)	0.968*** (0.007)	-0.285* (0.173)	0.036*** (0.014)	6.065	6.025	6.050	2.810 (0.44)	4.228 (0.15)	75.23
		Student	-0.002 (0.002)	0.000* (0.000)	0.025 (0.044)	0.702*** (0.144)	0.248 (0.243)	0.176* (0.100)	6.125	6.077	6.106	3.154 (0.37)	1.217 (0.66)	3.40
		GED	0.001 (0.001)	0.000*** (0.000)	0.000 (0.008)	0.955*** (0.007)	-0.072 (0.099)	0.048** (0.022)	6.119	6.071	6.100	2.861 (0.43)	3.754 (0.19)	34.78
	I-GARCH (1,1)	**Gauss**	0.000* (0.000)	0.000 (0.000)	0.031*** (0.007)	0.968			6.062	6.042	6.054	2.048 (0.60)	5.480 (0.08)	
		Student	0.000 (0.000)	0.000 (0.000)	0.046*** (0.008)	0.953			6.117	6.089	6.106	2.129 (0.58)	2.983 (0.29)	
		GED	0.000 (0.000)	0.000 (0.000)	0.037*** (0.007)	0.962			6.118	6.090	6.107	2.037 (0.60)	4.044 (0.16)	

Note: *** denotes significance at the 1% level, and ** at the 5% level and * at the %10 level. The standard deviations of coefficients are in parenthesis and the probability values of the residuals tests are also reported in parenthesis.

Table 2. BIST 30

	Model	Dist.	Parameters						In-Sample Criteria			Residuals Tests		
			c	ω	α	β	δ	λ	AIC	BIC	HQ	Lag(5)	ARCH-LM(5)	Half-Life
Pre-BISTECH Period	GJR-GARCH-in-Mean (1,1)	Gauss	0.003** (0.001)	0.000*** (0.000)	0.000 (0.011)	0.867*** (0.015)	-0.213* (0.125)	0.141*** (0.028)	5.544	5.509	5.531	3.307 (0.35)	1.029 (0.72)	10.92
		Student	0.002 (0.001)	0.000*** (0.000)	0.000 (0.011)	0.886*** (0.015)	-0.150 (0.127)	0.117*** (0.032)	5.612	5.571	5.596	3.525 (0.31)	1.300 (0.64)	12.46
		GED	0.002*** (0.000)	0.000*** (0.000)	0.002 (0.011)	0.874*** (0.017)	-0.113** (0.052)	0.125*** (0.036)	5.611	5.571	5.596	3.562 (0.31)	1.172 (0.68)	11.29
	I-GARCH (1,1)	Gauss	0.000 (0.000)	0.000 (0.000)	0.093*** (0.034)	0.906			5.502	5.485	5.495	3.603 (0.30)	1.439 (0.60)	
		Student	0.000** (0.000)	0.000 (0.000)	0.050*** (0.011)	0.949			5.594	5.570	5.585	4.283 (0.22)	3.681 (0.20)	
		GED	0.000 (0.000)	0.000 (0.000)	0.073*** (0.028)	0.926			5.592	5.569	5.583	3.848 (0.27)	1.986 (0.47)	
Post-BISTECH Period	GJR-GARCH-in-Mean (1,1)	Gauss	0.004 (0.002)	0.000*** (0.000)	0.002 (0.009)	0.971*** (0.003)	-0.311 (0.221)	0.035*** (0.013)	5.979	5.938	5.963	3.525 (0.31)	5.914 (0.06)	85.42
		Student	0.001 (0.002)	0.000*** (0.000)	0.004 (0.012)	0.947*** (0.011)	-0.052 (0.252)	0.051** (0.024)	6.024	5.977	6.006	3.634 (0.30)	4.284 (0.14)	29.86
		GED	0.000 (0.001)	0.000*** (0.000)	0.000 (0.007)	0.959*** (0.007)	-0.028 (0.128)	0.045** (0.020)	6.026	5.978	6.007	3.371 (0.34)	5.398 (0.08)	40.40
	I-GARCH (1,1)	Gauss	0.000* (0.000)	0.000 (0.000)	0.028*** (0.006)	0.971			5.975	5.955	5.967	2.604 (0.48)	6.938 (0.03)	
		Student	0.000 (0.000)	0.000 (0.000)	0.042*** (0.007)	0.957			6.023	5.996	6.013	2.661 (0.47)	3.817 (0.19)	
		GED	0.000 (0.000)	0.000 (0.000)	0.033*** (0.006)	0.966			6.025	5.998	6.015	2.569 (0.49)	4.998 (0.10)	

Note: *** denotes significance at the 1% level, and ** at the 5% level and * at the %10 level. The standard deviations of coefficients are in parenthesis and the probability values of the residuals tests are also reported in parenthesis.

Table 3. BIST bank

	Model	Dist.	Parameters						In-Sample Criteria			Residuals Tests		
			c	ω	α	β	δ	λ	AIC	BIC	HQ	Lag(5)	ARCH-LM(5)	Half-Life
Pre-BISTECH Period	**GJR-GARCH-in-Mean (1,1)**	**Gauss**	0.004 (0.004)	0.000*** (0.000)	0.009 (0.015)	0.846*** (0.046)	-0.253 (0.245)	0.104*** (0.034)	4.970	4.935	4.957	0.603 (0.94)	0.624 (0.84)	7.21
		Student	0.003 (0.004)	0.000** (0.000)	0.005 (0.016)	0.849*** (0.058)	-0.166 (0.223)	0.121** (0.047)	5.024	4.983	5.008	4.410 (0.20)	0.681 (0.82)	7.87
		GED	0.002 (0.006)	0.000** (0.000)	0.008 (0.016)	0.840*** (0.058)	-0.108 (0.349)	0.116** (0.046)	5.020	4.980	5.005	4.355 (0.21)	0.672 (0.73)	7.09
	I-GARCH (1,1)	**Gauss**	0.000 (0.000)	0.000 (0.000)	0.036*** (0.008)	0.963			4.939	4.921	4.932	3.973 (0.25)	1.260 (0.65)	
		Student	0.000 (0.000)	0.000 (0.000)	0.034*** (0.008)	0.965			5.006	4.983	4.997	4.072 (0.24)	1.568 (0.57)	
		GED	0.000 (0.000)	0.000 (0.000)	0.034*** (0.008)	0.965			5.003	4.979	4.994	4.055 (0.24)	1.412 (0.61)	
Post-BISTECH Period	**GJR-GARCH-in-Mean (1,1)**	**Gauss**	0.004 (0.009)	0.000 (0.000)	0.000 (0.022)	0.976*** (0.013)	-0.290 (0.575)	0.027* (0.013)	5.380	5.332	5.361	5.426 (0.08)	2.013 (0.46)	66.20
		Student	0.000 (0.003)	0.000*** (0.000)	0.010 (0.009)	0.942*** (0.010)	0.008 (0.249)	0.046** (0.022)	5.433	5.379	5.412	5.746 (0.06)	0.916 (0.75)	24.00
		GED	-0.000 (0.001)	0.000*** (0.000)	0.000 (0.005)	0.967*** (0.005)	0.038 (0.126)	0.036** (0.015)	5.424	5.369	5.402	5.293 (0.08)	1.837 (0.50)	40.62
	I-GARCH (1,1)	**Gauss**	0.000 (0.000)	0.000 (0.000)	0.020*** (0.004)	0.979			5.374	5.346	5.363	4.656 (0.14)	1.969 (0.47)	
		Student	0.000 (0.000)	0.000 (0.000)	0.042*** (0.010)	0.957			5.434	5.400	5.420	4.769 (0.12)	0.362 (0.92)	
		GED	-0.000 (0.000)	0.000 (0.000)	0.031*** (0.007)	0.968			5.424	5.389	5.410	4.651 (0.14)	0.802 (0.79)	

Note: *** denotes significance at the 1% level, and ** at the 5% level and * at the %10 level. The standard deviations of coefficients are in parenthesis and the probability values of the residuals tests are also reported in parenthesis.

Table 4. BIST basic materials

	Model	Dist.	Parameters						In-Sample Criteria			Residuals Tests		
			c	ω	α	β	δ	λ	AIC	BIC	HQ	Lag(5)	ARCH-LM(5)	Half-Life
Pre-BISTECH Period	GJR-GARCH-in-Mean (1,1)	Gauss	-0.000 (0.004)	0.000** (0.000)	0.000 (0.029)	0.723*** (0.102)	0.072 (0.263)	0.141** (0.055)	5.440	5.405	5.426	1.156 (0.82)	0.699 (0.82)	3.01
		Student	0.000 (0.002)	0.000** (0.000)	0.050 (0.041)	0.790*** (0.066)	0.029 (0.171)	0.109* (0.059)	5.572	5.532	5.557	1.041 (0.85)	0.591 (0.85)	6.23
		GED	0.000* (0.000)	0.000** (0.000)	0.021 (0.035)	0.767*** (0.080)	0.010 (0.011)	0.131** (0.061)	5.556	5.516	5.541	1.015 (0.85)	0.578 (0.86)	4.42
	I-GARCH (1,1)	Gauss	0.000 (0.000)	0.000 (0.000)	0.000 (0.000)	1.000			5.379	5.362	5.372	1.534 (0.73)	19.45 (0.00)	
		Student	0.001*** (0.000)	0.000* (0.000)	0.167*** (0.050)	0.832			5.569	5.546	5.560	1.124 (0.83)	0.455 (0.89)	
		GED	0.000*** (0.000)	0.000*** (0.000)	0.151*** (0.031)	0.848			5.540	5.517	5.532	1.264 (0.79)	0.041 (0.90)	
Post-BISTECH Period	GJR-GARCH-in-Mean (1,1)	Gauss	-0.003 (0.007)	0.000** (0.000)	0.005 (0.028)	0.798*** (0.092)	0.267 (0.411)	0.093* (0.052)	5.207	5.166	5.191	2.083 (0.59)	0.047 (0.89)	4.26
		Student	-0.005 (0.006)	0.000 (0.000)	0.011 (0.028)	0.826*** (0.097)	0.399 (0.371)	0.068 (0.051)	5.214	5.166	5.195	2.054 (0.60)	0.053 (0.87)	5.06
		GED	-0.005 (0.003)	0.000* (0.000)	0.010 (0.027)	0.820*** (0.097)	0.378* (0.207)	0.074 (0.051)	5.219	5.171	5.200	2.082 (0.59)	0.509 (0.88)	4.92
	I-GARCH (1,1)	Gauss	0.001** (0.000)	0.000 (0.000)	0.016*** (0.003)	0.983			5.195	5.175	5.187	1.483 (0.74)	2.964 (0.29)	
		Student	0.001** (0.000)	0.000 (0.000)	0.023*** (0.004)	0.976			5.210	5.182	5.199	1.438 (0.75)	1.919 (0.48)	
		GED	0.001** (0.000)	0.000 (0.000)	0.020*** (0.003)	0.979			5.213	5.186	5.203	1.450 (0.75)	2.222 (0.42)	

Note: *** denotes significance at the 1% level, and ** at the 5% level and * at the %10 level. The standard deviations of coefficients are in parenthesis and the probability values of the residuals tests are also reported in parenthesis.

Table 5. BIST Chem., petrol, plastic

	Model	Dist.	Parameters						In-Sample Criteria			Residuals Tests		
			c	ω	α	β	δ	λ	AIC	BIC	HQ	Lag(5)	ARCH-LM(5)	Half-Life
Pre-BISTECH Period	GJR-GARCH-in-Mean (1,1)	Gauss	0.000 (0.002)	0.000*** (0.000)	0.000 (0.040)	0.808*** (0.048)	0.037 (0.204)	0.162*** (0.044)	5.691	5.656	5.678	1.611 (0.71)	1.052 (0.71)	5.92
		Student	0.001 (0.002)	0.000*** (0.000)	0.016 (0.051)	0.830*** (0.037)	0.011 (0.194)	0.147*** (0.054)	5.794	5.753	5.778	1.521 (0.73)	1.150 (0.68)	8.39
		GED	0.000 (0.000)	0.000*** (0.000)	0.000 (0.013)	0.826*** (0.043)	0.038 (0.027)	0.160*** (0.047)	5.793	5.752	5.777	1.613 (0.71)	1.168 (0.68)	7.03
	I-GARCH (1,1)	Gauss	0.000* (0.000)	0.000 (0.000)	0.029*** (0.007)	0.970			5.635	5.618	5.628	1.263 (0.79)	3.427 (0.23)	
		Student	0.001*** (0.000)	0.000*** (0.000)	0.193*** (0.037)	0.806			5.790	5.766	5.781	1.677 (0.69)	0.931 (0.75)	
		GED	0.001 (0.000)	0.000*** (0.000)	0.190*** (0.039)	0.809			5.779	5.756	5.770	1.770 (0.67)	0.889 (0.76)	
Post-BISTECH Period	GJR-GARCH-in-Mean (1,1)	Gauss	0.009*** (0.001)	0.000 (0.000)	0.011* (0.006)	0.977*** (0.000)	-0.717*** (0.091)	0.002 (0.013)	5.884	5.843	5.868	2.473 (0.51)	0.485 (0.88)	68.84
		Student	0.010*** (0.002)	0.000** (0.000)	0.000 (0.006)	0.973*** (0.001)	-0.759*** (0.247)	0.025* (0.013)	5.989	5.941	5.970	2.551 (0.49)	0.286 (0.94)	51.39
		GED	0.009*** (0.003)	0.000* (0.000)	0.000 (0.011)	0.976*** (0.001)	-0.671** (0.289)	0.021 (0.021)	5.974	5.926	5.956	2.461 (0.51)	0.391 (0.91)	52.43
	I-GARCH (1,1)	Gauss	0.000* (0.000)	0.000 (0.000)	0.016*** (0.003)	0.983			5.879	5.858	5.871	1.731 (0.68)	0.820 (0.78)	
		Student	0.001*** (0.000)	0.000 (0.000)	0.023*** (0.004)	0.976			5.985	5.958	5.975	1.691 (0.69)	0.543 (0.87)	
		GED	0.001** (0.000)	0.000 (0.000)	0.020*** (0.003)	0.979			5.973	5.946	5.962	1.689 (0.69)	0.642 (0.84)	

Note: *** denotes significance at the 1% level, and ** at the 5% level and * at the %10 level. The standard deviations of coefficients are in parenthesis and the probability values of the residuals tests are also reported in parenthesis.

Table 6. BIST corporate governance

	Model	Dist.	Parameters						In-Sample Criteria			Residuals Tests		
			c	ω	α	β	δ	λ	AIC	BIC	HQ	Lag(5)	ARCH-LM(5)	Half-Life
Pre-BISTECH Period	GJR-GARCH-in-Mean (1,1)	Gauss	0.002* (0.001)	0.000*** (0.000)	0.000 (0.017)	0.812*** (0.023)	-0.206 (0.146)	0.232*** (0.049)	5.757	5.722	5.744	3.036 (0.40)	1.241 (0.66)	9.41
		Student	0.002* (0.001)	0.000*** (0.000)	0.016 (0.016)	0.838*** (0.022)	-0.130 (0.104)	0.183*** (0.053)	5.855	5.815	5.840	3.245 (0.36)	1.506 (0.59)	12.79
		GED	0.001*** (0.000)	0.000*** (0.000)	0.008 (0.012)	0.823*** (0.023)	- 0.087*** (0.027)	0.196*** (0.055)	5.851	5.810	5.835	3.608 (0.30)	1.427 (0.61)	9.67
	I-GARCH (1,1)	Gauss	0.001** (0.000)	0.000*** (0.000)	0.175*** (0.041)	0.824			5.703	5.686	5.697	4.321 (0.21)	1.448 (0.60)	
		Student	0.001*** (0.000)	0.000** (0.000)	0.136*** (0.029)	0.863			5.842	5.818	5.833	4.461 (0.20)	2.056 (0.45)	
		GED	0.000*** (0.000)	0.000** (0.000)	0.146*** (0.036)	0.853			5.832	5.809	5.823	4.675 (0.18)	1.610 (0.56)	
Post-BISTECH Period	GJR-GARCH-in-Mean (1,1)	Gauss	0.003 (0.005)	0.000 (0.000)	0.004 (0.012)	0.964*** (0.011)	-0.296 (0.461)	0.038*** (0.008)	6.055	6.014	6.039	2.951 (0.41)	2.734 (0.33)	59.17
		Student	0.000 (0.002)	0.000*** (0.000)	0.004 (0.013)	0.924*** (0.012)	0.000 (0.248)	0.065** (0.029)	6.109	6.061	6.090	2.931 (0.41)	1.560 (0.57)	17.61
		GED	0.002 (0.001)	0.000*** (0.000)	0.000 (0.005)	0.954*** (0.006)	-0.142 (0.167)	0.047** (0.021)	6.103	6.055	6.084	2.936 (0.41)	2.630 (0.34)	32.65
	I-GARCH (1,1)	Gauss	0.000* (0.000)	0.000 (0.000)	0.034*** (0.007)	0.965			6.050	6.030	6.042	2.147 (0.58)	2.949 (0.29)	
		Student	0.000 (0.000)	0.000 (0.000)	0.047*** (0.009)	0.952			6.106	6.078	6.095	2.185 (0.57)	1.561 (0.57)	
		GED	0.000 (0.000)	0.000 (0.000)	0.039*** (0.007)	0.960			6.101	6.074	6.090	2.120 (0.59)	2.009 (0.46)	

Note: *** denotes significance at the 1% level, and ** at the 5% level and * at the %10 level. The standard deviations of coefficients are in parenthesis and the probability values of the residuals tests are also reported in parenthesis.

Table 7. BIST electricity

	Model	Dist.	Parameters						In-Sample Criteria			Residuals Tests		
			c	ω	α	β	δ	λ	AIC	BIC	HQ	Lag(5)	ARCH-LM(5)	Half-Life
Pre-BISTECH Period	**GJR-GARCH-in-Mean (1,1)**	**Gauss**	0.000 (0.003)	0.000*** (0.000)	0.030 (0.027)	0.692*** (0.066)	-0.020 (0.181)	0.218*** (0.069)	5.285	5.250	5.271	2.703 (0.46)	0.277 (0.94)	3.77
		Student	-0.000 (0.002)	0.000** (0.000)	0.081* (0.047)	0.816*** (0.056)	0.043 (0.134)	0.087 (0.067)	5.489	5.449	5.474	3.090 (0.39)	0.301 (0.93)	11.53
		GED	0.000 (0.000)	0.000** (0.000)	0.057 (0.039)	0.787*** (0.065)	0.000 (0.000)	0.117* (0.068)	5.487	5.446	5.471	3.005 (0.40)	0.322 (0.93)	6.86
	I-GARCH (1,1)	**Gauss**	0.001** (0.000)	0.000*** (0.000)	0.249*** (0.053)	0.750			5.244	5.226	5.237	3.494 (0.32)	0.428 (0.90)	
		Student	0.000 (0.000)	0.000** (0.000)	0.157*** (0.045)	0.842			5.493	5.470	5.484	2.804 (0.44)	0.238 (0.95)	
		GED	0.000 (0.000)	0.000*** (0.000)	0.161*** (0.033)	0.838			5.483	5.460	5.474	3.472 (0.32)	0.273 (0.94)	
Post-BISTECH Period	**GJR-GARCH-in-Mean (1,1)**	**Gauss**	-0.001 (0.004)	0.000** (0.000)	0.080* (0.049)	0.535*** (0.141)	0.306 (0.281)	0.202* (0.121)	5.773	5.725	5.754	2.609 (0.53)	0.776 (0.80)	1.92
		Student	-0.002 (0.003)	0.000* (0.000)	0.071 (0.058)	0.614*** (0.160)	0.260 (0.240)	0.188* (0.102)	5.868	5.813	5.847	3.450 (0.32)	0.481 (0.88)	2.74
		GED	-0.003 (0.002)	0.000*** (0.000)	0.083 (0.085)	0.542*** (0.098)	0.348* (0.201)	0.205 (0.149)	5.868	5.814	5.847	3.131 (0.39)	0.568 (0.86)	2.09
	I-GARCH (1,1)	**Gauss**	0.000 (0.000)	0.000 (0.000)	0.043*** (0.012)	0.956			5.749	5.721	5.738	1.981 (0.71)	3.813 (0.19)	
		Student	0.001** (0.000)	0.000 (0.000)	0.232* (0.139)	0.767			5.853	5.819	5.840	2.584 (0.54)	0.326 (0.93)	
		GED	0.001** (0.000)	0.000 (0.000)	0.058*** (0.015)	0.941			5.851	5.817	5.837	1.952 (0.72)	2.221 (0.42)	

Note: *** denotes significance at the 1% level, and ** at the 5% level and * at the %10 level. The standard deviations of coefficients are in parenthesis and the probability values of the residuals tests are also reported in parenthesis.

Table 8. BIST food, beverage

	Model	Dist.	Parameters						In-Sample Criteria			Residuals Tests		
			c	ω	α	β	δ	λ	AIC	BIC	HQ	Lag(5)	ARCH-LM(5)	Half-Life
Pre-BISTECH Period	GJR-GARCH-in-Mean (1,1)	Gauss	-0.003 (0.003)	0.000*** (0.000)	0.000 (0.018)	0.781*** (0.050)	0.233 (0.197)	0.181*** (0.044)	5.702	5.667	5.688	2.513 (0.50)	2.988 (0.29)	5.07
		Student	-0.003 (0.002)	0.000*** (0.000)	0.000 (0.025)	0.820*** (0.048)	0.306* (0.182)	0.164*** (0.051)	5.783	5.742	5.767	2.987 (0.40)	2.989 (0.29)	6.72
		GED	-0.002*** (0.000)	0.000 (0.000)	0.000 (0.027)	0.804*** (0.110)	0.223*** (0.054)	0.172** (0.071)	5.783	5.743	5.768	2.414 (0.52)	2.804 (0.31)	5.99
	I-GARCH (1,1)	Gauss	0.000 (0.000)	0.000 (0.000)	0.056*** (0.016)	0.943			5.639	5.622	5.632	1.010 (0.85)	2.815 (0.31)	
		Student	0.000 (0.000)	0.000*** (0.000)	0.137*** (0.029)	0.862			5.764	5.741	5.755	1.171 (0.81)	1.442 (0.60)	
		GED	0.000* (0.000)	0.000 (0.000)	0.124*** (0.045)	0.875			5.759	5.736	5.750	1.237 (0.80)	1.304 (0.64)	
Post-BISTECH Period	GJR-GARCH-in-Mean (1,1)	Gauss	-0.000 (0.002)	0.000*** (0.000)	0.212*** (0.057)	0.614*** (0.092)	0.005 (0.229)	-0.025 (0.064)	5.989	5.948	5.973	3.706 (0.29)	1.867 (0.50)	3.37
		Student	-0.003 (0.003)	0.000* (0.000)	0.121** (0.057)	0.730*** (0.120)	0.297 (0.262)	0.007 (0.057)	6.028	5.980	6.009	2.709 (0.46)	1.869 (0.50)	4.45
		GED	-0.002** (0.001)	0.000** (0.000)	0.159*** (0.060)	0.684*** (0.105)	0.207** (0.097)	-0.001 (0.065)	6.030	5.982	6.012	3.785 (0.28)	1.722 (0.53)	4.06
	I-GARCH (1,1)	Gauss	0.000 (0.000)	0.000** (0.000)	0.250*** (0.071)	0.749			5.976	5.956	5.968	4.372 (0.21)	2.076 (0.45)	
		Student	-0.000 (0.000)	0.000 (0.000)	0.113 (0.119)	0.886			6.020	5.993	6.010	4.047 (0.24)	1.443 (0.60)	
		GED	-0.000 (0.000)	0.000 (0.000)	0.166*** (0.077)	0.833			6.023	5.996	6.012	4.325 (0.21)	1.641 (0.55)	

Note: *** denotes significance at the 1% level, and ** at the 5% level and * at the %10 level. The standard deviations of coefficients are in parenthesis and the probability values of the residuals tests are also reported in parenthesis.

Table 9. BIST hold and investment

	Model	Dist.	Parameters						In-Sample Criteria			Residuals Tests		
			c	ω	α	β	δ	λ	AIC	BIC	HQ	Lag(5)	ARCH-LM(5)	Half-Life
Pre-BISTECH Period	GJR-GARCH-in-Mean (1,1)	Gauss	0.001 (0.001)	0.000*** (0.000)	0.000 (0.012)	0.853*** (0.016)	-0.077 (0.121)	0.154*** (0.033)	5.701	5.666	5.687	3.426 (0.33)	0.444 (0.89)	9.59
		Student	0.000 (0.001)	0.000*** (0.000)	0.000 (0.012)	0.881*** (0.014)	0.017 (0.146)	0.109*** (0.032)	5.757	5.716	5.741	3.761 (0.28)	0.805 (0.79)	10.54
		GED	0.000 (0.001)	0.000*** (0.000)	0.000 (0.007)	0.871*** (0.014)	0.010 (0.079)	0.124*** (0.035)	5.748	5.707	5.732	3.717 (0.29)	0.661 (0.83)	10.06
	I-GARCH (1,1)	Gauss	0.000 (0.000)	0.000 (0.000)	0.109 (0.073)	0.890			5.655	5.638	5.648	4.083 (0.24)	0.922 (0.75)	
		Student	0.000 (0.000)	0.000 (0.000)	0.101* (0.059)	0.898			5.736	5.712	5.727	3.985 (0.25)	1.083 (0.70)	
		GED	0.000 (0.000)	0.000 (0.000)	0.098 (0.069)	0.901			5.726	5.703	5.717	4.044 (0.24)	1.065 (0.71)	
Post-BISTECH Period	GJR-GARCH-in-Mean (1,1)	Gauss	-0.001 (0.003)	0.000*** (0.000)	0.010 (0.009)	0.949*** (0.007)	0.122 (0.307)	0.031 (0.019)	5.991	5.950	5.975	3.021 (0.40)	5.193 (0.10)	29.13
		Student	-0.004 (0.003)	0.000* (0.000)	0.066 (0.061)	0.516** (0.215)	0.453 (0.316)	0.175 (0.125)	6.040	5.992	6.021	2.363 (0.53)	1.818 (0.51)	1.73
		GED	-0.003*** (0.000)	0.000** (0.000)	0.069 (0.058)	0.562*** (0.182)	0.329*** (0.040)	0.142*** (0.051)	6.039	5.991	6.021	2.613 (0.48)	2.063 (0.45)	1.96
	I-GARCH (1,1)	Gauss	0.000 (0.000)	0.000 (0.000)	0.033*** (0.007)	0.966			5.989	5.968	5.981	2.551 (0.49)	4.561 (0.12)	
		Student	0.000 (0.000)	0.000 (0.000)	0.040*** (0.007)	0.959			6.028	6.001	6.018	2.564 (0.49)	3.927 (0.18)	
		GED	0.000 (0.000)	0.000 (0.000)	0.036*** (0.006)	0.963			6.034	6.007	6.023	2.536 (0.49)	4.208 (0.15)	

Note: *** denotes significance at the 1% level, and ** at the 5% level and * at the %10 level. The standard deviations of coefficients are in parenthesis and the probability values of the residuals tests are also reported in parenthesis.

Table 10. BIST technology

	Model	Dist.	Parameters						In-Sample Criteria			Residuals Tests		
			c	ω	α	β	δ	λ	AIC	BIC	HQ	Lag(5)	ARCH-LM(5)	Half-Life
Pre-BISTECH Period	GJR-GARCH-in-Mean (1,1)	Gauss	0.000 (0.001)	0.000*** (0.000)	0.188*** (0.053)	0.541*** (0.064)	0.021 (0.121)	0.328*** (0.108)	5.643	5.608	5.629	1.840 (0.65)	3.538 (0.22)	6.18
		Student	0.000 (0.001)	0.000*** (0.000)	0.343*** (0.116)	0.520*** (0.077)	0.020 (0.093)	0.157 (0.138)	5.833	5.793	5.818	1.466 (0.74)	2.783 (0.32)	11.65
		GED	-0.000*** (0.001)	0.000*** (0.000)	0.253*** (0.056)	0.543*** (0.050)	0.060*** (0.007)	0.233*** (0.076)	5.828	5.787	5.812	2.375 (0.53)	3.037 (0.28)	7.64
	I-GARCH (1,1)	Gauss	0.001*** (0.000)	0.000*** (0.000)	0.422*** (0.052)	0.577			5.631	5.614	5.625	0.874 (0.88)	1.835 (0.50)	
		Student	0.001*** (0.000)	0.000*** (0.000)	0.471*** (0.076)	0.528			5.839	5.815	5.830	1.125 (0.83)	2.050 (0.46)	
		GED	0.000 (0.000)	0.000 (0.000)	0.053*** (0.009)	0.946			5.769	5.745	5.760	3.055 (0.39)	0.639 (0.84)	
Post-BISTECH Period	GJR-GARCH-in-Mean (1,1)	Gauss	-0.006* (0.004)	0.000*** (0.000)	0.062 (0.052)	0.553*** (0.099)	0.536* (0.324)	0.196** (0.085)	5.903	5.855	5.885	0.475 (0.99)	1.665 (0.69)	2.65
		Student	-0.005* (0.003)	0.000*** (0.000)	0.072 (0.068)	0.510*** (0.109)	0.437* (0.249)	0.290** (0.113)	6.001	5.946	5.979	0.625 (0.98)	4.288 (0.15)	2.48
		GED	-0.004*** (0.000)	0.000*** (0.000)	0.067 (0.071)	0.543*** (0.140)	0.404*** (0.072)	0.245*** (0.093)	6.003	5.948	5.982	0.641 (0.98)	4.224 (0.15)	2.65
	I-GARCH (1,1)	Gauss	0.000 (0.000)	0.000*** (0.000)	0.322*** (0.055)	0.677			5.874	5.846	5.863	1.046 (0.93)	8.793 (0.01)	
		Student	0.000 (0.000)	0.000** (0.000)	0.549*** (0.135)	0.450			5.982	5.948	5.969	1.282 (0.89)	5.945 (0.06)	
		GED	0.000*** (0.000)	0.000** (0.000)	0.454*** (0.114)	0.545			5.982	5.948	5.969	1.197 (0.91)	8.484 (0.01)	

Note: *** denotes significance at the 1% level, and ** at the 5% level and * at the %10 level. The standard deviations of coefficients are in parenthesis and the probability values of the residuals tests are also reported in parenthesis.

Table 11. BIST insurance

	Model	Dist.	Parameters						In-Sample Criteria			Residuals Tests		
			c	ω	α	β	δ	λ	AIC	BIC	HQ	Lag(5)	ARCH-LM(5)	Half-Life
Pre-BISTECH Period	GJR-GARCH-in-Mean (1,1)	Gauss	-0.001 (0.001)	0.000*** (0.000)	0.101*** (0.022)	0.828*** (0.016)	0.181 (0.150)	0.004 (0.030)	6.224	6.189	6.210	2.339 (0.54)	7.239 (0.03)	9.87
		Student	-0.000 (0.001)	0.000*** (0.000)	0.091*** (0.025)	0.850*** (0.022)	0.123 (0.145)	0.010 (0.043)	6.334	6.293	6.318	2.391 (0.52)	9.036 (0.01)	12.77
		GED	-0.000** (0.000)	0.000*** (0.000)	0.095*** (0.024)	0.834*** (0.021)	0.145*** (0.046)	0.009 (0.041)	6.326	6.285	6.310	2.302 (0.54)	7.445 (0.02)	10.27
	I-GARCH (1,1)	Gauss	0.000 (0.000)	0.000 (0.000)	0.119 (0.122)	0.880			6.209	6.191	6.202	1.694 (0.69)	5.613 (0.07)	
		Student	0.000*** (0.000)	0.000 (0.000)	0.134*** (0.031)	0.865			6.336	6.313	6.327	1.851 (0.65)	6.244 (0.05)	
		GED	0.000 (0.000)	0.000 (0.000)	0.126 (0.078)	0.873			6.323	6.299	6.314	1.590 (0.71)	4.875 (0.11)	
Post-BISTECH Period	GJR-GARCH-in-Mean (1,1)	Gauss	-0.003* (0.001)	0.000*** (0.000)	0.124*** (0.021)	0.718*** (0.026)	0.510** (0.255)	-0.036 (0.044)	6.920	6.873	6.902	1.301 (0.89)	2.257 (0.41)	3.49
		Student	-0.002 (0.003)	0.000** (0.000)	0.254** (0.101)	0.520** (0.143)	0.381 (0.510)	-0.111 (0.1090)	6.978	6.923	6.956	1.320 (0.88)	4.065 (0.16)	2.48
		GED	-0.001** (0.000)	0.000*** (0.000)	0.188*** (0.048)	0.605*** (0.047)	0.335*** (0.105)	-0.079 (0.079)	6.963	6.909	6.942	1.663 (0.80)	3.425 (0.23)	2.65
	I-GARCH (1,1)	Gauss	0.000*** (0.000)	0.000 (0.000)	0.002** (0.001)	0.997			6.894	6.866	6.883	2.646 (0.52)	8.108 (0.01)	
		Student	0.000*** (0.000)	0.000 (0.000)	0.005*** (0.001)	0.994			6.952	6.918	6.939	3.801 (0.25)	7.323 (0.02)	
		GED	0.000** (0.000)	0.000 (0.000)	0.003*** (0.001)	0.996			6.994	6.910	6.931	3.970 (0.23)	7.947 (0.02)	

Note: *** denotes significance at the 1% level, and ** at the 5% level and * at the %10 level. The standard deviations of coefficients are in parenthesis and the probability values of the residuals tests are also reported in parenthesis.

Table 12. BIST leasing, factoring

	Model	Dist.	Parameters						In-Sample Criteria			Residuals Tests		
			c	ω	α	β	δ	λ	AIC	BIC	HQ	Lag(5)	ARCH-LM(5)	Half-Life
Pre-BISTECH Period	**GJR-GARCH-in-Mean (1,1)**	**Gauss**	-0.000 (0.002)	0.000*** (0.000)	0.045 (0.034)	0.515*** (0.137)	0.081 (0.217)	0.311*** (0.108)	5.813	5.778	5.800	2.320 (0.54)	0.716 (0.95)	2.08
		Student	-0.003 (0.003)	0.000* (0.000)	0.055 (0.050)	0.599*** (0.183)	0.234 (0.239)	0.195 (0.139)	5.968	5.927	5.952	2.087 (0.59)	0.033 (0.99)	2.43
		GED	-0.000 (0.000)	0.000* (0.000)	0.058 (0.046)	0.722*** (0.141)	0.000 (0.000)	0.152 (0.121)	6.007	5.966	5.992	2.830 (0.43)	0.145 (0.97)	4.48
	I-GARCH (1,1)	**Gauss**	0.000* (0.000)	0.000*** (0.000)	0.222*** (0.045)	0.777			5.768	5.751	5.762	2.088 (0.59)	0.542 (0.87)	
		Student	0.000 (0.000)	0.000 (0.000)	0.155*** (0.059)	0.844			5.966	5.943	5.957	2.655 (0.47)	0.070 (0.99)	
		GED	0.000 (0.000)	0.000*** (0.000)	0.140*** (0.031)	0.859			6.004	5.981	5.995	2.312 (0.54)	0.145 (0.97)	
Post-BISTECH Period	**GJR-GARCH-in-Mean (1,1)**	**Gauss**	0.008*** (0.002)	0.000** (0.000)	0.404** (0.174)	0.572*** (0.158)	-0.413*** (0.143)	-0.258* (0.154)	5.267	5.226	5.251	7.420 (0.04)	1.331 (0.63)	4.19
		Student	0.003* (0.001)	0.000*** (0.000)	0.567** (0.222)	0.422** (0.111)	-0.138 (0.114)	-0.174 (0.195)	5.474	5.427	5.456	4.533 (0.19)	9.693 (0.00)	6.82
		GED	0.002*** (0.000)	0.000*** (0.000)	0.396*** (0.049)	0.528*** (0.042)	-0.145*** (0.016)	-0.180*** (0.068)	5.468	5.420	5.450	4.021 (0.25)	3.668 (0.20)	3.82
	I-GARCH (1,1)	**Gauss**	0.001*** (0.000)	0.000*** (0.000)	0.307*** (0.058)	0.692			5.238	5.218	5.230	2.348 (0.53)	1.836 (0.50)	
		Student	0.001*** (0.000)	0.000*** (0.000)	0.633*** (0.107)	0.366			5.480	5.452	5.469	4.412 (0.20)	24.70 (0.00)	
		GED	0.000*** (0.000)	0.000** (0.000)	0.484*** (0.147)	0.510			5.468	5.440	5.457	2.662 (0.47)	4.532 (0.13)	

Note: *** denotes significance at the 1% level, and ** at the 5% level and * at the %10 level. The standard deviations of coefficients are in parenthesis and the probability values of the residuals tests are also reported in parenthesis.

Table 13. BIST metal products, mach

	Model	Dist.	Parameters						In-Sample Criteria			Residuals Tests		
			c	ω	α	β	δ	λ	AIC	BIC	HQ	Lag(5)	ARCH-LM(5)	Half-Life
Pre-BISTECH Period	GJR-GARCH-in-Mean (1,1)	Gauss	0.000 (0.001)	0.000*** (0.000)	0.000 (0.030)	0.782*** (0.035)	0.043 (0.135)	0.296*** (0.056)	5.628	5.593	5.615	2.527 (0.50)	1.664 (0.55)	9.63
		Student	-0.000 (0.001)	0.000*** (0.000)	0.000 (0.044)	0.834*** (0.050)	0.120 (0.137)	0.164*** (0.042)	5.728	5.687	5.712	2.973 (0.41)	1.953 (0.48)	7.91
		GED	-0.001 (0.000)	0.000*** (0.000)	0.000 (0.039)	0.802*** (0.048)	0.173 (0.166)	0.219*** (0.058)	5.711	5.670	5.695	3.587 (0.31)	1.760 (0.52)	7.54
	I-GARCH (1,1)	Gauss	0.001*** (0.000)	0.000*** (0.000)	0.210*** (0.026)	0.789			5.575	5.558	5.569	1.947 (0.63)	1.239 (0.66)	
		Student	0.001*** (0.000)	0.000** (0.000)	0.134*** (0.029)	0.865			5.705	5.682	5.696	2.293 (0.55)	1.393 (0.62)	
		GED	0.000 (0.000)	0.000** (0.000)	0.157*** (0.035)	0.842			5.680	5.657	5.671	2.173 (0.57)	1.075 (0.71)	
Post-BISTECH Period	GJR-GARCH-in-Mean (1,1)	Gauss	-0.006*** (0.002)	0.000*** (0.000)	0.016** (0.007)	0.865*** (0.012)	0.567*** (0.208)	0.082*** (0.031)	6.006	5.965	5.990	1.502 (0.73)	1.937 (0.48)	8.65
		Student	-0.008* (0.004)	0.000** (0.000)	0.000 (0.040)	0.785** (0.068)	0.723* (0.408)	0.138** (0.055)	6.066	6.019	6.048	1.486 (0.74)	2.322 (0.40)	4.43
		GED	-0.007*** (0.001)	0.000*** (0.000)	0.000 (0.000)	0.818*** (0.018)	0.620*** (0.129)	0.118*** (0.038)	6.056	6.008	6.038	1.539 (0.73)	2.507 (0.36)	5.29
	I-GARCH (1,1)	Gauss	0.000 (0.000)	0.000 (0.000)	0.030*** (0.006)	0.969			6.000	5.980	5.992	2.348 (0.53)	3.138 (0.27)	
		Student	0.000 (0.000)	0.000 (0.000)	0.044*** (0.008)	0.955			6.052	6.025	6.041	2.197 (0.57)	2.257 (0.41)	
		GED	0.000 (0.000)	0.000 (0.000)	0.036*** (0.006)	0.963			6.050	6.023	6.039	2.281 (0.55)	2.685 (0.33)	

· Note: *** denotes significance at the 1% level, and ** at the 5% level and * at the %10 level. The standard deviations of coefficients are in parenthesis and the probability values of the residuals tests are also reported in parenthesis.

Table 14. BIST real estate

	Model	Dist.	Parameters						In-Sample Criteria			Residuals Tests		
			c	ω	α	β	δ	λ	AIC	BIC	HQ	Lag(5)	ARCH-LM(5)	Half-Life
Pre-BISTECH Period	GJR-GARCH-in-Mean (1,1)	Gauss	0.003 (0.003)	0.000*** (0.000)	0.002 (0.017)	0.813*** (0.042)	-0.198 (0.225)	0.111*** (0.031)	5.560	5.525	5.547	3.691 (0.29)	0.137 (0.97)	5.84
		Student	0.002 (0.002)	0.000*** (0.000)	0.074* (0.042)	0.834*** (0.050)	-0.093 (0.149)	0.077 (0.054)	5.713	5.672	5.697	2.660 (0.47)	0.109 (0.98)	9.11
		GED	0.000*** (0.000)	0.000*** (0.000)	0.052* (0.031)	0.807*** (0.042)	-0.044*** (0.015)	0.094** (0.044)	5.704	5.664	5.689	2.801 (0.44)	0.106 (0.98)	7.14
	I-GARCH (1,1)	Gauss	0.000 (0.000)	0.000 (0.000)	0.000 (0.000)	0.999			5.502	5.484	5.495	6.838 (0.05)	8.439 (0.01)	
		Student	0.000** (0.000)	0.000*** (0.000)	0.181*** (0.033)	0.818			5.713	5.690	5.705	2.599 (0.48)	0.110 (0.98)	
		GED	0.000 (0.000)	0.000*** (0.000)	0.186*** (0.033)	0.813			5.699	5.675	5.690	2.526 (0.50)	0.167 (0.97)	
Post-BISTECH Period	GJR-GARCH-in-Mean (1,1)	Gauss	-0.000 (0.002)	0.000*** (0.000)	0.284*** (0.088)	0.680*** (0.083)	-0.001 (0.210)	-0.180** (0.078)	5.976	5.936	5.961	3.835 (0.27)	1.310 (0.64)	5.15
		Student	-0.002 (0.002)	0.000*** (0.000)	0.177* (0.098)	0.487*** (0.120)	0.251 (0.202)	0.112 (0.128)	6.123	6.075	6.104	3.221 (0.36)	0.561 (0.86)	2.12
		GED	-0.001*** (0.000)	0.000*** (0.000)	0.208 (0.074)	0.531*** (0.127)	0.171*** (0.031)	0.030 (0.155)	6.114	6.066	6.095	3.438 (0.33)	0.639 (0.84)	2.47
	I-GARCH (1,1)	Gauss	-0.000 (0.000)	0.000*** (0.000)	0.343*** (0.089)	0.656			5.957	5.936	5.949	2.883 (0.42)	0.581 (0.85)	
		Student	0.000 (0.000)	0.000** (0.000)	0.468*** (0.121)	0.531			6.116	6.089	6.106	3.192 (0.37)	0.058 (0.85)	
		GED	0.000 (0.000)	0.000** (0.000)	0.426*** (0.124)	0.573			6.108	6.081	6.097	2.893 (0.42)	0.698 (0.82)	

Note: *** denotes significance at the 1% level, and ** at the 5% level and * at the %10 level. The standard deviations of coefficients are in parenthesis and the probability values of the residuals tests are also reported in parenthesis.

Table 15. BIST sports

	Model	Dist.	Parameters						In-Sample Criteria			Residuals Tests		
			c	ω	α	β	δ	λ	AIC	BIC	HQ	Lag(5)	ARCH-LM(5)	Half-Life
Pre-BISTECH Period	**GJR-GARCH-in-Mean (1,1)**	**Gauss**	-0.002 (0.002)	0.000*** (0.000)	0.321*** (0.104)	0.650*** (0.087)	0.145 (0.160)	-0.220** (0.102)	5.127	5.092	5.114	2.454 (0.51)	1.433 (0.61)	4.64
		Student	0.000 (0.000)	0.000*** (0.000)	0.604*** (0.206)	0.501*** (0.095)	-0.069 (0.085)	-0.212 (0.184)	5.371	5.331	5.356	3.953 (0.25)	2.234 (0.42)	692.73
		GED	0.000*** (0.000)	0.000*** (0.000)	0.464** (0.121)	0.526*** (0.049)	-0.023*** (0.002)	-0.185 (0.147)	5.391	5.351	5.376	3.881 (0.26)	2.262 (0.41)	6.41
	I-GARCH (1,1)	**Gauss**	-0.000 (0.000)	0.000*** (0.000)	0.308*** (0.044)	0.691			5.103	5.085	5.096	4.675 (0.18)	2.085 (0.45)	
		Student	-0.000 (0.000)	0.000*** (0.000)	0.493*** (0.094)	0.506			5.376	5.352	5.367	4.311 (0.21)	2.137 (0.44)	
		GED	0.000 (0.000)	0.000** (0.000)	0.456*** (0.109)	0.543			5.395	5.372	5.386	4.549 (0.19)	2.567 (0.35)	
Post-BISTECH Period	**GJR-GARCH-in-Mean (1,1)**	**Gauss**	0.001 (0.001)	0.000 (0.000)	0.081*** (0.018)	0.936*** (0.010)	-0.089 (0.095)	-0.058*** (0.018)	5.221	5.181	5.206	3.415 (0.33)	2.420 (0.38)	60.53
		Student	-0.001 (0.002)	0.000* (0.000)	0.213** (0.101)	0.664*** (0.138)	0.074 (0.137)	0.039 (0.103)	5.343	5.295	5.324	2.270 (0.55)	0.311 (0.93)	6.41
		GED	-0.000 (0.000)	0.000*** (0.000)	0.091*** (0.021)	0.903*** (0.019)	0.007* (0.004)	-0.040 (0.030)	5.348	5.300	5.330	2.962 (0.41)	1.869 (0.50)	27.53
	I-GARCH (1,1)	**Gauss**	-0.000 (0.000)	0.000 (0.000)	0.050** (0.024)	0.949			5.215	5.194	5.207	2.644 (0.47)	3.329 (0.24)	
		Student	0.000 (0.000)	0.000 (0.000)	0.274** (0.127)	0.725			5.349	5.322	5.338	2.307 (0.54)	0.094 (0.98)	
		GED	0.000 (0.000)	0.000 (0.000)	0.081 (0.065)	0.918			5.352	5.325	5.342	2.805 (0.44)	1.266 (0.65)	

Note: *** denotes significance at the 1% level, and ** at the 5% level and * at the %10 level. The standard deviations of coefficients are in parenthesis and the probability values of the residuals tests are also reported in parenthesis.

Table 16. BIST W and retail trade

	Model	Dist.	Parameters						In-Sample Criteria			Residuals Tests		
			c	ω	α	β	δ	λ	AIC	BIC	HQ	Lag(5)	ARCH-LM(5)	Half-Life
Pre-BISTECH Period	GJR-GARCH-in-Mean (1,1)	Gauss	-0.002 (0.001)	0.000*** (0.000)	0.000 (0.003)	0.822*** (0.015)	0.193 (0.127)	0.204*** (0.041)	5.668	5.633	5.665	1.604 (0.71)	2.103 (0.44)	8.90
		Student	-0.002* (0.001)	0.000*** (0.000)	0.000 (0.013)	0.869*** (0.016)	0.228** (0.112)	0.135*** (0.041)	5.724	5.683	5.708	1.613 (0.71)	3.697 (0.20)	10.69
		GED	-0.001* (0.000)	0.000*** (0.000)	0.000 (0.007)	0.861*** (0.017)	0.138** (0.056)	0.149*** (0.042)	5.731	5.690	5.715	1.706 (0.68)	2.847 (0.31)	10.48
	I-GARCH (1,1)	Gauss	0.000* (0.000)	0.000*** (0.000)	0.163*** (0.027)	0.836			5.617	5.599	5.610	1.623 (0.70)	3.457 (0.23)	
		Student	0.000** (0.000)	0.000*** (0.000)	0.124*** (0.025)	0.875			5.708	5.685	5.700	1.741 (0.68)	5.163 (0.10)	
		GED	0.000** (0.000)	0.000* (0.000)	0.132*** (0.032)	0.867			5.711	5.688	5.703	1.696 (0.69)	4.296 (0.15)	
Post-BISTECH Period	GJR-GARCH-in-Mean (1,1)	Gauss	0.007*** (0.000)	0.000*** (0.000)	0.001*** (0.000)	0.997*** (0.00)	-0.639*** (0.024)	0.005*** (0.000)	5.960	5.919	5.944	3.477 (0.32)	2.207 (0.42)	191.09
		Student	-0.007*** (0.002)	0.000 (0.000)	0.000*** (0.000)	0.999*** (0.000)	0.595*** (0.187)	-0.002*** (0.000)	6.034	5.986	6.015	3.445 (0.33)	2.253 (0.41)	652.92
		GED	0.006*** (0.000)	0.000 (0.000)	0.000 (0.000)	0.999*** (0.000)	0.519*** (0.063)	-0.001*** (0.000)	6.037	5.989	6.018	3.495 (0.32)	2.381 (0.39)	632.65
	I-GARCH (1,1)	Gauss	0.000 (0.000)	0.000 (0.000)	0.008*** (0.002)	0.991			5.955	5.934	5.947	3.936 (0.26)	2.593 (0.35)	
		Student	-0.000 (0.000)	0.000 (0.000)	0.026*** (0.004)	0.973			6.033	6.005	6.022	4.185 (0.23)	2.236 (0.42)	
		GED	-0.000 (0.000)	0.000 (0.000)	0.010*** (0.001)	0.989			6.038	6.010	6.027	3.930 (0.26)	2.545 (0.36)	

Note: *** denotes significance at the 1% level, and ** at the 5% level and * at the %10 level. The standard deviations of coefficients are in parenthesis and the probability values of the residuals tests are also reported in parenthesis.

Table 17. BIST wood, paper, printing

	Model	Dist.	Parameters						In-Sample Criteria			Residuals Tests		
			c	ω	α	β	δ	λ	AIC	BIC	HQ	Lag(5)	ARCH-LM(5)	Half-Life
Pre-BISTECH Period	GJR-GARCH-in-Mean (1,1)	Gauss	-0.001 (0.001)	0.000*** (0.000)	0.232*** (0.069)	0.582*** (0.062)	0.066 (0.139)	0.115 (0.086)	5.904	5.869	5.890	0.937 (0.87)	1.465 (0.60)	5.10
		Student	-0.001 (0.000)	0.000*** (0.000)	0.209*** (0.019)	0.744*** (0.026)	0.123 (0.075)	0.039 (0.073)	6.076	6.035	6.060	1.181 (0.81)	1.280 (0.65)	25.60
		GED	0.005 (0.002)	0.000*** (0.000)	0.204*** (0.073)	0.692*** (0.056)	0.000 (0.000)	0.077 (0.090)	6.059	6.019	6.044	0.923 (0.87)	1.512 (0.58)	10.56
	I-GARCH (1,1)	Gauss	-0.000 (0.000)	0.000*** (0.000)	0.433*** (0.063)	0.566			5.898	5.881	5.892	0.956 (0.86)	2.109 (0.44)	
		Student	0.000 (0.000)	0.000*** (0.000)	0.257*** (0.043)	0.742			6.081	6.057	6.072	0.976 (0.86)	1.449 (0.60)	
		GED	0.000 (0.000)	0.000*** (0.000)	0.301*** (0.064)	0.698			6.064	6.040	6.055	1.007 (0.85)	1.884 (0.49)	
Post-BISTECH Period	GJR-GARCH-in-Mean (1,1)	Gauss	-0.002 (0.003)	0.000*** (0.000)	0.053 (0.042)	0.689*** (0.081)	0.202 (0.264)	0.138** (0.064)	5.767	5.727	5.752	2.180 (0.57)	0.834 (0.78)	3.33
		Student	-0.000 (0.002)	0.000** (0.000)	0.045 (0.043)	0.755*** (0.081)	0.100 (0.214)	0.149** (0.068)	5.842	5.794	5.824	2.052 (0.60)	0.368 (0.92)	5.20
		GED	-0.001* (0.000)	0.000** (0.000)	0.049 (0.045)	0.704*** (0.106)	0.133** (0.065)	0.165** (0.076)	5.840	5.792	5.822	2.148 (0.54)	0.511 (0.88)	3.88
	I-GARCH (1,1)	Gauss	0.000 (0.000)	0.000*** (0.000)	0.293*** (0.053)	0.706			5.736	5.716	5.728	2.064 (0.60)	0.296 (0.94)	
		Student	0.000 (0.000)	0.000* (0.000)	0.156*** (0.047)	0.843			5.832	5.805	5.821	1.979 (0.62)	0.310 (0.93)	
		GED	0.000 (0.000)	0.000*** (0.000)	0.223*** (0.047)	0.776			5.826	5.799	5.816	2.038 (0.60)	0.255 (0.95)	

inconclusive evidence that the effects of sudden shocks on volatility have become more evident for most of the sub-indexes in the post-BISTECH period.

The β parameter shows the effect of the volatility of a previous period on current volatility. The beta parameter is statistically significant for all estimated models regardless of model type, period and distribution. These findings suggest that the current volatility is largely explained by the volatility of the previous period. After the BISTECH transition, the effect of the volatility of the previous period on current volatility decreased for the sub-sectors BIST Electricity; BIST Food, Beverage; BIST Insurance; BIST Leasing, Factoring and BIST Real Estate, while it increased for the other sub-sectors.

Our examination of the presence of asymmetries reveals that they exist before and after the BISTECH transition in both of the main indexes, BIST 100 and BIST 30. The positive sign of the λ parameter indicates that negative shocks increase volatility more than positive shocks. This effect is visible in both indexes. The effect of negative shocks on volatility increases for both the BIST 100 and BIST 30 after the BISTECH transition. As for the sub-indexes, we find that the BIST Banks; BIST Basic Materials; BIST Corporate Governance; BIST Electricity; BIST Technology; BIST Metal Products, Mach.; BIST W. and Retail Trade; BIST Chem., Petrol, Plastic; BIST Hold. and Investment; BIST Food, Beverage; BIST Leasing, Factoring and BIST Real Estate indexes have significant asymmetrical effects in the pre-BISTECH period. The λ parameter has a positive sign for these indexes, which suggests that negative shocks have a greater impact on volatility than positive shocks. However, the asymmetries disappear for the BIST Chem., Petrol, Plastic; BIST Hold. and Investment and BIST Food, Beverage indexes after the BISTECH transition. Furthermore, the asymmetry parameter returns to negative for the BIST Leasing, Factoring and BIST Real Estate indexes. The asymmetries emerge with a positive sign for the BIST Wood, Paper, Printing index in the post-BISTECH period. Lastly, there are no asymmetries in the BIST Insurance index in both periods, while negative and significant asymmetry parameters are observed in the BIST Sports index.

The δ parameter, which shows the relationship between risk and return, is statistically insignificant for most indexes in both periods. The relationship between risk and return is significant only for the BIST 100 and BIST 30 indexes in the pre-BISTECH period, but the sign of the parameter for these indexes is negative as opposed to what is expected. The parameter turns out to be insignificant for the BIST 30 index in the post-BISTECH period. The negative sign of the parameter suggests that returns are decreasing, while risk increases for main indexes in both periods. In addition, the risk and return relationship is only positive and significant for the BIST Technology; BIST Insurance and BIST Metal Products, Mach. Indexes, while it is negative and significant for BIST Chem., Petrol, Plastic; BIST Leasing; Factoring and BIST W. and Retail Trade in the post-BISTECH period.

Finally, we present the half-life of volatility values, which show the duration of volatility's return to its average after a shock. The increase in this value suggests that the effects of shocks on volatility have become more permanent. The duration of volatility's return to its average after a shock lasts about 11 days for BIST 100 and BIST 30 in the pre-BISTECH period. This rises to 75 days for BIST 100 and 85 days for BIST 30 in the post-BISTECH period. Therefore, it can be understood that the effect of shocks on the volatility of BIST 100 and BIST 30 becomes more persistent in the post-BISTECH period. In the other sub-indexes, mixed results are obtained again the duration of volatility's return to its average after the BISTECH transition increases dramatically for most of the indexes of BIST Banks; BIST Chem., Petroleum and Plastic; BIST Corporate Governance; BIST Hold. and Investment; BIST Sports and BIST W. and Retail Trade, while it declines in the majority of other indexes.

CONCLUSION

Technological developments are one of the most fundamental factors affecting market conditions today. These innovations integrating into the financial system can change its functioning. High-frequency trading and algorithmic trading, which are relatively new developments in financial markets, have significant effects on several market indicators such as liquidity, competition, price efficiency, market quality and volatility. However, the direction and magnitude of these effects is not yet fully known. The studies freshly emerging in this field usually examine markets in developed countries. Therefore, this study examines the effects of these two new technological processes on volatility by taking into account asymmetry, and risk and return for Borsa Istanbul. Unlike in other studies, a more general and long-term approach is preferred. To this end, the behaviors of the main and sub-sector indexes of Borsa Istanbul are examined and compared for the periods before and after the transition to the BISTECH system, which made HFT and AT activities possible. In this framework, data covering November 14, 2012 to June 7, 2018 is analyzed by using the GJR-GARCH-in-Mean and I-GARCH models.

Although the findings of the study do not give a definite conclusion in terms of understanding the effects of HFT and AT on volatility, it has demonstrated that, in general, there has been an increase in the volatility of some important indexes in the post-BISTECH period. Thus, evaluating the findings of the indexes that HTF and AT activities are more intense may be more informative. The companies included in the BIST 30 and BIST Banks indexes carry considerable weight within the composition of Borsa Istanbul. Furthermore, more than 50% of the shares of the companies in these two indexes are held by foreign and institutional investors. From this point, it can be assumed that the behaviors of these two indexes are more determinative in terms of understanding the effects of HFT and AT on the volatility of Borsa Istanbul. The findings show us that volatility increases significantly in these indexes for the post-BISTECH period. In particular, the duration of volatility returns to average after shock increases about 7 times for BIST 100 and about 8 times for BIST 30 after BISTECH transition. We also show that the impact of the volatility of the previous period on current volatility increases in the post-BISTECH period. Our results on volatility are in parallel with the results of studies examining developed country examples, including those of Zhang (2010), Kirilenko et al. (2011), Scholtus et al. (2014), Boehmer et al. (2015), Kalejian and Mukerji (2016), and Hasbrouck (2018). However, our findings do not provide sufficient evidence to argue that HFT and AT activities definitely increase volatility. Therefore, the results should be interpreted with caution, and this indirect implication that HFT and AT activities increase volatility needs to be supported by further investigation.

Consequently, and although innovations in financial technologies are important for market development, these developments can have significant disruptive effects on financial markets. Once a market function changes, it takes time for all market participants to adapt to this change. The markets may be very uncertain and fragile during these transition periods. HFT and AC activities can create potential negative externalities for other market participants, and thus it is likely that traditional investors could in particular be harmed. Therefore, regulatory authorities must closely monitor the technological developments in financial markets and design appropriate safeguarding mechanisms against the potential disruptive effects. Even though it is stated in the literature that HFT and AT activities contribute positively to market efficiency in the short term, the long-term consequences of these technologies are still uncertain.

This research can be improved in several ways. First, analyses can be repeated by selecting the companies with higher levels of HFT and AT activities. In addition, future research could focus on intraday volatility using high-frequency data. On the other hand, future studies, from a comparative perspective, could examine the effects of HFT and AT activities on market participants who are using and not using AT and HFT activities. These interrogations will help us to understand the effects of HFT and AT on developing country markets in a deeper way.

REFERENCES

Aitken, M., Cumming, D., & Zhan, F. (2015). High frequency trading and end-of-day price dislocation. *Journal of Banking & Finance*, *59*, 330–349. doi:10.1016/j.jbankfin.2015.06.011

Alexander, C. (2001). *Market models: a guide to financial data analysis.* John Wiley & Sons.

Alexander, C. (2008). *Market risk analysis: practical financial econometrics* (Vol. 2). John Wiley and Sons.

Baron, M., Brogaard, J., Hagströmer, B., & Kirilenko, A. (2017). *Risk and return in high-frequency trading.* Retrieved May 8, 2018, https://papers.ssrn.com/sol3/papers.cfm?abstract_id=2433118

Biais, B., & Woolley, P. (2011). *High frequency trading. Manuscript.* Toulouse University, IDEI.

Boehmer, E., Fong, K., & Wu, J. (2015). *International evidence on algorithmic trading.* Retrieved May 15, 2018, from http://citeseerx.ist.psu.edu/viewdoc/download?doi=10.1.1.471.8155&rep=rep1&type=pdf

Brogaard, J. (2010). *High frequency trading and its impact on market quality.* Northwestern University Kellogg School of Management Working Paper 66.

Brogaard, J. (2012). *High frequency trading and volatility.* Retrieved April 20, 2018, from http://ssrn.com/abstract=1641387

Brogaard, J., Hendershott, T., & Riordan, R. (2014). High-frequency trading and price discovery. *Review of Financial Studies, 27*(8), 2267–2306. doi:10.1093/rfs/hhu032

Chaboud, A. P., Chiquoine, B., Hjalmarsson, E., & Vega, C. (2014). Rise of the machines: Algorithmic trading in the foreign exchange market. *The Journal of Finance, 69*(5), 2045–2084. doi:10.1111/jofi.12186

Conrad, J., Wahal, S., & Xiang, J. (2015). High-frequency quoting, trading, and the efficiency of prices. *Journal of Financial Economics, 116*(2), 271–291. doi:10.1016/j.jfineco.2015.02.008

Engle, R., Lilien, D. M., & Robins, R. P. (1987). Estimating time varying risk premia in the term structure: The ARCH-M model. *Econometrica, 55*(2), 391–407. doi:10.2307/1913242

Engle, R. F., & Bollerslev, T. (1986). Modelling the persistence of conditional variances. *Econometric Reviews, 5*(1), 1–50. doi:10.1080/07474938608800095

Frino, A., Mollica, V., Monaco, E., & Palumbo, R. (2017b). The effect of algorithmic trading on market liquidity: Evidence around earnings announcements on Borsa Italiana. *Pacific-Basin Finance Journal, 45*, 82–90. doi:10.1016/j.pacfin.2016.07.003

Frino, A., Prodromou, T., Wang, G. H., Westerholm, P. J., & Zheng, H. (2017a). An empirical analysis of algorithmic trading around earnings announcements. *Pacific-Basin Finance Journal, 45*, 34–51. doi:10.1016/j.pacfin.2016.05.008

Glosten, L., Jagannathan, R., & Runkle, D. E. (1993). On the relation between the expected value and the volatility of the nominal excess return on stocks. *The Journal of Finance, 48*(5), 1779–1801. doi:10.1111/j.1540-6261.1993.tb05128.x

Groth, S. (2011). Does algorithmic trading increase volatility. *Empirical Evidence from the Fully-Electronic Trading Platform Xetra, proceedings of the 10th International Conference on Wirtschaftsinformatik.*

Gsell, M. (2008). *Assessing the impact of Algorithmic Trading on markets: A simulation approach* (No. 2008/49). CFS Working Paper.

Hagströmer, B., & Norden, L. (2013). The diversity of high-frequency traders. *Journal of Financial Markets, 16*(4), 741–770. doi:10.1016/j.finmar.2013.05.009

Hamzaoui, N., & Regaieg, B. (2016). The Glosten-Jagannathan-Runkle-Generalized Autoregressive Conditional Heteroscedastic approach to investigating the foreign exchange forward premium volatility. *International Journal of Economics and Financial Issues, 6*(4), 1608–1615.

Hasbrouck, J. (2018). High-frequency quoting: Short-term volatility in bids and offers. *Journal of Financial and Quantitative Analysis, 53*(2), 613–641. doi:10.1017/S0022109017001053

Hendershott, T., Jones, C. M., & Menkveld, A. J. (2011). Does algorithmic trading improve liquidity? *The Journal of Finance, 66*(1), 1–33. doi:10.1111/j.1540-6261.2010.01624.x

Hendershott, T., & Riordan, R. (2009). *Algorithmic trading and information. Manuscript*. Berkeley, CA: University of California.

Hendershott, T., & Riordan, R. (2013). Algorithmic trading and the market for liquidity. *Journal of Financial and Quantitative Analysis, 48*(4), 1001–1024. doi:10.1017/S0022109013000471

Jain, P. K., Jain, P., & McInish, T. H. (2016). Does high-frequency trading increase systemic risk? *Journal of Financial Markets, 31*, 1–24. doi:10.1016/j.finmar.2016.09.004

Jones, C. M. (2013). *What do we know about high-frequency trading*. Columbia Business School, Research Paper No. 13-11.

Kelejian, H. H., & Mukerji, P. (2016). Does high frequency algorithmic trading matter for non-AT investors? *Research in International Business and Finance*, *37*, 78–92. doi:10.1016/j.ribaf.2015.10.014

Kirilenko, A., Kyle, A., Mehrdad, S., & Tugkan, T. (2011). *The flash crash: the impact of high frequency trading on an electronic market.* Available at SSRN 1686004.

Liu, L. (2013). *High Frequency Trading and Its Impact on the Swedish Stock volatility* (Unpublished Master Thesis). Lund University, Sweden.

Manahov, V., Hudson, R., & Gebka, B. (2014). Does high frequency trading affect technical analysis and market efficiency? And if so, how? *Journal of International Financial Markets, Institutions and Money*, *28*, 131–157. doi:10.1016/j.intfin.2013.11.002

Martinez, V. H., & Rosu, I. (2013). High frequency traders, news and volatility. In *AFA 2013*. San Diego Meetings Paper.

Rachev, S. (2007). *Financial Econometrics: From Basics to Advanced Modeling Techniques*. John Wiley & Sons.

Scholtus, M., van Dijk, D., & Frijns, B. (2014). Speed, algorithmic trading, and market quality around macroeconomic news announcements. *Journal of Banking & Finance*, *38*, 89–105.

Zhang, F. (2010). *High-frequency trading, stock volatility, and Price Discovery.* SSRN eLibrary.

ADDITIONAL READING

Boehmer, E., Li, D., & Saar, G. (2018). The competitive landscape of high-frequency trading firms. *Review of Financial Studies*, *31*(6), 2227–2276. doi:10.1093/rfs/hhx144

Brennan, M. J., Huh, S. W., & Subrahmanyam, A. (2018). High-frequency measures of informed trading and corporate announcements. *Review of Financial Studies*, *31*(6), 2326–2376. doi:10.1093/rfs/hhy005

Brogaard, J., Carrion, A., Moyaert, T., Riordan, R., Shkilko, A., & Sokolov, K. (2018). High frequency trading and extreme price movements. *Journal of Financial Economics*, *128*(2), 253–265. doi:10.1016/j.jfineco.2018.02.002

Farjam, M., & Kirchkamp, O. (2018). Bubbles in hybrid markets: How expectations about algorithmic trading affect human trading. *Journal of Economic Behavior & Organization*, *146*, 248–269. doi:10.1016/j.jebo.2017.11.011

Golub, A., Grossmass, L., & Poon, S. H. (2018). Ultra Short Tenor Yield Curves For High-Frequency Trading and Blockchain Settlement.

Jiang, G. J., Lo, I., & Valente, G. (2018). High-Frequency Trading in the US Treasury Market around Macroeconomic News Announcements.

Li, K., Cooper, R., & Van Vliet, B. (2018). How Does High-Frequency Trading Affect Low-Frequency Trading? *Journal of Behavioral Finance, 19*(2), 235–248. doi:10.1080/15427560.2017.1376669

Malceniece, L., Malcenieks, K., & Putniņš, T. J. (2018). High Frequency Trading and Co-Movement in Financial Markets.

Menkveld, A. J. (2018). High-Frequency Trading as Viewed through an Electron Microscope. *Financial Analysts Journal, 74*(2), 24–31. doi:10.2469/faj.v74.n2.1

Mestel, R., Murg, M., & Theissen, E. (2018). Algorithmic trading and liquidity: Long term evidence from Austria. *Finance Research Letters, 26*, 198–203. doi:10.1016/j.frl.2018.01.004

KEY TERMS AND DEFINITIONS

Adverse Selection: Adverse selection is a problem created by asymmetric information. When sellers and buyers do not have same information level before the transaction in the market, the adverse selection problem arises.

Algorithmic Trading: Algorithmic trading is a system producing automated trading orders based on certain rules which use mathematical formulas run by computers.

BISTECH: BISTECH is a technological infrastructure that allows algorithmic trading and high-frequency trading operations in Borsa Istanbul.

Borsa Istanbul: Borsa Istanbul is an institution that provides storage and exchange services for Turkish and foreign-funded banks operating in Turkey's capital market.

Half-Life Volatility: Half-life volatility is a measurement that calculates the duration of volatility's return to its average after a shock.

High-Frequency Trading: High-frequency trading is an automated trading platform that transacts a large number of orders in fractions of a second.

Volatility: The fluctuation of the price of a security or the market in a short period of time. The price of a high-volatility security is characterized by rapid and extreme changes.

Section 3

FinTech and Islamic Finance

Chapter 9
Fintech and *Shariah* Principles in Smart Contracts

Norafni Farlina Rahim
Universiti Teknikal Malaysia – Melaka (UTeM), Malaysia

Mohammed Hariri Bakri
Universiti Teknikal Malaysia – Melaka (UTeM), Malaysia

Siti Norbaya Yahaya
Universiti Teknikal Malaysia – Melaka (UTeM), Malaysia

ABSTRACT

FinTech, or financial technology, is an emerging technology in financial transaction. It is disruptive technology which is changing the banking behavior for stakeholders. The thriving emergence of FinTech not only affects the conventional finance industry but also Islamic finance industry, as Islamic finance sector is also embracing FinTech as part of financial revolution. Thus, the Islamic FinTech emerges as faith-based FinTech. This is because Islamic FinTech claimed to comply with Shariah principle in their mechanism and smart contract. There is limited discussion on smart contract and Islamic FinTech and its Shariah principles. Hence, the Shariah principle in smart contract of Islamic FinTech need to be addressed. This chapter tries to delve into the smart contract concept in Islamic FinTech and Shariah principles in the mechanism. The review found that smart contract is currently in the early stage and so is Islamic FinTech. The scholars agreed that FinTech is a Maslahah (interest) to mankind's benefit. However, the smart contract is still in discussion and review.

DOI: 10.4018/978-1-5225-7805-5.ch009

INTRODUCTION

Fintech is defined as financial technology. As the financial industry moving toward modernism and globalization, technology is inevitable. The technology in finance has changing the banking behaviour of stakeholders in doing financial transaction. Financial technology has started with the evolution of Internet since 1990s which it implicates the lower cost of doing transaction (Lee and Shin, 2018). The emergence of internet and smart phone has accelerated the banking process and expedite the financial transaction. This change has evolved into new whole industry from traditional banking of brick-and-mortar to the new system in doing financial transaction called Fintech. Hence, it is considered disruptive technology, which means disrupt or complete changes the way to do things. This also means, consumer will no longer go to traditional banks to do their financial matters, rather they do it by apps and mobile. According to Lee (2017), Fintech is divided into two-traditional and emergent Fintech. Traditional Fintech is market players serve as facilitators, while emergent Fintech is rather a disruptor to the existing market. The first is considered to facilitate and supporting the existing financial industry, while the latter is deemed as innovator to the industry. Zovolokina, Dolata and Schwabe (2016) mentioned that Fintech is not a phenomena affecting entrepreneur, rather it is influenced by the combination of economic, technological factor and regulation.

The market of Fintech is lucratively attractive and potential for handsome profit. Surendra (2017) reported that estimation of investment in Fintech globally reaching up to USD 40 billion. Although it is reported that the users of Fintech globally is still small, as it is now in nascent stage, the report from Ernst & Young (2016) has shows that the growth rate of adoption is fast up to three times. Currently, the adoption index of Fintech globally is 15.5 percent and it is estimated can be tripled within a year, provided there are awareness on the adoption. This is quite fast compared to the report in 2016 by International Trade Adiministration (ITA) from US Department of Commerce which stated that the adoption rate can double within a year (ITA, 2016). In Indonesia, the transaction value via Fintech in 2016 is worth RPI 199 trillion (Dwi Marlina & Alex, 2017). In the case of Malaysia, Fintech in Malaysia is still in infancy stage but growing rapidly. Securities Commission (SC) is the first fintech regulator in ASEAN. SC has amended the Guidelines for Recognized Market, as part of regulatory framework for P2P lending, allowing small and medium-sized companies access for debt funding (Surendra, 2017). Minister of Finance II (year 2016-2018), Dato' Seri Johari Abdul Ghani has mentioned in Malaysia Fintech Expo 2018 that government of Malaysia will guarante the condusive economic environment to support the Fintech industry to ensure no glitch in the digital business (Hazwan Faisal, 2018). He also reporting that digital economy has contribute to the

Gross Domestic Product (GDP) about 17.8 percent in 2016 and estimated to reach 20 percent in 2020.

Islamic Finance sector has also embrace this change. In Malaysia, the Islamic banks are on Fintech too. Maybank, CIMB Bank, Hong Leong Bank and RHB Bank among the few that join Fintech, which some of them cooperate with local companies to come out with Fintech innovations like remittance and P2P (Nurul Aini & Ainulashikin, 2018). Smart contract could support the Islamic finance products in several areas like capital market, Islamic investment, takaful and many more (Siti Rohaya, Zam Zuriyati, Juliana, Farhana Hanim, & Norhayati, 2018). However, there are very limited discussion on the smart contract in Islamic Fintech with Shariah principles underlies. This is because the sector and industry itself is considered nascent (MIFC, 2016; BIS, 2017). Furthermore, the studies in Islamic Fintech and smart contract is currently underexplored (Alharby & Moorsel, 2017) and most of the studies in Islamic Fintech is hovering in concept, legal issues and regulation.

Thus, this chapter trying to delve the concept of smart contract in Islamic Fintech and its Shariah principles. The subject is important as smart conract is no longer a hype but a reality (Capegemini Consulting, 2016). It is so because smart contract able to overcome the problems in traditional contract (Capegemini Consulting, 2016). Furthermore, people nowadays are techno-literate and prefer less human interaction when dealing with financial transaction (Siti Rohaya et al., 2018; Nurul Aini & Ainulashikin, 2018).

LITERATURE REVIEW

Islamic Fintech

Islamic Fintech is one of the innovation in Fintech. Some reports separate Islamic Fintech as one of the business model in Fintech and some reports put Islamic Fintech as similar like any other Fintech, except that the business model of Islamic Fintech following Shariah guidelines. They are also known as Shariah-compliant Fintech, Shariah Fintech, or Halal Fintech which are all bring the similar meaning. Basically, Islamic Fintech carry the same jurisdiction as products in Islamic finance; which must be free from '*Maghrib*' elements; *maysir* (gambling), *gharar* (uncertainty) and *riba* (interest) (Muthiah, et al., 2017).

Although it is notable that Islamic Fintech is still positioning themselves around the world, its starts-up are growing tremendously all around the world, particularly in Muslim-majority countries like Malaysia, Indonesia, and United Arab Emirates. Surprisingly, non-Muslim countries like US and UK also have some numbers in this profitable digital business as reported by IFNFintech, RedMoney (2018). Kenya and

Switzerland also venturing in Islamic Fintech recently. This is because consumer, especially Muslim consumers and religious-minded person, aware of the financial technology and want to deal with it with faith.

However, Todorof (2018) argued that Islamic Fintech is somehow left behind and losing the huge populations of Muslim consumers. This is because the adherence to Shariah principles is strong which somehow make it quite strict to acquire wealth. This is because in Shariah point of view, wealth should be acquired by risk and labor. However, Todorof (2018) also positively mentioned that technology can accelerate the economies of Muslims particularly in Fintech industry, especially in P2P, remittance, crowfunding and mobile wallet. This can be done by having harmonization of standards and guidelines to minimize the risk. Despite the position of Islamic Fintech is still in infancy stage, its market will be robust and wider. This is because Islamic Fintech not only offers efficiency in mobile banking and low transaction cost, but also provide transparency and flexibility, which are vital elements in Shariah guidelines and *Maqasid al-Shariah* (objectives of Shariah).

The following are among the innovations in Islamic Fintech around the globe. It will be increased more soon as the invention is fast and the success stories are ubiquitous.

Though the Islamic Fintech is getting popular among consumers, the vital element in digital transaction need to be addressed. One of it is smart contract.

Smart Contract

Smart contract was first introduced by Nick Szabo in 1994. However, the information technology infrastructure at that time was not ready. Smart contract is defined as "a set of promise, specified in digital form, including protocols within which the parties perform on these promises" (Lauslahti, Mattila & Seppälä, 2017; Idelberger, Governatori, Riveret & Sartor, 2016). According to Szabo (1997), smart contract able to facilitate financial services and products such as loans intallments and credit card. The application of smart contract is not only for financial services such as banking and insurance, it also vastly applicable for energy, e-government, telecommunication, education, art and many more.

According to Laldin (n.d.), smart contract is more generic than traditional contract. The objectives of smart contract are to meet the conditions of common contract and to minimize the need for intermediaries. It also intended to reduce fraud loss and to lower arbitration and transaction cost (Laldin, n.d.; Siti Rohaya et al., 2018). Smart contract also needed to speed up the transaction process and to maximize transparency.

Table 1. Islamic Fintech landscape

Islamic Fintech Innovation	Islamic Fintech Apps
Alternative Finance	Liberis*, Ovamba Finance*, Primary Finance*
Blockchain and Cryptocurrencies	Ateon*, Bioonline, Everex*, HelloGold, OneGram, Ripple*
Crowdfunding & P2P Finance	570easi, Ammana Fintek Syariah*, Beehive, Blossom*, Croowd, DANAdidik*, EthisCrowd, Halal Launcher*, HalalSku*, IAP Integrated, Indves*, Investree*, Invoice Wakalah*, Kapital Boost, Launch Good*, Maliyya*, Mehrabane", MelkBaMa*, MercyCrowd*, MoneyFellows*, NusaKapital, PropTechCrowd, Qard Hasan*, Sadaqah Indonesia*, Shekra*, Seed Out, Stride Up*, Syarfi Teknologi Finansial*, Waqf World*, Yielders
Data & Analytics	Arabesque*, Capnovum*, Ideal Ratings*, MyFINB*
Digital Banks	Clearly*, HadaDBank*, MCash, Medina Digital Finance*, Ummah Finance*
Insurtech	InsureHalal*
Islamic Incubators / Ventures / Solution Builders	ConexCap, EthisVenture, Finocracy*, Goodforce Labs*, Mountain Partners*, Sedania Al Salam Capital
Personal Finance, Trading and Investments	AAM Commodities*, AbleAceRaakin*, Al-Iman, Bursa Suq Al Sila, CowryWise*, DDCap, EIGER Trading Advisors, Finerd*, Hajj Builder*, HelloGold, Investroo*, Sarwa Digital Wealth*, Sedania Al Salam Capital, Shariah Portfolio*, Tamasia
Payment, Remittance and Foreign Exchange	Ajar Online*, NowMoney*, Payfort*, PayHalal, PayTren, World Remit*
Technology, IT and Infrastructure	3i Infotech*, Aetins*, ALAMI Sharia*, Alpha Fintech*, AutoSoft Dynamics*, BIT Group*, CodeBase Technologies, Edgeverve Finacle*, Iprimitus Consultancy*, Path Solutions, PIBAS*, RM Applications*, Silverlake Axis, Temenos*, Trasset*
Robo Advisors	Farringdon Group, Wahed Invest, Wealth Simple*

*Companies without an official Shariah compliance recognition
Source: RedMoney (2018)

Smart contract was described by Siti Rohaya et al., (2018) have few stages that efficiently applied in financial technologies. The pre-defined smart contract set the specific terms and standards which the parties involved adhere. This will execute the smart contract which the informations are exchanged and the transaction take place. Digital asset can be traded via cryptocurrencies such as Bitcoin or Ethereum but for physical asset, the smart contracts require stocks or fiat money. The use of artifical intelligence (Ai) is applied in smart contract, which is widely applied in customer services, product sales and financial transaction.

How Smart Contract Working?

In a brief explanation, smart contract is created between two users. Then the terms and conditions of the contract is written as code. The smart contract then is placed in blockchain and after that the smart contract will execute itself upon the triggering event. Lauslahti (et al., 2017) had mentioned that the most simplest form of smart contract is vending machine. Vending machine is one of offer-acceptance mechanism where the "creator" of smart contract put pre-conditioned in the distribution of asset. When the terms and conditions in the smart contract are met, the contract will executed itself automatically (Lauslahti et al., 2017; Zerado & Fintech Network, 2017; Siti Rohaya et al., 2018).

Figure 1 shows the system in smart contract. Each contract will have 20 bytes of unique address. Once the smart contract is positioned into the blockchain, the contract algorithm cannot be changed. Users will send a transaction to the contract's address and it will be executed by miners network to reach a consensus of its yield. The contract's state then will be updated accordingly. The contract able to read or write its private storage, store money into its account balance and send or receive messages, send and receives money from user or other contracts, based on the transaction it receives (Alharby & Moorsel, 2017).

Advantage of Smart Contract Compared to Traditional Contract

Smart contract is claimed to have advantage in efficiency, security and impartiality in the agreement execution. Thus, it can lower the transaction cost and improving

Figure 1. Smart contract system
Source: Alharby & Moorsel (2017)

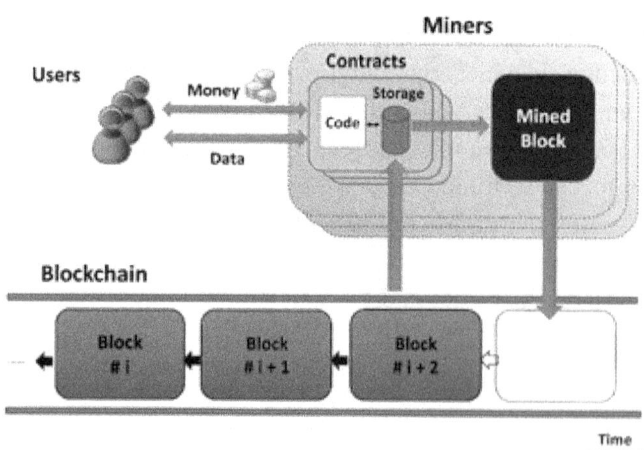

confidence and confidentiality between parties involved (Idelberger, Governatori, Riveret & Sartor, 2016). Traditional contracts on the other hand created by legal professional, which mostly contrain legal language. The public have hard time in deciphering the legal language which slowing down the transaction. Traditional contract also have too many printed documents and risk of losing it is high. This jeorpardize the safety and confidentiality of the transaction. It also heavily depend on the third parties for enforcement and if things go wrong, the parties involved need to rely on the public judicial system (Laldin, n.d). The data gathered by Capegemini Consulting (2016) has shows that traditional contract is exposed to the risk of fraud, overhead, and settlement delay. It was reported that average settlement days for loan in US is 20+ days while in Europe around 48 days. The same report also shows that £277 billion per day volume handled by UK's RTGS (Real-time-gross-settlement) system that went offline for 10 hours in 2014, delaying deals worth billions.

As mentioned previously, the smart contract can solve the problems in traditional contract. Smart contract is created by programmers where it is digitally written using programming code. It has pre-defined rule and consequences by stating obligations, benefits and penalties. It also reduce the potential of litigation and have auditable history of transaction. This is because the smart contracts has fully-digitalized the contracts. The report from Capegemini Consulting (201X) has indicated that by applying smart contract in loan market, the banks can generate extra income from fee around US 2-7 billion annually. In motor insurance service, insurers can save money because of the lower cost of settlement around US $21 billion annually. In customers' side, the loan is taking less day, lower processing fee and lower insurance premium.

Figure 2 shows the features that differentiate traditional contracts and smart contracts. From the figure we can infer that smart contracts is the better option compared to traditional contracts.

Figure 2. Differences between traditional contract and smart contract
Source: Laldin (n.d.)

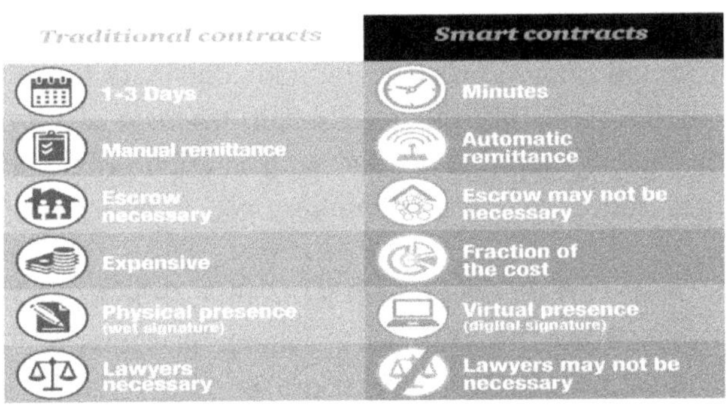

Smart Contract in Islamic Fintech

Smart contract is expected to to accelerate the digitalization of Islamic banking industry in Islamic capital market, Islamic investment, takaful and Islamic banking. Malaysia is so optimist on this that Malaysian Digital Economy Corp (MDEC) is launching Islamic Digital Framework that was formulated by Department of Islamic Development, Malaysia (JAKIM) and Amanie Advisors Sdn Bhd, which was lead by the prominent scholars of Islamic finance, Datuk Dr Daud Bakar. Similarly, Dubai also has launched Fintech Hive with aim to become the global hub of Islamic Fintech revolution.

Currently, smart contract is under scrutinization of laws and regulations. Capegemini Consulting (2016) has reported that year 2017-2018 are the year of take-off. Most of current studies has stated that blockchain technology is currently uses smart contract. It is so because blockchain is the ideal platform for smart contract due to its technology security and immutability (Shariyah Review Bureau, 2018; Alharby & Moorsel, 2017). The study of smart contract and blockchain however is limited because the industry is still in infancy stage. Furthermore, the regulators and legal scholars are cautious about this new technology. Currently, the legal status about smart contract in blockchain is regulated and influenced by state law (Lauslahti, et al., 2017).

According to Siti Rohaya et al., (2018), smart contract could support Islamic finance product. The terms and conditions in smart contract should be specific and must be executed within Shariah guidelines. According to Shariah Review Bureau (2018), smart contract make the Sukuk (Shariah-compliant bond) based on blockchain possible. It also can be applied to other Islamic financial product such as Takaful, crowdfunding and microfinance models. However the Bureau mentioned that the smart contract on blockchain must be differ from each other accordingly. Dadabhoy (2018) has mentioned that smart contract can be adopted possible automation in Islamic finance, Murabahah contract, collateralised Murabahah, Wakalah and Tahawwut Master Agreement.

According to Laldin (n.d.) smart contract in Fintech is considered *Maslahah* (public interest). This is because smart contract and Fintech is facilitating to the goodness of well-being. It provides good order of life and contribute to the civilization of mankind. Indirectly, it serve the objective of Shariah (*Maqasid-al-Shariah*). However, smart contract in Fintech should be in line with Shariah principles as guided by main sources of revelation i.e. *Quran, Sunnah, Ijma'* (consensus of scholars) and *Qiyas* (analogy).

However, the framework of smart contract in Fintech to be Shariah-compliant still in debate (Djafri, 2017; IRCIEF, 2018; Islamic Business & Finance; 2017). This is because the discussion on blockchain is still on-going as it is a new technology emerged to the public. Furthermore, blockchain is closely intertwined with cryptocurrency which currently under scrutinization of regulators, financial players, academicians and scholars. The complexities of the blockchain and smart contract, although proved to be more secure and sound, is also exposed to the risk similar as traditional financial risk. Smart contract also exposed to the fraud risk, issue of decentralization, market risk, human-nature elements outside of the contract, systemic risk, jusrisdiction issue, programmatic risk and many more (Laldin, n.d; Delmolino, Arnett, Kosba, Miller & Shi, 2015).

Shariah Principles and Issues in Smart Contract and Fintech

Similar with any contracts in Islamic finance, smart contract in Fintech also relies on the concept of Shariah. Shariah is Islamic guidelines based on Holy Quran, *Sunnah* (sayings and actions of the Prophet Muhammad PBUH), *Qiyas* (analogy) and *Ijma'* (scholars' consensus) as the primary source of the rulings. As mentioned before, the sale and buy contracts must be free from '*Maghrib*' elements; *maysir* (gambling), *gharar* (uncertainty) and *riba'* (interest) elements. At a glance, smart contract and Islamic Fintech has nothing to do with gambling like in casino, but in Islamic perspective, *maysir* prohibition here means the contracts should be free from betting, speculation and derivaties such as forwards, options and so on. It also must be free from *gharar* (uncertainty) which means dubious contracts, vague contracts and questionable buying and selling. *Riba'* (interest or usury) is the vital element that differentiate between conventional contracts and Islamic contracts. *Riba'* is strictly prohibited in the Quran as Allah said in Holy Quran "But Allah has permitted trade and forbidden riba'.." (Al-Baqarah: 275). The contracts also should abide other basic rules of *muamalat* (Islamic financial transaction) such as promoting justice, avoiding *tadlis* (cheating) and *ikrah* (coercion) in which the contracts cannot have deceptive contracts or advertisement, and adhere to other guidelines stipulated in financial transaction.

In Islamic finance contract, the product offered must have a valid contracts as stipulated in Quran, Sunnah, *Ijma'* (consensus) and *Qiyas* (analogy) There are many various valid contracts that have been used extensively by the traditional Islamic banks such as *Hiwalah* for credit card, *Bay' al Dayn* for Islamic accepted bills, *Wadiah* for saving accounts and many more. It means, every product in Islamic finance have gone through the tight process and procedure for product development stages to compliments the notion of Islamic finance for whole.

The same principles applies in smart contract in Islamic Fintech. Although Fintech is considered disruptive technology, it does not mean that Islamic Fintech can escape from the rulings, rather it extends the choices to the consumers to do their financial transaction in Shariah-compliancy. It means, the disruptiveness happens in the technological advancement in doing the transaction, but not its rules and principles. Smart contract and digital contract in Islamic Fintech should bind with Islamic values and the principles of muamalat, same way as Islamic finance products.

As mentioned before, the regulators and scholars are very careful with this new technology of financial transaction and it is still in debate. Djafri (2017) has reported from the workshop on Fintech and Islamic Finance organized by London School of Economics and Political Science (LSE) and Hamad bin Khalifa University (HBKU) that application of Fintech not intended to divert any legal ruligs of transaction (*Ahkam*), rather it is considered *Dhara'i* (means) to a benefit of people (*Maslahah*). The cyrptocurrency roundtable discussion organized by International Research Centre of Islamic Economics and Finance (IRCIEF) Islamic University College of Selangor (KUIS) has debate on the digital contract that mostly related with blockchain and cryptocurrency has find resolution that the use of cryptocurrency as settlement and remittance medium is fall under Shariah legal maxim: "All things are originally permissible and the willingness of the sides in implementing the contract (IRCIEF, 2018). After all, crytocurrency is backed by fiat money. This also under discussion as in report by Djafri (2017) mentioned that cryptocurrency have no instrinsic value. This result of this discussion is similar as in result of discussion by IRCIEF (2018) which also debating the instrinsic value and the *rawaj* (circulation) of cryptocurrency and blockchain. The same goes to the Shariah issue in smart contract. Islamic Finance & Business (2017) argued that the smart contract may have slight contradiction of Shariah principles in contract and the practicality of the contract execution. In other words, Shariah principles require the contract to be very details and transparent in order to preserve its validity in Shariah framework. However, some contract like solar energy purchase where the transaction volume and future prices is unknown. This may withdraw some potential buyer which makes the contract itself not self-executed. This is against the idea of smart-contract where the smart contract supposed to be self-executed. This has raise the debate on how 'smart' the contract under Shariah legislation.

Despite the debate on Shariah issues on smart contract and Islamic Fintech, the potential of the smart contract and Islamic Fintech is huge. This is because the application of smart contract is numerous. We cannot deny that digitalization of transaction and doing banking is our future. Smart contract and Islamic Fintech can soar higher with well-crafted regulatory framework. Shariyah Review Bureau (2018) has outlined how the Initial Coin Offering (ICO) oppose to Initial Public Offering (IPO) by cryptocurrency and blockchain which should pass Shariah screening. The Shariah screeening consist of two; business activities screening and financial ratio screening. The Shariah screening here is similar with the regulation under Securities Commission Malaysia (SC) to determine the Shariah-compliant stocks, unit trust and real estate investment. Business screening is a measure for the Shariah review to filter the business activities of the companies – if the companies involve with prohibited activities, while financial screening is the determination of ratio agreed by Muslim scholars include the interest bearing ratio and non-compliant ratio in the companies income. This proposal is one of the step to regulate the smart contract and Islamic Fintech to make it Shariah-compliant. This will make the smart contract and Islamic Fintech applicable to Muslim consumers who demand on faith-based transaction.

CONCLUSION

The application of smart contract in Islamic Fintech is widely applied. This is because it promotes transparency and legal binding which sounds attractive to the stakesholders in Fintech. The smart contract in Islamic Fintech is vital as it not only provide information, but act as legal contract between the parties involved. The existence of smart contract accelerate the digital economy of a country, especially in financial technologies.

The discussion above is explaining the Shariah principles and issues pertaining to the smart contracts in Islamic Fintech. The review of literature found that smart contract in Islamic Fintech is still in early stage and accepted with optimism. Most of researchers has found that smart contract will replace traditional contract soon due to its practicality and less transaction cost. However, it still under review and study by regulators, Shariah scholars and academicians. The scholars agreed that Fintech is *Maslahah* (interest) to benefit mankind by facilitating financial transaction but scholars are still contemplating and discussing on the issue of smart contract in blockchain and cryptocurrency.

To catch up with fast-paced technology of Fintech, the regulators and Shariah reviewer may start with the screening like proposal of Shariyah Review Board (2018) on imitating the Shariah regulatory framework by Securities Commission Malaysia (SC) in filtering the business entities and activities as well as financial ratios. This move though may have some slight drawbacks due to the complexities of the smart contract and its application in Islamic Fintech, but one step ahead is needed for betterment of regulatory framework for smart contract and Islamic Fintech. This will not only make the companies in Islamic Fintech uphold the Shariah principles, but also uphold transparency and integrity. Consequently, it will direct us to *khairu ummah* (better nation) in doing transaction with peace of mind and preserve our relationship with the Creator.

REFERENCES

Alharby, M., & Moorsel, A. V. (2017). *Blockchain-Based Smart Contracts: A Systematic Mapping Study. In Computer Science & Information Technology* (pp. 125–140). CS & IT.

BIS. (2017). *Sound Practices: Implications of Fintech developments for banks and bank supervisors*. Basel Committee on Banking Supervision.

Capegemini Consulting. (2016). *Smart Contracts in Financial Services: Getting from Hype to Reality*. Retrieved from https://www.capgemini.com/consulting-de/wp-content/uploads/sites/32/2017/08/smart_contracts_paper_long_0.pdf

Dadabhoy, I. (2018). *Introduction to FinTech and Smart Contracts (Slide)*. IIFM Seminar on Islamic Financial Markets, Kuala Lumpur, Malaysia.

Delmolino, K., Arnett, M., Kosba, A., Miller, A., & Shi, E. (2016). Step By Step Towards Creating A Safe Smart Contract: Lessons And Insights From A Cryptocurrency Lab. In *International Conference on Financial Cryptography and Data Security*, (pp. 79-94). Springer. 10.1007/978-3-662-53357-4_6

Djafri, F. (2017). *Summary Report of the LSE-HBKU Workshop on Fintech and Islamic Finances*. Center for Islamic Economics and Finance (CIEF), College of Islamic Studies, Hamad Bin Khalifa University at the London School of Economics.

Dwi Marlina, W., & Alex, F. R. (2017). Shariah Fintech: Positive Innovation in Consumer Perspective. *Proceeding International Seminar on Competition Policy and Law*, 101-120.

Ernst & Young. (2016). *Landscaping UK Fintech*. UK Trade and Investment.

Hazwan Faisal, M. (2018). Kerajaan komited perkasa Fintech di Malaysia. *Berita Harian*. Retrieved from https://www.bharian.com.my/bisnes/lain-lain/2018/03/396634/kerajaan-komited-perkasa-fintech-di-malaysia

Idelberger, F., Governatori, G., Riveret, R., & Sartor, G. (2016). Evaluation of Logic-Based Smart Contracts for Blockchain Systems. In J. Alferes, L. Bertossi, G. Governatori, P. Fodor, & D. Roman (Eds.), Lecture Notes in Computer Science: Vol. 9718. *Rule Technologies. Research, Tools, and Applications. RuleML 2016*. Springer. doi:10.1007/978-3-319-42019-6_11

International Trade Administration (ITA). (2016). *2016 Top Markets Report Financial Technology*. Department of Commerce.

IRCIEF. (2018). Roundtable Discussion On Cryptocurrency: Issues And Solutions. *IRCIEF KUIS*. Retrieved from http://www.kuis.edu.my/ircief/blog/2018/04/18/roundtable-discussion-on-cryptocurrency-issues-and-solutions/

Islamic Business & Finance. (2017). Is Fintech Shari'ah compliant? In Developing Islamic Fintech. CPI Financial FZ LLC.

Laldin, M. A. (n.d.). *Fintech and Smart Contract: Opportunities in Islamic Finance*. Retrieved from International Islamic Financial Market: http://www.iifm.net/sites/default/files/Session%206%20%20Fintech%20and%20Smart%20Contract%20Opportunities%20in%20Islamic%20Finance%20%20Prof.%20Dr.%20Mohamad%20Akram%20Laldin%20%28ISRA%29.pdf

Lauslahti, K., Mattila, J., & Seppälä, T. (2017). *Smart Contracts – How will Blockchain Technology Affect Contractual Practices?* ETLA Reports No 68. Retrieved from https://pub.etla.fi/ETLA-Raportit-Reports-68.pdf

MIFC. (2016). *Islamic Finance Technology and Innovation*. Bank Negara Malaysia.

Muthiah, A. Z. R., & Ro'fa, S., & Islamiyati. (2017). Crowdfunding Syariah Untuk Pengembangan Produk Perbankan Syariah Dari Perspektif Shariah Compliance. *Diponegoro Law Journal*, *6*(4), 1–16.

Nurul Aini, M., & Ainulashikin, M. (2018). Will Fintech Disrupt Islamic Banks? In Extending the Boundaries of Islamic Finance, Vol. 4, YTI Lecture Series (pp. 182-195). USIM Press.

RedMoney. (2018). *IFNFintech: Unlocking the Potential of Islamic Finance*. Retrieved from https://www.ifnfintech.com/issue/volume-2-issue-1

Shariyah Review Bureau. (2018). Decoding Compliance of an Iconic Offering (ICO). *Shariyah Review Bureau.* Retrieved from http://shariyah.com/wp-content/uploads/2018/08/ICO-with-changes.pdf

Siti Rohaya, M. R., Zam Zuriyati, M., Juliana, A. B., Farhana Hanim, M., & Norhayati, M. I. (2018). Artificial Intelligence, Smart Contract and Islamic Finance. *Asian Social Science*, *14*(2), 145–154. doi:10.5539/ass.v14n2p145

Surendra, E. (2017). *Introduction to Fintech in Malaysia*. Retrieved from https://www.imoney.my/articles/introduction-fintech-malaysia

Szabo, N. (1997). Formalizing and Securing Relationships on Public Networks. *First Monday*, *2*(9). doi:10.5210/fm.v2i9.548

Todorof, M. (2018). *Editorial: Shariah-compliant Fintech in the banking industry. ERA 2018*. Springer. doi:10.100712027-018-0505-8

Zavolokina, L., Dolata, M., & Schwabe, G. (2016). The FinTech phenomenon: Antecedents of financial innovation perceived by the popular press. *Financial Innovation*, *2*(16), 1–16. doi:10.118640854-016-0036-7

Zerado & Fintech Network. (2017). *Smart Contracts – From Ethereum to Potential Banking Use Cases*. Retrieved from https://blockchainapac.fintecnet.com/uploads/2/4/3/8/24384857/smart_contracts.pdf

KEY TERMS AND DEFINITIONS

Fintech: Technologically enabled financial innovation that could result in new business models, applications, processes, or products with an associated material effect on financial markets and institutions and the provision of financial services.

Islamic Fintech: Fintech with Shariah principles and Islamic values.

Murabahah: Cost plus profit margin.

Shariah: Islamic guidelines based from Quran, Sunnah, Qiyas (analogy) and Ijma' (scholars consensus).

Smart Contract: Digital contract of legal binding.

Tahawwut: A hedging process/mechanism that is used or offered by Islamic banks and financial institutions to help mitigate a specific type of risk (khatar or mukhatarah) or more (such as FX risk, market risk, liquidity risk, counterparty risk, etc.).

Wakalah: The contract of representative, which gives the *Muwakkil* (representative) the jurisdiction of doing things on behalf of the appointer.

Chapter 10
Blockchain for Islamic Social Responsibility Institutions

Moutaz Abojeib
ISRA, Malaysia

Farrukh Habib
ISRA, Malaysia

ABSTRACT

Blockchain and smart contracts are forming new systems to record and manage businesses with less need for intermediaries. The new systems are expected to offer high level of governance with lower cost as compared to the traditional technologies. While there is a continuous effort to apply this innovative technology in several businesses, Islamic finance in general—and Islamic social finance in particular—are facing few challenges that could be solved by such innovations. Islamic social finance institutions such as waqf are facing some challenges in enhancing its governance structure to ensure Shariah compliance as well as economic efficiency. This chapter explains how blockchain and smart contract technologies can help these institutions for better governance, lower transaction cost, more transparency, and higher trust, hence enhancing the business flexibility and market accessibility. It also presents some related cases that are currently under development as an evidence for the practicality of these technologies in the Islamic social finance arena.

DOI: 10.4018/978-1-5225-7805-5.ch010

INTRODUCTION

There are mainly two main trends that can be observed in the post financial crisis in 2007-2008. First, there is an outcry from various parts of the world to introduce social and ethical values to the financial system and institutions (Benedikter, 2012). The introduction of the Sustainable Development Goals (SDGs) and the Principles for Responsible Investment by the United Nations are some of the evidences. Second, due to various advancements in the technology including blockchain, there is a shift in the focus of innovation from merely digitalization of financial products and services to changing fundamental business models, products and services (Gomber, Koch & Siering, 2017). The current trend is towards more customer-centric approach and greater customization.

Islamic finance is another dimension of doing finance in compliant manner to Sharīʿah (Islamic law). Since the inception of Islamic finance almost four decades ago, it has not been able to demonstrate substantial divergence from the conventional finance (Khan, 2010). Due to adherence to Sharīʿah, it is claimed that Islamic finance is more refined form of ethical and social finance. However, in practice, the ethical and social aspect of Islamic finance is overshadowed by its commercial aspect (Sairally, 2007). The development achieved so far in the area of Islamic finance was focusing on the contractual forms of the financial transactions only. This approach, though, avoids elements prohibited by the Islamic law, but it results in the similar effect and outcome of conventional finance. Therefore, it fails to reflect Islamic social and ethical values. This study derives its motivation from such practices of Islamic finance and attempts to suggest development of Islamic social finance institutions through blockchain and smart contracts to support sustainable economic development. Moreover, currently, the Islamic social finance institutions are facing an array of challenges and issues which will be discussed throughout the chapter.

This chapter applies qualitative technique of literature review and tries to develop relevant concepts and ideas. This chapter is discursive in nature covering a technical subject of blockchain and smart contracts and link those concepts with Islamic social finance products. Furthermore, while there is an array of issues and challenges facing the implementation of these products in the contemporary world, this chapter explains how blockchain and smart contract technologies can help the social finance institutions for better governance, lower transaction cost, more transparency and higher trust; hence, enhancing the business flexibility and market accessibility. It also presents some related cases that are currently under development as an evidence for the practicality of these technologies in the Islamic social finance arena.

BACKGROUND

There are various Islamic social finance institutions proposed by the Islamic law which always played a pivotal role of sustainable economic development in a Muslim society throughout the history of Islam. The whole social ecosystem was an integral element of the financial empowerment program of the people which actively contributed in the financial inclusion, poverty alleviation and fruitful mutual community initiatives. However, recently, such important institutions have been generally failed to produce substantial impact within the Muslim society. Part of this problem is due to the challenges and issues faced by such institutions. Whereas another part of the problem lies in the fact that the commercial aspect of Islamic finance has captured most of the academic and professional attention at the expense of the Islamic social finance. One can easily notice the dearth need of quality academic literature in the topic from technology perspective.

The Islamic social finance institutions comprise of *zakat, sadaqat, waqf* and *qardh hasan* proposed by the Islamic law. A brief description of each of these institutions is given for a better understanding of the readership.

Zakat

Zakat is the transfer of ownership of a specific amount of money (or property) from someone who meets the certain criteria for the zakat to be obligated up on him/her to someone who deserves it by fulfilling certain criteria (Al-Jaziri, 2009). It is a form of obligatory charity; and one of the five pillars of Islam. Due to its importance, it is mentioned thirty-two times in the *Quran*. The beneficiaries of zakat consist of eight categories including poor and needy. The criteria for individuals to be beneficiaries of zakat is well-identified in Shariah.

Sadaqat

It is a form of charity which is given to someone voluntarily to seek the pleasure of Allah (SWT). Differently from *zakat*, the scope of *sadaqat* in terms of beneficiaries is very wide. *Sadaqat* could be financial or non-financial; however, in the context of this study, the term *sadaqah* is used to indicate financial form of charity.

Waqf

Waqf is a form of charity that is voluntary, permanent and irrevocably dedicated to Allah (SWT). *Waqf* can be either in kind, fixed assets, or cash. The donor of *waqf* (*waqif*) can specify the purpose of waqf which may vary from a general one such as helping poor and needy to a very specific one such as to help orphans with cancer. The *waqif* has also the right to specify the conditions for waqf. Is also worth to mention that the asset or property of *waqf* shall not be sold or distributed to charities, rather the benefits or revenue generated from investing waqf property. *Waqf* property is considered to be in the direct ownership of Allah, it can neither be gifted, traded, nor inherited (Ibn Abidin, 1992).

Qard Hasan

Qard means loan. In Islam, interest or usury is prohibited, therefore, *qard* should be interest-free. It is a transfer of ownership of a property to benefit from with the condition that a similar property is returned to the giver (Ibn Abidin, 1992). While *qard* may refer to any loan, *qard hasan* is used to refer to an interest-free loan which is given to seek Allah's pleasure. It also implies flexibility in terms of granting the debtor more time in case he or she is facing financial difficulty in returning the loan. It also implies encouraging, but not obliging, the creditor to forgo the loan partially or fully in such case.

What is Blockchain?

To explore and truly appreciate the full potential and efficient implementation of blockchain, it is pertinent to understand the technology, its benefits and limitations. This section will explore what blockchain is, and what it offers before explaining its implementation for Islamic social finance.

Definition

Blockchain is a distributed ledger technology which allows transactions to be recorded without the need for any central authority or intermediary. In other words, it allows users to verify and store transactions or data, not on a certain server operated by a centralised body as usual, rather on servers and computers operated by various participants of the network (known as nodes). Having such a decentralized system through traditional technology was extremely difficult due to the technical challenges in synchronising the data, reaching consensus among the users to implement any changes, as well as protecting the data integrity among others. Blockchain technology overcomes these challenges and ensures that the data is not manipulated.

Technically, 'blockchain is a database of immutable time-stamped information of every transaction that is replicated on servers' across the network (Hansen, 2015). Enabled by an open-source software usually, the transactions are recorded in blocks after verification process performed by the full nodes. Full nodes is a term used in blockchain refers to those who are authorized to verify a transaction before recording it and participate in forming and chapping the rules of a blockchain. To simplify, full nodes are playing a role similar to admin users in classical systems. Blockchain can be public in which any user could be a full node, or private in which the full nodes are necessarily part of the organisation. The blocks represent a set of information that vary according to the purpose of the blockchain. It could be accounting records, titles, amounts, text or any other form of info. These info are recorded in the blocks with info about time and sequence the record. Each block is connected to the next block with a hash function, forming a chain of block; therefore, the name of technology is blockchain.

In order to add a transaction within a block, and the block into the chain, a consensus of majority of the full nodes is required. Once a block is completed, it is verified by other full nodes, and subsequently, added to the chain. The nodes verification process involves solving mathematical problems enabled by software at the nodes' terminals. Once a block is added to the chain, all full nodes immediately update the copy of their ledger. With this setup, historical information cannot be altered or manipulated. This is why it is largely argued that blockchain offers higher degree of integrity without the need of a trusted intermediary or central authority.

Inception and Difference Between Cryptocurrencies and Blockchain

Cryptocurrencies are often cited as the use case for blockchain technology. This is due to the fact that blockchain was first introduced to the world by the famous cryptocurrency called Bitcoin. Bitcoin was introduced as peer-to-peer digital payment system, while the technology underneath was the blockchain. In other words, blockchain was used by Bitcoin as a platform to enable peer-to-peer transactions. Surely, Bitcoin is not the only cryptocurrency, there are around two thousand different cryptocurrencies exist as of September 25, 2018 (Coinmarketcap.com). All these cryptocurrencies are in principal the values stored on the distributed ledger. These entries show the amount of digital funds or value that each user owns. Each type of cryptocurrencies has its own objective, underlying technology, protocols and features.

Although blockchain and Bitcoin were introduced jointly to the world, they are not the same thing. The best quote explains this is the following: *blockchain is to Bitcoin, what the internet is to email. A big electronic system, on top of which you can build applications. Currency is just one (Marr, 2018).*

Beside cryptocurrencies, a blockchain platform can be used for other purposes, products, and services. In that sense, blockchain, being a digital technology platform, can be considered as neutral. It is up to the user of that platform to utilize such technology for either permissible purpose or otherwise. In that sense, it is Shariah compliant, because the hardware (mining machine), developers' software (virtual machine, Bitcoin core, for instance), and the resources (like electricity) required to operate a blockchain platform do not involve any impermissible element from Shariah perspective by default.

Types of Blockchain

Based on permission or restriction protocols, there are mainly three types of blockchain: private, consortium and public blockchain. Each type is briefly explained below.

Public Blockchain

Public blockchain is open source in which anyone can participate, without the need of permission. On such platform, anyone can download the code or software, and start running a full node on the local device, validating transactions in the network, thus participating in the consensus process. Due to the public nature, anyone can see or audit transaction on the public block explorer; however, the parties of a transaction remain anonymous.

There are few advantages of using public blockchain. It has a potential to disrupt current business models through disintermediation. Moreover, there is no need to maintain servers or system admins by the central authority, this radically reduces the cost of creating and running decentralized applications (DApps). Some examples of public blockchain are Bitcoin, Ethereum, and Litecoin.

Consortium Blockchain

It is also called federated blockchain. It operates under the control of a specific group of organizations which are allowed to perform the role of full nodes. As opposed to public blockchain, the structure does not give access to all persons to participate in the process of verifying transactions. The consensus process is controlled by a pre-selected set of nodes in which the protocol defines the minimum number required to sign every block in order for the block to be valid. The right to read the blockchain can either be public or restricted to the participants only.

This type of blockchain has some specific advantages. For example, it reduces transaction costs; avoids data redundancies; and replaces legacy systems. It is also helpful for simplifying document handling and getting rid of semi manual compliance mechanisms. The transaction processing in such blockchain is faster than a public blockchain, which means there is a potential for higher scalability. It also provides more privacy, but at the cost of lesser transparency. Consortium blockchain can be suitable for the traditional banking sector. Some of the examples are: R3 Corda (for banks); EWF (for energy), B3i (for insurance).

Private Blockchain

Private blockchain can be defined as a platform controlled by a single or centralized organization with restricted number of nodes within that organization. It is valuable for solving efficiency, security and fraud problems within traditional institutions, but the most important feature of decentralization is not available for private blockchain.

It has same advantages as of the consortium blockchain, but it is different from it in the sense that it has more restriction and is not distributed.

Use Cases of Blockchain for Social Purposes

Blockchain has the potential to disrupt large number of industries and sectors. Social aid is among those sectors that could be reshaped by this innovative technology. In fact, few examples already exist. To appreciate the implication, one needs to understand the challenges that faces social-aid programs and NGOs as well as the issues that these programs and organizations try to address.

The most significant problem in helping poor and refugees is distribution of aid. While there are an estimated 766 million people under poverty line (World Bank, 2017) and 25.4 million refugees (UNHCR, 2018), distributing aids is very challenging. Daily supply of foods to a huge number of populations is not an easy task. It requires many accountants, administrators and supervisors to keep track of all transactions from purchase to delivery. It requires time-consuming and costly processes to avoid mismanagement and ensure that the food reaches to the eligible person. Blockchain offers in this regard an important solution.

There are a couple of experiments already implemented by UNHCR. For instance, Ethereum blockchain is used by The United Nations World Food Programme (WFP) to help Syrian refugees in Zatari Camp in Jordan. The solution offers unique electronic coupons (e-coupons) representing an undisclosed amount of money podcasted to the shops in refugee camps. Using eye-scanning devices, refugees' identities are verified, and the aid is disbursed to the refugees by redeeming the e-coupons. The transaction is then recorded in the blockchain. This blockchain applications would minimize the traditional cost of sending money or food through a series of intermediaries. It could save up to 98% of the tradition fees of UNHCR (Juskalian, 2018).

Furthermore, apart from saving costs, blockchain application in refugees' aid programs would help solving another important challenge that is missing documentation. Refugees, due to the war, often loses their documentations in their journey from their towns and cities to the refugee camps. Blockchain would enable digitally-authenticated identification documents in which the refugees who have lost their passports or national identities can use the digital ID. 'Bitnation' for instance is a blockchain start-up working in developing a platform that can provide such service. This platform would use the blockchain technology to ensure that the ID is never stolen or manipulated. Ultimately, refugees would be able to obtain digital ID documents, which host governments can use to verify their identity. *To build trust in the blockchain identity, the service verifies a person's multiple social media accounts and links them to their social security number, passport and other documents (Bayram, 2018).*

SMART CONTRACTS

Definition

Blockchain platform can also run smart contracts. Smart contracts are simply self-executing contracts. As rightly explained by Kasri (2007), *smart contract is a term used to describe a computer program code that is capable of facilitating, executing, and enforcing the negotiation or performance of an agreement (i.e. a contract) using blockchain technology. The entire process is automated and can act as a complement or substitute for legal contracts where the terms of the smart contract are recorded in a computer language as a set of instructions.*

The success factor behind smart contract is the convergence of the terms and conditions of the contract into codes. This will enable the automatic verification process in which if the conditions are met, the contract is immediately concluded. In classical systems, the challenge are in finding a mechanism to enable this verification process to be performed without the need of going to a central authority to verify that the conditions are met. With blockchain, conditions, being written into lines of code, could exist across a distributed, decentralized blockchain network in which it could be verified against the pre-set conditions by anonymous parties, legal system, or external enforcement mechanism. Such structure could provide an alternative to the traditional legal system. Furthermore, it enables machine to machine commerce without enforcement by legal entities (Stark, 2018).

With smart contacts being a tool for solving the problem of trust between parties, trading can be made automatic. Put it simply, if someone want to sell his land against certain price, the price is set as condition in blockchain land registration system for example. If anyone pays the amount, this event will trigger the sale contract and transfer the ownership of the land. As a result, the sale contract is concluded and executed. This would minimise the transaction costs and make the transactions transparent and traceable. In addition, having the system on blockchain implies that the transaction is irrevocable which ensures that no individual party can manipulate the transaction. In fact, even if the contracting parties want to cancel the transaction, they would need to engage themselves in new reverse-sale transaction.

With the above explanation, it should have been made clear that smart contracts can revolutionize trading through its impact on the cost and risk factors. Smart contracts reduce the costs associated with the legal and regulatory infrastructures that are necessary to save the rights of the contracting partiesrisk of manipulation through non-discriminatory execution. By this, markets could be more efficient (Khan, 2017).

Inception

Though the concept and idea of smart contract was not always attached to blockchain, its application in reality was facing technical challenges which are solved today by blockchain. For instance, Nick Szabo, a legal scholar and cryptographer, in 1994 suggested some simple use of decentralized ledger for sale and purchase of securities (Blockgeeks, n.d). However, the actual birth of smart contracts has been delayed because of the lack of appropriate platform for applying the concept efficiently. This has been changed with the appearance of blockchain in 2009, when the discussions over its application came back. Today, thought smart contracts are still very limited and facing legal and technical challenges, the initial applications looks promising. With the fast-growing development and spread of blockchain applications, one can expect much further developments in smart contracts.

How Smart Contracts Work?

Smart contracts are basically just computer programs. The program code identifies parameters to play a role in triggering events in accordance to the terms and conditions of a contract. If certain conditions are fulfilled, then a specific pre-programed line of codes reflecting the contractual clause of the triggered condition will be executed. By this setup, the paper-based contracts are transferred into electronic format which anyone can see at real-time bases. This further allows a uniliteral application without a need of a trust.

These computer codes are not stored in a single database which could be manipulated by any party having control over it. Instead, it is replicated, stored and distributed over the network. This implies that there is no need to trust a centralised body as it is supervised by the network of computers that run the blockchain. It is also important to note here that the smart contracts allow an automatic enforcement of the penalties for instance according to the predefined rules.

The application of smart contracts is not limited to any specific type of contracts, neither to trade. Its application and setup could be very simple or very complex depend on the case. *Time-stamping services like ascribe (art registry) or governmental and semi-governmental registries (land titles, birth certificates, school and university degrees) are examples for simpler technological use cases. The regulatory aspects might be more complex. Decentralized autonomous organizations, on the other hand, are the most complex form of a smart contract (BlockchainHub, n.d).*

Use Cases of Smart Contracts for Social Purposes

According to Deloitte, though blockchain has a great potential in offering immutable data storing with transparency and traceability, smart contracts represent a next step of development in which the data not only stored efficiently, but it is also processed automatically in terms of execution of multi-party agreements. This automation does not just offer cheaper solution but also reduce human errors and risk of manipulation. Smart contracts can help in setting-up systems to ensure proper recording of donations, and at the same time to form contracts that ensure spending of these donations are in line of the specified purpose. This looks very promising for Islamic endowment that is called *waqf*. In Waqf, the donor has the right to force conditions related to the projects, timing, beneficiaries the endowment manger. Using blockchain and smart contract technologies, these conditions could be translated into a system able to enforce contracts between donors, entrepreneurs and *waqf* managers. In fact, the scenarios in which smart contracts can be implemented for charities and social projects are limitless. According to Gengler (2007), UNICEF is already working on some projects in this regard.

SOLVING ISSUES WITH BLOCKCHAIN AND SMART CONTRACTS

The introduction of the blockchain has offered a ray of hope for the reinforcement of social financeproducts and institutions in the modern Islamic finance sphere. The technology possesses various attractive features that are naturally required by all the stakeholders of such products and institutions to establish trust and reliability. This section deliberates the general model of blockchain solution, as well the product or institution specific features of blockchain.

General Model of Blockchain Solution

Rightly called as 'trust machine', blockchain offers an array of general features which are equally desired by all the Islamic social finance products or institutions. Some of those prominent features will be discussed in this section.

Traceability

From *qard hasan* to *sadaqat*, *waqf* and *zakat*, all social financeinstruments require traceability. They, being a lenders or donors, insist on receiving complete information about the utilization of funds. With limited capability of centralized governing bodies, maintaining full detailed records of all the transactions performed is always challenging. Once the funds are received and commingled, it is almost impossible to track each and every amount of fund. Consequently, tracking mechanisms for funds have become a huge cost, contributing to further inefficiencies of such products. With built-in feature of distributed and decentralized ledger, blockchain provides an end-to-end tracking mechanism and complete history of a transaction.

Transparency and Public Disclosure

Blockchain-based ledgers are distributed among all the network nodes, or at least among the full nodes who are responsible for transaction confirmation and block formation. Therefore, the participating nodes at a blockchain network are able to scrutinise all the transactions; and they keep updating the copy of the ledger in almost real time with the addition of a new block in which the process ensure obtaining consensus among them. Moreover, all the public keys and their history of transaction is available in the ledger for the nodes to verify and confirm. This mechanism offers full transparency and public disclosure to all the stakeholders of the blockchain network.

Compliance and Audit

One of the main concerning issues with the Islamic social finance products or institutions is the lack of complete data and reliable records to perform proper compliance review and audit. However, as mentioned earlier, blockchain can offer end-to-end traceability, transparency and public disclosure; therefore, the complete set of data is available. Subsequently, it is easy to perform a *bonafide* compliance review and audit to identify and rectify any irregularities. This feature is very crucial for the regulatory and legal authorities as well as other stakeholders to gauge genuine overall performance of such institutions.

Security

Centralized databases are prone to security threats because they have single point of failure. On the contrary, blockchain ledger system is distributed in a decentralized manner. The whole network depends on a huge number of anonymous nodes who maintain the ledger. With proper setup, the data would be protected even if the security of a few nodes is compromised. This reinsures safe working and viability of the institutions that digitize their products and processes and implement blockchain system.

Scalability

Although blockchain systems are currently facing some challenging in developing further scalability, they, at current stage, are still comparatively more efficient than traditional databases in terms of scalability. For instance, some blockchain systems claimed that they have already achieved the equivalent, or twice, the speed of 'visa' for transaction processing per second (Kaustav, 2018; VISA, 2018; Ripple, 2018). Moreover, they are less affected by the number of nodes as compared to the number of clients in usual databases. In other words, while traditional systems have some limitations in terms of number of users, this seems to be less applicable for blockchain systems. This factor of scalability has several advantages for products or institutions dealing with large numbers of individuals. A good example of such institutions are NGOs, charities, *waqf* among many others.

Fraud Prevention

Due to the usage of unique hash function distributed ledger technique, once the data is entered in the blockchain ledger, it is technically immutable. Since the records at the blockchain are unalterable, it is extremely difficult to corrupt those records or data entries. Moreover, since all the nodes at the network maintain a copy of ledger for verification, the probability of double record is zero. In fact, the problem of double records, or making fake copies of an asset or certificate, is one of the biggest issues in the digital world. Blockchain has successfully solved this issue. This strong security factor can ensure that once the data is securely inserted using the predefined protocols, the date cannot be manipulated either accidentally or maliciously. This will not only enhance reliability of records, but also prevent any fraud.

Product Specific Features

In addition to the general characteristics that could bolster Islamic social finance products or institutions, blockchain is customizable and hence able to provide some specific benefits. In other words, the possibilities to develop different blockchain systems with different technical features construct a unique opportunities to the institutions which have specific needs. Waqf, zakat and qard hasan are among these institutions. The following discussion deliberate how each one of institutions would benefit from blockchain.

Smart Contracts for Waqf

Smart contracts can be effectively used in *waqf*. For instance, a *waqf* deed can be converted into an algorithm or code. The algorithm can then be inserted in the blockchain platform in the form of a smart contract. The execution of the smart contract is automated to prevent using *waqf* property or fund outside of the stipulated conditions of the *waqf* donor (*waqif*). In this way, the *waqf* deed can be protected and adhered to. This is a simple example of how *waqf* can benefit from the application of a smart contract. From macro perspective, the use of smart contracts could further enhance the performance and efficacy of the *waqf* institution, due to improved compliance and audit mechanisms. Incorporating smart contracts could also reduce the cost, while further increasing the security, transparency and adherence to the *waqf* stipulations and traceability of the *waqf* funds.

Finterra's Waqf Chain is one of the examples of using blockchain for *waqf*.

Finterra is a company registered in Singapore with a couple of presence in other countries. It has developed a crowdfunding platform that uses blockchain and enable creating smart contracts for the different *waqf* projects. Initially, Waqf Chain allows participants to create project proposals to develop and invigorate endowment properties. Others can fund these project proposals by contributing funds. Using smart contracts, the relationship between the donors and receivers is formalized online which provides a more efficient way to raise money, manage and transfer ownership of *waqf*. Furthermore, the platform allows participations of auditors, Shariah and legal advisors to be engaged. The whole process is automated in blockchain in which digitalized token are generated to participating funders upon matching the funds with *waqf* projects proposals of their choice. *The tokens can be held to gain stakeholder rights and revenue-sharing or transferred and exchanged in the wider Finterra ecosystem and on other networks (Finterra, 2018).*

Among the key benefits that Finterra wants to achieve:

- Each project's 'real world' documentation is stored immutably and publicly for all stakeholder to see and review, ensuring safety and transparency of the project as it moves forward;
- Contribution, stakeholder voting, and special terms cannot be tampered with because they are enforced by blockchain consensus via smart contract;
- Token distribution and project revenue are handled automatically in the smart contract logic guaranteeing fairness and accounting accuracy for token holders;
- Specific project terms are encoded into (and enforced by) a smart contract in a tamper proof manner.

Transfer and Receipt of Zakat

One of the biggest challenges for *zakat* institutions is related to the costs associated with governance. This is because ensuring that the ownership of *zakat* funds has been transferred to the rightful recipients is a very crucial matter from Shariah perspective. Benefiting from the traceability characteristic of blockchain, this matter can be taken care of. Moreover, the procedures for engaging the donors and recipients of *zakat* can be facilitated using blockchain with smart contracts. The process can be automated and simplified. The credentials of recipients can be cross verified through wider integration of application programming interfaces (APIs). Their data can be globally shared in order to utilize *zakat* funds effectively, while avoiding any wastage of resources. And this could be done without jeopardizing the privacy of the recipients thanks to the developments of cryptography associated with blockchain.

The Global University for Islamic Finance (INCEIF), the International Federation of Red Cross (IFRC) and AidTech (fintech company) are currently developing an Islamic social finance mobile application that leverages blockchain technology for *zakat* and *ṣadaqat*. The App provides the users with several options in which they can choose the project. Once a project is selected and the payment is made, the transaction is registered on blockchain in which the disbursement to the end users is registered to. This structure allows the payer to get notifications once their *zakat* or *ṣadaqat* has reached the intended recipients. This offer higher transparency. The team is further working on developing a social scorecard to evaluate the projects. If it is implemented on blockchain, then users could get an access to reliable evaluations which no one is able to manipulate.

Qardh Hasan

Several institutions and market players are already enthusiastic about building online systems for Islamic microfinance. This includes building electronic crowdfunding platforms and peer-to-peer (P2P) systems to provide interest-free loan based on the Islamic concept of *qard hasan* (See for example, QardHasan.com). These platforms providing a virtual meeting points between the various parties. Receiving the loan requests and accepting to finance them are done online. Transfer of payments are also facilitated through internet. Yet, governance is a big challenge for such platforms. Currently, social financial institutions avoid involving in *qard hasan* because of high administrative cost. However, with the usage of blockchain and smart contracts, sound governance could be insured with minimal operating cost as the technological design could ensure high governance be construct. After going mainstream, blockchain and smart contracts will become an inevitable part of crowdfunding platforms. And, it can be assumed that *qard hasan* will be a widely-used viable product for social finance.

Challenges Facing the Technology and Their Solutions

Despite several benefits and promising features, blockchain and smart contracts are facing serious issues and severe challenges. Although, the proponents of this technology are optimistic about its future implementation, it is not free from many pitfalls at present. Some of the concerns are stated as follows.

Immature Technology

Blockchain and smart contracts are still at their infancy stage. At the moment, the technology may not be matured enough to be adopted for the mainstream application. That is why, most of the financial industry players are reluctant to start offering their financial products using blockchain and smart contracts. However, most big players currently testing the technology and hoping to roll-out their product when the time is right. This is only a matter of time, as the technology has already successfully received traction by the relevant industry players.

Lack of Human Talent

Due to the short history of this nascent technology, human expertise is lacking in programming and development. Developers who have achieved vast experience and skills are few and in high-demand. This situation has resulted in high price tag for acquiring such expertise. Education and training programmes for such an important technology are yet conducted by mainstream educational institutions. There should be specialized courses to fill up the dearth in the current human capacity development.

Governance Issues

Another problem is the governance of blockchain and smart contracts at organizational level. This is related not to the technology itself, rather to its implementation and design. Structuring the system involves a number of crucial decisions includes selecting the type of blockchain that is appropriate for an organization, identifying the parties to be involved as nodes, choosing the information to be input, among other decisions related to maintaining and sharing the data. Each option involves different risk, cost and benefit. Market players, particularly Islamic social finance institutions, should not adopt this technology because of the hype. They should carefully explore the technology and perform their own cost-and-benefit analysis before even having a pilot-project. They should not be carried away by the sentiments, rather they should base their decision on sound business logic.

Privacy and Security

Although transparency is a positive trait of this technology, it poses real challenge regarding data privacy and security of people and transactions. To protect privacy, blockchain solutions usually involves cryptography to mask the information of the transacting parties. However, it is argued that this can be breached by using meta-data collected through digital devices. One need to understand that such issue can be solved, but the solution may imply a trade-off between privacy and transparency. The best thing is to strike a good balance between transparency and privacy by developing highest standards and regulations for data privacy and cyber security.

Inflexibility

Immutability is a strong important feature of blockchain and smart contracts, however, it has appeared to be a double-edge sword. It makes this technology somewhat inflexible too. For example, if there are any bugs (technical errors in programming), they cannot be immediately and easily fixed due to the requirement of majority consensus and distributed nature of the blockchain ledger. In addition, they are visible to all the users, including hackers, due to open source code of smart contracts. This is purely a technical issue; and blockchain experts are working on it. However, the main concern is that there is a trade-off between flexibility and trust. Yet, it is possible for some market players to have customized blockchain solutions where there is a good mix of both.

Interoperability

Another major concern is integration of blockchain system with the current existing systems. Particularly, the financial institutions have already invested a huge amount of capital into their legacy traditional systems. Moreover, the legacy systems are well-tested and widely used for the financial products; they have been considered as reliable technology for long-time. On the other hand, blockchain technology is new at development stage; therefore, the blockchain technology cannot be adopted all at once. Furthermore, Blockchain provides a completely independent eco-system and technology framework. This is not only unique, but also more advanced than other technologies. For this reason, a gradual approach is more appropriate. In other words, breaking the implementing of the technology into stages looks as viable solution. At the first stage, the blockchain technology needs to be integrated with the current systems in order to further improve their efficiency. At the second stage, other technology infrastructure and supportive mechanisms should be devised and implemented. At the third stage, the whole blockchain framework should be tested and checked for any errors. At the fourth stage, an overall migration from the current system to the blockchain system should take place.

Regulatory and Legal Framework

Regulations and legal implications play an extremely crucial role in any sector. Their role is even stronger in the financial sector including the social finance part. As any other system, the blockchain and smart contracts technology requires a comprehensive regulatory and legal framework to support its adoption and implementation. Issues such as data privacy, legal status of smart contracts in courts, and others need to be examined and confidently responded. It worth noting here that regulatory and legal concerns regarding blockchain and smart contracts have been investigated with serious approach by beginning of 2018. There is indeed good development already; however, there is a lot to be done in terms of high standards, prudent guidelines, proper legislations, robust rules and regulations.

CONCLUSION

Blockchain technology, though still in its infancy stage, has already proved itself as a game changing breakthrough for the global financial sphere. In fact, its utilisation is not limited to the financial sector rather it carries promising features for non-financial sectors. The Islamic social finance institutions could be invigorated with the innovative and efficient use of the blockchain and smart contracts. The technology and such institutions can indeed have a perfect natural match because, interestingly, the blockchain addresses many, if not all, of the issues and problems currently facing the Islamic social finance industry in the contemporary world.

It is strongly believed that Islamic social finance could make a great step forward by adopting an innovative approach consisting of technological advancements like blockchain and smart contracts. Such adaptation would enforce these institutions and ensure a dynamically participation in the societal and economic development of the whole Muslim world. Such remarkable initiatives will also crystalise the ethical and social dimensions of Islamic finance in a robust manner.

REFERENCES

Al-Jaziri, A. R. (2009). *Islamic Jurisprudence According to the Four Sunni Schools*. Fons Vitae.

Bayram, A. S. (2018, June 25). Here Are Three Ways Blockchain Can Change Refugees' Lives. *World Economic Forum*. Retrieved from: https://www.weforum.org/agenda/2018/06/three-ways-blockchain-change-refugees-lives/

Benedikter, R. (2012, February 12). Social Banking and Social Finance: Building Stones Towards A Sustainable Post-Crisis Financial System? *The European Financial Review*, Retrieved from: http://www.europeanfinancialreview.com/?p=2027

BlockchainHub. (n.d.). *Smart Contracts*. Retrieved from: https://blockchainhub.net/smart-contracts/

Blockgeeks. (n.d.). *Smart Contracts: The Blockchain Technology That Will Replace Lawyers*. Retrieved from: https://blockgeeks.com/guides/smart-contracts/

Gengler, E. B. (2017, August 29). Leveraging Blockchain Technology for Corporate Social Responsibility. *Payments Journal*. Retrieved from: http://paymentsjournal.com/leveraging-blockchain-technology-for-corporate-social-responsibility/

Gomber, P., Koch, J., & Siering, M. (2017). Digital Finance and FinTech: Current Research and Future Research Directions. *Journal of Business Economics*, *87*(5), 537–580. doi:10.100711573-017-0852-x

HalalChain. (2018). *Halal-Chain White Paper*. Retrieved from: https://www.hlc.com/whitepaper.pdf

Hansen, E. (2015, July 29). The Blockchain, Explained. *Medium*. Retrieved from: https://medium.com/linkreply-blockchain/the-blockchain-explained-3300f4506890

Ibn Abidin, M. A. (1992). *Radd Al-Mukhtar Ala Al-Durr Al-Mukhtar*. Beirut, Lebanon: Dar Al-Fikr.

Investopedia. (n.d.). *Smart Contracts*. Retrieved from: https://www.investopedia.com/terms/s/smart-contracts.asp

Juskalian, R. (2018, April 12). Inside the Jordan Refugee Camp That Runs on Blockchain. *MIT Technology Review*. Retrieved from: https://www.technologyreview.com/s/610806/inside-the-jordan-refugee-camp-that-runs-on-blockchain

Kasri, N. S. (2017, July 18). Shariah Compliance via Blockchain and Smart Contract – The Case for Islamic Credit Card. *Halal Investing Journal*. Retrieved from: https://journal.wahedinvest.com/shariah-compliance-via-blockchain-and-smart-contract-the-case-for-islamic-credit-card

Kaustav. (2018, March 28). How Ripple (XRP) Outdid the Transaction Speed of VISA. *Global Coin Report*. Retrieved from: https://globalcoinreport.com/how-ripple-xrp-outdid-the-transaction-speed-of-visa

Khan, F. (2010). How 'Islamic' is Islamic Banking? *Journal of Economic Behavior & Organization*, *76*(3), 805–820. doi:10.1016/j.jebo.2010.09.015

Khan, N. (2017, January 9). *Smart Contracts - The Future of Islamic Banking*. Retrieved from: https://www.linkedin.com/pulse/smart-contracts-future-islamic-banking-nida-khan

Marr, B. (2018, February 16). A Very Brief History of Blockchain Technology Everyone Should Read. *Forbes*. Retrieved from: https://www.forbes.com/sites/bernardmarr/2018/02/16/a-very-brief-history-of-blockchain-technology-everyone-should-read/#5462f7f37bc4

PwC. (2017). *Blockchain, A Catalyst for New Approaches in Insurance*. Retrieved from: https://www.pwc.com/gx/en/insurance/assets/blockchain-a-catalyst.pdf

Ripple. (2018). *XRP The Digital Asset for Payments*. Retrieved from: https://ripple.com/xrp

Sairally, S. (2007). Evaluating the 'Social Responsibility' of Islamic Finance: Learning from the Experiences of Socially Responsible Investment Funds. In M. Iqbal, S. S. Ali, & D. Muljawan (Eds.), *Advances in Islamic Economics and Finance* (pp. 279–303). Jeddah, Saudi Arabia: Islamic Research & Training Institute.

Stark, J. (2018). *Fintech, Smart Contracts and Blockchain* [PowerPoint Slides]. Presentation at IIFM Seminar in Kuala Lumpur.

UNHCR. (2018). *Figures at A Glance*. Retrieved from: http://www.unhcr.org/figures-at-a-glance.htm

UNICEF. (2017, January 9). UNICEF to present 'Donercoin' at London Blockchain Week 2017. *UN Blockchain*. Retrieved from: https://un-blockchain.org/2017/01/09/unicef-to-present-donercoin-at-london-blockchain-week-2017

VISA. (2018). *Visa Acceptance for Retailers*. Retrieved from: https://usa.visa.com/run-your-business/small-business-tools/retail.html

World Bank. (2017). *No Poverty*. SDG Atlas. Retrieved from: http://datatopics.worldbank.org/sdgatlas/archive/2017/SDG-01-no-poverty.html

Chapter 11
Blockchain for Islamic Financial Services Institutions:
The Case of *Sukuk* Financing

Fatima Zaka
Information Technology University, Pakistan

Shazib Ehsan Shaikh
Information Technology University, Pakistan

ABSTRACT

By enabling better traceability of funds against specific assets, technologies should appeal to a significant segment of the lending market – one that is religiously conscientious. Such Islamic FinTechs should therefore be disruptive for the existing regime of Islamic financial services institutions who have problems managing credit risk and compliance. Islamic financial instruments are no stranger to controversy. It emerged from the scandals that gaining investor confidence for Islamic financial instruments such as the Sukuk, which is the Islamic alternative to bonds and securities, investors demand more transparency in Sukuk to make sure they are Shariah-compliant, thus making traceability to assets a special hindrance to current schemes of Sukuk. In this chapter, the authors will discuss how technology could be disruptive in Islamic banking and finance sector keeping Sukuk as a case. The authors will further elaborate on it by discussing the proposed model of blockchain that could solve the issue of traceability which could also boost investor confidence in Sukuk.

DOI: 10.4018/978-1-5225-7805-5.ch011

INTRODUCTION

Blockchain technology represents a generational opportunity to mutualize database infrastructure across entities within financial services. What that translates into is an enormous cost-saving, risk-reducing, and capital-enhancing opportunity. (Blythe Masters)

The societal disharmony that results from a large income gap between the rich and poor is essentially what Islamic models of financing aim to alleviate. By eyeing a fairer distribution of risk and return between lender and borrower, such models focus on aiding the buying of assets on credit rather than directly taking out loans. Islamic financing, in spirit, is not about earning from loans but about helping people buy assets on credit or earn a profit from businesses.

The authors believe that blockchain technologies can greatly facilitate the type of large-scale asset-funding required by modern businesses and developers of infrastructure. By enabling better traceability of funds against specific assets, these technologies should appeal to a significant segment of the lending market – one that is religiously conscientious. Such Islamic fintechs (what is fintech?) should therefore disrupt the existing regime of Islamic Financial Services Institutions (IFSIs) as they have problems managing credit risk and compliance.

Islamic financial instruments are no stranger to controversy, with scandals such as those involving Dubai Islamic Bank, Invest Dar and Goldman Sachs to name a few. This suggests that Islamic Banks could also have spurious projects similar to their conventional counterparts. The authors believe that these controversies primarily arise from a lack of investor confidence in the compliance of an Islamic financial instrument to Shariah guidelines. In 2012, Goldman Sachs' $2 billion Islamic bond programme faced a setback when it emerged that the Sukuk were not endorsed by Shariah scholars, hence making it a spurious programme that adversely affected investor confidence. The programme was also accused of being used to finance other non-Shariah programmes that involved the interest-bearing side of conventional finance - an accusation that was rejected by the bank, yet further damaged already waning investor confidence. With such scandals, it emerged that gaining investor confidence for Islamic financial instruments, such as Sukuk (pronounced su-kook' – plural of sak) - the Islamic alternative to bonds and securities, is more challenging than for conventional bonds. Investors demand more transparency in Sukuk to make sure they are Shariah-compliant, thus making traceability to assets a notable hindrance to current schemes of Sukuk. This may also lead to questions such as whether technologies like blockchain could effectively rectify trust issues and also improve investor confidence in Islamic financial instruments. It is also worthwhile to mention that the current scheme of Sukuk financing requires the contract to be an operating lease rather than a finance one.

As the authors build up their argument on the crucial role technology may play in upscaling the growth of Islamic financial institutions, it is important to first briefly discuss what Islamic banks do and how they are different from their conventional counterparts.

In this chapter, the authors will discuss how technology could be disruptive in Islamic banking and finance sector using Sukuk as a case. The authors will further elaborate by discussing our proposed model of blockchain that could solve the issue of traceability and lead to a boost in investor confidence in Sukuk.

ISLAMIC BANKING AND FINANCE

Islamic banking and finance refers to financial activity that complies with Islamic Shariah law. The transactions undertaken by Islamic Financial Services Institutions (IFSIs) are required to follow Islamic Shariah-based principles. This sector is currently valued at over US$2 trillion globally and is growing rapidly. There has been significant work done in countries such as Malaysia, Saudi Arabia, Pakistan, Dubai and also the United Kingdom, in promoting and expanding this sector. It is already considered a mature market providing an Islamic alternate to conventional banking products and solutions.

BACKGROUND AND TRENDS IN ISLAMIC FINANCE

Islamic finance is a significant niche in today's financial market. Some key statistics and trends should highlight this, as reported recently in the Islamic Financial Services Industry Stability Report 2017 (IFSB, 2017):

1. The total worth of the Islamic Financial Services Industry (IFSI) in 2016 was estimated at USD 1.89 trillion (2014: USD 1.87 trillion – at a time when assets of top 1000 global conventional banks declined by 2.6%);
2. Out of this, USD 318.5 billion were outstanding Sukuk, which registered a 6.06% expansion (the largest component of IFSI is Islamic banking, with USD 1.493 trillion in global banking assets, and this showed a slight decline);
3. Islamic banking assets, in the 2nd quarter of 2016, as a percentage of total banking assets' market share in Iran, Brunei, Saudi Arabia, Malaysia and the UAE were 100%, 100%, 51%, 28% and 25% respectively;

4. Around 80% of Sukuk issuances in 2016 were by national governments (sovereign Sukuk). Of these, more than 50% were by Malaysia, followed by Indonesia, UAE and Saudi Arabia. In the UAE, notable entities such as Etihad Airways and Dubai DP World Crescent Ltd. were the issuers, while in Saudi Arabia, the Islamic Development Bank makes a regular annual issue.

In keeping with the tradition of other Abrahamic faiths, Islam stipulates a strong prohibition on interest-based earnings. The legal maxim attributed to the final Prophet of Islam, Muhammad (peace be upon him), states that "profit comes with liability", thus requiring a lender to share in the risk of the investment (Iqbal and Mirakhor, 2011). Islamic jurists do, however, allow for the sale of real goods on credit at a higher price (vis-à-vis cash sales). This, in essence, is the foundation for most modern Islamic financing models, including Sukuk (Iqbal and Mirakhor, 2011; Usmani, 2000). When compared to conventional borrowing, such sales are described as "asset-backed" borrowing. The other basic model for Islamic finance is instituting partnerships where the lender is a sleeping partner and there is profit-and-loss sharing. Whether credit-sale or partnership, the conventional lender now faces more exposure to loss as their risk now extends beyond the borrower to the underlying investment itself. Thus, the IFSI have often combined their products with parallel rental agreements (called Ijarah or operating leases). The receiver of funds thus retains immediate usage of the asset and pays rent on the share that they do not own, until they have bought back the whole asset at maturity. Such sales with lease or "Ijarah Sukuk" are a significant component of the Sukuk market. International Islamic Financial Market (IIFM) estimated these to have around 35% of the international Sukuk market share in 2010-2015, but this share has declined to 16% in 2016 (IIFM, 2018). The growth of a specific form of partnership-based Sukuk (called Wakalah Sukuk) explains this displacement. These Sukuk increased from 43% of international issuances in 2010-2015 to 75% in 2016, according to IIFM (IIFM, 2018). IIFM do concede that the Wakalah contracts they reported included an element of Ijarah within them. The agreement is no longer focused on assets; rather the funding-provider now employs an agent (either the fund-raiser or usually a related party) to oversee a pool of assets. Of the profits, what is over and above a certain profit level is kept by the agent as an incentive for lucrative asset management. Ultimately, it is conscientious investors who have surplus funds and wish to avoid interest-bearing investments that are the target market for IFSI products. In certain Muslim majority economies, these funds otherwise remain in the informal sector as a form of abstinence from the banking sector (Abedifar, Hasan, & Tarazi, 2016).

ISLAMIC VERSUS CONVENTIONAL BANKING

The essence of Islamic banking, as discussed earlier, is that it is interest-free and also discourages risk-taking contracts. In order to achieve this, Islamic banking and finance encourages profit and loss sharing as well as contracts that limit liquidity risk. Hence, the incorporation of Islamic Joint Ventures (IJVs) is dominant within Islamic Financial Services Institutions (IFSIs) as they make the contracts more equity based. Islamic Joint Ventures are based on partnerships. It is very important to understand that in conventional banking, money is largely made through interest. The depositors make money on saving accounts through fixed interest and the banks make money through lending by charging fixed interest. Any product or transaction that has involves interest makes it non-Shariah-compliant, thereby making it non-Islamic.

The time value of money is the basis of investments under the conventional banking system. A fixed interest is charged over a fixed period of time on investments, such as on bonds. Islamic banking, on the contrary, encourages and promotes profit-making by exchange of goods and services.

FORMS OF FINANCING IN ISLAMIC BANKING AND FINANCE

There are two forms of financing in Islamic Joint Ventures:

1. **Mudarabah:** Mudarabah is a special type of Islamic Joint Venture Partnership in which one partner (rab-ul-maal) invests money, and the other partner (mudarib) runs the business on pre-agreed terms. The profit that is distributed between them is pre-determined. However, it is only the rab-ul-maal that bears any loss as the mudarib has not invested any capital in the joint venture;
2. **Musharakah:** In Musharakah, all parties contribute some part of the total capital. The profit ratio in Musharkah is decided with mutual consent but the loss incurred is equal to each party's investment proportion (Azmat and Skully, 2017).

Fintech as a Disruptive Technology in Islamic Banking and Finance Sector

If we consider the fact that fintech is already an almost US$ 2 billion industry with very promising growth trends, it becomes imperative to discuss the ways in which fintechs can also work alongside Islamic financial institutions. In order to stay competitive with their conventional counterparts, Islamic banks need to be more innovative in the products and services they offer. There are an increasing number of Islamic fintech companies in Asia as well as in Europe, offering solutions in peer-to-peer lending, digital wealth management and Islamic stocks. However, so far Islamic banks have been struggling to get into digital banking. The authors believe that Islamic fintechs could address this problem by providing unconventional solutions designed for Islamic Financial Services Institutions.

Islamic financing is predominantly asset-based. Keeping that in mind, the authors shall discuss how Islamic fintechs can be disruptive for IFSIs, as in the case of the disbursement of payments using blockchain, both for asset-based as well as asset-backed credit purchases, such as Sukuks and Islamic car financing (Ijarah). Blockchain also has a huge potential in Islamic Joint Venture (IJV) contracts, such as Murabaha and Musharakah for profit sharing.

While modern modes of Islamic financing have shown much promise, we believe that they could go further if the complexities behind asset ownership are made transparent to those investors and scholars who view them with skepticism. The remainder of this paper will show how this can be made possible by adopting blockchain technologies and how it has the potential of disrupting traditional IFSIs.

Asset-Based vs. Asset-Backed Financing

Islamic financial instruments are predominantly either asset-based or asset-backed, with the most commonly used instruments being Islamic car financing and Sukuk financing contracts. In asset-based financing, a loan is taken out against a real asset (which is tangible and physical in nature). In case of a default, the bank has to go through the legal process to settle the issue between the bank and the defaulter, such as the case of car financing, for instance. In other words, asset-based financing is a form of financing that provides companies with working capital and term loans. To elaborate this concept, an asset-based finance would be purchase order financing[1]. When a company cannot meet the cost of completing an order (this could be due to lack of funds available to cover the cost of raw material) has a poor credit history and not enough assets to offer as collateral to a bank, purchase order financing could serve as a better option. In this case, a failure to finance raw materials to complete the orders would leave a company operating under capacity. The asset-based lender finances the purchase of the raw material, and the purchase orders are then assigned to the lender. After the orders are filled, payment is made to the lender, and the lender then deducts its cost and fees and remits the balance to the company[2].

On the other hand, asset-backed financing is a type of financing which is backed up by collateralization of specific assets. Generally, it refers to securities backed up by short-term collateral, such as credit card receivables, car loans, leases, home–equity loans, royalties, etc.

One of the major differences between Islamic and conventional financing is that Islamic Shariah-based financing is primarily asset-based where ideally paper currency should not be taken into account for lending purposes, except for special cases where paper cannot be avoided. If you take a loan from an Islamic bank you do so against a guarantee, e.g. a loan is given against or is equivalent to the value of the real asset that you have shown as a guarantee. The bank owns the property as collateral and takes it as soon as you default. This is asset-backed financing.

Is Digital Banking and Finance Shariah-Compliant?

According to Shariah scholars belonging to the conventional school of thought, Islamic banking and finance is predominantly asset-based, meaning that resources behind any transaction must be physical and tangible in nature. However, among Shariah scholars, there are proponents for modernising banking and finance. They believe that Islam is an innovative religion that supports creativity and innovation in many aspects of life. By making Islamic financial instruments digital, not only would any issue related to traceability be solved, but by making the instruments tamper proof, investors' confidence could also be achieved. It is also believed by a majority in the field that innovation would make Islamic instruments sophisticated enough to keep up with modern trends and the growing needs of the financial markets. It is pertinent to understand that if technology driven methods are introduced in the Islamic banking and finance sector, without compromising on the basic requirements as highlighted by the Shariah law, this would make the Islamic Banking and Finance sector innovative and ultimately would reduce the cost of operations.

Sukuk

Sukuk are Shariah-compliant financial certificates that serve as an alternate to conventional bonds. Investing in bonds is not permissible under any Islamic jurisdictions as interest is involved, whereas an investor in Sukuk earns profit and not interest.

How do Sukuk work?

Party A (here, Party A could be any company known as the Originator) leases its assets to a Special Purpose Vehicle (SPV) for a predetermined period of time. The SPV then puts them on rent for that period. After renting it out, the SPV then issues a Sukuk equivalent to the amount of the assets that it had leased from Party A. The Sukuk holders get a partial share in those assets depending on the amount of investment they made in the Sukuk. Instead of interest like in conventional bonds, the Sukuk holders get the rent as a profit on their share of assets, which does not make it a debt contract. It is pivotal to understand that the ownership remains with the Originator, which means that it is not transferred, hence making the contract that of an operating lease in nature rather than a financing one.

There are different types of Sukuk contracts depending on the nature of the project and the mode of financing involved in the contract. Whatever the nature of the contract may be, the project has to be Shariah-compliant and no investment should involve interest payment. It is pivotal to note that Sukuk can be traded in the secondary market and the ownership can be transferred. The different types of Sukuk are as follows:

1. Mudarabah Sukuk
2. Musharaka Sukuk
3. Ijarah Sukuk
4. Murabaha Sukuk
5. Salam Sukuk
6. Istisna Sukuk
7. Hybrid Sukuk
8. Al Musaqa Sukuk
9. Ijarah Thumma Bai' Sukuk
10. Wakalah Sukuk

Later on in this chapter, the authors will be discussing how technology could disrupt the Islamic financial services institutions using the case of an Ijarah Sukuk as this is the most commonly used form of Sukuk financing.

BLOCKCHAIN TECHNOLOGY

Blockchain is a digital ledger that keeps a record of any information that has a value on a public platform (see Figure 1). This technology is also used for record-keeping in a chronological order. A node is connected through the internet for any user of the blockchain that has a copy of any transaction made on the blocks present in a particular blockchain. Multiple blocks can be added like a chain within the blockchain. Satoshi Nakamoto created this technology for allowing digital information to be distributed without being tampered or copied. Any economic transaction can be recorded on these ledgers that are then accessible from any system or to any user of that system. It is a continuously growing chain of blocks that have information stored on them which cannot be corrupted and are not easy to alter. The records remain on the blocks and are copied on the node permanently.

Figure 1. Blockchain
(Source: Satoshi Nakamoto's model)

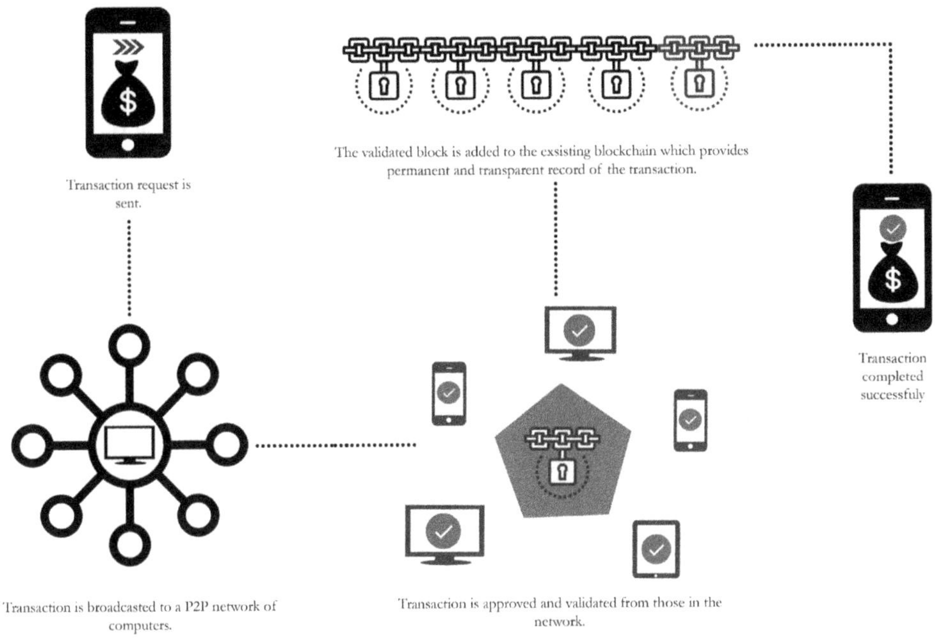

Not shown in the diagram is how the validating miners (the peer-to-peer nodes) encapsulate the blockchain with a new hash value, each time a new block is added. The hashing function relies on producing a new random number every time the blockchain is extended. The old blockchain, without the newly added block was already carrying a hash value. By adding a new hash value over the newly extended blockchain, the platform effectively places another lock on top of a previous lock. This compounding of hash values is what makes blockchains prohibitive to tamper with (Peck 2017). The "miners" are termed as such precisely because of the computing power required to set each new lock in the first place.

It is based on this technological architecture that cryptocurrencies, such as the renowned Bitcoin, have been made possible. In the case of Bitcoin, the block encapsulates the set of transactions for which Bitcoin was used as a currency. They cannot be reversed (i.e. are "immutable") due to the prohibitive computing power required to hack a chain of these blocks. However, this blockchain technology is open enough to encapsulate any type of transaction that needs to be made immutable and for which maintaining a devolved and distributed ledger will enhance trust (see Figure 1). As a result, others have developed Ethereum (Wood 2014), a blockchain platform for generalised transactions, i.e. not restricted to cryptocurrency exchange. Though it is a public blockchain platform using its own cryptocurrency, called "Ether", it is flexible enough to allow groups to implement their own "hyperledger" (Peck 2017; Zheng et al. 2017). They may employ a custom digital token to track exchanges, instead of speculatively traded digital currency, and can avoid the controversy of legitimacy among Islamic scholars (Al-Jazeera 2018).

It is believed that the crash in financial instruments such as the Credit Default Swaps (CDS) triggered off the 2007-2008 financial crisis. Proponents of blockchain technology are of the view that such a crisis can be controlled by making financial contracts more secure and this can be done by backing the traditional systems through blockchain technology (blockchain world, IEEE 2017).

Traceability of Funds in Islamic Financial Institutions

Apart from "riba" (money on money or interest), Shariah-compliant financial institutions should on principle also avoid "gharar" (risk). This means that all possible risks attached to a product or service provided by the IFSIs must be disclosed to the buyer or investor. In addition to this, any relevant information should also be conveyed to any party involved in a transaction. In order to eliminate any further risk, any person who does not own the product cannot sell it to another party. This factor of risk could also be connected to traceability of funds as well as assets involved in any transaction.

Traceability of assets and funds in any transaction involving Islamic financial instruments could be challenging for the parties involved. Trust issues could emerge as a result of lack of traceability anywhere in the transaction. Investors of Islamic financial instruments are generally more conscious about Shariah compliance issues, traceability of assets as well as how and where the funds are invested or utilised.

Traceability of Assets and Funds Using Blockchain Technologies in Islamic Financial Institutions

1. The authors believe that the issue of traceability of funds and assets using the blockchain technology would be beneficial for the following reasons:
    a. Any transaction based on blockchain technology is irreversible and tamper proof;
    b. It can also be accessible from anywhere and any system after it has been enabled with that software;
    c. The user of the program knows that the information embedded on the blocks will always remain there;
2. For any transaction of an Islamic financial instrument, it is vital to understand that all the building blocks involved in that instrument, whether an asset or a loan, have to be Shariah-compliant. Due to this, traceability of funds is a

major concern in traditional Islamic financial instruments. This problem can be ratified by introducing blockchain technologies in Islamic Financial Institutions for the following reasons:

a. It gives credibility to the instrument for being Shariah-compliant;
b. It gives credibility to the Islamic financial institution's claim of being truly Shariah-compliant;
c. It builds trust between the parties involved in the transaction, with the parties being the buyer and the seller;
d. It would encourage and promote the growth of the Islamic financial institutions as a market;
e. Due diligence of the product or service would not be an issue as the buyer of the instrument could trace the nature of the transaction on blockchain, know the history of the instrument, the type of funds that have been used for the transaction, whether Islamic or conventional, and the owner of the instruments in the past.

Traceability of assets is also a concern which may hinder investments in Sukuk as the investors could be sceptical about the origin, form and type of investment made on those assets. The authors feel that blockchain technology could help solve this issue as well.

Traceability ensures that trust is built between all the parties involved in the Islamic financial markets, including banks, financial institutions, consumers and any third parties, like clearing houses, etc. This process can be explained with the help of the model that we are proposing which is shown in Figure 4.

The Value of Blockchained Traceability in Sukuk

While the ideal mode is the "asset-backed" Sukuk where the underlying asset is "truly" sold to the Sukuk owners, some Sukuk defaults in the earlier part of this decade highlighted the need to recognize the prevalence of "asset-based" rather than "asset-backed" Sukuk (Radzi and Lewis, 2015). It came to the fore that only "beneficial ownership" had been sold and not the complete ownership. So while Sukuk holders could gain profit from the asset, at the time of default, they could not execute their resale (much like a trust). In fact, during the 2008 global financial crisis, the Sukuk that defaulted were all asset-based and not asset-backed. However, asset-backed Sukuk remain a small component of Sukuk issuances, due to the strong preference of the Sukuk issuer to retain practical ownership of the pledged assets.

The legitimacy of Sukuk among reputable Islamic jurists has a significant impact on valuations of Sukuk (Godlewski, Turk-Ariss, & Weill, 2016). Furthermore, beyond the requirement of interest avoidance and risk-sharing, Islamic financing is also explicitly meant to reduce uncertainty and speculative behaviour (Iqbal and Mirakhor, 2011). Hence, gambling and short-selling (selling an asset you do not yet own) are prohibited under Islamic law.

As a result, the authors believe that enhancing the traceability of funds to specific registered assets will enhance the tradability of Sukuk among investors who have avoided them in the past. A scepticism persists – especially with cases such as these "asset-based" defaults – that Islamic financing is a lion in sheep's skin. The perception exists that they function as conventional bonds, and originally simple Islamic models have been grafted to fit conventional models of finance (Lai, Rethel, & Steiner, 2017).

Sukuk issuance can actually take quite a complex legal form, as it often involves drawing up parallel contracts of sale, rental and agency between multiple parties. This is especially the case in Sukuk Wakala (Agency-based Sukuk), where up to three or four parties come between the Sukuk buyer and the underlying pool of assets being managed on their behalf (see Figure 1). This is in addition to the other parties (lawyers, corporate bankers, etc.) also involved in facilitating the set-up of such a venture. The authors, therefore believe traceability, especially of the kind brought by a blockchained distributed ledger, will greatly enhance investor confidence.

Figure 2 describes a typical Wakala Sukuk as explained above.

The value of blockchaining security issuances has already been made by others (Vakta, Maheswari, & Mohanan, 2016, p.5-6):

Figure 2. Complexity of roles in an agency-based (Wakala) Sukuk structure
(Source: Authors)

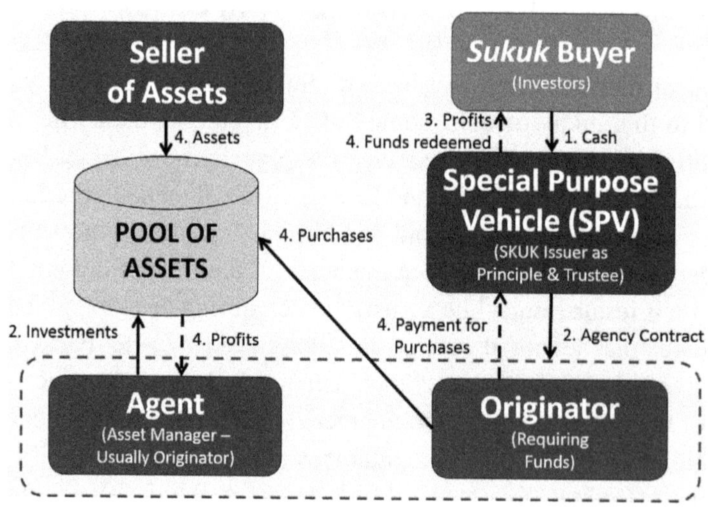

1. Data inconsistencies arise that lead to time-consuming reconciliations among the multiple parties;
2. Clearing and settlement times are elongated;
3. Risks arise when there are delays between advance payments and issuance of security;
4. Multi-step processes are also prone to greater errors.

The list is in fact longer than this. What the authors add is that:

1. The time from decision-to-issue to go-to-market takes days for conventional bonds, but takes from “a few weeks to a few years” for Sukuk (a key reason given for the decline in corporate Sukuk) (IFSB, 2017, p.22);
2. Traceability to the underlying asset is a key criteria for legitimizing Sukuk over bonds with Islamic jurists. Hence, the value of blockchaining Sukuk is even greater than that of blockchaining conventional securities as it affects the legitimacy, not just cost and time, of the business transaction. Further complications in traceability of Sukuk assets can arise, where there is actually a pool of assets instead of a set of easily identifiable and countable assets. Furthermore, there has been an appetite for granting the asset-seller (who then leases them back) flexibility in substituting assets within the pool with others, prior to Sukuk maturity. This is desirable where the issuance concerns a property developer who would like to sell off some real estate from within the pool. Hence, again, blockchained traceability can grant this flexibility to the issuer (Al-Amine, 2008). Additionally, for the buyer of the Sukuk, selling on their asset holdings can be more transparently carried out leading to greater liquidity in Sukuk.

The following section further explains how blockchains are understood to work. It is after this that the authors propose a model for blockchained Sukuk and elaborate on it in the following section.

Blockchain: A Secure and Distributed Ledger

A blockchain is essentially a distributed database of records, or public ledger of all transactions or digital events that have been executed and shared among participating parties. Each transaction in the public ledger is verified by consensus of a majority of the participants in the system (Crosby, Pattanayak, Verma, & Kalyanaraman, 2016, p. 7).

It should be clarified that this is a digital ledger that can keep record of any information that has any value. When a transaction takes place, this is added to a hashed blockchain on multiple machines in this network of ledgers. Once a pre-specified set of transactions is completed, the blocks are encapsulated in a hashed blockchain. As some have described it: "Each block becomes an independent banking statement whereas a blockchain is a complete history of all banking transactions."

The blockchain could be public or private or even based on an open source protocol. Given the distributed and strong hashing-based record-keeping, the need for active involvement of intermediaries to close agreements and broker trust (such as commercial banks, central banks and other agencies) is reduced. It is reported that consumers could save up to $16 billion in banking and insurance fees each year through the use of blockchain-based applications (Tapscott and Tapscott, 2017).

Proposed Model for Blockchained Sukuk

Figure 3 describes how a typical Ijarah Sukuk works.

To illustrate how Sukuk issuance can be blockchained that would help in resolve the issue of traceability as already discussed in the chapter, let us take the example of a common Ijarah Sukuk that is structured as a credit sale followed by a lease-back agreement (see Figure 2). The party requiring the funds that originally owns the assets is called the Originator. To manage the Sukuk as a trust, the creation of a Special Purpose Vehicle (SPV) is standard procedure. It is the SPV that buys (or even leases) the assets being pledged against the Sukuk and then rents it back to the Originator so that the SPV can generate a regular income for Sukuk buyers. How this can be processed as a blockchain is seen in Figure 3 and explained in the following steps (note that we have shown only one transaction per block for the purposes of illustration and it is the blockchain platform that will dictate the number and sequence of transactions included in a single block):

1. **Hash value initialized:** An initial hash value is created that will be used to secure the blockchain;

Figure 3. Sukuk where assets are sold then leased back (Ijarah Sukuk)
(Source: Authors)

2. **Asset registration:** A new block is created. For the Sukuk this would include the name of the parent company, details (such as date, nature and location of the asset, market value of the asset at that date, etc.). Important for Sukuk: the asset to be leased is registered with the appropriate legal authority for the jurisdiction of the contract (e.g. in Pakistan this would be with the courts). This would give it a status as a legal entity;
3. **Contract on asset with SPV registered:** A new block is created that shows the transaction details, the date on which the asset was sold or leased to the SPV and the market value of the sold/leased assets have been transferred adequately to the SPV;
4. **Lease-back of asset:** Assets are leased for rental income by the Originator for a fixed period of time. The new block will have that information as well as any other relevant information, such as the name of the parties involved, purpose of asset rental, and so on;
5. **Sukuk registration:** On a new block, SPV will show that the Sukuk are registered with the relevant securities regulating body (such as the Securities and Exchange Commission of Pakistan). The total value of the Sukuk, along with other details will also be part of information created on the block. Of course, this will also include the asset(s) against which certain Sukuk will have claim;
6. **Sukuk issuance:** A block will be created to show that SPV has issued Sukuk in the market;
7. **Sale of Sukuk:** As Sukuk subscription proceeds, the share of ownership against the Sukuk pool of assets will be registered for the subscriber;
8. **Profit recording:** Blocks shall record disbursement of any profits from the underlying asset;
9. **Final redemption:** On redemption, the value repaid at maturity at the prevailing market price plus additional details.

The major differences vis-à-vis the proposed conventional bond blockchain structure (Vakta, et al., 2016) is the registration of the asset with a legal authority (such as the Courts in Pakistan) and the registration of the Sukuk while listing the asset share entitlement with a securities regulator (such as the Securities and Exchange Commission). Conventional bonds may register collateral, but is not necessary to comply with this registration where "bearer bonds" are concerned.

As the objective of blockchain is to reduce intermediaries for the verification of a transaction, the extra steps for Sukuk may seem redundant. However, given that the legal climate is still in development with respect to blockchain, the regulatory intermediaries may offer their digital signatures being locked in with the asset-offering block for future efficiency.

Figure 4. Proposed blockchaining of lease-based (Ijara)
(Source: Authors)

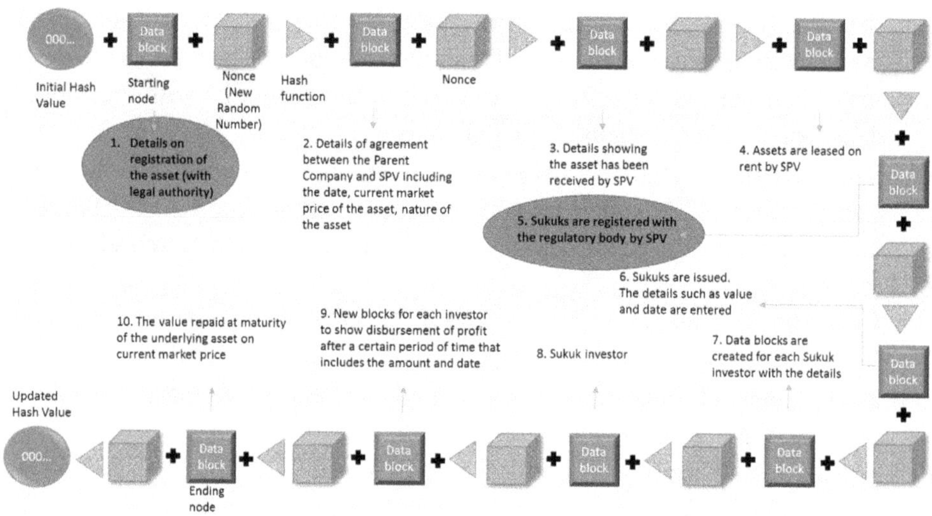

Also, it should be noted that the promise of our proposed approach is not that all offline transactions will be protected online by blockchains. The minimum viability for us is that all asset transfer transactions (which are only a subset) be recorded. We assume it is the transparency of missing any asset transfer step that will allow investors to exert pressure on Sukuk providers to ensure compliance.

CONCLUSION

The authors discussed that traceability of assets and funds in any transaction involving Islamic financial instruments could be challenging for the parties involved. Trust issues could emerge as a result of lack of traceability anywhere in the transaction. Investors of Islamic financial instruments are generally more conscious about Shariah-compliance issues, such as traceability of assets, as well ashow and where the funds are invested or utilised. The authors proposed that blockchain technology could solve these issues.

It has also been highlighted the need for credibility of Sukuk in the context of a practice of offering them as "asset-based" rather than "asset-backed". Sukuk transactions, as we have seen, involve a number of entity layers coming between the buyer and their asset – which can often allow incomplete asset sales and restricted "beneficial ownership" sales only. With blockchain, the authors have proposed not only an efficient and cost-saving solution, but one that goes to the core of the products' legitimacy. The future steps the authors foresee are experimentation with an open blockchain protocol such as Ethereum, to allow for further optimization of the blockchain set-up.

REFERENCES

Abdul Aziz, R., & Gintzburger, A. (2009). Equity-Based, Asset-Based and Asset-Backed Transactional Structures in Sharia'a-Compliant Financing: Reflections on the Current Financial Crisis*. *Economic Papers: A Journal of Applied Economics and Policy, 28*(3), 270-278. doi:10.1111/j.1759-3441.2009.00035.x

Abedifar, P., Hasan, I., & Tarazi, A. (2016). Finance-growth nexus and dual-banking systems: Relative importance of Islamic banks. *Journal of Economic Behavior & Organization, 132*, 198–215. doi:10.1016/j.jebo.2016.03.005

Al-Amine, M. A.-B. M. (2008). sukuk market: Innovations and challenges. *Islamic Capital Markets, 33*.

Azmat, S., Skully, M., & Brown, K. (2017). The (little) difference that makes all the difference between Islamic and conventional bonds. *Pacific-Basin Finance Journal, 42*, 46–59. doi:10.1016/j.pacfin.2015.12.010

Crosby, M., Pattanayak, P., Verma, S., & Kalyanaraman, V. (2016). Blockchain technology: Beyond bitcoin. *Applied Innovation, 2*, 6–10.

Crosby, M., Pattanayak, P., Verma, S., & Kalyanaraman, V. (2016). *BlockChain Technology: Beyond Bitcoin*. Retrieved from http://scet.berkeley.edu/wp-content/uploads/AIR-2016-Blockchain.pdf

Fanning, K., & Centers, D. (2016). Blockchain and Its Coming Impact on Financial Services. *Journal of Corporate Accounting & Finance, 27*(5), 53–57. doi:10.1002/jcaf.22179

Gheeraert, L. (2014). Does Islamic finance spur banking sector development? *Journal of Economic Behavior & Organization, 103*, S4–S20. doi:10.1016/j.jebo.2014.02.013

Godlewski, C. J., Turk-Ariss, R., & Weill, L. (2013). Sukuk vs. conventional bonds: A stock market perspective. *Journal of Comparative Economics, 41*(3), 745–761. doi:10.1016/j.jce.2013.02.006

Guild, J. (2017). Fintech and the Future of Finance. *Asian Journal Of Public Affairs, 10*(1). doi:10.18003/ajpa.201710

IFSB. (2017). *Islamic Financial Services Industry Stability Report 2017*. IFSB.

IIFM. (2018). *IIFM Annual sukuk Report*. IIFM.

Image: Difference between Operating and Financial Lease | eFM. (2018). Retrieved from https://www.google.com/imgres?imgurl=https://efinancemanagement.com/wp-content/uploads/2015/01/Difference-between-Operating-and-Financial-Lease.png&imgrefurl=https://efinancemanagement.com/sources-of-finance/difference-between-operating-and-financial-lease&h=615&w=1101&tbnid=SuYR9ukWCqO5pM:&tbnh=117&tbnw=211&usg=__iixUTyFeTHHgzPVdUX6VyshcHIA%3D&vet=12ahUKEwiBx-r814rbAhUMuxQKHZTuBu8Q9QEwAHoECAEQKQ.i&docid=JWNo8_x3cD7A2M&sa=X&ved=2ahUKEwiBx-r814rbAhUMuxQKHZTuBu8Q9QEwAHoECAEQKQ

Iqbal, Z., & Mirakhor, A. (2011). *An introduction to Islamic finance: theory and practice*. John Wiley & Sons. doi:10.1002/9781118390474

Lai, J., Rethel, L., & Steiner, K. (2017). Conceptualizing dynamic challenges to global financial diffusion: Islamic finance and the grafting of sukuk. *Review of International Political Economy, 24*(6), 958-979. doi:10.1080/09692290.2017.1373689

Peck, M. E. (2017a, October). Blockchains: How They Work and Why They'll Change the World. *Blockchain World, Spectrum IEEE.ORG*, 22-24.

Peck, M. E. (2017b, October). Blockchains: How Does Proof of Work Secure Blockchains. *Blockchain World, Spectrum IEEE.ORG*, 26-28.

Radzi, R. M., & Lewis, M. K. (2015). Religion and the Clash of "Ideals" and "Realities" in Business: The Case of Islamic Bonds (sukuk). *Thunderbird International Business Review, 57*(4), 295–310. doi:10.1002/tie.21706

Tapscott, A., & Tapscott, D. (2017). How Blockchain Is Changing Finance. *Harvard Business Review*.

Trautman, L. (2016). *Is Disruptive Blockchain Technology the Future of Financial Services?* Retrieved from https://papers.ssrn.com/sol3/papers.cfm?abstract_id=2786186

Usmani, M. (2007). *Sukuk and their contemporary applications*. AAOIFI Working Paper. Retrieved August 14, 2014, from http://www.ifseb.com/wp-content/uploads/2012/07/Sukuk-and-Contemporary-application-14-JAN-08.pdf

Usmani, M.T. (2002). *An Introduction to Islamic Finance*. Hague, The Netherlands: Kluwer Law.

Vakta, T., Maheswari, A., & Mohanan, N. U. (2016). *Blockchain Disruption in Security Issuance*. Retrieved from https://www.capgemini.com/wpcontent/uploads/2017/07/blockchain_securities_issuance_v6_web.pdf:Capgemini

Vishwanath, S., & Azmi, S. (2009). An Overview of Islamic Sukuk Bonds. *The Journal Of Structured Finance*, *14*(4), 58–67. doi:10.3905/JSF.2009.14.4.058

World Islamic Banking Competitiveness Report 2014-15. (n.d.). Retrieved http://www.ey.com/Publication/vwLUAssets/EY-world-islamic-banking-competitiveness-report-2014-15/$FILE/EY-world-islamic-banking-competitiveness-report-2014-15.pdf

KEY TERMS AND DEFINITIONS

Bearer Bonds: A fixed-income security that is retained and kept by the holder (bearer), and not the registered owner. Coupons for interest payments are physically attached to the security, and it is the bondholder's responsibility to submit the coupons to a bank for payment and redeem the physical certificate when the bond at maturity date.

Credit Default Swap: Credit default swap (CDS) is like an insurance against a default risk by a particular company. The company is called the reference entity and the default is called credit event. This contract takes place between two parties, called protection buyer and protection seller. Under the contract, the protection buyer is compensated for any loss originating from a credit event in a reference instrument. As a result, the protection buyer makes periodic payments to the protection seller.[3]

Fintech: Fintech is financial technology applied in financial services helping companies to manage the financial aspect of their businesses including new software, applications, processes and business models.

Hyperledger: It is an open source combined with efforts bent to advance cross-industry block chain technologies.

Ijarah: Ijarah is a type of contract in Islamic finance. It is an ownership of the right to the benefit of using an asset for a particular period of time in return for a payment.

Ijarah Sukuk: Ijarah Sukuk are certificates of equal value which are issued by the owner of an existing property or asset either on his own or through a financial intermediary, for the purpose of leasing it against a rental from the subscription proceeds. After subscription, the underlying becomes owned by the Sukuk holders.

Lease vs. Purchase Agreement: The methodology is to find the after tax cash outflows for each year under both alternatives. Then look at PV using after tax cost of debt (since the choice is between two financing techniques having very low risk).

Maturity: It refers to the final date of payment against any financial instrument.

Miner: Mining is a process of adding transactions to the large distributed public ledger of existing transactions which are known as the block chain. The person involved in mining is hence called a miner.

Mudarabah: It is a partnership contract in which one party provides the capital, whereas the other party (known as 'Mudarib') provides labour and expertise in running the partnership.

Musharakah: It is an Islamic partnership for financing contracts used by Islamic banking. An agreement between two or more parties (Islamic bank and its clients) where they to contribute the capital in cash or kind. Debts are not accepted. The partnership is in equal or varying amounts to establish a new project or share in an existing one.

P2P Lending: Peer-to-peer (P2P) lending is a method of debt financing that allows individuals to borrow and lend money minus the use of an official financial institution acting as an intermediary. Peer-to-peer lending removes the middleman from the process, but it also involves more time, effort and risk than the general brick-and-mortar lending scenarios.

Riba: In Islamic banking it is known as charged interest. Exploitative gains made in trade or business under Islamic law.

Shariah Law: Shariah Law is a set of religious principles which form a part of the Islamic culture. More precisely, it is the law of GOD. In Arabic its literal meaning is a way or path.

SPV: A special purpose vehicle/entity (SPV/SPE) is a "bankruptcy-remote entity" that is used to isolate or securitize assets and is often held off-balance sheet. It is also referred to as a "bankruptcy-remote entity" or "variable interest entities" since its operations are very limited.

Sukuk: A Sukuk is meant to be an Islamic certificate, similar to a bond in western finance. It complies with Sharia—Islamic religious law.

Wakala Sukuk: Wakala Sukuk is a form of sukuk structure that originates from the concept of a wakala which means an arrangement whereby one party entrusts another party to act on its behalf. A wakala is very similar to an agency contract in which there is a Principal and an Agent (manager). A principal (the investor) appoints an agent (wakeel) to invest funds on principal's behalf, into a pool of investments or assets and the wakeel lends its expertise and manages those investments for a particular period of time for profit making. In this type of contract, the principal agrees to pay fees to the wakeel for the services rendered.

Wealth Management: It is a very specialized field of financial service that combines financial and investment advice, accounting and tax services, retirement planning fee and legal advice and one estate planning to the clients for a fee.

ENDNOTES

1 https://www.investopedia.com/terms/a/assetbasedfinance.asp

2 https://www.investopedia.com/terms/a/assetbasedfinance.asp

3 https://economictimes.indiatimes.com/definition/cross-elasticity-of-demand

APPENDIX

Table 1. Financial versus operating lease

Finance/Capital Lease	Operating Lease
Long Term (5 yrs +)	Short Term (< 5 yrs)
Non-cancelable	Cancelable (at option of lessee)
Lessee makes payments for use of asset over predefined period of time	
Total payments made by lessee to lessor are greater than lessor's initial cost of the leased asset	Total payments made by lessee to lessor are less than lessor's initial cost of the leased asset
Leased term is 75% of estimated economic life of the asset	Economic life of the asset > leased term so asset's economic value > 0 at lease end
At beginning of lease, PV of payments = 90% of fair market value of leased asset	
Ownership transferred at end of lease period: lessee has option to buy at fair market value	At maturity, asset returned to lessor who may sell or release; lessee has option to renew lease
Lessee maintains asset	Lessor maintains the asset
Lessee insures asset	Lessee insures asset

Compilation of References

Abacı, M. (2018). *IT Yatırımlarımızın Yüzde 41'i Dijitalleşmeye Gidiyor*. Retrieved from http://m.sigortagundem.com/uploads/documents/akilliyasamdergisi-ocak2018-qnWW.pdf

Abdul Aziz, R., & Gintzburger, A. (2009). Equity-Based, Asset-Based and Asset-Backed Transactional Structures in Sharia'a-Compliant Financing: Reflections on the Current Financial Crisis*. *Economic Papers: A Journal of Applied Economics and Policy, 28*(3), 270-278. doi:10.1111/j.1759-3441.2009.00035.x

Abedifar, P., Hasan, I., & Tarazi, A. (2016). Finance-growth nexus and dual-banking systems: Relative importance of Islamic banks. *Journal of Economic Behavior & Organization, 132*, 198–215. doi:10.1016/j.jebo.2016.03.005

ABI (Giovanni Sabatini). (2017). *Indagine conoscitiva sulle tematiche relative all'impatto della tecnologia finanziaria sul settore finanziario, creditizio e assicurativo* [Cognitive survey on issues related to the impact of technology]. Retrieved from https://www.abi.it/DOC_Info/Audizioni-parlamentari/Presentazione%20per%20Audizione%20DG%20Commissione%20FInanze%20Camera%204%2012%202017.pdf

Accenture. (2018a). *What is Fintech and where is it headed?* Retrieved from https://www.accenture.com/ng-en/insight-fintech-did-someone-cancel-revolution/

Accenture. (2018b). *The future of Fintech and banking: Digitally disrupted or reimagined?* Retrieved from https://www.accenture.com/us-en/insight-future-fintech-banking/Accessed/28/5/2018

Acer, F. (2017). *Insurance Sector to Develop with InsurTech*. Retrieved from https://www.bankasurans.com.tr/sigorta-sektoru-insurtech-ile-gelisecek/

African Business. (2018, February). *Beyond the hype: what block chain could mean for Africa*. Author.

Ahmed, S. R. (2004). *Applications of data mining in retail business*. Paper presented at the Information Technology: Coding and Computing, 2004. 10.1109/ITCC.2004.1286695

Ahram, T., Sargolzaei, A., Sargolzaei, S., Daniels, J., & Amaba, B. (2017). *Blockchain technology innovations. In 2017 IEEE Technology & Engineering Management Conference* (pp. 137–141). Santa Clara, CA: TEMSCON.

Aitken, M., Cumming, D., & Zhan, F. (2015). High frequency trading and end-of-day price dislocation. *Journal of Banking & Finance*, *59*, 330–349. doi:10.1016/j.jbankfin.2015.06.011

Aït-Sahalia, Y., & Jacod, J. (2014). *High-frequency financial econometrics*. Princeton, NJ: Princeton Press.

Aït-Sahalia, Y., Mykland, P., & Zhang, L. (2005). How often to sample a continuous- time process in the presence of market microstructure noise. *Review of Financial Studies*, *18*(2), 351–416. doi:10.1093/rfs/hhi016

Al-Amine, M. A.-B. M. (2008). sukuk market: Innovations and challenges. *Islamic Capital Markets*, *33*.

Aldás-Manzano, J., Lassala-Navarré, C., Ruiz-Mafé, C., & Sanz-Blas, S. (2009). The role of consumer innovativeness and perceived risk in online banking usage. *International Journal of Bank Marketing*, *27*(1), 53–75. doi:10.1108/02652320910928245

Alexander, C. (2001). *Market models: a guide to financial data analysis*. John Wiley & Sons.

Alexander, C. (2008). *Market risk analysis: practical financial econometrics* (Vol. 2). John Wiley and Sons.

Alexander, L., Das, S. R., Ives, Z., Jagadish, H. V., & Monteleoni, C. (2017). Research Challenges in Financial Data Modeling and Analysis. *Big Data*, *5*(3), 177–188. doi:10.1089/big.2016.0074 PMID:28816500

Alharby, M., & Moorsel, A. V. (2017). *Blockchain-Based Smart Contracts: A Systematic Mapping Study. In Computer Science & Information Technology* (pp. 125–140). CS & IT.

Al-Jaziri, A. R. (2009). *Islamic Jurisprudence According to the Four Sunni Schools*. Fons Vitae.

Alotaibi, S., Furnell, S., & Clarke, N. (2016). A novel Taxonomy for mobile applications data. *International Journal of Cyber-Security and Digital Forensics*, *5*(3), 115–122. doi:10.17781/P002070

Amer, D. W., Barberis, J. N., & Buckley, R. P. (2015). The evolution of Fintech: A new-crisis paradigm? University of Hong Kong.

Andersen, T. G., & Bollerslev, T. (1997). Intraday periodicity and volatility persistence in financial markets. *Journal of Empirical Finance*, *4*(2), 115–158. doi:10.1016/S0927-5398(97)00004-2

Andersen, T. G., & Bollerslev, T. (1998a). Deutsche Mark-Dollar volatility: Intraday activity patterns, macroeconomic announcements, and longer run dependencies. *The Journal of Finance*, *53*(1), 219–265. doi:10.1111/0022-1082.85732

Anderson, T. G., Thyrsgaard, M., & Todorov, V. (2018). Time-varying periodicity in intraday volatility. *CREATES Research Paper.*

Anderson, T. G., & Benzoni, L. (2009). *Realized volatility. In Handbook of Financial Time series, Part III*. Springer Science & Business Media.

Anderson, T. G., & Bollerslev, T. (1998b). Answering the skeptics: Yes, standard volatility models do provide accurate forecasts. *International Economic Review*, *39*(4), 885–905. doi:10.2307/2527343

Anderson, T. G., Bollerslev, T., Diebold, F., & Labys, P. (2003). Modeling and forecasting realized volatility. *Econometrica*, *71*(2), 579–625. doi:10.1111/1468-0262.00418

Asare-Frempong, J., & Jayabalan, M. (2017). Predicting Customer Response to Bank Direct Telemarketing Campaign. *International Conference on Engineering Technologies and Technopreneurship (ICET2T)*, 1-4. 10.1109/ICE2T.2017.8215961

Asu, F. M. (2018). Fintech, threat to banking industry- CBN. *CIBN*. Retrieved from https://punch.ng.com/fintech-threat-to- banking-industry-cbn-cibn/Accessed 28/5/2018

Azmat, S., Skully, M., & Brown, K. (2017). The (little) difference that makes all the difference between Islamic and conventional bonds. *Pacific-Basin Finance Journal*, *42*, 46–59. doi:10.1016/j.pacfin.2015.12.010

BaFin. (2018). *Big data meets artificial intelligence: Challenges and implications for the supervision and regulation of financial services*. Retrieved from https://www.bafin.de/SharedDocs/Downloads/EN/dl_bdai_studie_en.pdf?__blob=publicationFile&v=11

Baker, M., Bradley, B., & Wurgler, J. (2011). Benchmarks as limits to arbitrage: Understanding the low-volatility anomaly. *Financial Analysts Journal*, *67*(1), 40–54. doi:10.2469/faj.v67.n1.4

Bakshi, G., & Kapadia, N. (2003). Volatility risk premiums embedded in individual equity options: Some new insights. *Journal of Derivatives*, *11*(1), 45–54. doi:10.3905/jod.2003.319210

Bakshi, K. (2012). Considerations for Big Data: Architecture and Approaches. *Proceedings of the IEEE Aerospace Conference*. 10.1109/AERO.2012.6187357

Ballings, M., Van den Poel, D., Hespeels, N., & Gryp, R. (2015). Evaluating multiple classifiers for stock price direction prediction. *Expert Systems with Applications*, *42*(20), 7046–7056. doi:10.1016/j.eswa.2015.05.013

Bandi, F., & Russell, J. (2005). *Realized covariation, realized beta and microstructure noise* (Unpublished paper). Graduate School of Business, University of Chicago.

Bandi, F., & Russell, J. (2008). Microstructure noise, realized variance and optimal sampling. *The Review of Economic Studies*, *75*(2), 339–369. doi:10.1111/j.1467-937X.2008.00474.x

Banerjee, P., Doran, J., & Peterson, D. R. (2007). Implied volatility and future portfolio returns. *Journal of Banking & Finance*, *31*(10), 3183–3199. doi:10.1016/j.jbankfin.2006.12.007

Barndorff-Nielsen, O., & Shephard, N. (2007). Variation, jumps and high frequency data in financial econometrics. *Advances in Economics and Econometrics. Theory and Applications, Ninth World Congress, CUP*, 328-372.

Barndorff-Nielsen, O., Hansen, P., Lunde, A., & Shephard, N. (2008). Designing realized kernels to measure the ex-post variation of equity prices in the presence of noise. *Econometrica, 76*(6), 1481–1536. doi:10.3982/ECTA6495

Barndorff-Nielsen, O., & Shephard, N. (2004). Power and bipower variation with stochastic volatility and jumps. *Journal of Financial Econometrics, 2*(1), 1–37. doi:10.1093/jjfinec/nbh001

Baron, M., Brogaard, J., Hagströmer, B., & Kirilenko, A. (2017). *Risk and return in high-frequency trading*. Retrieved May 8, 2018, https://papers.ssrn.com/sol3/papers.cfm?abstract_id=2433118

Bauwens, L., & Hautsch, N. (2009). *Modelling financial high frequency data using point processes. In Handbook of financial time series* (pp. 953–979). Berlin: Springer.

Bayram, A. S. (2018, June 25). Here Are Three Ways Blockchain Can Change Refugees' Lives. *World Economic Forum*. Retrieved from: https://www.weforum.org/agenda/2018/06/three-ways-blockchain-change-refugees-lives/

BeBeez. (2018). *Tutte le Fintech italiane (o fondate da italiani) finanziate da venture, angel, o altri investitori* [All the Italian Fintech (or founded by Italians) funded by venture, angel, or other investors]. Retrieved from https://bebeez.it/files/2018/06/FintechBeBeez-giu2018.pdf

Beckley, J. (2013). Innovation: Key to successful business. *BusinessNewsDaily*. Retrieved from https://www.businessnewsdaily.com/5167-innovation.html

Beikverdi, A., & Song, J. (2015). Trend of centralization in Bitcoin's distributed network. *2015 IEEE/ACIS 16th International Conference on Software Engineering, Artificial Intelligence, Networking and Parallel/Distributed Computing (SNPD)*, 1-6. 10.1109/SNPD.2015.7176229

Bekaert, G., & Wu, G. (2000). Asymmetric volatility and risk in equity markets. *Review of Financial Studies, 13*(1), 1–42. doi:10.1093/rfs/13.1.1

Benedikter, R. (2012, February 12). Social Banking and Social Finance: Building Stones Towards A Sustainable Post-Crisis Financial System? *The European Financial Review*, Retrieved from: http://www.europeanfinancialreview.com/?p=2027

Bergantini, D. (2013). Moment-based estimation of stochastic volatility. *Journal of Banking & Finance, 37*(12), 4755–4764. doi:10.1016/j.jbankfin.2013.08.008

Berger, R. (2017). *Copy Them? Work with Them? or Buy Them?* InsurTechs and the Digitalization of Insurance.

Berry, M. M. J., & Taggart, J. H. (1994). Managing technology and Innovation: A review. Research & Development Management, 24(4).

Betz, F. C. (1998). *Managing technological innovations: Competitive advantage from change*. New York: Wiley.

Biais, B., & Woolley, P. (2011). *High frequency trading. Manuscript*. Toulouse University, IDEI.

BIS. (2017). *Sound Practices: Implications of Fintech developments for banks and bank supervisors*. Basel Committee on Banking Supervision.

Bisoi, R., & Dash, P. K. (2014). A hybrid evolutionary dynamic neural network for stock market trend analysis and prediction using unscented Kalman filter. *Applied Soft Computing*, *19*, 41–56. doi:10.1016/j.asoc.2014.01.039

Black, F., & Scholes, M. (1973). The pricing of options and corporate liabilities. *Journal of Political Economy*, *81*(3), 637–654. doi:10.1086/260062

Blitz, D., & van Vliet, P. (2007). The volatility effect: Lower risk without lower return. *Journal of Portfolio Management*, *34*(1), 102–113. doi:10.3905/jpm.2007.698039

BlockchainHub. (n.d.). *Smart Contracts*. Retrieved from: https://blockchainhub.net/smart-contracts/

Blockgeeks. (n.d.). *Smart Contracts: The Blockchain Technology That Will Replace Lawyers*. Retrieved from: https://blockgeeks.com/guides/smart-contracts/

Boehmer, E., Fong, K., & Wu, J. (2015). *International evidence on algorithmic trading*. Retrieved May 15, 2018, from http://citeseerx.ist.psu.edu/viewdoc/download?doi=10.1.1.471.8155&rep=rep1&type=pdf

Bollerslev, T. (1986). Generalized autoregressive conditional heteroskedasticity. *Journal of Econometrics*, *31*(3), 307–327. doi:10.1016/0304-4076(86)90063-1

Bollerslev, T., Gibson, M., & Zhou, H. (2011). Dynamic estimation of volatility risk premia and investor risk aversion from option-implied and realized volatilities. *Journal of Econometrics*, *160*(1), 235–245. doi:10.1016/j.jeconom.2010.03.033

Bollerslev, T., & Zhou, H. (2002). Estimating stochastic volatility diffusion using conditional moments of integrated volatility. *Journal of Econometrics*, *109*(1), 33–65. doi:10.1016/S0304-4076(01)00141-5

Bolton, R. J., & Hand, D. J. (2002). Statistical fraud detection: A review. *Statistical Science*, 235–249.

Boston Consulting Group. (2016). *Global Corporate Banking 2016: The Next-Generation Corporate Bank*. Retrieved from http://image-src.bcg.com/Images/BCG-Global-Corporate-Banking-2016-Dec-2016_tcm80-217574_tcm9-167068.pdf

Boudt, K., Croux, C., & Laurent, S. (2011). Robust estimation of intraweek periodicity in volatility and jump detection. *Journal of Empirical Finance*, *18*(2), 353–367. doi:10.1016/j.jempfin.2010.11.005

Britten-Jones, M., & Neuberger, A. (2000). Option prices, implied price processes, and stochastic volatility. *The Journal of Finance*, *55*(2), 839–866. doi:10.1111/0022-1082.00228

Brogaard, J. (2010). *High frequency trading and its impact on market quality*. Northwestern University Kellogg School of Management Working Paper 66.

Brogaard, J. (2012). *High frequency trading and volatility*. Retrieved April 20, 2018, from http://ssrn.com/abstract=1641387

Brogaard, J., Hendershott, T., & Riordan, R. (2014). High-frequency trading and price discovery. *Review of Financial Studies*, *27*(8), 2267–2306. doi:10.1093/rfs/hhu032

Budale, D., & Mane, D. (2013). Predictive Analytics in Retail Banking. *International Journal of Engineering and Advanced Technology*, *2*(5), 508–510.

Budish, E., Carmton, P., & Shim, J. (2015). The high-frequency trading arms race: Frequent batch auctions as a market design response. *The Quarterly Journal of Economics*, *130*(4), 1547–1621. doi:10.1093/qje/qjv027

Canina, L., & Figlewski, S. (1993). The informational content of implied volatility. *Review of Financial Studies*, *6*(3), 659–681. doi:10.1093/rfs/5.3.659

Capegemini Consulting. (2016). *Smart Contracts in Financial Services: Getting from Hype to Reality*. Retrieved from https://www.capgemini.com/consulting-de/wp-content/uploads/sites/32/2017/08/smart_contracts_paper_long_0.pdf

Cappiello, A. (2018). Digital Disruption and InsurTech Start-ups: Risks and Challenges. In *Technology and the Insurance Industry*. Springer.

Carhart, M. M. (1997). On persistence in mutual fund performance. *The Journal of Finance*, *52*(1), 57–82. doi:10.1111/j.1540-6261.1997.tb03808.x

Carney, M. (2017). *The Promise of FinTech—Something New Under the Sun?* Retrieved from www.bankofengland.co.uk/publications/Documents/speeches/2017/speech956.pdf

Çavuşoğlu, R. (2018). *İkinci Nesil Insurtech Şirketine Dönüşmek İçin Çalışıyoruz*. Retrieved from http://m.sigortagundem.com/uploads/documents/akilliyasamdergisi-ocak2018-qnWW.pdf

Cb Insights, R. R. (2018). *Fintech Trends to Watch in 2018. A look back at fintech trends in 2017 and exploring what's ahead in 2018*. Retrieved from https://www.cbinsights.com/research/report/fintech-trends-2018/

Chaboud, A. P., Chiquoine, B., Hjalmarsson, E., & Vega, C. (2014). Rise of the machines: Algorithmic trading in the foreign exchange market. *The Journal of Finance*, *69*(5), 2045–2084. doi:10.1111/jofi.12186

Chen, L. (2016). From fintech to finlife: The case of fintech development in China. *China Economic Journal*, *9*(3), 225–239. doi:10.1080/17538963.2016.1215057

Chima, O. (2017, February 1). Expanding financial services through digital payments. *ThisDay*.

Christensen, K., Hounyo, U., & Podolskij, M. (2017) Is the diurnal pattern sufficient to explain the intraday variation in volatility? a nonparametric assessment. *CREATES Research working paper*.

Christensen, K., Oomen, R. C., & Podolskij, M. (2014). Fact or friction: Jumps at ultra-high frequency. *Journal of Financial Economics*, *114*(3), 576–599. doi:10.1016/j.jfineco.2014.07.007

Christie, A. A. (1982). The stochastic behavior of common stock variances: Value, leverage and interest rate effects. *Journal of Financial Economics*, *10*(4), 407–432. doi:10.1016/0304-405X(82)90018-6

Christoffersen, P., Diebold, F. X., & Shuermann, T. (1998), Horizontal Problems and Extreme Events in Financial Risk Management. The Handbook of Risk, 234, 155.

ÇipilM. (2016). Retrieved from https://tr.linkedin.com/pulse/blockchain-sigortac%C4%B1l%C4%B1%C4%9F%C4%B1-nas%C4%B1l-etkileyecek-mahir-%C3%A7ipil

Cocco, L., Pinna, A., & Marchesi, M. (2017). Banking on blockchain: Costs savings thanks to the blockchain technology. *Future Internet*, *9*(3), 25. doi:10.3390/fi9030025

Cochrane, J. (2005). *Asset Pricing* (Revised Edition). Princeton, NJ: Princeton University Press.

Cockerton, C. (2018). *FinServ 25: The most influential voices in banking*. Retrieved from https://thefinancialbrand.com

Conoscenti, M., Vetrò, A., & De Martin, J. C. (2016). Blockchain for the Internet of Things: A systematic literature review. *2016 IEEE/ACS 13th International Conference of Computer Systems and Applications (AICCSA)*, 1-6. 10.1109/AICCSA.2016.7945805

Conrad, J., Wahal, S., & Xiang, J. (2015). High-frequency quoting, trading, and the efficiency of prices. *Journal of Financial Economics*, *116*(2), 271–291. doi:10.1016/j.jfineco.2015.02.008

Conti, M., Kumar, S., Lal, C., & Ruj, S. (2018). A survey on security and privacy issues of bitcoin. IEEE Communications Surveys & Tutorials. doi:10.1109/COMST.2018.2842460

Conti, M., Nguyen, V. T. N., & Crispo, B. (2011). CRePE: Context-related policy enforcement for Android. In *Information Security* (pp. 331–345). Springer. doi:10.1007/978-3-642-18178-8_29

Corradi, V., & Distaso, W. (2006). Semi-parametric comparison of stochastic volatlity models using realized measures. *The Review of Economic Studies*, *73*(3), 635–667. doi:10.1111/j.1467-937X.2006.00390.x

Courtois, N. T., Emirdag, P., & Nagy, D. A. (2014). Could Bitcoin transactions be 100x faster? *2014 11th International Conference on Security and Cryptography (SECRYPT)*, 1-6. 10.5220/0005102804260431

CPAFRICA. (2018). *The rise and rise of Fintech in Africa*. Retrieved from https://www.cp-africa.com/2018/51/30/rise-rise-fintech-africa/

Crosby, M., Pattanayak, P., Verma, S., & Kalyanaraman, V. (2016). *BlockChain Technology: Beyond Bitcoin*. Retrieved from http://scet.berkeley.edu/wp-content/uploads/AIR-2016-Blockchain.pdf

Crosby, M., Pattanayak, P., Verma, S., & Kalyanaraman, V. (2016). Blockchain technology: Beyond bitcoin. *Applied Innovation*, *2*, 6–10.

Dadabhoy, I. (2018). *Introduction to FinTech and Smart Contracts (Slide).* IIFM Seminar on Islamic Financial Markets, Kuala Lumpur, Malaysia.

Dai, W. (2014). *Statistical methods in finance* (Unpublished doctoral dissertation). Princeton University, Princeton, NJ.

Delmolino, K., Arnett, M., Kosba, A., Miller, A., & Shi, E. (2016). Step By Step Towards Creating A Safe Smart Contract: Lessons And Insights From A Cryptocurrency Lab. In *International Conference on Financial Cryptography and Data Security*, (pp. 79-94). Springer. 10.1007/978-3-662-53357-4_6

Deloitte. (2018). *2018: Banking Outlook: Accelerating the transformation.* Retrieved from https://www2.deloitte.com/content/dam/Deloitte/tw/Documents/financial-services/tw-2018-Banking-Outlook-English.pdf

Derrig, R. A. (2002). Insurance fraud. *The Journal of Risk and Insurance, 69*(3), 271–287. doi:10.1111/1539-6975.00026

Deshmukh, A., Romine, J., & Siegel, P. H. (1997). Measurement and combination of red flags to assess the risk of management fraud: A fuzzy set approach. *Managerial Finance, 23*(6), 35–48. doi:10.1108/eb018629

Dhliwayo, C., & Governor, A. (2014). *Role of the banking sector in promoting growth & development of small and medium enterprises. In 2nd SME Banking* (pp. 1–17). Microfinance Summit.

Diao, X., & Tong, B. (2015). Forecasting intraday volatility and VaR using multiplicative component GARCH model. *Applied Economics Letters, 22*(18), 1457–1464. doi:10.1080/13504851.2015.1039696

Ding, X., Zhang, Y., & Liu, T., & Duan. (2015). Deep learning for event-driven stock prediction. *IJCAI (United States)*, 2327–2333.

Ding, X., Zhang, Y., Liu, T., & Duan, J. (2014). Using structured events to predict stock price movement: An empirical investigation. *Proceedings of the 2014 Conference on Empirical Methods in Natural Language Processing (EMNLP)*, 1415-1425.

Djafri, F. (2017). *Summary Report of the LSE-HBKU Workshop on Fintech and Islamic Finances.* Center for Islamic Economics and Finance (CIEF), College of Islamic Studies, Hamad Bin Khalifa University at the London School of Economics.

doi:10.1109/INFOTEH.2018.8345547

Dorfleitner, G. H., Weber, M., Schmitt, M., & Hormuf, L. (2017). *Fintech in Germany.* New York: Springer International Publishing, AG. doi:10.1007/978-3-319-54666-7

Drost, C. D., & Nijman, T. (1993). Temporal aggregation of GARCH processes. *Econometrica, 61*(3), 909–927. doi:10.2307/2951767

Dwi Marlina, W., & Alex, F. R. (2017). Shariah Fintech: Positive Innovation in Consumer Perspective. *Proceeding International Seminar on Competition Policy and Law*, 101-120.

Egloff, D., Leippold, M., & Wu, L. (2010). The term structure of variance swap rates and optimal variance swap investments. *Journal of Financial and Quantitative Analysis, 45*(5), 1279–1310. doi:10.1017/S0022109010000463

Elgendy, N. (2013). *Big Data Analytics in Support of the Decision Making Process* (MSc Thesis). German University in Cairo.

Ellickson, B., Sun, M., Whang, D., & Yan, S. (2018). *Estimating a local Heston model.* SSRN Archive. doi:10.2139srn.3108822

Elnagdy, S. A., Qiu, M., & Gai, K. (2016). *Understanding taxonomy of cyber risks for cybersecurity insurance of financial industry in cloud computing.* Paper presented at the Cyber Security and Cloud Computing (CSCloud), 2016 IEEE 3rd International Conference on. 10.1109/CSCloud.2016.46

Engle, R. (1982). Autoregressive conditional heteroscedasticity with estimates of the variance of United Kingdom inflation. *Econometrica, 68*(1), 1–22. doi:10.1111/1468-0262.00091

Engle, R. F., & Bollerslev, T. (1986). Modelling the persistence of conditional variances. *Econometric Reviews, 5*(1), 1–50. doi:10.1080/07474938608800095

Engle, R., Ghysels, E., & Sohn, B. (2008). *On the economic sources of stock market volatility.* SSRN Electronic Journal. doi:10.2139srn.971310

Engle, R., Lilien, D. M., & Robins, R. P. (1987). Estimating time varying risk premia in the term structure: The ARCH-M model. *Econometrica, 55*(2), 391–407. doi:10.2307/1913242

Engle, R., & Sokalska, M. (2012). Forecasting intraday volatility in the US equity market. multiplicative component GARCH. *Journal of Financial Econometrics, 10*(1), 54–83. doi:10.1093/jjfinec/nbr005

Ernst & Young. (2016). *Landscaping UK Fintech.* UK Trade and Investment.

Eroğlu, M. A. (2018). *Her Aşamada Müşteriye Dokunmalıyız.* Retrieved from http://m.sigortagundem.com/uploads/documents/akilliyasamdergisi-ocak2018-qnWW.pdf

European Central Bank. (2016). *Financial Stability Review.* Retrieved from https://www.ecb.europa.eu/pub/pdf/other/financialstabilityreview201611.en.pdf

European Commission. (2003). *Commission Recommendation of 6 May 2003 concerning the definition of micro, small and medium-sized enterprises.* Retrieved from https://eur-lex.europa.eu/LexUriServ/LexUriServ.do?uri=OJ:L:2003:124:0036:0041:en:PDF

European Commission. (2010). *European SMEs Under Pressure: Annual Report on EU Small and Medium-Sized Enterprises. SME performance review.* Retrieved from https://ec.europa.eu/docsroom/documents/15767/attachments/1/translations/en/renditions/native

Eurostat & OECD. (2005). *Guidelines for collecting and interpreting innovation data-the Oslo manual* (3rd ed.). Paris: Author.

Evry. (n.d.). *Big data in banking for marketers: How to derive value from big data.* Whitepaper. Retrieved from https://www.evry.com/globalassets/insight/bank2020/bank-2020---big-data---whitepaper.pdf

Fama, E. F., & French, K. R. (1993). Common risk factors in the returns on stocks and bonds. *Journal of Financial Economics, 33*(1), 3–56. doi:10.1016/0304-405X(93)90023-5

Fama, E. F., & French, K. R. (2006). Profitability, investment and average returns. *Journal of Financial Economics, 82*(3), 491–518. doi:10.1016/j.jfineco.2005.09.009

Fang, Y., Fataliyev, K., Wang, L., Fu, X., & Wang, Y. (2014). Improving the genetic-algorithm-optimized wavelet neural network for stock market prediction. *International Joint Conference on Neural Networks (IJCNN)*, 3038-3042. 10.1109/IJCNN.2014.6889969

Fanning, K., & Centers, D. (2016). Blockchain and Its Coming Impact on Financial Services. *Journal of Corporate Accounting & Finance, 27*(5), 53–57. doi:10.1002/jcaf.22179

Fawcett, T., & Provost, F. (1997). Adaptive fraud detection. *Data Mining and Knowledge Discovery, 1*(3), 291–316. doi:10.1023/A:1009700419189

Financial Stability Board. (2017). *Artificial Intelligence and machine learning in financial service: Market developments and financial stability implications.* Retrieved from http://www.fsb.org/wp-content/uploads/P011117.pdf

FinTech Network. (n.d.). *Four Blockchain Use Cases for Banks.* Retrieved from https://blockchainapac.fintecnet.com/uploads/2/4/3/8/24384857/FinTech_blockchain_report_v3.pdf

Fleming, J., Kirby, C., & Ostdiek, B. (2003). The economic value of volatility timing using "realized" volatility. *Journal of Financial Economics, 67*(3), 473–509. doi:10.1016/S0304-405X(02)00259-3

Ford, N. (2017). Should established banks fight or assimilate Fintech? *African Banker, 41.*

Fraser, J. G., & Bouridane, A. (2017). Have the security flaws surrounding BITCOIN effected the currency's value? *2017 Seventh International Conference on Emerging Security Technologies (EST)*, 50-55. 10.1109/EST.2017.8090398

Frazzini, A., & Pederson, L. H. (2009). Betting against beta. *Journal of Financial Economics, 111*(1), 1–25. doi:10.1016/j.jfineco.2013.10.005

Frino, A., Mollica, V., Monaco, E., & Palumbo, R. (2017b). The effect of algorithmic trading on market liquidity: Evidence around earnings announcements on Borsa Italiana. *Pacific-Basin Finance Journal, 45*, 82–90. doi:10.1016/j.pacfin.2016.07.003

Frino, A., Prodromou, T., Wang, G. H., Westerholm, P. J., & Zheng, H. (2017a). An empirical analysis of algorithmic trading around earnings announcements. *Pacific-Basin Finance Journal, 45*, 34–51. doi:10.1016/j.pacfin.2016.05.008

Gabor, D., & Brooks, S. (2017). The digital revolution in financial inclusion: International development in the fintech era. *New Political Economy, 22*(4), 423–436. doi:10.1080/13563467.2017.1259298

Gai, K., & Li, S. (2012). Towards cloud computing: a literature review on cloud computing and its development trends. Paper presented at the Multimedia Information Networking and Security (MINES), 2012 Fourth International Conference on. 10.1109/MINES.2012.240

Gai, K., Qiu, M., & Elnagdy, S. A. (2016). *Security-aware information classifications using supervised learning for cloud-based cyber risk management in financial big data.* Paper presented at the Big Data Security on Cloud (BigDataSecurity), IEEE International Conference on High Performance and Smart Computing (HPSC), and IEEE International Conference on Intelligent Data and Security (IDS), 2016 IEEE 2nd International Conference on. 10.1109/BigDataSecurity-HPSC-IDS.2016.66

Gai, K., Qiu, M., Jayaraman, S., & Tao, L. (2015). Ontology-Based Knowledge Representation for Secure Self-Diagnosis in Patient-Centered Teleheath with Cloud Systems. Paper presented at the Cyber Security and Cloud Computing (CSCloud), 2015 IEEE 2nd International Conference on. 10.1109/CSCloud.2015.72

Gai, K., Qiu, M., Sun, X., & Zhao, H. (2016). *Security and privacy issues: A survey on FinTech.* Paper presented at the International Conference on Smart Computing and Communication.

Gai, K., Qiu, M., Thuraisingham, B., & Tao, L. (2015). *Proactive attribute-based secure data schema for mobile cloud in financial industry.* Paper presented at the High Performance Computing and Communications (HPCC), 2015 IEEE 7th International Symposium on Cyberspace Safety and Security (CSS), 2015 IEEE 12th International Conferen on Embedded Software and Systems (ICESS), 2015 IEEE 17th International Conference on. 10.1109/HPCC-CSS-ICESS.2015.250

Gai, K. (2014). A review of leveraging private cloud computing in financial service institutions: Value propositions and current performances. *International Journal of Computers and Applications, 95*(3), 40–44. doi:10.5120/16578-6268

Gai, K., Qiu, M., & Sun, X. (2018). A survey on FinTech. *Journal of Network and Computer Applications, 103*, 262–273. doi:10.1016/j.jnca.2017.10.011

Gai, K., Qiu, M., Tao, L., & Zhu, Y. (2016). Intrusion detection techniques for mobile cloud computing in heterogeneous 5G. *Security and Communication Networks, 9*(16), 3049–3058. doi:10.1002ec.1224

Gai, K., Qiu, M., Zhao, H., Tao, L., & Zong, Z. (2016). Dynamic energy-aware cloudlet-based mobile cloud computing model for green computing. *Journal of Network and Computer Applications, 59*, 46–54. doi:10.1016/j.jnca.2015.05.016

Garcia, R., Lewis, M., Pastorello, S., & Renault, E. (2011). Estimation of objective and risk-neutral distributions based on moments of integrated volatility. *Journal of Econometrics, 160*(1), 22–32. doi:10.1016/j.jeconom.2010.03.011

Gengler, E. B. (2017, August 29). Leveraging Blockchain Technology for Corporate Social Responsibility. *Payments Journal.* Retrieved from: http://paymentsjournal.com/leveraging-blockchain-technology-for-corporate-social-responsibility/

Geroge, G., McGalan, A. M., & Prabhu, J. (2012). Innovation for inclusive growth: Towards a theoretical framework and a research agenda. *Journal of Management Studies, 49*(4).

Gheeraert, L. (2014). Does Islamic finance spur banking sector development? *Journal of Economic Behavior & Organization, 103*, S4–S20. doi:10.1016/j.jebo.2014.02.013

Gifari, A., Anggorojati, B., & Yazid, S. (2017). On preventing bitcoin transaction from money laundering in Indonesia: Analysis and recommendation on regulations. *2017 International Workshop on Big Data and Information Security (IWBIS)*, 143-148. 10.1109/IWBIS.2017.8275116

Giot, P. (2005). Market risk models for intraday data. *European Journal of Finance, 11*(4), 309–324. doi:10.1080/1351847032000143396

Glancy, F. H., & Yadav, S. B. (2011). A computational model for financial reporting fraud detection. *Decision Support Systems, 50*(3), 595–601. doi:10.1016/j.dss.2010.08.010

Global FinTech Survey. (2016). *Customers in the spotlight: How FinTech is reshaping banking*. Retrieved from https://www.pwc.com/jg/en/publications/fin-tech-banking-2016.pdf

Glosten, L., Jagannathan, R., & Runkle, D. E. (1993). On the relation between the expected value and the volatility of the nominal excess return on stocks. *The Journal of Finance, 48*(5), 1779–1801. doi:10.1111/j.1540-6261.1993.tb05128.x

Godlewski, C. J., Turk-Ariss, R., & Weill, L. (2013). Sukuk vs. conventional bonds: A stock market perspective. *Journal of Comparative Economics, 41*(3), 745–761. doi:10.1016/j.jce.2013.02.006

Gomber, P., Kauffman, R. J., Parker, C., & Weber, B. W. (2018). On the Fintech Revolution: Interpreting the Forces of Innovation, Disruption, and Transformation in Financial Services. *Journal of Management Information Systems, 35*(1), 220–265. doi:10.1080/07421222.2018.1440766

Gomber, P., Koch, J., & Siering, M. (2017). Digital Finance and FinTech: Current Research and Future Research Directions. *Journal of Business Economics, 87*(5), 537–580. doi:10.100711573-017-0852-x

Groth, S. (2011). Does algorithmic trading increase volatility. *Empirical Evidence from the Fully-Electronic Trading Platform Xetra, proceedings of the 10th International Conference on Wirtschaftsinformatik.*

Gsell, M. (2008). *Assessing the impact of Algorithmic Trading on markets: A simulation approach* (No. 2008/49). CFS Working Paper.

Guilbaud, F., & Pham, H. (2013). Optimal high-frequency trading with limit and market orders. *Quantitative Finance, 13*(1), 79–94. doi:10.1080/14697688.2012.708779

Guild, J. (2017). Fintech and the Future of Finance. *Asian Journal Of Public Affairs, 10*(1). doi:10.18003/ajpa.201710

Guo, Y., & Liang, C. (2016). Blockchain application and outlook in the banking industry. *Financial Innovation, 2*(1), 24. doi:10.118640854-016-0034-9

Güzey, P. (2018). *Dijital projelerin yüzde 80'inden fazlası başarısızlıkla sonuçlanıyor.* Retrieved from http://m.sigortagundem.com/uploads/documents/akilliyasamdergisi-ocak2018-qnWW.pdf http://blokzincir.bilgem.tubitak.gov.tr/blok-zincir.html https://fintechistanbul.org/category/insurtech/

Hagströmer, B., & Norden, L. (2013). The diversity of high-frequency traders. *Journal of Financial Markets, 16*(4), 741–770. doi:10.1016/j.finmar.2013.05.009

HalalChain. (2018). *Halal-Chain White Paper.* Retrieved from: https://www.hlc.com/whitepaper.pdf

Hamzaoui, N., & Regaieg, B. (2016). The Glosten-Jagannathan-Runkle-Generalized Autoregressive Conditional Heteroscedastic approach to investigating the foreign exchange forward premium volatility. *International Journal of Economics and Financial Issues, 6*(4), 1608–1615.

Hansen, E. (2015, July 29). The Blockchain, Explained. *Medium.* Retrieved from: https://medium.com/linkreply-blockchain/the-blockchain-explained-3300f4506890

Hansen, P. R., & Lunde, A. (2005). Realized variance and market microstructure noise. *Journal of Business & Economic Statistics, 24*(2), 127–161. doi:10.1198/073500106000000071

Hasbrouck, J. (2018). High-frequency quoting: Short-term volatility in bids and offers. *Journal of Financial and Quantitative Analysis, 53*(2), 613–641. doi:10.1017/S0022109017001053

Hassani, H., Huang, X., & Silva, E. (2018). Digitalisation and big data mining in banking. *Big Data and Cognitive Computing, 2*(3), 18. doi:10.3390/bdcc2030018

Hayashi, T., & Yoshida, N. (2006). *Estimating correlations with nonsynchronous observations in continuous diffusion models* (Unpublished Working Paper). Columbia University, New York, NY.

Hayikader, S., Hadi, A., Hanis, F. N., & Ibrahim, J. (2016). Issues and security measures of mobile banking apps. *International Journal of Scientific and Research Publications, 6*(1), 36–41.

Hazwan Faisal, M. (2018). Kerajaan komited perkasa Fintech di Malaysia. *Berita Harian.* Retrieved from https://www.bharian.com.my/bisnes/lain-lain/2018/03/396634/kerajaan-komited-perkasa-fintech-di-malaysia

Hecq, A., Laurent, S., & Palm, F. (2012). Common intraday periodicity. *Journal of Financial Econometrics, 10*(2), 325–353. doi:10.1093/jjfinec/nbr012

Hegazy, O., Soliman, O. S., & Salam, M. A. (2015). Comparative study between FPA, BA, MCS, ABC, and PSO algorithms in training and optimizing of LS-SVM for stock market prediction. *IJACR, 35*.

Hendershott, T., Jones, C. M., & Menkveld, A. J. (2011). Does algorithmic trading improve liquidity? *The Journal of Finance*, *66*(1), 1–33. doi:10.1111/j.1540-6261.2010.01624.x

Hendershott, T., & Riordan, R. (2009). *Algorithmic trading and information. Manuscript*. Berkeley, CA: University of California.

Hendershott, T., & Riordan, R. (2013). Algorithmic trading and the market for liquidity. *Journal of Financial and Quantitative Analysis*, *48*(4), 1001–1024. doi:10.1017/S0022109013000471

Heston, S. (1993). A closed-form solution for options with stochastic volatility with applications to bonds and currency options. *Review of Financial Studies*, *6*(2), 327–343. doi:10.1093/rfs/6.2.327

He, W., Tian, X., Shen, J., & Yaohang, L. (2015). Understanding Mobile Banking Applications' Security risks through Blog Mining and the Workflow Technology. *36th International Conference on Information Systems*, 1-10.

Hu, F., Qiu, M., Li, J., Grant, T., Taylor, D., McCaleb, S., ... Hamner, R. (2011). A review on cloud computing: Design challenges in architecture and security. *CIT. Journal of Computing and Information Technology*, *19*(1), 25–55. doi:10.2498/cit.1001864

Hull, J., & Basu, S. (2016). *Options, futures and other derivatives*. Pearson Education India.

Hussain, M., Al-Haiqi, A., Zaidan, A., Zaidan, B., Kiah, M., Iqbal, S., ... Abdulnabi, M. (2018). A security framework for mHealth apps on android platform. *Computers & Security*, *75*, 191–217. doi:10.1016/j.cose.2018.02.003

Hussain, M., Zaidan, A., Zidan, B., Iqbal, S., Ahmed, M., Albahri, O., & Albahri, A. (2018). Conceptual framework for the security of mobile health applications on Android platform. *Telematics and Informatics*, *35*(5), 1335–1354. doi:10.1016/j.tele.2018.03.005

Iansiti, M., & Lakhani, K. R. (2017). The truth about blockchain. *Harvard Business Review*. Retrieved from https://hbr.org/products/the-truth-about-blockchain/R1701J-PDF-ENG

Iansiti, M., & Lakhani, K. (2017). The Truth About Blockchain. *Harvard Business Review*, *95*(1), 118–127.

Ibn Abidin, M. A. (1992). *Radd Al-Mukhtar Ala Al-Durr Al-Mukhtar*. Beirut, Lebanon: Dar Al-Fikr.

Idelberger, F., Governatori, G., Riveret, R., & Sartor, G. (2016). Evaluation of Logic-Based Smart Contracts for Blockchain Systems. In J. Alferes, L. Bertossi, G. Governatori, P. Fodor, & D. Roman (Eds.), Lecture Notes in Computer Science: Vol. 9718. *Rule Technologies. Research, Tools, and Applications. RuleML 2016*. Springer. doi:10.1007/978-3-319-42019-6_11

IFSB. (2017). *Islamic Financial Services Industry Stability Report 2017*. IFSB.

IIFM. (2018). *IIFM Annual sukuk Report*. IIFM.

Image: Difference between Operating and Financial Lease | eFM. (2018). Retrieved from https://www.google.com/imgres?imgurl=https://efinancemanagement.com/wp-content/uploads/2015/01/Difference-between-Operating-and-Financial-Lease.png&imgrefurl=https://efinancemanagement.com/sources-of-finance/difference-between-operating-and-financial-lease&h=615&w=1101&tbnid=SuYR9ukWCqO5pM:&tbnh=117&tbnw=211&usg=__iixUTyFeTHHgzPVdUX6VyshcHIA%3D&vet=12ahUKEwiBx-r814rbAhUMuxQKHZTuBu8Q9QEwAHoECAEQKQ.i&docid=JWNo8_x3cD7A2M&sa=X&ved=2ahUKEwiBx-r814rbAhUMuxQKHZTuBu8Q9QEwAHoECAEQKQ

ImagineNation. (2018). *8 reasons why innovation is important to businesses today*. Retrieved from https://www.imaginenationa.com.au/innovation-blog/8reasons-innovation-important-business-today/Accessed 28/5/2018

Innovationxchange. (2018). *Importance of innovation in business*. Retrieved from https://www.ixc-uk.com/importance_of_innovation_in_Business.html/Accessed 28/5/2018

International Trade Administration (ITA). (2016). *2016 Top Markets Report Financial Technology*. Department of Commerce.

Investopedia. (2018a). *What is the financial services sector?* Retrieved from https://www.investopedia.com/ask/answers/030315/what-is-the-financial-services-sector.asp/Accessed 28/5/2018

Investopedia. (2018b). *Why fintech will drive business models of the future?* Retrieved from https://www.investopedis.com/articles/markets/080716/why-fintech-will-drive-business-models-future.asp/Accessed 28/5/2018

Investopedia. (n.d.). *Smart Contracts*. Retrieved from: https://www.investopedia.com/terms/s/smart-contracts.asp

Iqbal, Z., & Mirakhor, A. (2011). *An introduction to Islamic finance: theory and practice*. John Wiley & Sons. doi:10.1002/9781118390474

IRCIEF. (2018). Roundtable Discussion On Cryptocurrency: Issues And Solutions. *IRCIEF KUIS*. Retrieved from http://www.kuis.edu.my/ircief/blog/2018/04/18/roundtable-discussion-on-cryptocurrency-issues-and-solutions/

Islamic Business & Finance. (2017). Is Fintech Shari'ah compliant? In Developing Islamic Fintech. CPI Financial FZ LLC.

Isobe, T., Morishima, M., Yoshitani, G., Koizumi, N., & Murakami, K. (1996). Voice-activated home banking system and its field trial. In *Proceedings of Fourth International Conference on Spoken Language Processing* (pp. 1688-1691). Philadelphia: IEEE. 10.1109/ICSLP.1996.607951

Ivanauskienė, N., Auruškevičienė, V., Škudienė, V., & Nedzinskas, Š. (2012). Customer perceptions of value: Case of retail banking. *Organizations and Markets in Emerging Economies*, *3*(1/5), 75–88.

Jacob, F. (2015). *Risk estimation on high-frequency financial data*. Wiesbaden, Germany: Springer. doi:10.1007/978-3-658-09389-1

Jacod, J., Li, Y., & Zheng, X. (2017). Statistical properties of microstructure noise. *Econometrica*, *85*(4), 1133–1174. doi:10.3982/ECTA13085

Jain, P. K., Jain, P., & McInish, T. H. (2016). Does high-frequency trading increase systemic risk? *Journal of Financial Markets*, *31*, 1–24. doi:10.1016/j.finmar.2016.09.004

Johnson, B. (2010). *Algorithmic Trading & DMA: An introduction to direct access trading strategies* (Vol. 200). London: 4Myeloma Press.

Jones, C. M. (2013). *What do we know about high-frequency trading*. Columbia Business School, Research Paper No. 13-11.

Jones, C., Ramanau, R., Cross, S., & Healing, G. (2010). Net generation or Digital Natives: Is there a distinct new generation entering university? *Computers & Education*, *54*(3), 722–732. doi:10.1016/j.compedu.2009.09.022

Judmayer, A., Stifter, N., Krombholz, K., & Weippl, E. (2017). Blocks and Chains: Introduction to Bitcoin, Cryptocurrencies, and Their Consensus Mechanisms. *Synthesis Lectures on Information Security, Privacy, &. Trust*, *9*(1), 1–123.

Juskalian, R. (2018, April 12). Inside the Jordan Refugee Camp That Runs on Blockchain. *MIT Technology Review*. Retrieved from: https://www.technologyreview.com/s/610806/inside-the-jordan-refugee-camp-that-runs-on-blockchain

Kasri, N. S. (2017, July 18). Shariah Compliance via Blockchain and Smart Contract – The Case for Islamic Credit Card. *Halal Investing Journal*. Retrieved from: https://journal.wahedinvest.com/shariah-compliance-via-blockchain-and-smart-contract-the-case-for-islamic-credit-card

Kaushik, A., Choudhary, A., Ektare, C., Thomas, D., & Akram, S. (2017). Blockchain—Literature survey. *2017 2nd IEEE International Conference on Recent Trends in Electronics, Information & Communication Technology (RTEICT)*, 2145-2148. 10.1109/RTEICT.2017.8256979

Kaustav. (2018, March 28). How Ripple (XRP) Outdid the Transaction Speed of VISA. *Global Coin Report*. Retrieved from: https://globalcoinreport.com/how-ripple-xrp-outdid-the-transaction-speed-of-visa

Kawai, Y. (2016). Fintech and the IAIS. *IAIS Newsletter, 52*. Retrieved from https://www.iaisweb.org/file/61139/iais-newsletter-june-2016-final

Kelejian, H. H., & Mukerji, P. (2016). Does high frequency algorithmic trading matter for non-AT investors? *Research in International Business and Finance*, *37*, 78–92. doi:10.1016/j.ribaf.2015.10.014

Kenny, R., Hope, B., DeBold, T., & Yang, S. (2015). *'Flash Crash' a perfect storm for markets*. Retrieved from http://graphics.wsj.com/flash-crash-timeline/

Kent, A. (2015). *High Frequency Decomposition and Trade Arrivals* (Unpublished Working Paper). University of Colorado, Boulder, CO.

Khan, N. (2017, January 9). *Smart Contracts - The Future of Islamic Banking*. Retrieved from: https://www.linkedin.com/pulse/smart-contracts-future-islamic-banking-nida-khan

Khan, F. (2010). How 'Islamic' is Islamic Banking? *Journal of Economic Behavior & Organization*, *76*(3), 805–820. doi:10.1016/j.jebo.2010.09.015

Kirilenko, A., Kyle, A., Mehrdad, S., & Tugkan, T. (2011). *The flash crash: the impact of high frequency trading on an electronic market.* Available at SSRN 1686004.

Kirilenko, A., Kyle, A. S., Samadi, M., & Tuzun, T. (2017). The Flash Crash: High-frequency trading in an electronic market. *The Journal of Finance*, *72*(3), 967–998. doi:10.1111/jofi.12498

Kou, G., Peng, Y., & Wang, G. (2014). Evaluation of clustering algorithms for financial risk analysis using MCDM methods. *Information Sciences*, *275*, 1–12. doi:10.1016/j.ins.2014.02.137

KPMG. (2016). *Nuovi modelli distributivi nel settore bancario* [New distribution models in the banking sector]. Retrieved from https://assets.kpmg.com/content/dam/kpmg/pdf/2016/06/it-modelli-distributivi.pdf.pdf

KPMG. (2017). *Sigortacılık, Teknolojiyle Yeniden Doğdu* [Rebirth of insurance business with technology]. Retrieved from https://home.kpmg.com/tr/tr/home/media/press-releases/2017/07/sigortacilik-teknolojiyle-yeniden-dogdu.html

Kuo Chuen, D.L.., & Teo, E.G. (2015). Emergence of fintech and the LASIC Principles. *Journal of Financial Perspectives, 3*(3).

Lahmiri, S., & Boukadoum, M. (2015). An ensemble system based on hybrid EGARCH-ANN with different distributional assumptions to predict S&P 500 intraday volatility. *Fluctuation and Noise Letters*, *14*(1), 1550001. doi:10.1142/S0219477515500017

Lai, J., Rethel, L., & Steiner, K. (2017). Conceptualizing dynamic challenges to global financial diffusion: Islamic finance and the grafting of sukuk. *Review of International Political Economy, 24*(6), 958-979. doi:10.1080/09692290.2017.1373689

Laldin, M. A. (n.d.). *Fintech and Smart Contract: Opportunities in Islamic Finance*. Retrieved from International Islamic Financial Market: http://www.iifm.net/sites/default/files/Session%206%20%20Fintech%20and%20Smart%20Contract%20Opportunities%20in%20Islamic%20Finance%20%20Prof.%20Dr.%20Mohamad%20Akram%20Laldin%20%28ISRA%29.pdf

Larimer, D. (2016). *Blok Zinciri Ve Sigorta.* Retrieved from https://www.blokzinciri.org/yazi/blok-zinciri-ve-sigorta/

Lauslahti, K., Mattila, J., & Seppälä, T. (2017). *Smart Contracts – How will Blockchain Technology Affect Contractual Practices?* ETLA Reports No 68. Retrieved from https://pub.etla.fi/ETLA-Raportit-Reports-68.pdf

Lee, H., Surdeanu, M., MacCartney, B., & Jurafsky, D. (2014). On the Importance of Text Analysis for Stock Price Prediction. *LREC*, 1170-1175.

Lee, I., & Shin, Y. J. (2018). Fintech: Ecosystem, business models, investment decisions, and challenges. *Business Horizons*, *61*(1), 35–46. doi:10.1016/j.bushor.2017.09.003

Lee, M. C. (2015). Factors influencing the adoption of internet: An integration of TAM and TPB with perceived risk and perceived benefit. *Electronic Commerce Research and Applications*, *8*(3), 130–141. doi:10.1016/j.elerap.2008.11.006

Lenard, M. J., & Alam, P. (2004). The use of fuzzy logic and expert reasoning for knowledge management and discovery of financial reporting fraud. *Organizational data mining: Leveraging enterprise data resources for optimal performance*, 230-262.

Leong, C., Tan, B., Xiao, X., Tan, F. T. C., & Sun, Y. (2017). Nurturing a FinTech ecosystem: The case of a youth microloan startup in China. *International Journal of Information Management*, *37*(2), 92–97. doi:10.1016/j.ijinfomgt.2016.11.006

Levy, S., & Hino, H. (2016). Emotional brand attachment: A factor in customer-bank relationships. *International Journal of Bank Marketing*, *34*(2), 136–150. doi:10.1108/IJBM-06-2015-0092

Li, J., Qiu, M., Ming, Z., Quan, G., Qin, X., & Gu, Z. (2012). Online optimization for scheduling preemptable tasks on IaaS cloud systems. *Journal of Parallel and Distributed Computing*, *72*(5), 666–677. doi:10.1016/j.jpdc.2012.02.002

Li, J., Todorov, V., & Tauchen, G. (2017). Jump regressions. *Econometrica*, *85*(1), 173–195. doi:10.3982/ECTA12962

Lim, S. H., Kim, D. J., Hur, Y., & Park, K. (2018). An Empirical Study of the Impacts of Perceived Security and Knowledge on Continuous Intention to Use Mobile Fintech Payment Services. *International Journal of Human-Computer Interaction*, 1–13. doi:10.1080/10447318.2018.1507132

Li, Q., Wang, T. J., Li, P., Liu, L., Gong, Q., & Chen, Y. (2014). The effect of news and public mood on stock movements. *Information Sciences*, *278*, 826–840. doi:10.1016/j.ins.2014.03.096

Liu, L. (2013). *High Frequency Trading and Its Impact on the Swedish Stock volatility* (Unpublished Master Thesis). Lund University, Sweden.

Li, X., Xie, H., Chen, L., Wang, J., & Deng, X. (2014). News impact on stock price return via sentiment analysis. *Knowledge-Based Systems*, *69*, 14–23. doi:10.1016/j.knosys.2014.04.022

Li, Y., Dai, W., Ming, Z., & Qiu, M. (2016). Privacy protection for preventing data over-collection in smart city. *IEEE Transactions on Computers*, *65*(5), 1339–1350. doi:10.1109/TC.2015.2470247

Luo, J., Su, W., & Huang, A. Q. (2017, July). Bit-energy: An innovative bitcoin-style distributed transactional model for a competitive electricity market. In 2017 IEEE Power & Energy Society General Meeting (pp. 1-5). IEEE. doi:10.1109/PESGM.2017.8274639

Lustig, C., & Nardi, B. (2015). Algorithmic Authority: The Case of Bitcoin. *2015 48th Hawaii International Conference on System Sciences*, 743-752. 10.1109/HICSS.2015.95

Macedo, B. E. (2018). Security in the Future of WealthTech. *The WealthTech Book: The FinTech Handbook for Investors, Entrepreneurs and Finance Visionaries*, 279-281.

Machler, M. (2016). *InsurTech Paving the Way to Change the Insurance Regulatory Landscape?* Retrieved from http://www.icir.de/fileadmin/Documents/Policy_Platform/180426_ICIR_JB_PP_InsurTech.pdf

Mak, M. K. Y., Ho, G. T. S., & Ting, S. L. (2011). A financial data mining model for extracting customer behavior. *International Journal of Engineering Business Management*, *3*(3), 59–72.

Manahov, V., Hudson, R., & Gebka, B. (2014). Does high frequency trading affect technical analysis and market efficiency? And if so, how? *Journal of International Financial Markets, Institutions and Money*, *28*, 131–157. doi:10.1016/j.intfin.2013.11.002

Mancini, C. (2003). *Statistics of a Poisson-Gaussian process* (Unpublished Working Paper). Dipartimento di matematica per le Decisioni, Universita di Firenze, Florence, Italy.

Mancini, C. (2004). Estimaton of the characteristics of jump of a general Poisson-diffusion process. *Scandinavian Actuarial Journal*, *1*(1), 42–52. doi:10.1080/03461230310017009l

Markowitz, H. (1952). Portfolio selection. *The Journal of Finance*, *7*(1), 77–91.

Marous, J. (2018). *FinServ 25: The most influential voices in banking*. Retrieved from https://thefinancialbrand.com

Marr, B. (2018, February 16). A Very Brief History of Blockchain Technology Everyone Should Read. *Forbes*. Retrieved from: https://www.forbes.com/sites/bernardmarr/2018/02/16/a-very-brief-history-of-blockchain-technology-everyone-should-read/#5462f7f37bc4

Martinez, V. H., & Rosu, I. (2013). High frequency traders, news and volatility. In *AFA 2013*. San Diego Meetings Paper.

McKinsey. (2017). Blockchain Technology in the Insurance Sector. In *Proceedings of the Quarterly Meeting of the Federal Advisory Committee on Insurance (FACI)*. McKinsey & Company.

McNally, S., Roche, J., & Caton, S. (2018). Predicting the Price of Bitcoin Using Machine Learning. *2018 26th Euromicro International Conference on Parallel, Distributed and Network-based Processing (PDP)*, 339-343. 10.1109/PDP2018.2018.00060

Merton, R. C. (1976). Option pricing when underlying stock returns are discontinuous. *Journal of Financial Economics*, *3*(1-2), 125–144. doi:10.1016/0304-405X(76)90022-2

Merton, R. C. (1980). On estimating the expected return on the market: An exploratory investigation. *Journal of Financial Economics*, *8*(4), 323–361. doi:10.1016/0304-405X(80)90007-0

MIFC. (2016). *Islamic Finance Technology and Innovation*. Bank Negara Malaysia.

Mitra, S., Pal, S. K., & Mitra, P. (2002). Data mining in soft computing framework: A survey. *IEEE Transactions on Neural Networks*, *13*(1), 3–14. doi:10.1109/72.977258 PMID:18244404

MobileworldwideLive. (2017). *Bharti Airtel identifies African consolidation markets*. Retrieved from https://www.mobileworldwide.com/featured-content/top-three/bharti-airtel-identifies-african-consolidation-markets

Montier, J. (2013). *Hyperinflations, Hysteria, and False Memories*. GMO LLC.

Moore, R. (2017). *Technology is an enabler of business growth*. Retrieved from https://m.fin24.com/Tech/opinion/technology-is-an-enabler-of-business-growth-20170612

Morales, M., Brizan, D. G., Ghaly, H., Hauner, T., Ma, M., Reza, S., & Rosenberg, A. (2014). *Application of Social Network Analysis in the Estimation of Bank Financial Strength During the Financial Crisis*. NLP Unshared Task in PoliInformatics. Retrieved from https://www.researchgate.net/profile/Michelle_Morales4

Moreira, A., & Muir, T. (2017). Volatility-Managed Portfolios. *The Journal of Finance*, *72*(4), 1611–1644. doi:10.1111/jofi.12513

Morgan, R. (2017). The Top Fintech Trends Driving the Next Decade. *American Bankers Association. ABA Banking Journal*, *109*(5), 22.

Moro, S., Cortez, P., & Rita, P. (2015). Business intelligence in banking: A literature analysis from 2002 to 2013 using text mining and latent Dirichlet allocation. *Expert Systems with Applications*, *42*(3), 1314–1324. doi:10.1016/j.eswa.2014.09.024

Muller, P., Caliandro, C., Peycheva, V., Gagliardi, D., Marzocchi, C., Ramlogan, R., & Cox, D. (2015). *Annual report on European SMEs*. Retrieved from http://ec.europa.eu/DocsRoom/documents/16341/attachments/2/translations/en/renditions/native

Mulligan, G. (2017). *Over 300 fintech start-ups active in Africa*. Retrieved from https://www.disrupt-africa.com/2017/06/0ver-300-fintech-startups-active-in-africa/

Muthiah, A. Z. R., & Ro'fa, S., & Islamiyati. (2017). Crowdfunding Syariah Untuk Pengembangan Produk Perbankan Syariah Dari Perspektif Shariah Compliance. *Diponegoro Law Journal*, *6*(4), 1–16.

Mykland, P. A., & Zhang, L. (2005). A tale of two time scales: Determining integrated volatility with noisy high-frequency data. *Journal of the American Statistical Association*, *100*(472), 1394–1411. doi:10.1198/016214505000000169

Nelson, C. (2017) Fintech marches on. *African Banker*, *41*.

NetConsulting. (2017). *Le aziende del Fintech in Italia 2017*. Retrieved from https://www.pwc.com/it/it/industries/FinTech/docs/2017-FinTech-report.pdf

Ngai, E., Hu, Y., Wong, Y., Chen, Y., & Sun, X. (2011). The application of data mining techniques in financial fraud detection: A classification framework and an academic review of literature. *Decision Support Systems*, *50*(3), 559–569. doi:10.1016/j.dss.2010.08.006

Nguyen, T., & Shirai, K. (2015). *Topic modeling based sentiment analysis on social media for stock market prediction*. Association for Computational Linguistics.

Nopp, C., & Hanbury, A. (2015). Detecting Risks in the Banking System by Sentiment Analysis. In *Proceedings of the 2015 Conference on Empirical Methods in Natural Language Processing* (pp. 591-600). Lisbon, Portugal: Association for Computational Linguistics. 10.18653/v1/D15-1071

Nurul Aini, M., & Ainulashikin, M. (2018). Will Fintech Disrupt Islamic Banks? In Extending the Boundaries of Islamic Finance, Vol. 4, YTI Lecture Series (pp. 182-195). USIM Press.

Okonji, E. (2018, July 9). FG urged to adopt blockchain technology to boost FDI. *Thisday*.

Okuda, T., & Shoda, S. (2018). AI-based chatbot service for financial industry. *Fujitsu Scientific and Technical Journal*, *54*(2), 4–8.

Oladeji, A. (2018). *African Fintech startups are revolutionizing banking*. Retrieved from https://syncedreview.com/2018/03/17/african-fintech-startups-are-revolutionizing-banking/

Organization for Economic Cooperation and Development. (2002). *Frascati Manual*. Retrieved from https://stats.oecd.org/glossary/detail.asp?ID=2688

Patel, J., Shah, S., Thakkar, P., & Kotecha, K. (2015). Predicting stock and stock price index movement using trend deterministic data preparation and machine learning techniques. *Expert Systems with Applications*, *42*(1), 259–268. doi:10.1016/j.eswa.2014.07.040

Pathak, J., Vidyarthi, N., & Summers, S. L. (2005). A fuzzy-based algorithm for auditors to detect elements of fraud in settled insurance claims. *Managerial Auditing Journal*, *20*(6), 632–644. doi:10.1108/02686900510606119

Peck, M. E. (2017a, October). Blockchains: How They Work and Why They'll Change the World. *Blockchain World, Spectrum IEEE.ORG*, 22-24.

Peck, M. E. (2017b, October). Blockchains: How Does Proof of Work Secure Blockchains. *Blockchain World, Spectrum IEEE.ORG*, 26-28.

Phua, C., Lee, V., Smith, K., & Gayler, R. (2010). *A comprehensive survey of data mining-based fraud detection research.* arXiv preprint arXiv:1009.6119

Piotrowska, A. I., Polasik, M., & Piotrowski, D. (2017). Prospects for the application of biometrics in the Polish banking sector. *Equilibrium. Quarterly Journal of Economics and Economic Policy*, *12*(3), 501–518.

Pratali, P. (2003). Strategic management of technological innovations in the small to medium enterprise. *European Journal of Innovation Management*, *6*(1), 18–31. doi:10.1108/14601060310456300

Premoli, F. (2017). *The impact of digital innovations on the current banks' offering towards SMEs*. Retrieved from https://www.politesi.polimi.it/handle/10589/136364

PwC. (2017). *Blockchain, A Catalyst for New Approaches in Insurance*. Retrieved from: https://www.pwc.com/gx/en/insurance/assets/blockchain-a-catalyst.pdf

Qiu, M., Chen, Z., & Liu, M. (2014). Low-power low-latency data allocation for hybrid scratch-pad memory. *IEEE Embedded Systems Letters*, *6*(4), 69–72. doi:10.1109/LES.2014.2344913

Qiu, M., Ming, Z., Li, J., Gai, K., & Zong, Z. (2015). Phase-change memory optimization for green cloud with genetic algorithm. *IEEE Transactions on Computers*, *64*(12), 3528–3540. doi:10.1109/TC.2015.2409857

Qiu, M., Ming, Z., Wang, J., Yang, L. T., & Xiang, Y. (2014). Enabling cloud computing in emergency management systems. *IEEE Cloud Computing*, *1*(4), 60–67. doi:10.1109/MCC.2014.71

Qiu, M., Sha, E. H.-M., Liu, M., Lin, M., Hua, S., & Yang, L. T. (2008). Energy minimization with loop fusion and multi-functional-unit scheduling for multidimensional DSP. *Journal of Parallel and Distributed Computing*, *68*(4), 443–455. doi:10.1016/j.jpdc.2007.06.014

Qiu, M., Zhang, L., Ming, Z., Chen, Z., Qin, X., & Yang, L. T. (2013). Security-aware optimization for ubiquitous computing systems with SEAT graph approach. *Journal of Computer and System Sciences*, *79*(5), 518–529. doi:10.1016/j.jcss.2012.11.002

Rachev, S. (2007). *Financial Econometrics: From Basics to Advanced Modeling Techniques*. John Wiley & Sons.

Radzi, R. M., & Lewis, M. K. (2015). Religion and the Clash of "Ideals" and "Realities" in Business: The Case of Islamic Bonds (sukuk). *Thunderbird International Business Review*, *57*(4), 295–310. doi:10.1002/tie.21706

Rajaobelina, L., Brun, I., & Toufaily, É. (2013). A relational classification of online banking customers. *International Journal of Bank Marketing*, *31*(3), 187–205. doi:10.1108/02652321311315294

Ranco, G., Aleksovski, D., Caldarelli, G., Grcar, M., & Mozetic, I. (2015). The effects of Twitter sentiment on stock price returns. *PLoS One*, *10*(9), e0138441. doi:10.1371/journal.pone.0138441 PMID:26390434

RedMoney. (2018). *IFNFintech: Unlocking the Potential of Islamic Finance*. Retrieved from https://www.ifnfintech.com/issue/volume-2-issue-1

Ripple. (2018). *XRP The Digital Asset for Payments*. Retrieved from: https://ripple.com/xrp

Rizzi, M. (2018). *FinServ 25: The most influential voices in banking*. Retrieved from https://thefinancialbrand.com

Romānova, I., Grima, S., Spiteri, J., & Kudinska, M. (2018). The Payment Services Directive 2 and Competitiveness: The Perspective of European Fintech Companies. *European Research Studies Journal*, *21*(2), 5–24.

Rossi, E., & Fantazzini, D. (2015). Long memory and periodicity in intraday volatility. *Journal of Financial Econometrics*, *13*(4), 922–961. doi:10.1093/jjfinec/nbu006

Ross, S. A. (1989). Information and volatility: The no-arbitrage martingale approach to timing and resolution irrelevancy. *The Journal of Finance*, *44*(1), 1–17. doi:10.1111/j.1540-6261.1989.tb02401.x

Ryu, H. S. (2018). Understanding benefit and risk framework of fintech adoption: Comparison of early adopters and late adopters. *Proceedings of the 51st Hawai International conference on system sciences*. Retrieved from https://hdl.handle.net/10125/50374

Ryu, H.-S. (2018). Understanding Benefit and Risk Framework of Fintech Adoption: Comparison of Early Adopters and Late Adopters. *Proceedings of the 51st Hawaii International Conference on System Sciences*. 10.24251/HICSS.2018.486

Saad, M., & Mohaisen, A. (2018). Towards characterizing blockchain-based cryptocurrencies for highly-accurate predictions. *IEEE INFOCOM 2018 - IEEE Conference on Computer Communications Workshops (INFOCOM WKSHPS)*, 704-709. 10.1109/INFCOMW.2018.8406859

Saha, A. K. (2017). *Review of Design of Speech Recognition and Text Analytics based Digital Banking Customer Interface and Future Directions of Technology Adoption*. Retrieved from https://arxiv.org/ftp/arxiv/papers/1712/1712.04640.pdf

Sairally, S. (2007). Evaluating the 'Social Responsibility' of Islamic Finance: Learning from the Experiences of Socially Responsible Investment Funds. In M. Iqbal, S. S. Ali, & D. Muljawan (Eds.), *Advances in Islamic Economics and Finance* (pp. 279–303). Jeddah, Saudi Arabia: Islamic Research & Training Institute.

Saju, J. C., & Shaja, A. S. (2017). A Survey on Efficient Extraction of Named Entities from New Domains Using Big Data Analytics. *2nd International Conference on Recent Trends and Challenges in Computational Models (ICRTCCM)*, 170-175. 10.1109/ICRTCCM.2017.34

Sánchez, D., Vila, M., Cerda, L., & Serrano, J.-M. (2009). Association rules applied to credit card fraud detection. *Expert Systems with Applications*, *36*(2), 3630–3640. doi:10.1016/j.eswa.2008.02.001

Sanicola, L. (2017, February 13). What is fintech? *Huffington Post*.

Sayani, H. (2015). Customer satisfaction and loyalty in the United Arab Emirates banking industry. *International Journal of Bank Marketing*, *33*(3), 351–375. doi:10.1108/IJBM-12-2013-0148

Schaefer, A., Moormann, J., & Rosemann, M. (2012). The rise of smartphone apps: Opportunities for customer-centric retail banking. *Banks and Bank Systems*, *7*(1), 73–82.

Schanz, K. U. (2015). *The Technology and Data Revolution in Insurance: A Brave New World?* Middle East Insurance Review.

Scholtus, M., van Dijk, D., & Frijns, B. (2014). Speed, algorithmic trading, and market quality around macroeconomic news announcements. *Journal of Banking & Finance*, *38*, 89–105.

Schueffel, P. (2017). Taming the beast. A scientific definition of Fintech. *Journal of Innovation Management, 4*(4).

Schwert, G. W. (1989). Why does stock market volatility change over time? *The Journal of Finance, 44*(5), 1115–1153. doi:10.1111/j.1540-6261.1989.tb02647.x

Seljan, S., & Gašpar, A. (2009a). First Steps in Term and Collocation Extraction from English-Croatian Corpus. *Proceedings of 8th International Conference on Terminology and Artificial Intelligence*. Retrieved from http://ceur-ws.org/Vol-578/paper21.pdf

Seljan, S., Dalbelo Bašić, B., Šnajder, J., Delač, D., Šamec-Gjurin, M., & Crnec, D. (2009b). Comparative Analysis of Automatic Term and Collocation Extraction. *2nd International Conference "The future of information sciences (INFuture 2009): Digital resources and knowledge sharing"*, 219-228.

Seljan, S., & Dunđer, I. (2014). Combined Automatic Speech Recognition and Machine Translation in Business Correspondence Domain for English-Croatian. *World Academy of Science, Engineering and Technology (WASET) - International Journal of Computer, Electrical, Automation. Control and Information Engineering*, *8*(11), 1980–1986.

Seljan, S., Dunđer, I., & Gašpar, A. (2013). From digitization process to terminological digital resources. In *36th International Convention on Information & Communication Technology Electronics & Microelectronics (MIPRO)* (pp. 1053-1058). IEEE.

Seljan, S., Stančić, H., & Dunđer, I. (2017). Extracting Terminology by Language Independent Methods. In L. N. Zybatow, A. Stauder, & M. Ustaszewski (Eds.), *Forum Translationswissenschaft: Translation Studies and Translation Practice* (pp. 141–147). Frankfurt am Main: Peter Lang GmbH.

Shadrin, A., & Leonov, P. (2018). Risks Evaluation of Financial-Economic Activity and Their Management in the System of Economic Security of the Organization. *KnE Social Sciences, 3*(2), 427–435. doi:10.18502/kss.v3i2.1573

Shariyah Review Bureau. (2018). Decoding Compliance of an Iconic Offering (ICO). *Shariyah Review Bureau.* Retrieved from http://shariyah.com/wp-content/uploads/2018/08/ICO-with-changes.pdf

Sharma, A., & Panigrahi, P. K. (2013). *A review of financial accounting fraud detection based on data mining techniques.* arXiv preprint arXiv:1309.3944

Sharpe, W. (1964). Capital asset prices: A theory of market equilibrium under conditions of risk. *The Journal of Finance, 19*(3), 425–442.

Shcherbak, S. (2014). How should Bitcoin be regulated? *Eur. J. Legal Stud., 7*, 41.

Shelkovnikov, A. (2016). *Blockchain Applications in Insurance; Deloitte Report*. London, UK: Deloitte LLP.

Shiller, R. (1981). Do stock prices move too much to be justified by subsequent changes in dividends. *The American Economic Review, 75*, 421–436.

Shreve, S. E. (2004). *Stochastic calculus for finance II: continuous-time models*. Springer Science & Business Media. doi:10.1007/978-1-4757-4296-1

Shukla, A. (2017). *What is innovation? Why innovation is important?* Retrieved from https://www.paggu.com/getting-into-roots/what-is-innovation-why-innovation-is-important

Singleton, T. W., & Singleton, A. J. (2010). *Fraud auditing and forensic accounting* (Vol. 11). John Wiley & Sons. doi:10.1002/9781118269183

Siti Rohaya, M. R., Zam Zuriyati, M., Juliana, A. B., Farhana Hanim, M., & Norhayati, M. I. (2018). Artificial Intelligence, Smart Contract and Islamic Finance. *Asian Social Science, 14*(2), 145–154. doi:10.5539/ass.v14n2p145

Society for Worldwide Interbank Financial Telecommunication. (2017). *63 companies shaping Africa's fintech ecosystem*. Retrieved from https://medium.com/@gomedici/63.companies-shaping-africas-fintech-ecosystem-352720312629

Somal, H. K. (2017). Big Data & Analytics: Tackling Business Challenges in Banking Industry. *Business and Economics Journal, 8*(2).

Srivastava, U., & Gopalkrishnan, S. (2015). Impact of big data analytics on banking sector: Learning for Indian banks. *Procedia Computer Science, 50*, 643–652. doi:10.1016/j.procs.2015.04.098

Stark, J. (2018). *Fintech, Smart Contracts and Blockchain* [PowerPoint Slides]. Presentation at IIFM Seminar in Kuala Lumpur.

Stewart, H., & Jürjens, J. (2018). Data security and consumer trust in FinTech innovation in Germany. *Information & Computer Security, 26*(1), 109–128. doi:10.1108/ICS-06-2017-0039

Sun, M. (2016). *Modeling volatility using high-frequency data* (Unpublished doctoral dissertation). UCLA, Los Angeles, CA.

Sun, N., Morris, J. G., Xu, J., Zhu, X., & Xie, M. (2014). iCARE: a framework for big data-based banking customer analytics. *IBM Journal of Research and Development, 58*(5-6), 4:1-4:9.

Surendra, E. (2017). *Introduction to Fintech in Malaysia*. Retrieved from https://www.imoney.my/articles/introduction-fintech-malaysia

SVB. (2015). *Cybersecurity report 2015*. Retrieved from https://www.svb.com/uploadedFile/Content/TrendsandInsights/Reports/CybersecurityReport/cybersecurity-report-2015.pdf

Szabo, N. (1997). Formalizing and Securing Relationships on Public Networks. *First Monday, 2*(9). doi:10.5210/fm.v2i9.548

Tapscott, A., & Tapscott, D. (2017). How Blockchain Is Changing Finance. *Harvard Business Review*.

The Bain.com. (2016). *Divide and Conquer: A Guide to Winning SME Banking Strategies*. Retrieved from http://www.bain.com/publications/articles/divide-and-conquer-a-guide-to-winning-sme-banking-strategies.aspx

Todorof, M. (2018). *Editorial: Shariah-compliant Fintech in the banking industry. ERA 2018.* Springer. doi:10.100712027-018-0505-8

Todorov, T. (2009). Estimation of continuous-time stochastic volatility models with jumps using high-frequency data. *Journal of Econometrics, 148*(2), 131–148. doi:10.1016/j.jeconom.2008.10.005

Torres-Toukoumidis, A., & Marín-Mateos, P. (2017). Gamification in mobile applications for banking services in Spain. *Revista de Ciencias de la Administración y Economía, 7*(13), 59–72.

Trautman, L. (2016). *Is Disruptive Blockchain Technology the Future of Financial Services?* Retrieved from https://papers.ssrn.com/sol3/papers.cfm?abstract_id=2786186

Traynor, P., Butler, K., Bowers, J., & Reaves, B. (2017). FinTechSec: Addressing the Security Challenges of Digital Financial Services. *IEEE Security and Privacy, 15*(5), 85–89. doi:10.1109/MSP.2017.3681060

Tu, K. V., & Meredith, M. W. (2015). Rethinking virtual currency regulation in the Bitcoin age. *Washington Law Review (Seattle, Wash.), 90*, 271.

Turban, E., Sharda, R., & Delen, D. (2010). *Decision Support and Business Intelligence Systems (required).* Prentice Hall Learning Outcomes.

Turner, D., Schroeck, M., & Shockley, R. (2012). *Analytics: The real-world use of big data in financial services.* Retrieved from https://www-935.ibm.com/services/multimedia/Analytics_The_real_world_use_of_big_data_in_Financial_services_Mai_2013.pdf

Ünan, S. (2018). *Sigortacılığın Kişisel Veri İmtihanı.* Retrieved from http://www.sigortacigazetesi.com.tr/sigortaciligin-kisisel-veri-imtihani/

UNHCR. (2018). *Figures at A Glance.* Retrieved from: http://www.unhcr.org/figures-at-a-glance.htm

UNICEF. (2017, January 9). UNICEF to present 'Donercoin' at London Blockchain Week 2017. *UN Blockchain.* Retrieved from: https://un-blockchain.org/2017/01/09/unicef-to-present-donercoin-at-london-blockchain-week-2017

Usmani, M. (2007). *Sukuk and their contemporary applications.* AAOIFI Working Paper. Retrieved August 14, 2014, from http://www.ifseb.com/wp-content/uploads/2012/07/Sukuk-and-Contemporary-application-14-JAN-08.pdf

Usmani, M.T. (2002). *An Introduction to Islamic Finance.* Hague, The Netherlands: Kluwer Law.

Usta, A., & Doğantekin, S. (2017). *Blockchain 101.* İstanbul: Kapital Medya Hizmetleri A.Ş.

Vakta, T., Maheswari, A., & Mohanan, N. U. (2016). *Blockchain Disruption in Security Issuance.* Retrieved from https://www.capgemini.com/wpcontent/uploads/2017/07/blockchain_securities_issuance_v6_web.pdf:Capgemini

Vallois, V., & Guenane, F. A. (2017). Bitcoin transaction: From the creation to validation, a protocol overview. *2017 1st Cyber Security in Networking Conference (CSNet)*, 1-7. 10.1109/CSNET.2017.8241988

Van Loo, R. (2018). *Making Innovation More Competitive: The Case of Fintech*. 65. *UCLA Law Review. University of California, Los Angeles. School of Law, 232*. Retrieved from https://ssrn.com/abstract=2966890

Vasco Data Security. (2016). *Mobile Banking Applications: Balancing Security and Convenience*. Retrieved from https://www.vasco.com/images/Mobile-Banking-Applications-White-Paper-redux-MondayApril4_tcm42-46736.pdf

Velankar, S., Valecha, S., & Maji, S. (2018). Crypto-currency price prediction using machine learning. *2018 20th International Conference on Advanced Communication Technology (ICACT)*, 144-147.

VISA. (2018). *Visa Acceptance for Retailers*. Retrieved from: https://usa.visa.com/run-your-business/small-business-tools/retail.html

Vishwanath, S., & Azmi, S. (2009). An Overview of Islamic Sukuk Bonds. *The Journal Of Structured Finance*, *14*(4), 58–67. doi:10.3905/JSF.2009.14.4.058

Welch, O. J., Reeves, T. E., & Welch, S. T. (1998). Using a genetic algorithm-based classifier system for modeling auditor decision behavior in a fraud setting. *International Journal of Intelligent Systems in Accounting Finance & Management*, *7*(3), 173–186. doi:10.1002/(SICI)1099-1174(199809)7:3<173::AID-ISAF147>3.0.CO;2-5

Wells, J. T. (2007). Forensic Accounting and Fraud Investigation for Non-Experts. *The CPA Journal*, *77*(2), 14.

Whang, D. (2012). *Volatility at High Frequency* (Unpublished doctoral dissertation). UCLA, Los Angeles, CA.

World Bank. (2017). *No Poverty*. SDG Atlas. Retrieved from: http://datatopics.worldbank.org/sdgatlas/archive/2017/SDG-01-no-poverty.html

World Economic Forum. (2017). *Beyond fintech: A pragmatic assessment of disruptive potential in financial services*. Retrieved from https://www.weforum.org/reports/beyond-fintech-a-pragmatic-assessment-disruptive-potential-financial-serrvice

World Islamic Banking Competitiveness Report 2014-15. (n.d.). Retrieved http://www.ey.com/Publication/vwLUAssets/EY-world-islamic-banking-competitiveness-report-2014-15/$FILE/EY-world-islamic-banking-competitiveness-report-2014-15.pdf

Yalçın, G. F. (2018). *Sigorta Teknolojileri İçin Üretim Zamanı* [Time to Produce Insurance Technologies]. Retrieved from http://fintechtime.com/tr/2018/02/sigorta-teknolojileri-icin-uretim-zamani/

Yan, S. (2017). *Estimating stochastic volatility within a trading day* (Unpublished doctoral dissertation). UCLA, Los Angeles, CA.

Yeşilyurt, H. (2015). Cyber Security Risks And Solutions in The Financial Services Sector: Payment Systems And Supply Chain Integrity. *CBÜ Sosyal Bilimler Dergisi, 13*(2).

Yıldız, Y. (2017). *Turkey's digital insurance innovation*. Retrieved from https://www.worldfinance.com/markets/turkeys-digital-insurance-innovation

Yue, D., Wu, X., Wang, Y., Li, Y., & Chu, C.-H. (2007). *A review of data mining-based financial fraud detection research*. Paper presented at the Wireless Communications, Networking and Mobile Computing, 2007. WiCom 2007. International Conference on. 10.1109/WICOM.2007.1352

Zavolokina, L., Dolata, M., & Schwabe, G. (2016). The FinTech phenomenon: Antecedents of financial innovation perceived by the popular press. *Financial Innovation, 2*(16), 1–16. doi:10.118640854-016-0036-7

Zerado & Fintech Network. (2017). *Smart Contracts – From Ethereum to Potential Banking Use Cases*. Retrieved from https://blockchainapac.fintecnet.com/uploads/2/4/3/8/24384857/smart_contracts.pdf

Zhang, F. (2010). *High-frequency trading, stock volatility, and Price Discovery*. SSRN eLibrary.

Zhang, F. (2010). The effect of high-frequency trading on stock volatility and price discovery. *SSRN eLibrary*.

Zhang, D., & Zhou, L. (2004). Discovering golden nuggets: Data mining in financial application. *IEEE Transactions on Systems, Man and Cybernetics. Part C, Applications and Reviews, 34*(4), 513–522. doi:10.1109/TSMCC.2004.829279

Zhang, L. (2006). Efficient estimation of stochastic volatility using noisy observations: A multi-scale approach. *Bernoulli, 12*(6), 1019–1043. doi:10.3150/bj/1165269149

Zhang, L. (2011). Estimating covariation: Epps effect, microstructure noise. *Journal of Econometrics, 160*(1), 33–47. doi:10.1016/j.jeconom.2010.03.012

About the Contributors

Abdul Rafay is a practitioner cum academician. For more than 23 years, Mr. Rafay has been working as a freelance advisor, consultant & trainer to a wide variety of public & private sector national and multinational companies in the areas of Financial Technology, Corporate Finance, Financial Policy & Implementation, Auditing & Assurance, Accountancy, Corporate Tax Management and System Consultancy. He has been providing consultancy to various industries including Textile, Auto Assembling, Footwear, Industrial/Agro Chemicals, Ice Cream/Dairies, Glass/Ceramics, Healthcare, Mining/Natural Resources, Packaging/Paper Sacking, Steel/Pipe Casting, Rice Processing, Brokerage/Co-operative Financing, Software Development, Real Estate, Printing/Publishing, and Construction/Civil Engineering, etc. Mr. Rafay is a Fellow member of the Institute of Chartered Accountants of Pakistan. He is also member of various national and international professional bodies including Institute of Internal Auditors (IIA), USA; Association of Certified Fraud Examiners (ACFE), USA. Since 2001, he has been a life time member of Lahore Tax Bar Association. He has served as Co-regional Director (Founding) of Lahore-Islamabad Chapter of Professional Risk Managers International Association (PRMIA), Washington, USA (2011-2013). In 2012, he was nominated as Member: Education & Training Committee (ETCOM) of The Institute of Chartered Accountants of Pakistan (ICAP). He is also a member of ICAP's "Islamic Finance working group" which is closely in liaison with State Bank of Pakistan and other stakeholders for Islamic Finance Accounting and Auditing Standards. He is Alumni of Rausing Executive Development Center (REDC), Lahore University of Management Sciences (LUMS), Pakistan. In 2014, International Finance Corporation (World Bank Group) selected him for Training of Trainers (ToT) for Corporate Governance Action Planning for SMEs. He is also an approved trainer for Institute of Financial Markets of Pakistan (IFMP) established by Securities and Exchange Commission of Pakistan, the corporate regulator. In 2013, his name got included in the list of "Certified Directors" as per Clause (xi) of The Code of Corporate Governance 2012 issued by SECP. Since 1994, Mr. Rafay has also been associated with teaching in some of the top business schools of Pakistan. His specialized subjects of interest include: Strategic Corporate Finance, Financial Derivatives, Investments/Portfolio Analysis, International Financial Reporting Standards, Corporate Restructuring (Mergers & Acquisitions), Financial Statement Analysis & Corporate Taxation. He also served as an instructor in Civil Services Academy, Pakistan to train the CSS Officers selected by Federal Public Service Commission of Pakistan (FPSC). Currently he is a Professor of Finance & Accounting at University of Management & Technology, Pakistan. He has published more than two dozen research papers in indexed journals of repute in addition to contributing a chapter "Structural Mix of Credit Portfolios in Islamic Banking System: Evidence from a South Asian Economy (2017)" to edited Book "Advances in Islamic Finance, Marketing, and Management: An Asian Perspective" published by Emerald Group Publishing Limited, UK.

* * *

Moutaz Abojeib is a trainer and Islamic finance consultant. He is currently a Researcher at the International Shari'ah Research Academy for Islamic Finance (ISRA), Malaysia. He holds a Ph.D. in Islamic Finance and has clocked up 10 years of work experience in finance and banking consultancy. This includes his service at some European Investment Bank projects in the MENA region, and his work in the area of internal audit with several financial institutions. He has also conducted training in Syria, Malaysia and Indonesia. His current research areas are Islamic economics, Islamic microfinance, and Fintech including, but not limited to, blockchain applications for Islamic finance.

Syed Shahzaib Ali is working as a Data Scientist at MTBC Rawapindi, Pakistan. He received bachelor's degree in Computer Science from National University of Computer and Emerging Sciences, Islamabad. Currently, he is also pursuing his Masters in Computer Science from National University of Science and Technology (NUST), Islamabad. His research interests include Natural Language Processing, Machine Learning and Data Mining techniques.

Muhammad Adeel Ashraf is working as a Research Associate in the Department of Computer Science, School of Systems and Technology, University of Management and Technology, Pakistan. He has completed his Master of Science in Computer Science in 2016. His research interests include Software Engineering, Algorithms, Security, Blockchain, Bioinformatics, and machine learning.

Benjamin Enahoro Assay teaches mass communication at Delta State Polytechnic, Ogwashi-Uku, Nigeria. He holds BA and MA degrees in mass communication from Delta State University, Abraka and University of Nigeria, Nsukka respectively.

Assay is on the verge of being awarded a doctorate degree in mass communication by the Benue State University, Makurdi, Nigeria. He has published articles in scholarly journals, and contributed chapters in several books locally and internationally. His research interests cover areas such as information and communication technology and national development; international communication and comparative media studies, media, democracy and good governance, population and health communication, and public relations and advertising. He is a member of several professional bodies, including African Council for Communication Education (ACCE) Nigeria Chapter, Advertising Practitioners Council of Nigeria (APCON), Association of Communication Scholars and Professionals of Nigeria (ACSPN), Nigeria Institute of Public Relations (NIPR), National Association for Research Development (NARD), among others.

Mubashar Nazar Awan is currently working as a Graduate Research Assistant in the Department of Computer Science, National University of Computer and Emerging Sciences, Islamabad, Pakistan. He received his Bachelor's in Software Engineering from the International Islamic University, Pakistan. Currently, he is working on Natural Language Processing and Machine Learning.

Salah-u-din Ayubi is currently studying Master of Science in software engineering in Pakistan. He possesses two years of experience in web-based application and android application development. His research interests include FinTech Security, Blockchain, Android Security, Data mining, Machine learning and software system design.

Mirjana Pejić Bach is a Professor at the Department of Informatics at the Faculty of Economics & Business. She graduated at the University of Zagreb, Croatia where she received her Ph.D. degree in Business, submitting a thesis on "System Dynamics Applications in Business Modelling" in 2003. She is the recipient of the Emerald Literati Network Awards for Excellence 2013 for the paper Influence of strategic approach to BPM on financial and non-financial performance published in Baltic Journal of Management. Mirjana was also educated at MIT Sloan School of Management in the field of System Dynamics Modelling, and at OliviaGroup in the field of data mining. She participates in number of EU FP7 projects, and is an Expert for Horizon 2020.

Mohammed Hariri Bakri obtained PhD in Finance from Universiti Teknologi Mara, Malaysia (UiTM). His expertise is in securitization, financial planning, Waqf, Islamic Finance accounting, financial engineering, micro finance in technopreneurship. He is currently a senior lecturer in Faculty of Technology Management in Universiti Teknikal Malaysia Melaka (UTeM).

Mirza Omer Beg is currently working as an Assistant Professor in the Department of Computer Science, National University of Computer and Emerging Sciences, Pakistan. He received his PhD from the University of Waterloo, Canada. His research interests include compiler optimization, Memory Hierarchy Optimizations, Constraint Programming and Graph Theory. Currently, he is working on Green Computation which attempts to connect sustainable optimization techniques with machine learning and natural language processing.

Syeda Nisar Fatima received her MSc. (Information Technology) in 2016 from Minhaj University of Lahore, Pakistan. Currently, she is pursuing her Master of Science in Information Technology) at University of Management and Technology, Lahore, Pakistan. She has published 3 international conference papers. Her current research interests include Operating System Security, FinTech Security, Privacy, mHealth Security, Mobile Operating System Security, and Internet Security.

Farrukh Habib obtained PhD in Islamic Finance from INCEIF; the Global University of Islamic Finance. Previously he acquired a master's degree (M.Sc.) in banking and finance from Queen Mary, University of London, UK. He is a renowned expert in Shariah, Finance and FinTech with a diverse experience and strong educational background. He is Researcher at ISRA; co-editor of ISRA Journal of Islamic Finance (indexed by ESCI and SCOPUS); and Senior Advisor of HalalChain (HLC). He also advises various Islamic FinTech projects, with the focus on Blockchain and tokenized economy. He is also actively involved in training, consultancy, public speaking at international events and writing for journals, books, business magazines and reports.

Owais Hakeem is currently working as Lecturer in the Department of Computer Science, School of System and Technology, University of Management and Technology, Pakistan. His research interests include Cloud Computing, Distributed Computing, Fog Computing and IoT.

Mercan Hatipoglu is currently an Assistant Professor of Finance at Cankırı Karatekin University. Previously he was he was research assistant in Department of Business Management at Eskisehir Osmangazi University between 2011 and 2015 years. He obtained his PhD degree in Finance from Eskisehir Osmangazi University. His recent research interests include risk management, financial markets, volatility spillover in emerging markets. Dr. Hatipoglu has written extensively on financial economics and econometrics as well as Islamic banking. He teaches International Financial Management, Investment, Capital Markets and Econometrics courses at undergraduate and graduate level.

Muzammil Hussain is currently working as an Assistant Professor in the Department of Computer Science, School of Systems and Technology, University of Management and Technology, Pakistan. He completed his Ph.D. from University of Malaya, Kuala Lumpur, Malaysia (and he got Bright Sparks Program scholarship from the University of Malaya for his PhD studies). He has served as Research Associate for more than three years (2013-2017) in the Department of Computer Systems and Technology, Faculty of Computer Science and Information Technology, University of Malaya, Kuala Lumpur, Malaysia. He led or member for many funded research projects and he has published more than 11 research articles in various international journals. His potential research areas include, network security, FinTech Security, Blockchain, Android Security, IoT Security, SDN Security, and Internet Security.

Zunair Hussain is a software quality assurance engineer in Amco IT Systems. He has done many project related to web applications, desktop applications and mobile applications. He is currently perusing Mphil (Software Engineering) from University of Management and Technology, Pakistan. His research interests include networks security, cryptocurrencies, software defined network, software engineering and blockchain.

Shaukat Iqbal is a Professor and Dean at School of Systems and Technology, University of Management and Technology, Lahore, Pakistan. Dr. S. Iqbal has more than 24 years of professional experience. Out of which, he has served Pakistan Atomic Energy Commission for a period of sixteen and a half years in the capacity of Junior Scientist to Principal Scientist. He has made valuable contributions towards research with more than 50 scientific publications in well reputed national and international journals. His research interest includes Computer Systems Engineering, Numerical Computing & Computer Security. Dr. Iqbal holds PhD degree in Computer System Engineering from Ghulam Ishaq Khan Institute of Engineering Sciences and Technology, Pakistan.

Stefania Marrara earned her PhD in Information Engineering. She possesses long experience as a PostDoc in the Academy and is responsible of the cooperation with Universities and other research centres, and she collaborates within several projects of the Consortium and of the Start-Up Find Your Doctor. http://www.findyourdoc.org/ She is member of the International Journal of Web Engineering and Technology (IJWET) Editorial Board.

Sobia Mehrban is a researcher in Department of Computer Science, School of Systems and Technology, University of Management and Technology, Pakistan. She is an active researcher and working on a funded research project. She completed her Master of Science in Information Technology with excellent grades in 2016. She is working as a member of a research project at University of Management and Technology, and she has published numerous research articles in various international journals and conferences. Her potential research areas include, Privacy, FinTech Security, Information Security, Blockchain, Operating System Security, IoT security, Android Security, and Internet Security.

Muhammad Umar Munir is an IT professional based in Pakistan and a graduate of Computer Science. For past two years he has been successfully running a software development startup. He specializes in .NET framework development coupled with Xamrin mobile app development platform as well as C# desktop based applications programming. His core interests are in R&D related to databases, business intelligence as well as in machine learning. He has been doing research on latest technologies such as cryptocurrencies and automated trading models as well as research and development of algorithms based on Python which have been adopted by leading financial institutions.

Ghulam Mustafa is currently working as Assistant Professor at School of Systems and Technology (SST), University of Management and Technology (UMT), Pakistan. Previously, he was a full-time researcher in High Performance Computing and Networking Lab (HPCNL), at Al-Khwarizmi Institute of Computer Science (KICS), University of Engineering and Technology (UET-Lahore), Pakistan. He has worked on various funded R & D projects in lead roles. He received the PhD degree in computer science from UET (Lahore), Pakistan. His research interests include parallel and distributed computing, cloud computing, scientific computing, virtualization, operating systems, compilers, system & data security and open source software development. He also holds the position of director final year projects, in the department of informatics and systems of SST.

Muhammad Waqas Nadeem is working as an Assistant Lecturer in the Department of Computer Science, Lahore Garrison University, Pakistan. Currently he is enrolled in MS(Computer Science). Previously he received his Bachelor of Science in Computer Science in 2017. His potential research areas include, network security, FinTech Security, Blockchain, Android Security, IoT Security, Machine Learning, Big Data, Neural Network, Deep Learning, Natural Language Processing.

Norafni Farlina Rahim is working as a lecturer in Department of Muamalat at Islamic College of Johor (MARSAH), a college under State Religious Council of Johor, Malaysia (MAIJ). She obtained her Master degree from Universiti Sains Islam Malaysia (USIM) focusing on Halal product specializing in consumer behaviour in Halal cosmetics and pharmaceuticals. Currently she is pursuing doctoral study in Technology Management at Universiti Teknikal Malaysia Melaka (UTeM) specializing in technology adoption of Financial Technologies. She also wrote book chapters with Emerald Publishing Group and USIM Press in the field of Halal perception and marketing, and Islamic social finance, respectively. Her research interests are Halal studies, economics and international trade, consumer behaviour, Islamic finance, financial technologies, and technology adoption.

Taner Sekmen is currently an Assistant Professor in the Department of Economics at the Eskişehir Osmangazi University where he has been a faculty member since 2010. He completed his Ph.D. degree in Economics at Anadolu University. His research interests include monetary policy, financial stability and financial markets. He has published several articles on the topics such as optimal monetary policy, macro prudential policies, Islamic banking and volatility spillover in emerging markets.

Sanja Seljan is a full professor in Information and Communication Sciences, Faculty of Humanities and Social Sciences, University of Zagreb, Croatia. She writes and presents widely on issues of machine translation, natural language processing, data analysis and educational technologies. She is a member of various program and review boards of international conferences and journals, co-editor of seven publications. She is a project manager and collaborator in the domain of information and communication sciences.

Shazib Ehsan Shaikh is an Assistant Professor of Decision Sciences at Information Technology University, Pakistan. He obtained PhD in Informatics from University of Manchester, UK. His research interests include informatics and decision sciences.

Amir Topalovic is the CEO of Consorzio per il Trasferimento Tecnologico C2T, Italy. He is enrolled at Doctoral studies at University of Sarajevo, Bosnia and Herzegovina with the topic Utilization of knowledge discovery in databases in SMEs.

Siti Norbaya Yahaya obtained her PhD in Risk Management from Aichi Institute of Technology, Japan. Currently she is a senior lecturer in Faculty of Technology Management and Technopreneurship at Universiti Teknikal Malaysia, Melaka (UTeM).

Da Yan is currently an Assistant Professor at the Department of Computer Science, the University of Alabama at Birmingham. He received his Ph.D. in Computer Science from the Hong Kong University of Science and Technology in 2014. He is the sole winner of Hong Kong 2015 Young Scientist Award in Physical/Mathematical Science, and the recipient of DASFAA 2011 Best Paper Award. He has developed a comprehensive platform of systems, collectively called BigGraph@CUHK, for data-intensive iterative big graph analytics. Dr. Yan regularly publishes in 1st-tier conferences and journals like SIGMOD, PVLDB, SIGKDD, ICDE, WWW, TKDE, TPDS, SoCC, EuroSys, etc. He was invited as the 1st author to write 2 books in Foundations and Trends in Databases and Springer Briefs in Computer Science, respectively, and a book chapter in Encyclopedia of Big Data Technologies. He also regularly serves as the reviewers of top journals including TODS, VLDBJ, TKDE, TPDS, WWWJ, TNSE, etc., and serves in the program committees of top conferences such as SIGMOD 2019, PVLDB 2018, IJCAI 2017, ICPP 2018, ICA3PP 2017, IRI 2017-2018, ICPADS 2016, etc. Dr. Yan is the leading program co-chair of the BIOKDD 2018 workshop held in conjunction with SIGKDD 2018, and serves in the PCs of a number of other workshops on database and data mining research.

Sibo Yan is currently a senior associate at the Economics and Valuation Group of KPMG LLP. He graduated from the University of California at Los Angeles (UCLA) with a Ph.D. in Economics and Statistics in 2017. He was a teaching and research fellow at the department of Economics, UCLA from 2012-2017. His research commits to innovative modeling of high-frequency financial prices. He introduces new techniques to measure financial volatility in the very short run, which overcomes market micro-structure defects that bothered traditional asset pricing research. He is invited to present at many international economics and finance conferences like ICNTEF, INFINITI, AIER, WFA, etc. He also serves as a reviewer and member of the INFINITI 2018 international finance conference. Dr. Yan is the 2018 Encore winner of the best associate at KPMG LLP EVS group. His research interests include high-frequency financial econometrics, risk management, return predictability and deep learning with applications in finance.

İsmail Yıldırım is an Associate Professor at Department of Insurance and Actuary, Hitit University, Corum-Turkey. He received PhD in Finance with his thesis entitled as “Stress Testing in The Risk Measurement Of Insurance Companies: An Implementation in Turkish Insurance Sector”. He has published several international articles and book chapters in the field of insurance. His research interests include insurance business, risk management and insurance, Islamic insurance.

Fatima Zaka is currently working as a Teaching Fellow of Finance at the Information Technology University (ITU), Pakistan. She had worked for over 6 years at prestigious organisations including United Nations Development Programme, Deloitte (UAE) and LUMS. She holds MSc degree in Finance and Accounting (with Distinction) from University of Sheffield, UK. Her research interests include role of FinTech in Islamic Banking and Finance and entrepreneurial finance.

Index

I

L

M

P

Q

R

S

www.ingramcontent.com/pod-product-compliance
Lightning Source LLC
LaVergne TN
LVHW081334300926
849161LV00008B/1970